BBL BOOKS

Also by Bradley Lewis

Long Island Purgatory
Dissolution
Bad Day In Beverly Hills
Cul De Sac
Another Bad Day In Beverly Hills
God's Helix
Great White Doctor
Hollywood's Celebrity Gangster, The Incredible Life and Times of Mickey Cohen
The Bloomingdale Code
Mickey Cohen: The Rat Pack Years
    The Elder Statesman's Life and Times   1960-1976
Mickey Cohen and the West Coast Mob
    Washington's Crackdown on Vegas and Los Angeles   1950-1960
My Father, Uncle Miltie
Mickey Cohen: The Gangster Squad and the Mob, The True Story of Vice in Los
    Angeles 1937-1950

BBL BOOKS
New York   Los Angeles
1st Edition
2015

FOR MR

Almost True Hollywood Stories   Bradley Lewis

PROLOGUE
Brantley

     Five long years have elapsed since I moved west — way out
west — to the Left Coast, about as far west as I could relocate
in the U.S. short of considering Hawaii. My New York friends had
repeatedly warned me but mostly chided me about moving to La-La
Land. I disregarded the majority of the tidy-but-funny shorthand
descriptions of life on the edge on the continent. Things
couldn't possibly be as awful and as silly as described, even if
Los Angeles was consistently the butt of jokes on *The Tonight
Show*, as well as one-liners repeated by any New Yorker who

fancied himself several cuts above Tinseltown – which was most everyone, from doormen to elected officials. Everyone is in show business; they don't have real bagels, pastrami, or pizza; valley jokes; celebrity scandals; you have to drive everyplace; it's not a city, just a big suburb. *There must be some redeeming value,* I thought.

The singles scene in New York had reduced me to one of its brain-dead captives, despite never having been a big drug consumer. Still, cocaine on the smoked glass dining table was a required staple within certain Big Apple social loops. Visitors often helped themselves to 'takeout' – stealing much more than I ever consumed. During a few destructive episodes, debauchery had no set limits. Exhaustion or death, whichever came first. So far my luck had held out, and I had not ended up in the emergency room of any of the local hospitals. Famous Bellevue was walking distance. Real New Yorkers thought nothing of walking two miles for a slice of pizza and the Bellevue ER was only a few blocks from my cave in the sky, but its reputation was so mixed among locals, even health professionals like me, that it wasn't considered a true emergency destination. Risking death by not heading to Bellevue and instead taking a cab or ambulance ride to St. Vincent's, or further uptown to Lenox-Hill, was considered the way to go in the event that impending doom became an evident and harsh reality that required immediate medical care.

I followed the general pattern of my city-dwelling predecessors and often escaped to the confines of my floating skybox. Even on summer weekends, I usually resisted the invitations to visit the Hamptons, suggested by pretentious friends who flew out via seaplane or drove their luxury gas-guzzlers for hours in heavy traffic. The Jitney was okay,

2

especially for the snoozers and heavy drinkers. I had no
interest in a pop culture version of an enjoyable long summer
weekend that included celebrity sightings in shops and chichi
restaurants. For others, Fire Island would suffice, but did not
quite offer the same celebrity-spotting opportunities as the
Hamptons. Besides, who cares about famous people who only rent
for the summer?

During the last couple of years, Manhattan was slowly
losing its attraction for me, and my life had become what is
best described as 'stale'. My body was no longer able to make
the transition from late-night club-hopping to early hours
office surgery. Weekends had become my escape. Sometimes on
weekdays, when I had to teach uptown at the hospital, I often
enlisted a colleague to substitute for me. Instead of teaching
on the clinic floor, I chose instead to entrench myself in bed
with cold Chinese food that was now stuck to the insides of the
soggy, white cardboard containers. While I ate the tasty
congealed leftovers, I absorbed the contemporary television
comedy scene. *Friends*. *Seinfeld* reruns. *Everybody Loves Raymond*.
(I didn't get the last one right away, so I had called it
Everybody Loves Raymond, But Me.) The choice of shows really
didn't matter. I enjoyed watching the narrative patterns,
however sparse. The current batch of mediocre shows were
derivative of older ones, and many could be traced all the way
back to *I Love Lucy*. The new programs that survived pilot week
reminded me somewhat of 'experimental' theater, perhaps from ten
to fifteen years earlier. What was once considered avant-garde,
and relegated to small Off-Off performance venues, was now part
of a popular sitcom, with its writers being touted as creative
geniuses.

I wasn't bad at my job; I just didn't like it. After I had
finished my education at Columbia P & S - the Ivy League hotshot

postgraduate school for health sciences and related professions
- I picked up extra cash as a model and an actor, something I
was originally exposed to as a child and then subsequently told
by my parents – the same ones who had originally suggested
performing - what a horrible life path the creative world would
make for me.

Instead, as a young adult, I wrote academic journal
articles, and received a 'professor' title to go with my
hospital appointment. The research and its associated reportage
had reached a boredom level of biblical proportions. I wanted to
write, but not scientific mumbo-jumbo, where fancy jargon and
doctor-style purple prose was the accepted format. Anything but
that. I wandered around Off-Broadway and points further south,
eventually seeing several of my plays mounted. After a few turns
as a soap opera actor, and then as a carpet pitchman (Kaufman)
in commercials, I was hooked. I didn't know exactly on what, but
it wasn't lancing oral abscesses or having to suture someone
after bloody and stinky surgeries. The Oral Surgery unit in the
hospital was somewhat interesting, but in private practice all I
chose to do was root canal surgery. Lucrative? Yes! Boring?
Incredibly. But, it was a decision I had made, mostly having to
do with a dislike of blood, as well as hospitals. I was a
surgeon who shared a phobia with Captain Hook. Staring at blood
could make me violently ill.

The students at Columbia knew and teased me for being Mr.
Kaufman Carpet. I starred in local commercial breaks during the
evening news and then much later into the night - interrupting
Johnny Carson. During thirty second spots, I endlessly – the
commercials were repeated ad nauseam - extolled the virtues of
the plush carpet quality. It was a shameless stint that led to
street-recognition, the first step toward making my way out to
Hollywood. Vanity? Ego? Shameless need for attention? Probably

4

all of the latter and therefore what better venue could there be
to satisfy those needs than life inside Los Angeles?

Despite the newfound attention, just once I wanted to hear
someone in my elevator say, "Oh, you're that writer guy, aren't
you?", instead of "Hey. It's Mr. Kaufman Carpet!" The
recognition didn't have to be because I was famous, although I
did envy the Tom Clancys of this world – he had recently plunked
down a few million for an apartment just under three thousand
square feet. I much preferred the sound of 'writer'. At least
'writer' opened up some people's minds to envision a person
whose life was filled with all sorts of glamorous experiences
and provocative ideas, even though in reality the lives of most
creative people were quite ordinary, some bordering on dull.

During my hospital training days, I had watched my father
die in a second-rate hospital on Long Island. Not known for his
timing, he chose the day that my mother was recuperating from an
abdominal hysterectomy at Downstate Medical, performed by a
famous surgeon related to opera star Beverly Sills. When the
call came from my mother, even though I had been estranged, I
nonetheless sped out in my white Porsche to the isolated house
on the island. I found two police paramedics struggling to start
an I.V. I watched them fail several times. Without asking where
they were taking him, I followed them to a tiny, local hospital,
where I had a final chat with Father. He was more concerned
about feeding Daisy, the family dog, but did also ask repeatedly
if I had finished my postdoctoral education. Later, there I was,
a hospital administrator for the renowned Oral Surgery unit at
St. Luke's-Roosevelt, having just watched my father die, begging
the pompous, God-complex resident in a third-rate hospital to
give me a Valium.

Now my mother was gone, too, after two years in and out of
cancer treatment centers. The last big cancer trip that she took

was for questionable alternative care in Mexico. She had been in remission for a few months after I had seen her, and then she slowly succumbed. I last saw her at one of those hotshot facilities, and she had been in good enough spirits to flirt with my older friend Ed, who had accompanied me to the clinic.

I began to feel very alone. The summer was over everywhere but in my head. Through slit-like eyes I watched the daylight break through the bare window. I hobbled to the tireless view and checked the imposing downtown skyline that was that day dwarfed by a dense cloud cover. Unexpected fall showers often gathered quickly during early September - washing away the sooty air. My body ached. I was getting too old for those unforgiving marathon sessions. A year of new lows was finally taking its toll. I could blame a lot of things, but ultimately it was all me.

"Oh, fuck," I said aloud, after a few minutes back in the sack. I pulled the designer quilt off my body with a decisive tug of my right hand. I had never used the WASP-described 'f'-word until I had moved to Manhattan to attend New York University College of Dentistry. Now the word had become one of my favorites. Apparently, the further I went with my education, the more curse words were at my disposal. I spotted a vibrator buried under the quilt. It didn't resemble anything I had seen before, although toys were a familiar variable during these escapades. I was also tiring of my device-oriented friends.

Now, who had brought the intimidating phallic piece? Was she gone? I thought back. Nothing. Blocked. Not a clue.

I found it tough to make my way to the kitchen. Down a narrow hall, it was off of the living room - a moderately sized space with an oversized glass dining table that reflected the sun as it shone through the large bay windows. Not that morning.

6

The horrible smog was at its best. I could make out the East River, while the 59th Street Bridge looked as if it was about to disappear in a darkish haze. The words of the Simon and Garfunkel song played on auto inside my head, "Slow down, you move too fast..." *Yup*. I needed a change. My time in New York City was coming to an end. *Shit*, I told myself. *You sold your practice*. I had developed seller's remorse, and had slipped back into my old destructive ways. That's what had led to this most recent bash, or so I told myself.

The kitchen was to my right. It had a small counter, built into a corner next to the refrigerator. Empty Chinese food containers. Condom wrappers. White powder. A rock. I wet my finger and picked up a little sample. I put it to my lips. Cocaine. The discarded items jarred my memory. Lily and I had taken a few last snorts before giving up for the night. We had popped Valium to come day and get some sleep. She took a five. I took two tens. Then we sat down to a feast of Chinese. I didn't have any food. It always surprised me how she could eat after doing so much coke. It never occurred to me that I was the one on the binge and that she, as a latecomer, had hardly touched the stuff.

Lily and I had been seeing each other, on-and-off, for almost four years. The last two years she had lived in a zillion dollar brownstone on Beekman Place, courtesy of an older commodities mogul, who years back had cornered the orange juice futures market and luckily got off with a slap on the wrist and huge fines. After the legal brouhaha had died down, they remained married and he commuted back and forth from the city to a Kings Point mansion, leaving behind an emotionally blind wife who tolerated his long stays on the Island as well as abroad. Lily had designed and kept up the city coop, while devoting two weekends a month to go down on Mr. Juice Futures.

Now I recalled more of last night, really the last night that I had been awake. I had been knocked out for a whole day after Lily had gone. When the doorbell rang, I staggered to the door and checked through the peephole before opening the door.

Lily rushed in and said, "I had given up. I was going to call the police. I kept calling and coming back to knock on the door."

"I guess I was pushing the physical envelope."

"You don't push the physical envelope," she said. "You stuff it until it can't be closed, and then you look for a larger envelope to fill up. It looks to me like you passed legal-size yesterday, and ended up with something more like a FedEx box for golf clubs."

Lily always made me laugh. She was always saving me from something. Yet, she was the one who had introduced me to coke, and might have felt guilty that I was up to binging two weekends a month. When I referred to her as my nursemaid, she said that it was nothing of the sort. She loved me. She cared about me. *Yeah. Yeah. Yeah.* After lambasting me for five minutes, Lily took off.

My relationship maturity was somewhere between a young cinematic Woody Allen and the real life Tom Cruise - rumored sexuality aside. Lily was a great sexual partner, and probably more of a friend than I was willing to admit. *Love?* I didn't have a clue. I never trusted her. She hadn't told me that she was living with another guy until I had known her for over a year.

After signing the closing papers for the sale of my practice, I had needed cash in order to jump start my weekend. A near closing time trip to the Chase Manhattan branch uptown on Madison Avenue yielded me about two grand. I also had my credit cards in case I ran out of funds, which often disappeared along

8

with the coke. I had kept my office bank account, so I still had some business checks. I had burnt out on surgery within ten years, a product of the stench of infections, family turmoil, too much coke, and partners that didn't have my best interests at heart. I had about thirty thousand left in the office account. I figured that I could make it another six months. Wishful thinking. Not with the quality of coke I was buying. Not with the restaurant tabs at Daniel, Nobu, and every other new over-hyped million-dollar restaurant.

Before deciding on Los Angeles, I had contacted people from Montego Bay, Jamaica as well as Portland, Oregon. The Portland administrators offered me the job running a university department, while keeping an intramural practice. Not for me. I was through with the hypocrisy of the American model of health professional education. I did want to run away, but not to Jamaica.

Hollywood. I wonder how much the drugs had to do with the selection. Somehow, I had managed to pass the over-scrutinized exam to become licensed in California. The process included a lot of contacts, money, and tutoring. Nothing on the exam was remotely related to my surgical field. Funny, the day I received the license I was cleared to take a scalpel to anyone.

The final choice did not come without some history. There was that lingering thought in the back of my mind that I could somehow resurrect my writing. I had gotten some accolades years back as a playwright wunderkind of sorts, to the dismay of my family who feared I would follow my singing grandmother into 'show business', the equivalent of curse words in our house.

Plans for two prior trips out west had fizzled because I missed the flights. Too much partying. I wasn't ready to go. I had to clean up my act, but at that time I wasn't getting anywhere. Each time before I had planned to leave, I had made

9

dates with women that I knew in Los Angeles. But even if I had made it to L.A., it would have been more of the same from the minute I stepped off the plane.

Rock bottom? It was for me, but too many of my friends were living the same life as if it was normal. I wanted out, like those 'opt out' offers on the Internet that don't allow vendors to share your personal information. I was convinced that they did it anyway – once they identified you as an Internet addict. In a similar local manner, there was no keeping my social life quiet. Money and drugs beget many acquaintances, and some, as mentioned, who saw me as a source of cash and coke.

Juice. I grabbed the container, and drank from it in short gulps. When I waltzed past the living room I moved closer to the windows. *Dreaming?* No. I was awake. The urge to pee was real. There was something wrong out there. That wasn't smog. *The bridge. Why so dark?* FDR Drive was jammed with cars. So what else was new?

What a weekend it had been, or more like what a weekend I had hoped it had been. After arriving home from work on Friday, I had made a few desperate phone calls – the usual drill. Within an hour, I had contacted two of my best female friends, not necessarily coke whores, but I can't recall seeing either one of them within the last year unless I had scored some nose candy, and guaranteed that the white miracle worker would be waiting for them upon their arrival.

The coke was generally spread out in a mound on a big glass sunburst dining table. I knew that once I had I left the room, they would help themselves, filling their personal vials. I was only a warm-up for them, and was considered quite an amateur. On occasion, both of them had smoked crack, and would head out from my place for points uptown. I knew that trading sex for the coke was unspoken, but always a distinct possibility.

So, this last time, soon after their arrival, I got right to the point. 'Blunt' was the operative plan.

"Why don't you two go down on each other while I watch?" It wasn't very sophisticated, but this was not a highlights reel from a Miss Manners seminar.

"You are such a jerk," Melissa responded quickly. The disapproval showed on her face. The close-legged body language that followed was a big stop sign. One-on-one with Terry might work for Melissa, but she didn't need me around for that, and wasn't about to do something designed solely for my benefit.

Terry didn't seem to care one way or the other; she merely smiled like a little girl. I certainly didn't want to waste the coke, while hearing about whom they were fucking and who they could fall in love with, so I made my stance clear.

"Hey. We all strip down. Rub the coke all over our bodies and take it from there." That was my way to let them know that they should leave.

Terry giggled.

A few seconds later, lanky Melissa was on her way out the door, stopping to search for her purse. Terry followed her. She said something silly like "Keep it real", which to many was still accepted colloquial usage.

I knew that Terry would keep in touch; perhaps returning later during my self-abuse spree that she knew would follow. She cared about me; at least she was human. I had too many acquaintances interested only in the side benefits, which often included lavish dinners out before heading back for the coke, or during the coming down time, tons of booze and sensational Chinese takeout. That went for the men, too. Contacts meant everything, and business survival was at the top of the list. Real friends proved to be a rare commodity; the closest thing was the television show bearing that name.

Now, parts of the weekend was coming back to me, in a
series of guilt-ridden scenes that made me laugh at my own
arrested development as a human being. Somehow, it always seemed
like fun while it was taking place. But, never the following
day. The longer I stayed awake whatever transpired became less
of any redeeming value - social, sexual, or otherwise.

After the girls left, I watched some of the adult channels.
Shameless porn videos. The coke took over. A series of phone
calls to people I hadn't talked to in years. At three A.M. I
called the Hampshire House to contact a young female executive
at Morgan Stanley. I had had lunch with her a week prior at the
Pierre. Her grandparents were the founders of a chain the size
of Wal-Mart. I had put on my best behavior, until that moment.
All common sense and dignity were thrown overboard, while I
clung tightly to the remnants of self-destruction and sophomoric
debauchery.

"Hello," on the receiving end was enough to get me started.
She didn't sound as if she had been asleep, although it was
unlikely that she was up at that late hour.

"Hey. It's Brantley. How's it going?"

"Okay. Brantley who?" She was polite, but firm.

Then I took off. "You know you looked great in that white
pants suit the other day. I watched you when you got up to go
the ladies' room. No panty line." I was at my worst. Sometimes I
came off as funny. It would have made an amusing scene in any
number of Hugh Grant movies. Reality always had a way of
diminishing cinematic humor.

"Oh. I think you want my granddaughter." To her credit, the
older woman I had disturbed in the middle of the night never
became angry.

The house operator had connected me to a family member of the same name. I called back and pursued the granddaughter who soon told me politely, "I'm not into this."

Within my stupor, I apologized and dialed on. I couldn't reach anyone else that I knew. Bored, I called an escort service number. A 'friend' had given it to me. His coworkers had used the service for his birthday party - thrown in the real estate office where they worked. He performed on the CEO's desk with a soap opera actress who supplemented her income by mingling for big dollars with rich junkies and boring, wealthy businessmen, some Metro North and Amtrak commuters to and from Connecticut.

I sang the old Doublemint chewing gum commercial while I waited for a confirmation on my credit card. "Double your pleasure, double your fun, with Doublewhore, Doublewhore, Doublewhore fun!" I found myself terribly funny.

About twelve hours of coke, champagne, and then the valium followed. I didn't remember most of what went on. I did eventually get my show – I think. The escort girls obliged the juvenile excesses, particularly since I was handing out hundred-dollar tips to go with fresh snorts of coke. Fake handcuffs, maybe oral sex, and a pretend spanking. The only problem was I couldn't remember who did what to whom or if I imagined the whole thing. I had a way of doing that on coke, mixing reality with fantasy.

Most of these encounters resulted in me talking endlessly for hours about the ribald possibilities. I threw in a few political speeches concerning the Middle East, the probability of man's ultimate failure, including every philosopher I could remember from Contemporary Civilizations I, a mandatory course at Queens College, CUNY. I had only read the synopses for CC II, when I found out that nobody in the class read the actual assigned material.

This time a bunch of my cash was missing. Much more than I had handed out as tips. I had found a check that belonged to one of the girls. It was from a podiatry clinic on Austin Street in Forest Hills, Queens, She had endorsed the back and I had given her the last of my money, part of my new coked-up check-cashing service. The check couldn't have possibly been legit. I didn't even know if the name on the check was hers. I tossed it in the trash. Why make trouble? I didn't want any publicity for my escapades, so the police were out of the question.

The working girls must have seen the loneliness. It was part of the business. Manhattan can be a lonely place. And they, in keeping with their own mixed morality, made the best of my depressive life, and took whatever they could. I was also missing a ring that I had made by a custom jeweler with the comedy/tragedy theatrical faces.

After Lily had been gone about twenty minutes, I made my way to the master bedroom, which had great southern views. The windows turned on a central hinge. I opened one to its fullest, limited by a rubber stopper, a wise safety mechanism. The air smelled bad. *Smoke*. It was smoke! I rubbed my eyes, and then the unimaginable became a reality.

The World Trade Center was gone. Not just from view – it was no longer in sight.

What happened during the next few days became daily world news. All eyes were on New York, and its now-I'm-a-hero-too Mayor leading the city through the worst tragedy in its history. Only a few months earlier, he had been scorned in the tabloids for his messy public divorce.

Everyone that I knew was in emotional shambles, exacerbated by the constant pictures of Ground Zero, an image from which there was no escape. If there ever was an extra impetus to

14

propel me out of Manhattan, this tragedy was it. I made plans to be on my way. During the next few weeks, a few of us helped unload trucks for the Red Cross. I even worked on a chow line for celebrity chef Bouley who was providing bulk meals for the throngs of volunteers needed downtown. Sadly, when the dust literally settled, while the EPA was accused of dragging its feet on the quality of the air, even the Red Cross appeared confused about how to handle its new monies. The celebrity chef was skewered for charging too much for his 'charity' - the audacity of making a profit off of such horrific times.

When the time arrived to leave for Los Angeles, Lily wished me luck, but also let me have it at the same time. "Don't continue to fall into this parody routine. You've become your own walking cliché. For years you were critical of everyone who didn't have a future, and now you look like an aging, Jewish Holden Caulfield or would that be Caulfeld - man?" Lily could still keep me laughing. She knew that I had already gotten the message before she pinpointed my useless life in a way that I clearly understood. We both had tears in our eyes when it was finally time to go. We grabbed each other in a desperate hug.

She spoke first. "I guess we don't have enough for us to stay together."

I was sorry that she had said it, but it was true. The harder reality was that Lily could not give up her life with the rich and famous, and even if I had had the money that she needed, I know that I couldn't spend my time traipsing around art shows and sitting on yachts near San Tropez, while taking downers with my champagne. Christmas week at Caneel Bay had even less appeal.

The American Airlines jet to Los Angeles was about twenty-five percent full.

Lily had warned me about flying so soon after the World Trade Center disaster.

"Don't be silly. The odds of anything else happening are pretty slim." At least that's what I told her. I don't think there was anyone who flew that day that didn't have some level of fear.

Sitting on the plane was at once calming, while simultaneously eerie. I was finally leaving my home behind, perhaps taking that first step toward truly growing up. Above those thoughts was the constant memory of the last few weeks - thousands of people gone. I tried instead to think about the fantasy ahead, conceivably misguided by popular culture influences like the television show *Lifestyles of the Rich and Famous*. Yet, those things associated with Hollywood people were inherently a real part of and a basis for my relocation. Life would be easier with the ocean on the left. I thought of all the advantages; sitting in a relaxed office, opening my desk window to let the warming Santa Ana winds fill the room, driving to work in a Jeep, sporting Hawaiian shirts, eating healthy by avoiding foods colored black, the old Woody Allen line about being able to "turn right on red" at intersections, Wolfgang Puck, and better karma. I knew the publicized drill well and had bought into the notion that a producer had once introduced to me with his thick Hungarian accent, reminiscent of Bela Lugosi, "It's a very agreeable way to live."

Then reality hit. I would never see a real bagel again, and I would be forced to eat processed pastrami on soggy sourdough bread or a roll. Goodbye Eli's, Balthazar, and the Carnegie. Hello Nate 'n Al's and its Wonder Bread with a hole in it bagels. Goodbye Hamptons chatter. Hello Santa Barbara and Hawaii, with people everywhere who say 'awesome' much too often.

The flight attendants were pleasant, and hardly on edge.
However, the captain made an impassioned speech before the
flight. The result was more unsettling than anything else. It
came off wrong, a false bravado that need not have been
expressed. Something like, "I'm going to get this plane where
it's going," and other promises that I had taken for granted
before I had stepped into the jet bridge in order to board.

"Can I get you a drink, sir?" asked a pretty middle-aged
flight attendant.

"A double scotch. Do you have any single malt scotch?"
Before she could answer, I changed my order. "Club soda. With a
lime."

"No scotch?"

I shook my head 'no'. I hadn't had a drink in almost two
weeks. This would be a bad time to start.

My carry-on suitcase contained three of my most valuable
possessions, copies of plays that I had written over the last
ten years. The trio were my best work, at least on paper, and
once I got settled it was my intention to adapt them as
screenplays. I couldn't get arrested in New York as a
playwright. Oh, a few hundred diehard theater aficionados knew
who I was, but it wasn't much beyond that. A handful of famous
actors appeared in my plays, but I never seemed to move uptown.
One time there was hope that Gulf & Western/Paramount was going
to put up the money, but they instead went with Tommy Tune and
Twiggy. I can't blame them; there were no dancing parts in my
plays. The only music was the screeching of family members in
dark comedies with titles like *The Last Days of An Addicted
Player*, last read at the American Place Theater. Yeah, I know
the title had a silly ring to it, but I was evolving from a doc
to a writer. A weird change. I dunno, but this is how it

happened. I was hell-bent on living the Hollywood dream, or lack thereof.

I would soon meet a lot of new people, some key to my west coast education. Most were very different from anyone I had known in the past. One thing I would learn quickly was that the friendly Hollywood veneer was only that, an outer coating not unlike the blinding reflection that came from the rows of over lit milk displays in mile long designer food markets and the artificial sparkling teeth that everyone sported. The contrast made my prior novel world appear homogenous.

Soon after I had arrived, I realized that I was inside the home of the hidden agenda.

CHAPTER ONE
Mickey, Brantley
Ira, Neil
Brian
Heather

The remainder of the flight had come off without a hitch.
Once off the plane, I didn't take long to have a 'Dorothy
moment'. Just traipsing through the airport told me that I
wasn't in my Kansas any longer. Outside in the bright sun, I
squinted in vain as I searched for any sign of a skyscraper.
From my little vantage point I could feel the expansiveness,
something that made me feel small, but it wasn't the same
dwarfing sensation of a cave dweller floating high over the
Manhattan skyline. Oddly enough, and perhaps apropos, a newly
found freedom crept slowly through my body like a convict's
first peek outside the prison walls - the very sense of
discovery that L.A. newcomers marveled about to one another over
cocktails at Spago. It wouldn't take long to realize that most
people who had relocated to Los Angeles firmly believed in the
myth perpetuated from years of movies like *Beach Blanket Bingo*
and the media's one-sided presentation of the popular culture
that exuded from the locally based entertainment industry. I
became an instant buyer for whatever they were selling.

My old friend Mickey Isles owned an apartment on the chic
Marina Del Rey Peninsula, the manmade competition to Malibu and

home to the yachting circle. He had stayed with me years ago,
when he had come to work in Manhattan. He had passed the dental
boards the first time around in the east, but he succumbed like
many playboy students to getting the cold shoulder during the
California exams. He would have to try again. In the interim, he
had made the best of an awkward situation. He would work in New
York and bask in the party scene until the next exam rolled
around. More than once when I had entered my New York apartment,
I found Mickey sprawled out on the living room floor with his
current date.

Mickey had suggested that I stay at his beach condo. It was
a generous offer, but I intended to get my own apartment as soon
as possible. Mickey was single and leading the bachelor life
about as well as anyone in Hollywoodland. His apartment was a
penthouse overlooking the sand. He shared an office in Beverly
Hills and also owned a budget dental factory in the Valley
which, in his own words, "turns out more coin than the mint in
Washington."

I took a cab from the airport. It was about a twenty-minute
ride. Mickey was not home when I arrived, but his houseguest
was. It wasn't the palm trees, the Spanish architecture, or the
sight and sound of waves at the beach that told me I was in La-
La Land. It was the vision of Les as he opened the door to
Mickey's penthouse - muscle beach incarnate.

I took a step back. Muscles on top of muscles, stuffed into
a little bikini brief. I prayed that when he turned around that
it wasn't a G-string. I lucked out. His body was covered with
oil, just like in the endless beach commercials. He had been on
the terrace, staring out through a telescope at topless
sunbathers.

"Hey, you must be the professor." He grabbed my hand.

20

"I'm Brantley." I tried to see his eyes behind the mirror-finished Oakleys, the expensive-but-popular sunglasses.

"Nice to meet you." His smile was a picket fence of teeth. The glare behind him or reflecting off him was almost blinding. "I'm Les." Nobody in L.A. used last names. I would learn later on that his was Guagliano. Italian was an excellent guess.

"Owww!" I tried to get my hand out of the vice.

"Sorry, Doc." He chuckled.

Les never walked. He had a variety of speeds that he used with the aplomb of Baryshnikov. Everything about him was gentle, except his handshake.

He insisted on grabbing the larger suitcase that I had checked for my flight. I held on to the carry-on. I had put some of my things in storage. I could always get them later, as the majority was winter clothing. The only thing I might have needed was my computer, but I would end up getting a newer, discounted model at one of the zillion local electronic stores. My mother's basement became home to my furnishings, soon to be appropriated without my permission by my sister and her new husband.

"Mickey threw me out of my room. That's where you're staying." There was a bit of a displaced child in his voice. Les stood slightly slumped, like a defeated boxer willing to take another shot from his opponent. Next to Les, Mike Tyson was a brain surgeon.

"Oh. That's not necessary. I can sleep out here." I pointed to the endless pastel sofa that covered every inch of wall space.

"That's mine. Hey, don't worry." Les patted my shoulder. "Mickey wants it this way." It was clear that Mickey was the boss.

I was curious as hell, but I was not about to ask who Les was and what he was doing here. Mickey was not gay, but this

could have been a curiosity fling. If that were the case, I
would not risk getting my head handed to me by Les for making
any stupid sexual references.

Mickey didn't like women, but they were his first sexual
choice. Mickey was one of the handsomest men I had ever seen.
His friends liked to tease him by calling him the 'Jewish Tom
Cruise'. He made the most of it with a modicum of social charm
and was able to persist in a world that was becoming more
hostile to misogynist social lives. He had built his dental
practice mostly with single female patients, who raved to their
parents and others about his great skills. When the girls
married, he often got the new husband and then the children as
patients.

I let Les show me to his/my room.

Mickey didn't make an appearance the rest of the day. I
went to sleep early. I wanted to keep my promise to be a good
Scout for as long as possible. I don't know how much time had
passed before I was shaken awake by a pair of massive hands. I
was too scared to scream. I thought I was back in Manhattan. My
building had been hit by an airplane. *Falling.*

"Doc!"

A huge head was almost nose to nose with mine.

I heard Mickey. He was laughing. A light came on.

Les? I thought.

The body straddled me. "I wanted to get a look at the guy
who pushed me out." I thought we had gotten past the
displacement issue. I looked beyond him. I could see Les with
Mickey. Who was this other behemoth?

"Hello," I said. It was polite and muffled. A smart choice,
since I thought I was hallucinating.

"So you're the smart cocksucker."

22

Under the circumstances, I said a clever thing. "Right." I could smell him. Like Old Spice or Brut gone sour - spiked with a garlic olive oil. His sweaty, greasy skin was divided into a map by his bulging veins.

"Meet my brother Lou," said Les. He was proud.

"Twins," I gasped loud.

Lou stood up and plopped on the mattress like a kindergartener.

"Now you met both the boys," said Mickey. "Clear out, guys."

Lou jumped off the bed as if it was a trampoline. He danced like Les, and the two disappeared, giggling like little boys.

Mickey leaned over the bed. We shook hands. "Go back to sleep. I'll be home in the morning. We can talk." He was comforting, like a parent.

"Mickey. Thanks. Thanks for everything."

"Hey. You helped me once. Big time." He turned, flicked off the light, and closed the door behind him.

I awoke later to a ruckus in the living room. Mickey's room was to the right of that, facing the beach. I opened the door to my room. Three naked butts faced me in the moonlight. Their owners were facing the ocean. Les and Lou had a woman sandwiched between them. Another woman, topless, was watching television from the sofa, eating the largest bowl of cereal I had ever seen - a green ceramic with little inlays of fruit on the sides.

I slowly closed the door.

Welcome to Hollywood.

The next morning, I tiptoed out of my room. The kitchen was a wide open expanse that ran almost the entire width of the apartment. Les and Lou were on a conference call. I would find, as they were that morning, that they were usually dressed in sleeveless muscle shirts and tiny shorts.

"Fuck you, you dirty piece-of-shit-son-of-a-bitch." Les glanced over to Lou for encouragement, who was listening on an extension phone.

Les continued. "Just send us the mother-fucking money. That's it. The mother-fucking money. The money. Send the money."

I hustled backwards toward my room, but Les signaled for me to come ahead. I stopped, and headed into the area between the breakfast counter and the appliances, which included a six-burner cooktop with a grill and barbecue. A green concoction filled the glass blender. I tried a little in a paper cup that I pulled from a dispenser on the water cooler. I immediately spit it into the sink. It tasted like my mouth had been dragged on the ocean floor under a wave. I grabbed a clean mug from an overhead cabinet and poured some coffee. I could tell that it was decaf. One of the first things that I realized was that most people in L.A. pretended to be healthy, even if they stayed up all night doing drugs and alcohol.

The phone call wound down. "Okay, we're set on this." Les put the phone down.

"Bye, Dad. I love you," said Lou just before he disconnected the call.

I made a mental note to never find myself on the wrong side of either one of them.

"Your father?" It was my meekest presentation.

"Yeah," said Lou. "We're from Great Neck." He was calm, and appreciated my interest.

"On the island?" I asked, knowing full well.

"You know it?" asked Les.

"My orthodontist was there. He was above the movie theater. I went once every two weeks for a million years, and my canines are still crooked. He took out one lower canine by mistake."

They roared as if I were Billy Crystal.

Sober, the twins were still menacing, but even more childlike, if humanly possible.

"Brantley," a voice boomed from the other side of the condo.

I jumped to attention and moved briskly around the smooth white floor-to-ceiling archway that led past the patio entrance and into Mickey's bedroom. As soon as I made the turn I could see Mickey in the wall-to-wall mirror. He enjoyed showing off his body, trim and muscular, with a healthy-sized limp appendage that seemed out of place on a Jewish body.

"Help yourself to anything. I'll be right out."

"Okay," I answered. Mickey moved out of sight. *Thanks for letting me see your dick*, I thought, as I retreated from the bedroom to the living room/kitchen area.

When Mickey emerged from the bedroom, the Guagliano boys stopped what they were doing, as if waiting for orders. Mickey was wearing blue jogging shorts, and a sleeveless terry vest.

Lou asked him, "Want some of our shake?"

Les was already pouring out the concoction. "It's got seaweed. The professor didn't care for it."

"I'll take it later." The tone of Mickey's voice was enough to end the conversation and dismiss the boys.

"Let's go jogging," said Les. He put down the blender jar, and wiped his hands on his bare stomach.

Lou picked up a pair of sunglasses from the counter.

Mickey said, "I'll catch up with you. Are you taking the beach route?"

"Yeah," said Les.

"Catch you later, Doc." Lou opened the door, and let Les go ahead. "He's older."

Les playfully slapped Lou across the face as he went past. "Moron."

Lou placed his hand on the offended cheek. "Hey, don't fuckin' do that." He nudged Les from behind.

The door slammed, and the tumult continued in the hallway.

"How'd you sleep?" asked Mickey. He sprawled out on a white lounge chair, his feet propped up on its oversized matching ottoman.

"Great. I usually don't get up this late, but I'm still on New York time."

"It takes a while to adjust."

I sat near him on the wall-to-wall sofa. I feared that my rear would disappear into the bulbous fabric. I was surprised how firm the cushion was. I ended up sitting up in a way that made me quite uncomfortable. This furniture was designed for gazing only. Even after trying a few adjustments, there was no way to get my back in a comfortable line with the sofa.

"This is a beautiful place," I said. That's not what I was thinking, although the drop-dead view was something out of a travel magazine. I could hear the ocean through the open terrace door.

"I like it." Mickey could be smug.

"What's not to like?" I could make a list, beginning with the mattress in my bedroom.

"How come you're out here?" He had come right to the point. "Everyone said that you had it made it bigtime in New York. You were on your way to becoming King of the Jews."

I decided to be candid. "I guess I can't take the city anymore. It's not for everyone, and I felt like I was wasting away. Going nowhere. After 9/11, I figured it was time to move on."

"Do you know anyone here?" He must have seen the look on my face. "Other than me?"

I lied. "Sure. Plenty." I didn't want him to feel responsible for me.

"Here's the deal. I'll pay you a third of your gross."

I wasn't expecting a job offer. I didn't want to seem eager even though I was. "Fifty per cent."

Mickey laughed. "You're acting like you don't have any money."

"If I didn't have any money, why would I negotiate?" It was a valid point, but a weak one.

Mickey paused. The percentage didn't matter much to him. This was a game. He didn't need me to work for him, but he knew I could increase his revenue by keeping the root canal surgeries in his office, instead of referring it to an outside specialist. To him, it was gained revenue, and from somebody he trusted. Health care professionals in tightknit places like Beverly Hills or Woodland Hills in the Valley were not above undercutting one another with remarks passed subtly to patients.

"Forty."

"No."

Mickey raised his voice. "Nobody in my office gets fifty per cent. I might be able to do that in Beverly Hills. We charge double what we get in the Valley. Endo is a gold mind in Beverly Hills." Endo was short for Endodontics.

"How much do you get?"

"I get over a thousand for a molar."

I did the calculations in my head. "Hey. I'm happy you're giving me a job."

"Brantley. You once helped me. Now I'm helping you." It was old school quid pro quo, but I gladly welcomed it.

"Thanks."

"Don't thank me. Get over to the Valley office as soon as you can. There's a Mustang convertible in the garage. The keys are over there." He pointed to a little breakfast bar on the other side of the kitchen. "And get a California driver's license as soon as possible. They'll treat you like scum without it."

I didn't grasp the magnitude of that statement until later on when I tried to cash a check in a supermarket. My I.D. might as well have said Afghanistan. After a little coaxing, the manager suggested a cash advance on one of my credit cards.

"How long does it take to drive to the Valley?"

"Not long." Mickey moved his head from side to side. He sprung up and waltzed to the picture window. "I played golf with Jimmy Caan yesterday."

"Oh, yeah? What's he like? He grew up not too far from me."

"He's great." Mickey never said anything negative about celebrities. He took it for granted that they were part of his territory.

"I thought the movie about gambling was sensational."

Mickey became smug. "You mean *The Gambler*." He now owned everything connected to James Caan. An essential to star-fucking.

"Right."

I had to keep in mind that almost everyone I would meet was an expert on show business, particularly movies. Even though I had treated many celebrities in my New York office, I was to become star struck as I made my way through the intricate Hollywood maze that lie ahead.

"Hey. I've got to jog." He turned his back toward me and moved quickly for the door. He was gone in a flash. No goodbye. That was Mickey.

I glanced around the apartment. It was really quite lavish. Original art. I recognized a Frank Stella. Could it be? There was a small sculpture garden on the terrace. *This stuff cost a bundle.* Mickey knew how to make money, but this was an unusually expensive layout. Prime beach penthouse. We were talking millions.

Mickey was always in deals, or at least pretended to be. He was the type of person who knew everyone, never letting on how or why he was friends with someone. If he didn't know someone personally, he always knew a contact who was 'tight' with the person in question. That went for business moguls as well as celebrities.

Every weekend was party time. Sleep was an impossibility on Friday or Saturday night. If there wasn't noise coming from the beach, it would be somewhere in the apartment, where Les or Lou would carry on until they passed out.

The upcoming Friday I was invited to a big bash that was taking place in a penthouse condo a few buildings away. Mickey commanded that I attend. "There'll be a lot of women there."

The building's owner and only penthouse resident was an Englishman named Colin who had made a fortune selling ladies underwear. The two ground floors of the three-story building was occupied by several women, all of whom insisted they were either models or actresses. Who was I to be judgmental? There wasn't a nicer place to live or party anywhere. Colin was an elegant 'landlord', making sure that every detail was attended to, right down to the exquisite palms and brightly colored flowers that lined the perimeter of the shore building.

I arrived around eight-thirty. The place was already jammed. The first woman that I met was strikingly attractive - auburn hair, halter top, white jeans, and sandals. She smiled continuously while we chatted. I grabbed a bottle of beer from a roving waiter.

"The new Woody Allen movie was funny. He goes blind and has to direct a movie. Blind! Can you believe it?"

"I think he can be very funny." I sipped my beer gingerly. I was in an environment where taking a slide back down debauchery lane would be easy. My plan was to be sociable, eat, and go home at a reasonable hour. I was now working half a day on Saturday mornings.

Another girl joined us. After a few minutes she revealed that she was once married to a baseball player who lost a big game by letting a ground ball dribble under his glove and through his legs. Suddenly it hit me; I had seen the play. The name Buckner came to mind. I didn't dare ask. If it was him, he had handed the World Series to the Mets.

She blurted it out. "Have you heard of him? Bill Buckner?"

"I think so." I excused myself before she went on. Who knew if anyone in Hollywood was telling the truth?

I kept mingling, bumping into an occasional television actor. It was hard to spot them. Everyone blended together. Les or Lou kept introducing me to actresses that they knew. I gave up trying to tell the muscle boys apart. I decided that it didn't matter. I settled on Les-Lou, the generic meld of the two hulks. For now on, that was it, Les-Lou.

I was amazed by how petite, almost emaciated, some of the actresses were in person. However, it made sense when it came to casting. Some of the leading men were so short that they had to be matched with tiny women in order to achieve their macho screen image, particularly in action adventures.

I soon met two funny younger guys, Ira Packer and Neil Hous. They shared an apartment near Mickey's building. Ira and Neil were set to start medical school at UCLA, although Neil made it very clear that that part of his life was going to be short-lived. He mentioned his show business aspirations as if it were his destiny, lowering his voice to an almost religious tenor. I told him that I had written some plays when I was in dental school.

"Write me a screenplay," Neil said. "I can shop it for you. I've got contacts."

From the way that he spoke it was hard to doubt him, but at that moment getting my life a little more settled was more important than adapting one of my plays for the movies. Part of me wanted to get to work writing, but Neil was definitely a long shot, as I would also learn was everything else connected to Hollywood. An often repeated line was that everyone in Hollywood had two jobs – their day job and show business. For a brief moment I thought of a bigger story, one that involved all of these new people. I was suddenly planning to write about this party and everything else that was going to happen. *That's it*, I told myself, *a story about Hollywood. Maybe with a prologue that starts out in New York.*

Ira and Neil were a delightfully strange pair. They spoke freely about everything, and never hesitated to poke fun at one another.

For the next year, almost everywhere I saw Mickey, I saw Ira and Neil.

Les-Lou joined us with a young man in tow. "Doc. I want you to meet a pal of ours."

"Hi," I said. I extended my hands.

"Hi. Brian Denkler. Nice to meet you."

"Brian is an agent," said Les-Lou.

"Not yet. I'm an assistant."

"Yeah, but to one of the big shots," said Les-Lou.
When Les-Lou released his shoulder, Brian began to tell me his
life story, as if I should have been enraptured. I listened. It
didn't sound much different than my own upbringing on Long
Island, albeit without freezing temperatures and snow.

Brian Denkler still lived at home with his parents in
Encino. His father, a prominent plastic surgeon, was so
entrenched in the entertainment business that he viewed his
son's foray into the agency business as a connection for new
patients. Dr. Denkler had tried to mold his son into a new-
styled agent; one that came armed with the best education money
could buy, and was steadily replacing the more gruff, uneducated
scumbags from an earlier era.

The road for Brian had been a long, convoluted one, but he
had stuck it out. Never a good high school student, he moved
from the tennis team to the golf team, one year reaching second
string on an already mediocre tennis squad. Even with a year of
Kaplan SAT study, Brian could only squeak out a little over
eight hundred for both the verbal and math sections combined.
So, it was the two-year Santa Monica City College for Brian, and
hopefully then another two years at UCLA. Based on his grades,
his father could only arrange credit for about one year, when a
miracle occurred. Out of the blue, Brian was accepted into a
program at USC, where it took him five more years to graduate.
Dr. Denkler had all the connections, including Wimbledon seats
for the last twenty years, which he used to his best advantage
as 'gifts'.

Lately, Dr. Denkler was disappointed with his son's slow
progress at CAA in Beverly Hills. Despite the hands-on breeding,
Brian was still learning to be an agent. That meant getting his
boss's laundry out of the dry cleaners and running to the

supermarket when it was discovered that the stash of mixed nuts was running low on cashews. Originally stuck in a rut for nearly two years as an assistant at William Morris, his gopher life had been one long struggle, in contrast to the cushy existence of his home life. He finally quit Morris when one of his father's connections had materialized at CAA.

Les-Lou dragged over two young women. "This is Brantley. I told you he was a piece of ass."

"Hi, Brantley. I'm Heather." She was pretty and petite - her hair fashioned in the again popular ponytail. She wore the standard beach uniform - braless t-shirt and cut-off, faded jeans.

The other woman clung to Les-Lou. They were all high on something.

"We're going in the hot tub," said Les-Lou.

He grabbed his new friend and Heather followed.

She turned her head back and said with a smile, "Join us."

"I promised to speak with Colin." I had lied.

My own hesitation stunned me. Suddenly I had become moral and responsible. I had to have been out of my mind. I was in the debauchery capitol of the world and I was pretending to be a monk. There could have been a worse pretense - choosing the priesthood as my model for alleged celibacy.

I silently laughed at my own silly joke. I downed the rest of my drink and placed the bottle on an expansive marble-topped table, situated up against a wall in the long party room.

A few minutes later, I wove my way out to the Jacuzzi. It was every man's dream of California, just like in what once were called beach B-movies, but now *Spring Break*, some with a bromance plot. Les-Lou was in a soft embrace with his friend. I slipped closer. Heather popped up out of the water. "Hi. You decided to come." She was topless. I felt like her breasts were greeting me - all pink from the warm water. *Should I shake hands? Breasts included?*

"Hey, Brantley. Take off your clothes," said Les-Lou. He pointed to his pile of clothes next to the tiled steps.

"Hey, thanks. No. I've got a big day tomorrow at the office." I was out of my mind for refusing.

Heather plunged her body back into the water. "Ooo! It's cold if you stay out too long."

Les-Lou persisted. He sounded as if it was more of a favor to take the extra woman off his hands. "Come on, professor. Don't you know how to have a good time?"

The irony was killing me. "I do. Can I please take a rain check?"

Les-Lou was no longer paying attention. He ran his tongue over his friend's shoulder. Heather moved closer to the giggling twosome. Apparently, I was not actually needed.

I took one last look and then found the stairs down to the sand in order to cool down and head back to Mickey's condo.

Later that night, I was awakened around one A.M. by the sound of an engine straining. I had a headache and needed some liquid. A stop at the mammoth refrigerator produced a bottle of cherry-flavored Powerade. While I replenished my electrolytes, I made it to the terrace and unlocked the sliding glass door. The ocean air felt good against my face.

That night, the moonlight was not strong enough to illuminate the beach. The only visible portions of the sand were the strips closest to the small streets between buildings. Light shone in from the streetlights, but only enough to cover a limited hemisphere of land.

A small truck was backing up to the sand. Bodies darted in and out of the lit semicircle, disappearing and reappearing quickly. I looked further down the beach, but could see nothing.

34

If I had to guess, they were night surfers loading their boards.
But this late? I didn't know the culture, but to begin with this
wasn't really a popular surf area. I heard Mickey's voice. I
spotted Les-Lou. He was shouting to driver. "You dumb mother-
fucking-shit-for-brains asshole." The driver responded. It was
the other Les-Lou. "You told me to back it up." There were
others milling about. Everyone moved quickly, depositing the
last of the boards on the truck. I recognized Ira and Neil. They
worked at a hectic pace. Ira kept glancing skyward, as if a
helicopter was hovering, or was about to. Les-Lou nearly tore
off the truck door. He removed his brother and shoved him toward
the sand. "Get the stuff in here."

The stuff? I didn't want to watch anymore, but I did. The
boys were up to no good.

"Brian. You drive."

I watched as the baby-agent-in-training slid in behind the
wheel. The truck was loaded in minutes and the group disbanded
quickly.

Drugs?. It had to be. Too cynical? I found it hard to
believe that these boys loved the surf enough to be playing with
boards in the middle of the night. I also knew Mickey. Money was
money. Whatever it was had to benefit him. Mickey knew how to
delegate when it came to deals. If it was something on the
fringe, he had a way of keeping his distance, even while
controlling a major share of the profits.

I didn't want to know. I returned inside, closed the
sliding door, and made sure that it was locked, the way I had
found it earlier. I returned to my room, at first shocked at my
discovery, but as time went on realized that it had made perfect
sense. Les-Lou needed money to live, particularly the lavish
Hollywood life, and what better way than to work behind the
scenes in an industry that needed their assistance as suppliers.

Even if the whole thing was innocent – and I knew that that was
unlikely – I went to sleep with the notion that I wasn't long
for this beach scene.

The next morning everything crystallized. I needed to live
closer to my office, somewhere with a little less sex, drugs,
and fog. The perverse mixture of coastal life in Los Angeles was
a dark study in contrasts, producing a feeling that mixed the
simple tranquility of the sand and water with the constant
promise of decadence. Everyone seemed to know it and accept it,
but me. Seemingly 'normal' families existed within the tangled
web that attracted thousands of newcomers every year, those who
showed up only for the wicked extras. People came to mingle with
the rich and famous - from Malibu to Playa Del Rey, with
hundreds of frivolous beach scenes portrayed like Annette
Funicelo or Steve Martin. The true *Beach Blanket Bingo* and *L.A.
Story*, their respective movies, lie further beneath the
Pollyanna surface.

The façade of Marina Del Rey resembled any other pristine,
upscale harbor town, but its underbelly seemed to attract the
worst and the best of new money, show business, saved dot.com
bucks, derivatives crooks, or the spoils of flipping real estate
in wild market upswings. Oh, and drugs. It was a far cry from
the public Jones Beach on the east coast, where thousands lined
up in cars every warm summer day to burn like discarded sardines
on the dirty-dark sand. When the day was over, they bitched all
the way home in bumper-to-bumper traffic, while spraying
themselves with Solarcaine and trying to brush sand out of
irritated body crevices.

I sat on the terrace with one of Mickey's remote
telephones. I positioned the telescope so that I could check the
topless sunbathers while I spoke. If I focused on an appealing
subject, it would only take seconds to snap off a series of

shots through the telescope lens. I had them made into post
cards which I sent to my friends in New York with a variety of
cornball travel expressions like "wish you were here". I usually
sent off the first batch following the first big snow storm in
the city.

One thing I learned in a short period of time was that
gossip was cheap, particularly if it wasn't about anything
connected to reality. That meant most everything except the
movie business, because that was the artificial pervasive
reality that bound everyone together. I decided to carry a small
tape recorder with me at all times. I felt a story developing, a
series of unique characters whose exploits could provide a
glimpse into the new millennium Hollywood existence. I was
hooked on writing the story.

Little did I know that the next person I would meet was to
become a bonanza of insight. Movie producer Sean Daren would
become my entrée into the heart of the beast. He was an insider,
a lifelong example of someone exposed to the sights and sounds
of Hollywood. We were mirror images; I wanted to get into 'the
business' and he wanted to get out. His life provided the
perspective that I didn't know, what my world would become if my
dream of writing materialized. I felt that if I interviewed
enough people, I could write a decent book. The key would be to
capture the perspective of people like Sean, in particular, from
his own point of view, and that of the throngs of people who
dipped in and out of his life on a daily basis. It sounded like
a delicate and difficult task to balance, but certainly worth a
try. But, best of all, Sean had an apartment for rent.

I began by recording my phone call to our mutual
acquaintance, Laurel Leff, in Manhattan. She was on her fourth
husband and had retired from selling stock at a high-flying firm
that specialized in pink sheets and new issue companies. A

"hello" was all that was needed to get her talking extensively about someone. She hadn't seen Sean in years and spoke about him mostly in the past tense.

"I always liked Sean. He had a sweet, hidden, sensitive side that made him very likeable. I don't know how he ever survived in Hollywood. I made him a ton of money in Amazon.com, the hot Internet stock. I got him in and out and he made over one hundred percent on his money. Others made more, but I had to get him out. I know that he needed the cash. He was tired of just making those cheap movies, although it made him a nice living. He always has a plan to fold his company into something bigger, but he can't ever come up with an idea. He kept telling me he'll make it big. I wanted to believe him. I still want to believe that he can do it, but I know Sean has one weakness, he's too human underneath it all. And human does not cut it out there."

Laurel's information seemed like an overabundance of preparation to discuss renting Sean's apartment. The last line remained in my mind, and served as a small clue for insight into my new education, the kind that I would learn to relish - freely volunteered by so many. Trite aphorisms in the form of allegedly friendly warnings would soon become part of my new vocabulary.

A young, curt voice answered the phone - the kind I was learning to adjust to on the coast. "Sean Daren Productions." I would meet a series of these revolving interns, people dying for production experience and willing to be enslaved for the privilege.

I reminded myself to be polite. "My name is Brantley - "

She had no intention of listening. She was very busy. "Hold on please."

I waited about fifteen seconds, during which time I envisioned her munching on a croissant. *Almond?* I wondered.

She came back. "Sean Daren Productions."

"I'm Brantley - " She cut me off again.

When she returned, her impatience had magnified. "You are?"

I bit my lower lip. "Dr. Brantley Benjamin. Laurel Leff asked me to call Sean about an apartment." I was being smart, using only his first name.

"We'll have to get back to you." Everything was 'we' in my new environment.

I wanted to make sure that my message was clear. "Will you tell Sean that I'm calling about an apartment?" I didn't realize that anything uttered on my end was meaningless to her.

"Do you have a number where he can reach you?" She spoke with finality. "He'll have to return." That was part of the industry shorthand language.

I gave her my number and she was gone in a flash.

Meanwhile, I made a few more calls to answer apartment ads from the local shore papers. The phone rang as I was leaving for the office. Already in the hall, I ducked back inside and ran to the kitchen phone.

I raised the volume on the answering machine as a message was already arriving. "Brantley. It's Lily. How's it going in La-La Land? I will try - "

I pushed the speakerphone button. "Hi. It's me."

"How's it going?"

"Not bad. I still feel like it's another world." I picked the phone up off the cradle.

"Duhhhhh. It is."

"I know."

"I miss you."

"I miss you, too."

"Any chance for me to come out and visit?"

"It's your call. If you like getting foot searched at the airport. Imagine actually having a foot fetish and getting assigned to the foot and shoe search posse."

"Ha! Do you really want me to come out?"

"Lily. I just said that it's fine. Listen, I've got a lead to rent an apartment. The owner is a retired movie executive or something."

"Doesn't that describe half the population?"

"I know, and the other half are actors."

"Have you started working yet?"

"Yes. Let me fill you in later. I have to get to the office."

"Okay. Speak to you later."

"Bye."

"Bye-bye."

I hung up the phone. It was good to hear Lily's voice. I did want her to visit. Why didn't I just come out and say it? Because I was afraid that she'd take it to mean that I wanted her to leave New York, and it was important for me to make it on my own. I knew better, there was no way she would ever leave the comfort of the moneyed crowd. It would never be more than a visit. The rest was pure fantasy.

Working in Beverly Hills was a stark contrast to Manhattan. Not only was the office design refreshing – big, wide open spaces with actual sunlight finding its way into the treatment rooms – but the people were actually calmer. They didn't explode while in the office, as many New Yorkers did. There was no shouting. No throwing of umbrellas, hats, or newspapers. In fact, nobody wore a hat, despite the constant sun. Also, it really never rained in Southern California. Newspapers? Maybe a copy of the *Hollywood Reporter*, the light-weight – in size and content – entertainment bible. Getting hit by that was nothing compared to even a daily-sized *New York Times*. But so far not a single patient had even hinted about anything critical enough that would warrant launching an object at the front desk manager or throwing something to the floor in disgust as they exited a treatment room.

I had already resigned myself to the daily drudgery of again performing root canal work all day, while listening to the buzz in the hallway outside the treatment rooms.

"Oh, my god, " Cheryl, the front office manager, would murmur every time a celebrity popped in. Cheryl would stop in her tracks and pretend to remove a speck of dirt from the sliding glass that separated her from the plush waiting room.

A slight woman would plop herself into one of the Marcel Breuer chairs. Her body was dwarfed by the chair design, her willowy arms rested on the flat, leather armrests like toothpicks.

She would state her name across the room to Cheryl. Cool. Calm. But loud enough for everyone to hear. The other patients tried not to take notice. But, it was impossible.

Cheryl would repeat the celebrity's name as if she was announcing a winner at the Academy Awards. She might as well have been doing just that, because the tiny-framed patient was often a bona fide movie star, someone who would be recognized as quickly in Cannes as in Des Moines.

Nobody became so star struck in New York. Celebrities walked the streets relatively virtually unnoticed. Sometimes people would corner someone famous, but I always thought that the stalkers were more likely from out of town, or at least Long Island or New Jersey. For the most part, nobody ever stopped anyone on the streets or in stores. Not so in Beverly Hills. My theory was simple; celebrities who hung out in Beverly Hills were looking for the attention.

I grew to expect the flow of celebrities coming to my office. I had had my share in New York, but the system in Beverly Hills was just not the same. Hugh Downs, the well-known television journalist, had to be the brightest patient I ever treated, or at the very least someone who wasn't ashamed of appearing intelligent. He needed medical clearance to go to the South Pole with the Navy. His own dentist didn't want to make the call regarding his oral health, so I, as a specialist, was asked to take responsibility. Hugh Downs had an acute mind and was willing to ask the right questions and absorb the information regarding his condition. He had an uncanny ability to pick out the important details of what was being said, and was able to formulate an intelligent decision on what should be done. We both arrived at the same conclusion, that he should have preventive root canal therapy before traveling to the South Pole. He had suggestive symptoms, so I could not sign the Navy release form required for the trip. There would be no health care practitioners around, and if his borderline case became worse, Hugh would be in agony, with a possible infection, thousands of miles from nowhere. It was a pleasure to treat him, a genuine character in a tricky business. He would talk about it later in interviews and reference it in *People Magazine*. My only regret was that he never once mentioned my name.

After my most recent day at the office, I headed over to Rochester Big & Tall. I was both, and for certain items accepted the 'big and tall' mantra as a must. I needed some casual slacks, something along the line of the popular Polo chino, the one that had its logo discreetly but still obviously tattooed on the ass of its devoted followers. I would settle for whatever

Rochester had in stock. The store was walking distance from my
office building.

When I arrived, a giant of a man with a booming voice was
on a cell phone. He was trying to hold a conversation with the
tailor and a salesman, while making a point into the phone about
his career. The voice and frame were unmistakable - the comedian
Brad Garrett, Raymond's brother on the popular sitcom *Everybody
Loves Raymond* (*But me.*) There was some concern about the
stitching on certain jeans, perhaps the quality of the fabric
was not exactly what Brad had in mind. He was polite but firm,
and seemed to know his subject matter. When the conversations
all died down, I mentioned that I had recently seen him in the
movie *Bleacher Bums* on television. He seemed genuinely
apologetic about his performance. I stopped him quickly to tell
him that I thought he was sensational. "It was one of the best
ensemble pieces I had ever seen. Besides, it was so hard. They
had you sitting for so long – facing the field." Then he gave me
some insider information about how the director let the actors
improvise their lines. He appeared happy. He thanked me and
headed for the fitting room. I was hustled by the sales staff to
finish my business, for fear that I was a disruptive fan on the
verge of causing a scene. Brad won an Emmy the next time around,
and said one of the funniest lines during the show, that he
hoped his win would open up opportunities for other Jews in show
business.

That night was my first formal cocktail party in town. I
had written my name on the back of a postcard that had asked if
I would be willing to serve on a City of Beverly Hills
committee. I thought that there wasn't a chance in hell that I
would be selected. I was not politically connected locally, and
if that part of the system worked anything like it did in New
York, sending out the cards was only a formality. The fix was

already in. Brantley Benjamin was not a likely choice. Wrong. I was accepted. Either they were hard up for bodies on the committees and felt that as a newcomer I had no hidden agenda and would keep my mouth shut, or someone I didn't know that knew me sent out the acceptance letters and included me as a joke. Really, who cares what an oral surgeon thinks about local politics?

The follow-up letter asked if I wanted to be part of the Business Triangle Planning Commission, a goals deal of some kind. It sounded like fluff since the group had no power, but I was in, eager to glad hand the locals. The list of names slated to move the city ahead were many of the top businessmen in town - the boss at Neiman Marcus, the Polo shop owner, developers from Rodeo Drive, and venerable founders of famous jewelry and curio shops. Somebody on that list was going to need a root canal. A thousand bucks was a thousand bucks. The party was at the incredulous Doheny Estate - Greystone Mansion - north of Sunset Boulevard. This palace had once been a residence belonging to the oil tycoon of Teapot Dome Scandal fame, and was now owned by the city, open to the public for everything from summer theater to automobile promotions.

I kept my tape recorder on inside the pocket of my sports jacket. Comedian Marty Ingels, probably more famous for being married to Shirley Jones, joked with me as he worked the crowd in his white suit.

One of the next people I chatted with was the actress Heather Renner - the young lady from the no t-shirt Jacuzzi interlude with Les-Lou. I found it impossible to tell her age. She could have been anywhere from twenty-five to almost forty. She exuded sex, from her constant smile down to her form-fitting skirt. We made no mention of the Jacuzzi. I didn't know whether she had forgotten me or just preferred to forget the incident.

44

Perhaps she took it all in stride. It was not something I needed to bring up.

Heather was smart, and had spent a great deal of time hanging with the Hollywood elite, an education not available at any institution of higher learning. I listened as Heather gave me her version of life in town. "The old adage that everyone has two jobs in Hollywood is really true. You don't have to be in the business to end up spending almost all of your free time schlepping around to promotions connected to entertainment. The most recent example was the opening and subsequent closing of the Planet Hollywood restaurant in Beverly Hills. We got to speak to all the movie stars - Willis, Arnold, Sly. That's business as usual in town...When residents wanted to get rid of those noisy gas blowers that the gardeners used they got Peter Graves as their spokesperson. Out here it's all intertwined and that's why I like it. It makes things more exciting." I said something about development, and Heather went on. "On the horizon? Beverly Hills is finally talking to different movie theater companies. I think it's time. You know we don't allow movie theaters to operate in Beverly Hills. It's coming. It's show biz. The people want it, but are so afraid that the riffraff will drive here to see a movie. If they posted a sign that said 'locals only', then it would be fine with everyone."

I also received an earful about Sean. She appeared to know him quite well. I was quickly learning that Hollywoodland was a very small town. She gave me Sean's home phone number and volunteered details about the interior of his new house, as well as how he was feeling about his life in general, including his mock attachment to his dog. I was amazed by what people volunteered. She behaved as if she knew Sean better than he did.

"Call him. It's fine. Sean likes to make money. He'll be glad to rent you the apartment."

I happily took the number and that night would leave a
message for him at home.

I was tired when I left the cocktail party, and was looking
forward to plopping on my bed with a beer and a bag of popcorn,
where I would listen to my recordings from that night. My beeper
went off while I was walking the almost half-mile to the parking
lot.

I checked with my answering service. A man named Donny
wanted to speak with me. It was an emergency. I immediately
called him back.

"Yeah, hello." The voice was gruff and assertive.

"This is Dr. Benjamin."

Assertive turned out to be an understatement. "Yeah, yeah.
My dentist, Zweiger, told me to call you. God, I hate him! He
says I need a root canal job and he can't do it and you're the
best. I can be at your office in half an hour. I'm in real
fucking pain. I took two Percodan since four this afternoon, and
it still hurts like a mother."

I glanced at my watch. It was almost eight. "I'm sure
you're uncomfortable. Can you be at my office at seven in the
morning?" It was the way things were done in Beverly Hills. "You
can increase the pain pill to every three hours."

Donny had other ideas. "Hey. What is this? Can't you do
something? I'm not going to wait around like this. Zweiger said
you'd take care of me."

I would find out subsequently that what Donny didn't reveal
was that Dr. Zweiger had told him two weeks ago to make an
appointment with me. I never blamed people for putting it off,
particularly since most infected cases didn't hurt in the
beginning. That was the nature of the toothache business; people
always became desperate after dark. A lot of theories had been

suggested, some scientific, indicating a relationship to anxiety levels, lack of motion, and head position.

None of those concepts were worth a damn, especially when someone was already hurting. "Okay. I can meet you at my office."

"Good. You're a good guy, doc." He said it with such finality. I didn't want to be on the other side of his current good graces.

That night I would meet an original character unlike any others I would come across in my new town. On the outside, he appeared simple and of less than average intelligence. He obviously had chosen a style that was purposely designed to deceive others. For most situations his overt bullying provided a short cut entrée to suit his needs. And from there he had a variety of schmoozes and passive-aggressive modes for every occasion. What a piece of work!

Donny was a thin man who wore conservative but expensive sport clothing like a button-down Polo shirt and matching golf jacket. He could pass for a college preppy with his sandy hair and ageless smile.

The meeting in the office was unremarkable medically, but the conversation was anything but ordinary. Once I gave him an injection and he was out of pain, Donny popped the question. "How much is this going to cost?" Few patients would ask about money at a time like that, just moments before the revved up drill would be inserted in his mouth, perhaps followed by a scalpel to drain his swelling.

"My fee for a molar, without surgery, is twelve hundred dollars, and I don't think this one will need complicated surgery." The fees varied, depending on how many roots were involved.

"Zweiger said it would be around a grand."

47

I stood firm. "He doesn't know my precise fees and this is a four-rooted molar, somewhat of a rarity. Once I take a look at it with the microscope, who knows, there might even be a fifth." That was stretching it, but the average was generally three.

Donny reached into his pocket, pulled out a wad of cash, and peeled off ten one-hundred dollar bills. "Here, it's a grand. Let's call it even."

I hesitated. "You can pay when you come back in tomorrow or the next day. I'll need to see you again to finish my work. It might even take two more trips." Some people assumed that cash payments entitled them to a discount, since if the situation were reversed they wouldn't report the income.

Donny had another angle. "Take the money, Doc. You know, I know a lot of people in town." While we waited for the anesthetic to take full effect, Donny rattled off many high profile names. He made it clear that he was well connected to the entertainment business, but he had 'other' interests, pieces of businesses ranging from the Chin Chin restaurant chain and Spago to a Lexus car dealership on Wilshire Boulevard. "Yeah, I know Wolfie Puck."

I accepted the money. I didn't want any trouble with Donny or his referring dentist, but especially from Donny.

Donny smiled in a way that made me feel sullied. "You're okay, doc." He meant it to come off as reassuring, which it did on some level.

That night, I only needed to work on Donny for about five minutes. He had a non-vital case, an infected tooth which required only making an opening to a chamber inside, in order to relieve the pressure and provide possible drainage. In most cases the patient received instant relief, and made the doctor appear like a hero. This time was no exception.

When we were finished, Donny continued to chatter. I didn't have anyplace to go, so I listened. He was funny, in a gruff sort of way. He made it clear that he wasn't gay, citing multiple recent sexual conquests, mostly actresses I had never heard of. I pretended to be impressed. The experience was a new one for me, and Donny was, as he would subsequently say about himself, 'a trip and a half.'

People and events that I had witnessed in the first few weeks repeated themselves in twisted patterns. Some would mix up their roles, and hidden agendas would become mangled like the remains of last year's bondage apparel. Locals traipsed the streets by day, disguised in rudimentary outfits of old jeans and sunglasses. Some were on their way to the 'ENT man' to have their sinuses washed, for fear of having a coke drip from their nostrils continue like the leaky faucets in their million-dollar homes. Cocaine was still around, but it was played down since most of the regulars had taken to smoking it.

The eyes were kept covered most of the day, hiding the blood shot irritated pools which signaled the revelry of the night before. Daily prescriptions needed to be filled for Vicodin, Valium, Prozac, Zoloft, and a regular supply of Zithromax, the newer antibiotic for warding off just about anything except anthrax. Pills were easy to score from doctors on an 'as needed basis', 'PRN', as it would be written on a prescription.

Actual allergies existed as well, though never directly attributable to the aromas inside Spago, where diners' bodies became odoriferous sponges. Patrons also absorbed a disturbing emotional air along with the wafting from the pricey cuisine that confused critics by its longevity in a town not known for its decent food. Diners in this world would eat anything served on a plate, provided that there were the requisite adjoining tables of celebrities, and an authoritative waiter who nearly ordered the amateurs' meals for them.

People traveled in lavish automobiles with the air conditioners on three-hundred-sixty-five days per year, and lately looked down on the traffic from their lofty perches inside over-the-top SUVs. Everything was drive-in - from money to eyeglasses, with proposals probably in the works for urology exams. "Can I take your sample, please?" Cell telephone waves oscillated the brains of the active lot like old zombie sci-fi movies. The constant cerebral scramble took place mostly in cars or attached to the ear of a diner who held the phone in one hand. Some kept an earpiece in place and spoke into a dangling mike, while begrudgingly downing a luncheon salad of curiously colored vegetables. Apologies were rare even after a phone played a loud ring song in the middle of dining conversation.

By nightfall everyone would be back in business, starting all over as bodies would transform magically into their designer nighttime armor, ready to do social battle in a world that thrived as much on its own frail human condition as it did in depicting it artificially in movies.

This is a story of insiders as much as it is my story. My success depended upon learning everything I could in order to survive. If I were able to put all the tales together, I might capture the heart and soul of Hollywood, if either ever existed.

CHAPTER TWO
Sean
Sean, Heather
Sean, Linda
Brantley
Sean, Bob

Sean had been managing to survive a typical Malibu
February. The seasonal highlights included the closing of Malibu
Canyon due to mudslides and falling rocks - nothing unusual.
Soon the Pacific Coast Highway would be completely closed due to
giant mudslides. Eventually, a one-hundred-forty-foot-long
retaining wall partially collapsed, damaging two adjacent homes.
Even the local Malibu courthouse was closed because of the
cascading sludge.

The local news deemed it a "routine" evacuation.

"Déjà vu all over again," said Sean as he skipped past a
recessed plasma television in his bedroom, designed to place the
screen flush against the wall. *Another fire*, he though.

The fire departments had an insurmountable task fighting
natural powers that far exceeded those of living deities inside
Hollywoodland and its muddy suburbs. No warning fax. No gossipy
e-mail. The publicity departments at the studios alerted no one
in advance. The wind came up on cue, as if the legendary

Selznick had risen from his celluloid grave to burn Malibu as in *Gone With The Wind*'s Atlanta. But this was no dress rehearsal.

If it wasn't Selznick, it had to be another of the equally mercurial moguls - Mayer, Lasky or maybe one of the Warners. A movie deity's sweet revenge, pulling a few strings on earth from the hereafter was the only possible explanation. The universal god couldn't be that cruel or vindictive. Besides, someone always had an axe to grind with these new people "in the business". Who better than one of the moguls who had to finally face the fact that he wasn't immortal?

The seven, ten, and twenty million-dollar homes sat perched, ready for a dirty slide into the ocean. Why were their inhabitants stupid enough to live in an area ravaged by mud and fires? Wasn't it always a Hollywood insider running from the fires on the local news? Go figure.

Sean checked the television, where the local news was hell-bent on scaring the entire city. "Fuck 'em. I've got my own problems."

He was a new resident of Malibu Canyon Road. Not much earlier, he had gotten a telephone call from a charming officer at the fire department, who had calmly told Sean to immediately evacuate his home.

No time that day for philosophizing as he searched for his three-year-old Doberman's leash. George Roy was named after the director who had given wunderkind Sean a job as an A.D. - assistant director - when he was only nineteen.

"George Roy. Why can't you find your own fucking leash?"

Sean paused and inhaled deeply. He surveyed the expansive open room whose glass windows overlooked the ocean. Darkness was about to set in, while the ocean still glistened innocently in a sepia sunset that no longer caused him to linger.

Sean found the leash wrapped around the faux metal umbrella stand by the front door. Sean picked it up, and dangled it as he shuffled. "George Roy. Here, boy. Let's go."

The leash made a dull sound when the metal clasp hit the white marble floor.

George Roy was nowhere in sight.

Sean bolted into his private office, wondering if he should take any personal belongings with him. The fire wasn't that close to his house, but with the shifting winds anything was possible. The situation was a difficult one for him, trying to decide which things in his life were actually valuable or mattered. He paused, reminding himself that he had a safe deposit box at the Wells Fargo Wealth Management Bank in Beverly Hills. The box contained everything important to him, a series of legal documents outlining his assets that also named his sole beneficiary, his daughter. The idea of his demise made him think in jagged flashbacks, mostly incomplete images of what once was or could have been.

He had removed all his marital pictures when his wife had left him two years ago. He thought about the circumstances, which even for Sean were dirty and tacky. Despite everything he had been exposed to in the entertainment industry, he had a very simple and moral code when it came to his wife, something he ultimately learned that she did not share. She had a lengthy affair with one of the Rosenberg brothers - high flying hustlers who had inherited some cash from their grandfather. Sean couldn't tell them apart. After several mishaps in business, the Rosenberg brothers started the short-lived-but-popular Santa Monica Safari. The customers drove along the beach in electric dune buggies, and ogled wild safari animals which were fenced in on one side by the shoreline and on the other by an elaborate faux design resembling a natural habitat.

The Safari was a big hit until Heather decided she was
going to "feed the kitty." She had been Sean's guest, who had
been invited by the Beverly Hills City Council. Well-fortified
with four margaritas, Heather stopped her dune buggy and opened
the protective plastic bubbletop. Standing on the bucket seat
she began hand feeding a young adult tigress some guacamole and
chips, part of a tricolor fusilli with extra virgin olive oil
and balsamic vinaigrette box lunch from the fabled Hillcrest
Country Club - usually intended for take along supper for the
Hollywood Bowl. What began as a routine photo op for the
photographer from the *Beverly Hills Courier* became a failed Jeff
Corwin safari adventure.

The tigress knocked Heather from the dune buggy, and then
backed off a bit, after turning its head away from the spilled
chips.

"Too spicy," said Sean, alluding to the snack and thinking
that the episode was over, since the tigress was well on her
way. Instead, the tigress turned and charged. However playful
its intention, the result bordered on a chilling catastrophe.

Before Heather could right herself, the tigress pushed
Heather face first into the sand.

"Don't move," shouted one of the guides.

Heather was reduced to guttural sighs as the tigress
sniffed around her lower body, tearing away the flimsy black
miniskirt to reveal a well-known fact in Hollywood - Heather
never wore underwear.

Click. Click. The newspaper photographer was about as
shameless as Heather, and since he felt safe still inside his
own vehicle, he rapidly used his telephoto lens to its best
advantage. Dozens of tourists captured the moment on videotape,
sandwiching the footage somewhere between the kids shaking hands
with Pluto at Disneyland and a close-up of Tom Cruise eating his

dinner at The Grill in Beverly Hills. All images were saved for posterity, to be seen back home in places stretching from Des Moines to Taiwan.

Within seconds, the safari experts had the tigress distracted while Sean covered Heather's butt with his golf jacket.

"Why the fuck are you laughing at a time like this?" yelled Heather as she was helped back into the dune buggy.

"I'm not laughing. You could have been killed or worse, your ass could have been destroyed." Sean was unable to resist the humor in the near tragedy, revealing at once his lack of sensitivity for Heather or anyone else's trauma, training that had come from years in the business and parents who had taught him to limit his emotional investments. He had developed a distance from human suffering that could only also be appreciated by career politicians or actors.

Heather wasn't physically hurt, but anyone's brush with death would surely make the top ten topics at the next therapy session. Her discussions would include how to make the most out of the public humiliation and psychological trauma. Her psychiatrist, Barry Leiberwolf, proved helpful, but he drew the line at agreeing to testify that her life was scarred beyond repair. She also sought out the help of local dermatologist, Dr. Manciewitz, who even with the different surname spelling still claimed ties to the famous movie family. Heather was rightfully livid and publicized her medical ordeal, although all Dr. Manciewitz was responsible for was repairing the scratches on the delicate and popular rear soft tissue.

One photo caption in the local paper was unavoidable. "City Council Protects Rear and Closes Safari Park." Worse for the Rosenbergs, videotaped footage of the incident made its way to CNN, making Heather's ass, albeit slightly blurred for the benefit of viewers, the most exposed visual image on cable television during a two-day period. This prompted some networks to run stories about the safety of theme parks in general, while others jumped on the inappropriateness of displaying the image as part of the news. The segment became one of the popular ones for twenty-four hour news networks, which relied on a bunch of resident talking heads to discuss and critique news in methods that no longer resembled what was once called journalism.

Heather eventually received an undisclosed settlement from the Rosenbergs' insurance carrier, despite her aggressive pleas with her own attorneys to stage a televised trial.

Overzealous pundits, local and otherwise, partially blamed Shawn for the episode, something about how stupid it was for him to continue his friendship with the Rosenbergs after one of them had broken up his marriage. Sean's brief fling with Heather was curtailed following the media coverage of the incident. There wasn't much to the relationship in the first place. They remained friends, always helping each other when a deal of any kind materialized. Heather regularly used Sean as an entrée to a variety of entertainment moguls, but more than anything else enjoyed receiving the Academy's free movies which were distributed to members prior to voting for the awards. This also went over bigtime with the locals. New Yorkers who were newly smitten with Hollywoodland kissed ass to be in line for the passed around DVDs.

With his mind refocused on finding George Roy and getting the hell out from Malibu, he glanced around. The only picture remaining on display was of Sean's parents, taken at a Bar Mitzvah in the seventies. He picked it up, studying their expressions as if for the first time. He heard his father rattling off many old-world Yiddish expressions, a simple mini-parable that when pieced together from his historic library became a bible for living - advice-laden 'facts of life' that often meant little or nothing to the ears of a child.

"Nifter-shmifter, a leben macht er?" "What difference does it make as long as he makes a living?"

Sean had made most of his money in the movie business, but was always open to new deals in emerging cash-rich arenas. He was more cautious today, having taken a bath on both WorldCom and Enron, while smartly agreeing to sell his AOL stock when it was at an all-time high. He kept his eye on emerging markets, while watching entertainment conglomerates that were still growing, with agents sliding directly into corporate executive suites. Some actors became politicians first and corporate moguls later. Sean dreamed of building a restaurant chain like The Hard Rock Café, once the darling of new businesses. He fantasized about 'folding' his movie business into a new shell company, but knew that he needed a seductive gimmick, particularly in the downturn economy reeling from the devastating financial and psychological effects of 9/11.

Sean felt disoriented as he moved around his office with George Roy's leash in his hand. He was still a handsome man, hiding his near fifty-one years with the requisite hair plugs and preventive tuck, pulled back behind his ears. His tall build made him tower over most everyone in the business. Whenever the wiry Sean would bring his slender frame into a room, people would notice. Sean was once at a party with movie star Tim Robbins and Conan O'Brien. People in the room were dwarfed by the three giants who towered over the miniscule leading men, most of whom wisely stayed on the other side of the room. The only time Sean blended in with the crowd was at Laker games, where the fans had more impressive and richer giants to ogle.

On the wall beside him was an original movie poster from *I Spit On Your Pasta*, a largely sought after cult classic that was

made for virtually nothing, and continued to make oodles of
money for Sean. He glanced at the poster, smiled, and went to
his office safe to remove the last few valuable items that he
kept in the house. Ten thousand in cash, a second series of
credit cards, his passport, a collection of photos featuring his
daughter and others of movie stars (already packed neatly into a
small black leather Gucci portfolio with a wrap-around leather
strap), an encrypted document with all his computer access
numbers and passwords, and letters of credit from overseas banks
where he held numbered accounts and stock in 'street names'. He
had everything he needed to continue his life as usual,
including a cell phone with a backup battery, and several
government issue food bars. He always kept extra water in his
car. After all, earthquakes were always a viable alternative to
a fire.

He was almost out of the office when he paused and rushed
to the wall. After a quick push upward to release the wire, and
then a pull toward him to separate the securing Velcro, the
movie poster was firmly in his grasp. *I Spit On Your Pasta* was
as much a part of Sean as anything else.

Back in his spacious living room, he glanced around at the
pretty pastel shaded furniture, 'courtesy' of Kreiss Imports.
Tom Kreiss and his brothers had also customized furniture for
basketball player Magic Johnson, so Sean had them do the same
thing for him, since his old furniture was uncomfortably small.
As Sean made his way around the house, his only thoughts were
the price tags that matched the items. He told himself that it
was very unlikely that his entire home would burn down. He had
homeowner's insurance, a Chubb Masterpiece plan, which was
considered one of the best in the industry.

George Roy was nowhere to be found. Sean felt that he had
done his moral best to find him. *How much time do you spend*

looking for a dog in a crisis? Dogs are smart; they can fend for themselves. Sean imagined a beach landing with soldiers, paramedics, firemen, and police. Robert Duvall led the way, reenacting the famous pre-surfing blow-up-the-beach scene from *Apocalypse Now*. This time the landing was filled with movie stars.

Sean, as did most of his friends and neighbors, envisioned everything in terms of a movie reference. This scene would end with Sean stranded inside his burning house, screaming out for George Roy, who is finally rescued by Tom Cruise, whose special elevator shoes allow him to catapult up a tree in order to prevent the spread of the fire to the house. Alternatively, it might be Kurt Russell, who played a firefighter in *Backdraft*; he would chop down the front door with an axe and come running through the flames with George Roy under his arm.

Sean chuckled to himself. He knew that he was a good writer, but who had the time to sit in front of a machine? There were plenty of hacks in town for that. Besides, writers were at the low end of the Hollywood food chain. Some line producers – part of the daily bread and butter people - made more money and commanded more respect on a film set. Most writers, however famous or large their literary contribution, never even made it to the set. The caterers were in greater demand when it came time to begin production. By the first day of principal photography, everyone seemed to forget that the scenes always began on a blank page, most often created by a single author. Rewrites by committee were routine, whose members included wives of studio producers, pathologically egomaniacal actors tailoring every word to their liking, and uncredited private script doctors who possessed 'artistic' license to hack away as they went. The number of story credits and screenwriters for ninety minutes of entertainment sometimes numbered six or seven.

Earlier, Sean had already taken two Zanax pills. It was his only reliable method to relax, and the fashionable choice by colleagues and doctors-to-the-stars. Even with the extra dose he felt his heart flutter, again prompting him to give up on finding his pet.

He imagined the headline. "Producer Dies In Worst Malibu Fire To Date." Then he wondered if his public relations firm had a complete list of his movies. It would be awful if his obit didn't have all his credits. Worse, if someone celebrated died within a day or two of his demise, and that was certainly likely given the size of the country and its obsession with celebrity, he might be relegated to a corner of a page, or perhaps passed over entirely. He could always count on the *Los Angeles Times* for something – they catered to show business people – but he was thinking more of *The New York Times* and continuing coverage on CNN.

"Where the fuck are you? George Roy. Come here boy. George Roy! Where are you?" His voice sang out with a legitimate ring of concern. He opened his front door and deposited the things to save outside.

He paused, glanced back toward the house, and reentered. He was committed to saving George Roy. "Hollywood Producer Sacrifices Himself To Save Pet." He liked that one.

Sean began darting around the house without a plan. The expanse was all on one floor, and it seemed to go on forever, with angles shooting off into a new hallway just when it appeared as if a room was coming to a walled end. The architect who had built the house initially presented a plan that he had proudly labeled as "some of my best work". When Sean heard how much it might cost, he redesigned the house without ridiculous additions like a Koi pond and moat-styled lap pool, instead settling for some of the architect's more "adequate work".

Sean began to panic; beads of sweat formed on his forehead.
His attachment to George Roy bothered him because he desperately
wanted to feel unemotional, while at the same time clinging to
what might tragically become his last and only contact with
legitimate human feeling. He had always viewed emotional
dependency as a sign of weakness. Through it all he wasn't ready
to accept that George Roy might be gone, lost forever up the
hill across from the ocean, in the scorching heat, deadly fumes
and swirling flames. At once Sean would bolt out the front door,
ready to run up the hill, ignoring the shouts of police and
firefighters, past the yellow tape fire lines, all to save
George Roy. It would be beyond heroic, the kind of heroism known
only to moral men, and Sean knew that he could be that kind of
man. His daughter Katherine would surely read his obituary in
the *Hollywood Reporter*. There was no way they could leave Sean
out of that rag. She would cry at ever believing her father to
be anything but the most human, kind, considerate, and self-
sacrificing man, and he had proved it by saving George Roy, and
losing his own life in the process.

Once out the door once again, Sean realized that he wasn't
about to sacrifice anything or anyone, particularly himself, to
find George Roy. As soon as he was safe in the car, an all black
Land Rover, he would report that George Roy was missing and hope
that the fire department or one of the neighbors had him in tow.

Sean rushed over to his driveway, and to his mixed delight
was greeted at the car by his faux best friend. "George Roy.
George Roy! You little bastard. You've been sitting there the
whole time."

He was nonetheless relieved to see George Roy waiting
patiently by the driver's door with the keys to the car at his
side on the ground. George Roy knew the routine. It was Sean who
was sometimes out of it. George Roy had gotten the keys, slipped

out the doggie door, and waited as he usually did for Sean to eventually come outside. Even on clearer thinking days, Sean could forget his keys as well as panic about leaving the house, sometimes returning to check the gas lines to the kitchen and close the fireplace flues, plus a series of other moderately neurotic exercises fueled by the bundle of money he had put into his house - but all done today under the guise of saving George Roy.

Sean's shrink and everyone's best friend, Barry, had told him that his behavior was normal. They should concentrate instead on other things like getting Sean off Zanax. Two years was a long time, but Barry avoided words like 'addiction', preferring instead 'slight chemical dependency'.

Barry would intone frequently, "It's more psychological than anything else."

He had a knack for establishing close relationships with all his patients. Most people liked him, and thought that he was for real. They didn't have people like Barry in New York. I, after meeting him, would never figure out if I liked him or not.

In sessions, Sean would be pumped up by Barry. "Compared to most people in this industry, and most people in and around the little world of Hollywood, you are actually a nice guy. You pay your alimony and child support, and kick in twenty thousand per year for each of your sister's sons, both in high tuition colleges, neither one of them with a major that he understands. So you're a Hollywood good guy, not exactly a pure soul, but a soul who perseveres in an industry that is full of stories that at first blush would appear to be almost true, but hard to believe by other industry or life standards. So what? You might call your life 'almost true' Hollywood stories, since if you retell things just the way they happened, it's hard for outsiders to understand or believe them anyway. You're very bright; you might even say brilliant. Brilliant people often appear simple, because they don't have an agenda. They speak directly. You can do that. I always thought that you could have made a decent doctor or even some kind of scientist. In this town, people of less intelligence don't answer in any simple way, they are on the make, and therefore often give complicated scenarios to hide their agenda and lack of any real intelligence. So, you do a little of both, but in the end you're a damned good salesman. You don't really have any other choice. Your business dictates your behavior. But you play it as good as anyone can, but you are really smarter than most of them. And when you sell, you are really selling a movie, not just the idea to get money into your account and worry about the movie later."

What a great out to have in life, a shrink who supported his every move. Sean needed Barry, and Barry knew how to keep his patient's ego inflated to just the right pressure.

Sean's thoughts quickly returned to his money-making skills, having a cool, calming effect on the hectic moment. It was his comfort zone, the real fuel for his existence. He knew how to turn a dollar. He used the meager proceeds from his movies to amass a small but profitable film library. When the money markets crashed in the late eighties, Sean was able to pick up a solid collection of movies at bargain rates. He knew who was strapped for cash, and was able to pry *Prison Boyfriend*, *Eviscerator*, *Hospital Volunteers*, *Voodoo Vibrator*, and his other personal favorite, *Night of the Bloodletters*, from his 'colleagues'. NOTB was nothing less than a classic in the B-movie world. Sean was quick to let anyone know that it was as good as any of the "best of Roger Corman. It's as good as anything he has ever made. And if you ask him, and I did, he even said so." Sean had no illusions about the comparison, knowing full well that in the first place, the industry snobs thought little of these types of movies. But, the money flowed in regularly from movies like NOTB, and that transmuted to an address on Malibu Canyon Road.

As Sean put the framed poster into the car, his thoughts returned to the one movie that had really turned his life around. *I Spit On Your Pasta* was not originally slated for a full theatrical release. Most of Sean's movies went straight to video or now DVD, an outcome for major studio flops as well. By hiring out-of-work television actors, and two or three ancient movie stars, Sean accidentally ended up with a half decent movie without spending a tenth of the cost of a major studio production. His longtime investing pal, Dave Stirling, came up with some distribution money for a four city opening. Rex Reed recently reviewed the movie as part of a small NYC film festival for the ultra hip *New York Observer* saying, "I don't know where he dug up the cast...But it was just a gas!"

ISOYP was about a group of people who had decided to eat and "fuck ourselves to death", the often repeated line uttered by the senior member of the cast. Sean naturally borrowed the concept, as he did for all his movies, from previous work. That idea was taken from a Luis Buñuel movie, *The Discreet Charm of the Bourgeoisie*. Sean also lucked out when he hired a young director named Lou Bradley, who had just spent ten years off and off-off Broadway. Because of his theater background, Lou was able to force some reasonably interesting dialogue into the movie. That, coupled with Sean's lack of interest in anything literary, unless he wrote it himself, proved a positive combination for creating lively dialogue. After watching ISOYP, people exited the theaters still laughing, despite the awkward plot line and occasionally having been drawn in to the macabre and disgusting elements of the food and fuck feast. The movie's off-beat, dark comedic appeal fell flat in the scenes that Sean had a hand in, spiraling away from any original momentum and landing back in B-movie hell. He had insisted on full frontal nudity for the men, most of which was cut or reduced to split second takes. But Sean's love for the scatological was unavoidable. "A gorgeous woman farting. That's funny. People laugh at that." He may have been right, but it made it harder for Lou to balance the movie. Even with Sean's input, Lou managed to turn out one of the great low-budget weird comedies of the year. Robert Vaughn received a special mention as the Rabbi who came to make a shiva call, got drunk, and ended up eating himself to death via a pile of shellfish. His last words included, "I can't believe the Talmud told us not to eat shrimp. Somebody must have tried a bad piece their first time. This stuff is sensational!"

ISOP eventually grossed eighteen million worldwide. That wasn't bad for a picture that cost less than one million to make. It made Sean a rich man for the second time in his life, with the help of a bankruptcy filing, and a marvelous accountant who managed to eliminate the word 'profit' from the production company's vocabulary and balance sheets.

Sean never forgot the experience, and how everything somehow fell into place. It was a rare accomplishment for an independent moviemaker, and since then he had no such comparable luck, despite trying his best to copy every new trend. Lately, nothing seemed to be working, and the competition from independent filmmakers had put many of Sean's colleagues out of business. Even the big studios were doing what used to be called 'independents'. Kids with hand-held cameras could end up making a bundle. With costs skyrocketing, to make something like ISOYP would run well over five million. Sean knew that that was no excuse, but he was becoming desperate for another moneymaker. He racked his brain day and night to figure out a way to make his next movie deal work. He desperately needed a windfall.

He did have an idea. It had come to him about a month ago, in an unexpected way, as had all his great ideas. *Beverly Hills Cannibals*. He didn't know anything else about the movie, but he was clear on the title. That's how he started all his creative projects, using the title as the sole driving force. It had worked before, so why not now? He also wanted to "work in" something about 9/11, but that might be a separate movie. He wasn't sure, but he knew never to tamper with what he considered to be his own special genius.

His 'partners' didn't always share his enthusiasm, but they played along most of the time, since money came in from enough of Sean's projects to keep their attention artificially riveted on his every word. Sean would get the 'idea' and then they would do all the work. Most of the days in the office were quiet - except for 'idea' days. One time Sean burst into the office after *Driving Miss Daisy* had won Best Picture at the Academy Awards. He flew in with his usual flushed face, while he slid his lower lip on his upper incisors. Gary and Bob, his on-again-off-again co-producers and line producers, knew to stop what they were doing and wait until the words exploded from Sean's mouth.

"*Driving Miss Daisy Crazy*," he said, almost delirious. "We'll make a killing. Like a cross between *Whatever Happened to Baby Jane* and *Gaslight*. Get a list of cancelled sitcoms from the last five years. We can get that old broad, you know, Getty or something. The one from *Golden Girls*."

"She dead." It was Gary, and he was always a realist.

"So what. You know the type." Sean sat on top of Bob's desk. That annoyed Bob, but only Gary was aware of Bob's criticisms of Sean. Bob never got in Sean's way. "Too many

cartons of free cigarettes to give up. Besides, I'm getting to
old – what am I saying – I'm way too old to get a studio job",
is what Bob had told his sister when she complained about all
the shit he had taken from Sean.

Bob was already making script notes on the new project. He
was a trooper, never denying the possibility of any idea. He
rattled off the words like a short order cook receiving another
order of an 'egg-white omelet.' "Okay, I think I got it, you
want to do a scary movie where the schvartze scares the old
white bitch to death?"

That single logline crystallized it for Sean. "It'll be a
cult hit," he screamed. "It will out gross *I Spit On Your
Pasta*."

The day he had thought of *Beverly Hills Cannibals*, Sean was
getting his hair cut on North Bedford Drive in Beverly Hills, at
the famous Penner Salon. He was waiting for Stanley, the owner,
to finish cutting Betty White's hair, when he overheard the
front desk receptionist, Ed, say something that sounded like
"Beverly Hills Cannibals". Sean believed that Ed was referring
to some commotion outside in front of the shop, and that that
was Ed's way of dismissing the local riff-raff, who were
probably arguing over a rare parking space.

The expression stuck. And it sounded so right. Sean only
needed to develop a story. That usually meant doing a sequel
from something he already owned, or "ripping off" an existing
plot line that had already made money. He was always careful to
change enough of the original story to avoid litigation. If he
ran out of ideas he would 'borrow' one of his partners' movie
plots, since they weren't in a position to refuse a deal over
derivative material. Even outsiders would think twice about
suing, since in order to collect on a judgment, a movie had to
show a profit, at least on paper. Columnist Art Buchwald learned

that the hard way, in the process of exposing Eddie Murphy's
theft of one of his screenplay stories - that it was easy to
show no net profits, and taking "monkey points', net points, was
essentially worthless.

As soon as Sean and George Roy were safe in the oversized
vehicle, his thoughts focused back on the fire. The trip from
the house was a slow, tortuous, almost two-mile run to the
Pacific Coast Highway, where schadenfreude crowds had already
gathered in the hope of witnessing a tragedy. *This could be
awful. The whole fucking thing could go up in smoke.* People like
Sean never thought about why they had originally moved to
Malibu, and as a result left themselves vulnerable to the fire
and mudslide wrath of the Hollywood gods. Many in the business
had flocked there automatically when the big bucks started to
roll in. It wasn't a choice thing. It was just something they
did. Sean had dreamed of living in Malibu while he squirreled
away cash until he had a 'spare' five-hundred thousand to put
down on a lot. He had never thought about the fires before he
moved. He had fought battle after small battle with the worst
"scum-sucking vermin in the world," in order to get that house.
And now, "the whole fucking thing could go up in smoke." As he
drove down the hill towards Pacific Coast Highway, he kept
repeating the words aloud

It would be a shame. A lot of people hadn't even seen the
new house. The most important one would have been Sean's father.
Sean needed to show him what he had. "Look, dad. It's all mine."
Sean wanted to enjoy the expression on his father's face when he
viewed the property. But it would never happen. His father had
died before the house was completed.

The fatherly advice from the past filled Sean's thoughts
like some computerized playback. His father was a hard-working

pharmacist, who took advantage of neighborhood contacts and changing social trends to make a little extra money.

"You get a good education working through the night. A little bit of everything comes in at night. You learn a lot about commerce, from the bottom up," was how Sean's father described his early work experiences in his little, retail pharmacy.

Sean suspected, but never really knew, that his father had made a tidy fortune on the side by selling Quaaludes, federal narcotic prescription blanks, and the occasional vial of pharmaceutical cocaine. By the time the pharmacy was investigated, Sean's father had quit and reinvested the money in coin-operated arcades. At about the same time, the Atari Company was expanding and pinball was being replaced by electronic video games. With strong Italian partnering, Sean's father moved on again, ultimately trading up for part of a brokerage firm called John Muir and Company. That run was also short lived, but it was the run of runs, making Sean's father quite wealthy buying and selling a ton of new issue stocks.

Sean finally got around to thinking about the people who were close to him. He had recently been dating Linda Stirling, the daughter of investor Dave Stirling, a wealthy Southern California businessman, drowning in oodles of third generation money, with a perverse interest in the movie business.

Linda loved to tell the story of how they had met and would do so frequently at charity events whenever they were stuck at a table with strangers, waiting for the delivery of the dreaded rubber chicken entrée.

"Sean was the most handsome man I had ever seen. The moment I set eyes on him, it was one of those instant attractions. He was tall, well-dressed. He was so different. He rarely wore a coat and tie. After all, he was in the movie business and ties

were definitely out. He still keeps a ancient picture in his
office where he is wearing a tie, an old black-and-white of a
Bar Mitzvah party. He must have been in his early twenties, and
he's like standing behind one of the tables, you know the way
the photographers have half of the people at a table stand in
the back? So Sean sticks out because, you know, he's very tall,
maybe six-five, and he is really towering over the people, like
he was stuck there - out of place. He had on one of these very
thin ties, with his collar opened and the tie loosened. He
looked like a movie star, or a drunken basketball player. I
still think Sean wants to be an actor. Look at him. He's a
handsome, imposing guy."

Sean politely smiled whenever Linda made that speech. She
could handle anyone in public, particularly Sean. He was
generally quiet around her, and it gave him a much needed break
from his daily grind. "She's royalty," was how he had described
Linda to Bob and Gary after they had first met.

That's just about how Linda and Sean's relationship had
actually started - pure sexual attraction. But the difference
between them and the rest of Hollywood was that when the sex had
dried up, people usually didn't hang around to find out what the
aftermath would be like. Lately, things had cooled for Linda and
Sean, despite having their paths cross regularly due to Sean's
ongoing association with her father Dave. Overall, the
relationship wasn't over.

Sean's daughter Katherine had an entirely different take on
her father, and kept him on his toes. While he continued to
drive, he thought about his last luncheon meeting with her, and
how she had stirred elements of his soul that he thought and
hoped had died long ago. Lunch was at Kate Mantilini, a Wilshire
Boulevard industry hangout and insider staple for scheduled
meetings, walking distance from the Writer's Guild movie

theater. Mantellini was owned by Marilyn and Harry Lewis. Harry was a former actor who with Marilyn had built a chain of popular Hamburger Hamlet joints. When the chain was sold, they hung on to Mantilini and Hamlet Gardens, the latter also a company town retreat, with one son a chef and the other keeping his eye on the till.

That day, Katherine had to muster more nerve than usual to get the words out. More than Sean could have realized. She always took risks with her father, because she believed that if she remained passive and didn't go full throttle when she had him alone, she might lose more than his present focus and end up with an estrangement of sorts or just a distant polite arrangement.

She began with, "Do you think God really exists or do you accept the old view that the whole religion thing is just one of man's complete deceptions, and if you accept it as a deception, is that why you feel comfortable making those kinds of movies that you do?"

The long frown on Sean's face said it all. "I don't know." She always challenged him, unabashed in her own personal investigation. She spoke for a long time while Sean's face twisted, perhaps in mock agony, as he toiled over her ideas.

"You must still have a fix on your own morality, even if you continue to make the kinds of movies that you make. You might think that believing in God is my substitute for the lost father, but I think I can have both. I know this might really floor you, but you know that I believe in God. Maybe it's because everyone in our house was so afraid of you. I simply needed more love, hoping to care for the infant in me that never seemed satisfied."

Sean pushed his favorite food away - frog's legs. He listened intently, prompting the passing waitress to think that he didn't like his food.

"Are those okay?" she asked. "Let me get you another plate."

"They're fine. I'm not hungry." He gave the plate to the waitress.

Katherine could really shake him up. He knew that she meant well, and he was willing to listen, but it was rare for him to follow anyone's advice. He tolerated his daughter's guru friends, even putting one up at his old house. Lately, he preferred the luncheon meetings. Katherine was leading her own life as a production assistant, and he thought that it was important for him to keep his distance.

Sean had to make his way down the hill and into the 'safe' zone on Pacific Coast Highway. He found himself stymied in a slow line of expensive cars, trailing a silver Corniche convertible. It must have made a funny scene, the rich running from the hills in their garish vehicles.

"Fuck the house. It's just a house," Sean said aloud. The love for his house was now gone, in case it wouldn't be there when he returned. In just a few seconds, the house that he had built from scratch was no longer part of his life, lumped in with the other dismissed histories of his past.

There were more important things than the damn house. He had only half of his financing for his next picture, some from Dave Stirling. To most that would seem like a blessing. He had run all over town to dig up the funds. He almost picked up a decent chunk of the money from an Indian movie producer he had met through the famous tennis-playing Amritraj brothers. Sean was going to add some cash left over from his trading in Amazon.com - luckily before the big tech dive. He knew that he would have to pay taxes on it, but wouldn't worry about that until the end of the year. By then, his accountant could come up with some scheme to hide the profits.

The Indian guy was tough, arrogant, and rich. He had financed some low budget movies that were coining money all over the world. Sean had pitched him project after project, script after script. Finally he pitched the idea about *Beverly Hills Cannibals*. He got the call some time later. *This might be doable*, Sean thought after the brief conversation.

"This isn't bad. I want to get involved," was all the Indian big shot had said.

"I knew you'd like it." Sean had no idea which project he was talking about.

"It needs a little work," said the Indian.

"Yeah. The ending sucked, right?" asked Sean, figuring that he'd play it safe since everyone always wanted to rewrite the endings. He didn't even remember pitching an entire story to the Indian. Sean would have to draw it out of him in bits and pieces.

"Awful, and we need more tits and ass," the Indian said, giving away his age and perspective.

"Sure..sure…When can we talk in person?" Sean didn't have any problem with additions or changes, since there was no script and no story.

"This week. This is a good one. Let's get going," said the Indian.

Later that week later the Indian did a flip-flop, a typical one-eighty move. "I don't know. Why don't you take a look at this other screenplay? I think I'd rather go with something like this." All along he had wanted Sean to look at one of *his* projects. Nothing new.

As Sean continued to drive toward the PCH, there was considerably more traffic winding its way down. Apparently, everyone had decided to leave their homes about the same time or else the media trucks had blocked the highway, making it difficult for people to navigate once they reached the beach, causing a logjam all the way up the hill.

Sean's tongue moved uncontrollably and lashed out with wild strokes at the side of his gums, the area that was most recently curetted by Dr. Mosher San, yet another fabled Beverly Hills periodontist. Either the rich and the famous in Beverly Hills had the worst periodontal disease in the world, or like everything else within Hollywood health care, were being overtreated and ripped off. Dr. San had been Sean's periodontist for about five years, immediately following the havoc news created by his onset of moderate periodontitis, a diagnosis meant to conjure up images of being toothless, which in Sean's business could quickly lead to becoming homeless. As Sean had told his friends, it was the fancy disease description for someone with "farshtunkena gums" and a lot of money. "If you're poor they probably tell you that you have lousy gums and it's hopeless." After getting the diagnosis, Sean had shuffled around depressed and nearly suicidal for two weeks. All he could envision was a fixed image of himself as a toothless panhandler, trying to eke out a living on Rodeo Drive, and sleeping in the park on Santa Monica Boulevard, which at least had a public bathroom.

In those days, Sean had been taking Prozac, prescribed after only one visit to Dr. Marder, a onetime disciple of the hip Bedford Drive analysts. Neither the Prozac nor heavy drinking helped avoid the gum issue.

At the first visit with Dr. San, Sean had asked if smearing cocaine on his gums could have caused the problem.

"It couldn't help it," was Dr. San's quick, meant-to-be-cool answer. A lot of his patients were coming in with inflamed gums, secondary to recreational cocaine use. Most of the real damage was caused by simply not flossing and brushing. People up for days on coke were unlikely to pay attention to oral hygiene, or any other kind of hygiene. The local proctologists and gynecologists reported some interesting cases of inflamed body orifices after heavy coke binging.

At the same time as Sean's gum work, Dr. Marder kept arbitrarily fiddling with Sean's dose of antidepressants. The Doctor didn't believe in blood tests for accuracy. Besides, Sean had never told Dr. Marder about his recreational drug habits. Marder was too square. It was during that period that a friend told Sean about Barry, a hip, younger shrink who was rumored to have Stallone, Hawn, and Katzenberg as patients. Whether it was true or not didn't matter. Sean hit it off with Barry at a party, who made an on the spot diagnosis - Sean was not suffering from any real clinical depression. Zanax was the new medication to go with the progressive point of view - generalized dysthymia with an acute anxiety problem.

Daily meetings ensued with Barry, tapering off to once a week when Sean's insurance coverage had maxed out. Sean took full advantage of the fact that Barry had a weakness for anything remotely connected with show business, resulting in favored appointment slots and lots of free medication.

"I get so excited just being on the set during filming," Barry would say.

Sean had given Barry tickets to industry parties, places where Barry rubbed skewered chicken with stars from the past and present, everyone from Kirk Douglas to Jim Carey. Most of the actors who Sean knew well were mostly unemployed television

veterans who would naturally work for cheap day rates in his
movies. Barry loved it all.

One of the first people Barry met through Sean was a very
attractive and bright actress named Robin Mattson. Robin had
just finished filming a movie with a then virtually unknown Nick
Nolte and perhaps lesser known Don Johnson. She had been
considering working in one of Sean's projects. Barry stuttered
when he had first met her at one of Sean's parties, and actually
asked for her autograph. Years later Robin would sell cookware
in over-exuberant infomercials with Florence Henderson, the two
giving record setting 'mugging' performances in front of
prepared food. "I know her," Barry would tell anyone willing to
show the slightest bit of interest, particularly when Robin
became an immensely popular soap opera actress.

Being enamored with the business was only the beginning;
Barry was a real sucker when it came to plunking down his own
cash for projects. He was often available for quick option
money, usually a twenty-five thousand dollar minimum. That would
entitle Barry to follow the entire production process, from
rewriting the screenplay to all the way up through opening night
screenings. Some of those were held in moderately sized
'private' theaters with buffet areas reminiscent of the overdone
salad bars in all-you-can-eat restaurants.

Sean was annoyed by those little tissue tears in his mouth.
It made him sad to think that any part of his anatomy was in
shreds. "Fuck you San and your fucking brutal hygiene bitches."
The girls did pride themselves on chrome spittoons filled with
blood. Working with high-speed suction cuspidors no bigger than
tiny soup bowls was a challenge for both the patient and the
sadistic scraper. One misguided spit of bloody saliva, and
whatever Sean wore to the office was ruined. He felt compelled

to bring a wardrobe change to appointments with San. And this, despite the strangling bib.

"God. Why are you doing this to me? First, the Indian fucks with me...and now my fucking gums. Do you want to fuck up my whole life?" What little faith he had surfaced during anxiety-provoking moments like that one.

Sean popped another Zanax as he inched down the hill. In a closed thermos cup at his side was a store-bought Bloody Mary mix with vodka, a fifty-fifty combination. Sean grabbed it from its position inside its techno-perfect holder, recessed within the leather-thickened console. He gulped from the little opening and washed down the pill.

"Shit. My voicemail," Sean said out loud. He realized that if the house burnt down, he would lose the current messages, which were separate from his cell phone voicemail.

He pushed the speed dial button to his home, waited for his machine to pick up, and when it did punched in his code to retrieve his messages.

"Hello, Sean. It's Gary. I've got Lew Shawn attached to doing our scouting in Vegas for the same price as the last picture. He wants his usual perks, you know, sex, drugs, and a boxed set of Vic Damone CDs."

Sean chuckled and pushed the button in order to move ahead to the next message.

It was a stranger's voice.

"Hi. This is Dr. Brantley Benjamin. I'm a friend of Laurel Lefrak's. She said to get in touch with you when I'm out on the coast, and that you might have an apartment that I could look at. Well, I'm here. Heather Renner gave me your home number and I also left a message at your office. Please give me a call when it is convenient. Thank you." (When I had left my number I was already feeling that I had been too aggressive. I had a lot to learn about what constituted aggression in Sean's world.)

Sean continued on to the next message without much thought. He did have a place at Horn-Sunset Towers to rent, but thought it was a longshot renting to some transient doctor from New York. For Sean, it sounded like a short-term deal at best. Whatever. He would meet with this Brantley guy because Laurel had recommended him. Sean kept up his 'relationships' with a lot of people. Some had taken to calling it 'networking', but to Sean it wasn't the same thing. Networking seemed so obviously shallow and deliberate, even in Sean's business. *Hi. I'm only calling to stay in touch. Hope some day we can make money for each other. Got to go now. I have forty other calls to make this hour.*

Sean listened to the beeping sounds. Then the next message arrived.

"*My Big Fat Greek Wedding!*" is catching on," said Bob. "It did good money on two screens, one here and one in the Rotten Apple." Movie talk was Bob's life, and he could smell a break-out money maker.

Another message. "Hi, Dad. I hope everything is okay. I saw the news. There's a lot of fire trucks and stuff on the PCH. Are you okay? I've got my cell. Call me. Love you."

"That was your last message," said the monotone electronic voice.

Sean needed another drink. He downed the last of the Bloody Mary, holding the cup at an extreme angle in order to get the last few drops out. He'd have to wait almost an hour for another drink. He was always careful not to get a DUI on PCH. That was a deadly and common combination for people in the business. Officers were used to pulling over drunken movie people who lived in Malibu, but if you got the wrong cop on the wrong night you could end up under arrest, like Nick Nolte and his famous mug shot. For a few years, Sean had carried a vial of urine in the car, all ready to go in case it went that far at the station. His attorney friend, Kyle Bixler, who often represented movie people for more serious crimes, had procured a few police vials for Sean. The other ploy that had worked for a few years was to ask the officer if you could give him or her another urine sample after you had supplied the first. If they refused, then they were denying some kind of basic right and the case had to be thrown out. That eventually changed and there was really no easy way around a DUI. You had to stay under the legal limit. That's where the Zanax really helped.

"Damn," said Sean out loud. He forgot to get his weekend shirts out of the cleaners. He panicked and thought about heading back to the house, because the blazer he had taken with him was black, and he didn't want to wear anything but a black shirt with it. He wondered if the cleaners might still be open, and he could bail out his black shirts.

"Just relax," he said. He pushed the CD switch and listened to Tony Bennett. He didn't like him all that much, but all the company people were playing Tony again. It did have a calming effect, because it made him think of something that made him smile. His insurance agent, who was a big Tony fan, in conjunction with a flexible appraiser from the bank, had helped Sean arrange for a homeowners policy that exceeded the value of the house by about three-hundred-and-fifty thousand dollars. Sean never signed some of the needed documents and left the 'minor' forgeries to his agent.

Further down the hill, his mind flashed back to the moments before he had evacuated. He had left the television in the living room tuned to MSNBC. Pat Buchanan, back with Bill Press on a new network, was mouthing off about something, still not satisfied with anything Clinton did while he was in office. Sean really despised the right wing. He had a vision of Pat Buchanan being gang raped by a bunch of transvestites, who first tied him up, spanked him, and then took turns fucking him in the ass. Then they revealed that they were all Republicans.

The sonofabitch might like it, Sean thought.

Then he laughed. "Sonic tongue cleaner," he said. Dr. San had sold him an electronic sonic kit for taking care of his mouth, including the never-used attachment that reminded Sean of a mini waffle maker.

At the bottom of the hill on Pacific Coast Highway, Sean saw a bizarre, surrealistic scene consisting of different colored fire trucks, television crew vans with satellite dishes, and dozens of Explorers, Suburbans, a few Hummers, and the old standard for the industry, the Land Rover. He slowed as he reached the disorganized intersection. The sun had almost disappeared over the horizon, but the highway was bright with artificial lights. Traffic was stalled on both sides of the PCH.

Malibu is on fire! he said to himself. He parked his car on the gravely shoulder and scurried along the side of the road. He could see the fire blazing in the distance, on both sides of the highway.

The fiery and black cinders fell from the darkened sky like incendiary manna, food to the news crews scurrying around looking for people to interview. This was going to give them something to report on for three consecutive days and nights. The scene had become surreal. As Sean shuffled amongst the turmoil, he felt as if he was an extra in one of his own trashy movies. *This can't be real.*

With the ocean as a backdrop on one side and the burning hills on the other, Hollywood television reporter and film commentator David Sheehan was conducting a live interview with a woman who looked a little like Sean's Aunt Marge. He rubbed his eyes, thinking that he should have eaten before taking the pills with booze. Sean moved a little closer to see Shirley MacLaine giving an animated, almost funny interview about the evacuation.

That was typical Hollywood. Anyone famous would be treated as an expert on any subject, if they decided to speak. Sean walked over and listened as David spoke to Shirley. It was as if she was part of the Army Corp of Engineers and David was doing his best to play Dan Rather.

Hollywood, thought Sean. *Oy!* Even he could be a cynic.

The traffic was moving again, albeit slowly in one lane south toward Santa Monica and Beverly Hills.

Sean returned to his car and pushed another code for speed dialing. He prided himself on the ease with which he had adapted to new technologies, but stopped short when it came to e-mail on his telephone. He secretly hoped that it wouldn't become an industry standard, because there would be no choice left but to use the feature.

"Hello," said the deep, baritone voice. It was Bob. He was sitting at home with his legs raised high in his new Relax-The-Back recliner. A table to his left supported a healthy sized pitcher of martinis and an open tin of Planters salted cashews. His flat screen plasma television filled half the wall in his den, with the other half sporting a map of the world with clocks set to different time zones. He didn't have a clue as to which cities it was set to, and didn't care. He enjoyed the look.

"Bob, baby. The place is burning down. I'm going to be homeless," said Sean.

"Are you okay?" was barely discernable through a mouthful of nuts.

Sean handled everything matter-of-factly. "Yeah, yeah. I'm down on PCH. I can't go back up tonight."

81

Bob had been expecting the call. "I'll tell the security guard at the gate to let you in. They have a key in the office. I have a date tonight, so just let yourself in. The fridge is loaded and there as those minuscule frozen diet shit things to eat in the freezer."

"Date with who?"

"It's not Melanie Griffith. She's busy posing naked with Antonio."

"Come on. Who's your date?"

"What's the difference?"

"The difference is maybe she has a friend." Sean was less than half-serious.

"Yeah, right. We can rent a limo and make out in the back and then switch - just like college...I'll let security know that you're coming."

"I should be there in about thirty."

"Oh, I might still be here."

"Then make me a Bloody Mary."

"I don't have any mix."

"No tomato juice?"

Bob sounded a tinge annoyed. "I don't know."

"The last time I was at your house I brought two bottles of the mix."

"Heather likes it. It goes fast when she's around." Bob occasionally dated Heather Renner, who I would learn lived in the same building where Sean had his rental apartment above Sunset Boulevard. It sure was a small town. Everyone was connected in some way, however insignificantly.

"Oh, great."

"Stop at the liquor store at Beverly Glen."

"Okay. I'll see you in the morning then."

Sean pushed the 'end' button.

82

"Right," answered Bob after the call had disconnected.

Bob flipped a small lever and his chair shot him forward, almost hurling him to the floor. He was quietly fuming. He wanted no part of Sean's problems, yet something unwritten in their relationship said that Sean had to get his way. That was how Bob was able to fill the role as Associate Producer or Line Producer on almost every one of Sean's projects. The title didn't matter. Bob just worked his ass off during a shoot, from providing coke for demanding stars to making sure that craft service didn't short them on any food items. Bob's personal intake demands were simple – Snickers bars and Dr. Pepper. But the guys who schlepped the lights around needed to be fed real food. Bob had always warned the acting extras that if they wanted anything substantial to eat they had better beat the grips to the buffet tables. For some of the aging stars, even the hot tray service would not suffice and Bob would need to be certain that their favorite restaurant food was on hand. Sometimes Sean would hand deliver a hot corned beef sandwich, bagel and lox, fettuccine Alfredo, or something more esoteric, as if he had made it himself. And it best be inside a bag from the star's designated restaurant. As needed, Sean would add, "And Wolfgang says 'hello'."

The prior night had been a simple one for Bob. His friend and my patient, Donny, called to say that he had met a few women through an escort service in the Valley. It had happened before, and it was Donny's way of keeping a hand in Sean's business. In exchange, Bob would tip Donny off about any new projects. Sometimes Donny would bring in a fading star or a writer/director who would work cheap. That way, Donny could pick up a point or two on the producer's side of the financing.

Donny had a knack for making deals in businesses that he'd never heard of. People listened to him and he got his piece of someone else's pie. I would learn from Donny that, "Sean was a good guy. I used to bring guys from the beach over to his office. A lot of guys hanging around Venice Beach wanted to be in the movies. Like that's a fucking surprise. One thing with Sean. He never screwed me out of a nickel. It's not like he paid a lot, but he did pay. And he never bullshitted me. I've been bullshitted all over the place from some of the biggest cocksuckers in town. It's part of the game. If Sean made any projects from anything I brought in, he always gave me a piece."

I would actually run into Sean that night, but of course not realize who he was. Mickey suggested that I buy my booze at the same liquor and caviar store that Sean frequented. "They have a great selection of champagne and good prices. Caviar, too. In the back. Unbelievable stuff. The owner's son has some connection with the Iranian Beluga. " I didn't have Mickey's cash flow, so I planned to pass on the fish eggs.

Once I had arrived, the store didn't seem so reasonably priced to me, but I was able to find something to keep in my fridge. I had an old habit of being well-stocked. While I was browsing the chilled selections, Sean entered. He moved with precision, as if he were on a mission. He was an imposing figure, and the response of the staff showed the effect.

An older man who was working in the back quickly came forward, and made his way rapidly down the aisle. "Mr. Daren. What do you need?" He had a slight accent and wore a plain, long-sleeved white shirt and ill-fitting grey dress pants with a black belt and ornate shiny buckle.

A girl behind the counter smiled and said, "I will put it on your account," while she took a pen in hand and began to write.

"How are you?" Sean didn't wait for an answer. "I need two bottles of Bloody Mary mix and two Grey Goose." His head moved around like a spy checking the room.

She answered, "Right away, Mr. Daren."

I heard the name, but it didn't sink in.

I got the feeling that this was someone very important in town, at least that's what the people in this store thought.

"Any caviar tonight?" The man asked with a broad smile, gesturing with one arm toward the back of the store.

"What have you got?"

The man waved his arm for Sean to follow, and the two headed down the aisle. I peered toward the back and I could see a huge walk-in refrigerator. It was dimly lit, but the steel front reflected what little light there was across a tiny table that was covered by a smooth slab of white material, suitable for mixing or spreading.

The man entered the refrigerator and returned with a tub of caviar that he strained to carry in two hands. After carefully removing the plastic wrap-lined lid, he spooned out a helping that could choke a horse, and offered it to Sean as a sample.

Sean tasted a little, and hurried back toward the front of the store, savoring the taste experience slowly. "Give me three ounces."

"Very good. Very good." The man was elated and began to measure the often-worshiped delicacy. He said to a younger man, dressed in an almost identical fashion, "Get his other things. See if he will be needing any wine or champagne today."

"Right away," said the younger man. He trailed Sean like a personal valet.

Everyone in the store spoke with an accent. My best guess was that they were from somewhere in the Middle East, a group that I would learn generally referred to themselves as

'Persian'. I would become educated to the fact that the bulk of these émigrés were from Iran. They never mentioned the country, with some choosing instead to be identified as Armenians. Those of Jewish descent, and that was the vast majority, were somewhat assimilated into Jewish-American culture, a mainstay of its own in Hollywood, but tended to keep their distance and support only their own synagogues.

Within minutes, Sean's items were all packed and ready to go. A third man helped Sean to his car after a woman in traditional Iranian garb rang everything up on an antiquated cash register and then posted it to Sean's account.

I, on the other hand, was treated like the stranger that I was. Nobody smiled and the woman behind the counter never glanced up when she eventually took my credit card. Suspicion would have been an understatement.

On the way to Bob's condo, Sean left a message for his daughter. "Hey, I'm fine. I'm going to spend the night at Bob's. If it burns, it burns. It's just a house. Love ya…"

The next day Bob woke early, preferring to nap later in the day rather than sleep late. One of the many screenplay submissions could easily put him to sleep. Sean was still asleep in the guest bedroom.

Bob crept into the stark, white kitchen and began to prepare a bowl of cereal with the aplomb of a diamond cutter. He always ate cereal soon after he woke up, whether it was in the morning, the middle of the night, or even after a nap. His housekeeper, Rosa, always left a bowl of fresh fruit on the table.

Bob mused over his numerous cereal choices, often a dozen. Nearby were cereal bars with fruit and two tins of powder additives from the health food store, the latter usually reserved for shakes. When his meal was prepared, he sat down to read *The New York Times*, which Rosa had brought in early that morning and propped up nicely on a chrome holder so that Bob could read it without having to lean over or support it with his hands.

About halfway through his cereal, his eyes caught an article about fiber. He read the article carefully, not lifting his cereal spoon once. He rose after completing the article, picked up the cereal bowl and slid it down a long counter, meeting it at the sink. He carefully placed the bowl into the sink, dumped its contents into the InSinkErator, and threw the switch. "Die", he said aloud, waited a few seconds, and turned off the electric food assassin. He turned and confronted the cereal boxes on the counter top with his arms outstretched wide as if he were about to make a speech, and finally leaned on the counter with his head slightly sagged. Then he slowly gathered up the boxes, one at a time, holding each at arm's length, as if he were examining an old photo of a long lost friend. He then dumped each one into a large trashcan, the kind with a swinging top. He pushed the top hard with his hand, and it squeaked back and forth. He waited for each next window of opportunity, and swoosh, the cereal flew inside its metal coffin, making a dull muffled thud on the way down. When all the boxes were inside the aluminum mausoleum, he turned on the cereal bars and murdered them as well, along with the vats of additives.

Bob opened the refrigerator door and removed an amorphous shape that was wrapped in tinfoil. He carefully removed the foil to reveal a cold veal parmesan hero sandwich, left over from his dinner earlier that week at Matteo's Little Taste of Hoboken. He thought it was the best Italian hero in town. He sat down at the table and muttered to himself while he ate, smiling and laughing between bites. "I'm glad that's over. Fiber is no longer any

good for the colon. Fucking outrageous!" He kissed his hand
after licking off a little tomato sauce and then patted the
newspaper article. "Thank you!"... "There is a god..."

Bob thought about his date. All of his dates had to include
sex, or there was no sense dating. He had started to see Barry-
the-Shrink about a year after Sean had begun. He initially
confided in Barry that he was getting tired of his dating
ritual, but didn't know any other way to behave. "I never spent
a great deal of time concentrating on my sex life, like most of
the guys who came up with me. It was what it was. When I got
older, I stopped dating most of the younger women. It wasn't the
fashion any longer, you know, but I guess I had done so much
when I first starting working in the business that I got tired.
Don't get me wrong. I played the game the way everyone played. I
helped set up a lot of parties for a lot of people. It was part
of the business. Sean was always hiring actors on their way up
or on their way down. Demands were part of the job. We once got
the brother of a movie star to do one of our movies. He had the
worst coke habit of anyone I'd ever met. Since we were shooting
in Sean's house, one of the bathrooms was set aside to be
Charlie's little coke room. He would be in and out of that room
all day. Charlie, who everyone knew was more or less gay,
promoted this idea that he was some sort of ladies' man. There
were always three or four girls hanging around the set. I don't
think Charlie ever touched one of them. For him it was good P.R.
Me? Well, that's another story. I was the producer. It went with
the territory. Now I go out mostly because I don't want to be
alone. But if there is no sex, I think she doesn't like me. Is
that nuts?"

Barry had spoken 'off the record' to Sean about Bob, but
never during one of Sean's sessions. "I never thought Bob needed
any treatment, but we spoke about a lot of things on a variety

of subjects. He's a throwback to old Hollywood, like a tough Warner or a Lasky, not quite there with an exterior executive shine, like some of the young Turks today. Years ago, he probably would have been hired as the muscle for one of the studios. He's smart when it comes to movies, but you already know that. He can talk on any subject. Very few people know this but Bob worked intelligence during the Vietnam War. He actually is in love with the movie business. He once told me that he always wanted to be around movies, ever since he was a kid. It was magic to him, just like to a lot of people. He said that he was the Will Rogers of script readers. 'I never read a screenplay that I didn't like.' He has another one. You must have heard it. Oh, yes. 'There are no truly bad screenplays. Only bad directors, actors, and producers.' He does genuinely love the work."

Bob washed down his sandwich with a cold beer, and started to read a new screenplay. He lit a cigar, which he would finish on the way to the office. Then it was back to cigarettes.

Sean didn't awaken in time to see Bob for breakfast. When he did, he immediately turned on the local news. After minutes of viewing more of the same grandstanding, he realized that the fire had not done anywhere near the damage that had been predicted yesterday. He hastily turned off the television. His thoughts were already consumed by his need to find something, anything, to get out of what he considered a deepening rut.

CHAPTER THREE
Brantley
Sean
Barry
Mal, Ricky, Gary, Bob, Sean, Barry
Sean, Gary, Bob, Barry, Heather

That morning the Pacific Coast Highway remained closed.
Every local network continued to run a story on the moribund
artery and by noon the national stations were all on board with
the impending horrors. CNN, MSNBC, and FOX aired the story a few
times every hour. Since 9/11, any news story that involved fire
naturally focused on firemen, and the cable news jocks were
quick to interview the firefighters and related civil servant
pundits, even before the usual celebrity bullshit. I was
fascinated by a city that had yearly problems on one of its
major thoroughfares, and yet was ineffectual in effecting any
sort of change. The natural elements in Hollywood played a large
supporting and imposing role in everything that went on.

I had to be in my office super early following an
unexpected long night after dinner with Donny, and fortunately
didn't need to traverse the PCH route to get to work. After I
had seen Donny for his emergency, he kept calling me and
insisting upon taking me to Matteo's for a late dinner. It

didn't take long to learn that 'no' was not an option with
Donny. Once inside the classic restaurant with red leather
booths, it was clear that Donny was a regular. Everyone knew
him, and he was quick to say hello to anyone in the business,
from producer to actor. Some of the responses were quite cool,
but Donny was unfazed by what people thought of him.

"Have the steak and peppers and the Sinatra pasta,"
commanded Donny. He also insisted that the maitre d' seat us at
the Sinatra table in the rear, even though we were only two. It
was the largest booth and faced the entire main room. I would
also learn that the steak and peppers were another link to the
crooner's eating habits.

Donny talked nonstop while he ate. He was going to help me,
because I had helped him. He went on about Sinatra, how both he
and the singer had been friends with the deceased owner Matty
Jordan (Matteo Giordano). Donny knew the history of all of the
oil paintings, and pointed out one depicting the rear view of a
bald man.

"Bullets Durgom. He was something."

I was lectured on everything Donny knew about Bullets.
Basically, George "Bullets" Durgom was a well-known celebrity
agent/manager, but judging by some of the outrageous stories, he
led a rather colorful life. Having Sinatra and Sammy as clients
certainly helped.

I didn't dare let Donny know that Sinatra had been a
patient in my New York office. Donny was not someone that you
one-upped.

During dinner my beeper went off. I called on my cell phone
to reach my answering service. The operator said, "We have a
Diane on the line."

That was all the information that they had. 'Diane'. Within
a few moments I realized that I was talking to Diane Keaton. I

made arrangements to meet her for an emergency. The wife of
Harold Becker, a well-known director, who was also one of my
patients, had referred her. I recalled one his movies, *Sea of
Love,* with Al Pacino.

Donny was hard to convince to let me go back to the office.

"Hey. It's nine-fucking-thirty. Can't it wait until
morning?"

When he realized that I was leaving, he automatically
assumed that I would take him with me. He thought nothing of it,
but I kept coming up with reasons why it wasn't such a good
idea. It seemed like a natural to him, while to me it was a
little bizarre. People in New York City didn't seem to have time
for things like this, latching on to the guy who recently did
some root canal work for them. Granted, a celebrity was
involved, and that had its own special set of weird protocols
and power structures.

Donny kept on. "I know her, well sort of. It will be good
if I'm there."

A few moments later, I had Donny convinced that it would be
unprofessional for me to bring him to the office. He smiled, but
wasn't buying anything that I said.

Then, as if it never really mattered, he dismissed me.
"Okay, if you have to go, I'll see you. I'll get this." It was
now an order and I quickly stood up to leave.

When I rose, I took out my credit card. "No, let me get
this." I soon learned that was the wrong move with Donny, and
many other people in town.

He took the card from my hand as if it now belonged to him.
"Okay, if you insist." He waved the card in the air and it was
grabbed by a passing waiter before Donny could bring his arm
back down.

"I'm going to send you plenty of business." It was his direct way of letting me know that I was going to be paid back, so my buying dinner would feel as if it was a worthwhile endeavor, rather than one of Donny's mini-cons. Transparent or not, Donny had his own protocol, and I would learn that he never deviated from it.

"If I have any deals for you, can I call you?"

"Sure," I answered, knowing I didn't have the big money that Donny would be after.

His parting words were, "Tell Diane I said 'hello'."

"Sure."

I couldn't and I didn't.

Diane was a charming, sweet, sensitive woman whom I wished I could spend time with outside the office. I didn't dare ask. Woody Allen. Al Pacino. I was not like either one of them. I kept it purely professional.

The case turned out to be a very difficult one - no reflection on the famous and extremely talented actress. It always seemed to work out that way. One way or another, celebrity patients who were nice had difficult cases, while those with the routine cases made themselves high maintenance inside and outside the office. There were exceptions.

George Peppard managed to get under my skin every time he was in my office. He had a strange way of rolling the word 'Doctor' off his tongue, as if he were mocking the relationship. The case was a bitch, one of the hardest with blocked calcified canals and I worked on it forever, never satisfying his old-time referring dentist and perhaps a former drinking buddy. George had persuaded the dentist, who appeared – as many Beverly Hills doctors did - quite friendly with him, to 'teach' him the technical details of the procedure. With the little added knowledge, George became my partner in suggesting what we should do next at each visit. Because my office worked on a flat fee for service system, the extra hours with George offered no compensation beyond the pleasure of his company.

After his treatment was completed, whenever I saw him in public I avoided him. He knew it, because I was once brought to the table across from his in the narrow booths at the rear of the barroom inside Matteo's. We exchanged lightning-quick glances when I was nearly on top of him. While he looked back at his date, I waltzed with mine to the front reception area of the restaurant to let them know that I needed to change tables.

Sean dragged himself into Bob's kitchen, wearing only his blue briefs. The coffee machine was still heating, and he helped himself. Black. No sugar.

George Roy trailed him.

"Yes. I'm on it." Sean opened the refrigerator and sifted through Bob's leftovers. "Ah. A little steak." He ripped the plastic wrap off the plate and placed it on the floor. "Knock yourself out, George. It looks like it's from The Grill On The Alley." The large remains of Bob's thirty-dollar steak from a 'company' hangout had become George Roy's breakfast.

As Sean sipped his coffee, he begrudgingly watched the Channel 7 local news. An African-American Cal Trans worker was being interviewed regarding the PCH debacle. Behind him, a pastel tinted bulldozer pushed dirt around, much the same way a four-year-old might play in the mud. *The whole thing smells of a setup.* Despite the choice of material for most of Sean's movies, he still understood the nuts-and-bolts of production, be it movies, TV, or news.

"We have a lot to consider before wrapping things up here," said the worker with all the aplomb of a Senator addressing the media throngs.

To Sean, the whole thing sounded like boilerplate copy and definitely rehearsed. *That guy should be a manager in McDonalds,* Sean thought and laughed. He had made a joke to himself about 'wrapping' up the burgers.

"And why is that? How soon will you open the PCH?" asked Bonita Williams, the perky reporter for 7, decked out in a bright yellow rain slicker, overalls, and a blue Dodgers baseball cap. This was the same outfit that she wore for floods and El Niño reports, and on this dubious occasion, she had substituted the Dodgers hat for her usual waterproof western-styled hat, probably a big ol' Stetson.

"You see that area right behind me?" the worker asked the calamity-loving audience. He turned to face the hillside, careful to keep his profile inside the live shot.

Sean noticed that there wasn't a speck of dirt on the worker. That's probably why they picked him. No sense showing the world that the mud in Malibu can actually make anyone dirty.

The handheld camera followed the Cal Trans worker's pointed finger up the hillside. A chunk of the hillside foliage had just slid down to the highway's pavement, and was still smoldering on cue. The remaining giant, irregular hole made the hill look as if it had been hit by a Scud missile.

"We have to shore that up before finishing the cleanup here," said the worker, who then turned back to face the camera.

Sean took another swallow of his coffee. He checked his pulse as he listened.

"That's the story here. This is Bonita Williams, live at Pacific Coast Highway in Malibu. Back to you guys in the studio."

Sean felt that his pulse was fast. He checked it again.

"Oh, shit," he said as he raced to the coffee maker.

He began opening all the drawers and shelves around the
machine. In one overhead compartment up and to his left, he
found what he was looking for.

"God damn it! Caffeine. Fucking caffeine!" he screamed, as
he tossed the coffee bag down in disgust. The bag opened wide
between the 'S' and the 'T' in 'Starbucks,' spilling its
contents onto the countertop.

"Bob. Get your ass in here. How dare you give me caffeine!
Bob! Bob! Get in here, you dirty bastard!" Sean expected
everyone to recall his personal needs and act accordingly.

After a few seconds, Sean realized that Bob had already
left.

By that time, Bob was sitting in the office, talking with
Gary, who sat at a smallish desk on the other side of the room.

"When the fuck is he going to get here?" Gary jumped up
from his desk.

"Take it easy, you know Sean. Why are you so angry so early
in the day? Your face is beet red."

"I do take it easy, and that's the problem. But I flush
easily when I am anxious. It's uncontrollable."

Bob wasn't easily revved up and he had a half dozen or so
speeches ready to go, as needed. "Cool down. You've known for
years that Sean is a master at not working. You know the drill,
so why fight it? He'll waltz into the office later, make a few
phone calls, and wonder what we're going to do for lunch. Look.
I don't have his skills or his chutzpah. God bless him for
those. He put food on our table for a long time, and I don't
mind admitting it. So he has no clue about how to write a movie.
It doesn't matter. He's a great promoter, and he knows how to
make the most out of this bullshit film library. He always buys
me cigarettes, even though I'm trying to stop. I take it as a

joke. Now that he's hooked up with Linda Stirling, he may be headed for the big time, and that means a bigger deal for us. Don't get me wrong. Sean will never be a mogul. Sean wants to be liked. I think in this business wanting to be liked is the kiss of death, but Sean works it in nicely. People do like him, and he is still able to keep it all going. Go figure. So don't forget it."

Gary paused, easily intimidated by Bob. He spoke quietly, "Sorry. I have some phone calls to make." He rushed to an inner office, the one usually reserved for Sean.

Bob smiled. He shook his head, and then buried it in the screenplay that he wanted to finish before lunch.

When Sean left Bob's condo, he headed straight back to his house. The route was tedious, since the PCH was not available. Along the way, he made a cell call to Bob.

"Production offices." Bob spoke into a tiny microphone.

"Bob, I walked George Roy and left him on your patio with the screen door open a bit in case he wants to come in."

"But is the alarm on?"

"Yeah, but what the fuck do you have that's worth stealing?"

"My record collection is worth a fortune."

"Uh-huh. And so are my old Converse sneakers."

"Is the alarm on?"

"I did the whatchumacallit…the…"

"Bypass?"

"Yes. The way you showed me. Take it easy. You've got security guards running all over the place."

Bob abruptly changed the conversation. "The Indian called."

"Any money?"

"No."

"Then, fuck him."

"Some guy named Brantley called. He said he left a message with Susan."

"I know about him. He called me at home."

"That's it. Nobody else wants you."

"Right. I'll be in around eleven-thirty."

"Okay." Bob rarely paid attention to anything having to do with Sean and time or appointments.

"Tell Gary I want to go the Chinese place."

"I'll wait until you get here. His hormones are raging already this morning."

Sean laughed. "See you, later."

"Okay."

The street leading to Sean's house was completely flooded. *Maybe the fire department had doused the houses*. As soon as he was closer to his house, he identified the problem. One of his sprinkler pipes had burst, shooting a geyser straight up into the sky. A two-inch brook flowed over his driveway, right up to and under the front door.

Sean spoke to himself in a muted voice. "Stay calm. Stay calm. Get everything under control, and then kill the plumbers. Bob will have 'Ralphie and Louie' pay them a visit." It was an office joke, but nevertheless a connection to two real-life gumbas from the Bronx.

The drain in the driveway was blocked by muddy leaves. Sean parked his car and began to slosh his way to the front door.

He opened the front door, and was greeted by the worst. "Shit," he said quietly.

The checkerboard marble floor was flooded. He moved further inside where he could see his soaked carpets. He hurriedly returned outside, quickly closed the door, and marched around

the house, searching for the water main. He knew that it was
somewhere on the side, toward the back.

When he turned off the water main, the sprinkler pipe
continued to erupt. Then he realized that his contractor had
illegally connected his sprinkler water to the street source, so
that Sean's sprinkler activity would not show up on the monthly
meter charges. Sean had no way to stop the flow of water.

"They got you, Daren."

He had great insurance, a Masterpiece Chubb policy, but
figured the best way to go was to get the contractor back to the
house as soon as possible. If any problems ensued he could sue
or have his insurance carrier subrogate the claim, maybe against
the city. The contractor would know a way to leave Sean
blameless.

He got into his car and called the Department of Water and
Power. He would need someone to turn off the water main in the
street.

The person who finally picked up was slow. "What's the
address?"

"I gave you my address already. How soon can you get
someone up here to turn off the water?" Sean screamed.

"Within thirty minutes."

"Is there someone else I can call?"

"No. I make the calls. We have people up there already,"
said the dispatcher. "Because of the mudslides and fires."

Sean was surprised by the answer.

After he hung up, he left a message for the plumber and the
contractor. They would fix the broken sprinkler, eventually.

Sean drove away feeling anxious. The broken sprinkler was a
minor wound. His mood was linked to the combination of fears
from last night, about losing the house. He had a strange
feeling of vulnerability, which he didn't like, causing him to

almost cease functioning. He had felt the same way after the last earthquake.

He made another call on his car phone. He waited for the voicemail. "Barry. It's Sean. I have to talk to you. I know you don't have hours this morning. I'm on the way to your house," he said, as if it were routine.

Barry was listening and chimed in after pushing the speakerphone. "Did something happen to your house?"

"No. Well, yes. I'll tell you later," said Sean.

Barry lived in the Beverly Hills flats. The only way that Sean could get to Barry's house was to first drive North to Mulholland, the road that ran about half-way between the San Fernando Valley and towns south, including Beverly Hills. Sean would take Mulholland inland toward Beverly Hills. Once he hit Beverly Glen, he'd travel south past the expanse of hillside homes, and then east into Beverly Hills. Normally, the PCH would take him directly into Santa Monica, and then he'd head east. Either way, the trip was annoying. Long-range highway planning was never a priority for the Westside of Los Angeles.

Barry lived north of Santa Monica Boulevard, in the seven-hundred block of Maple Drive. The beautiful block, as the name implied, was lined by mature trees, and multi-million dollar price tags.

Sean parked his car out front and rang the doorbell. A pleasant housekeeper let him inside. He had never bothered to learn her name. He had an easy system for use around town. With a big smile he said, "Buenos dias, señora." That always did the trick.

Sean walked through the house, stopping in the all-too-white living room. From that vantage point, he could see Barry floating in his pool. He was gesturing for Sean to come outside.

Barry was talking very loud and Sean could hear him through the sliding screen door. "I am not buying into any tech stocks. Over is over. I can find better bargains in Afghanistan."

Sean chuckled as soon as he took in the full view of the ridiculous sight. Barry was lodged inside an oversized banana float. His face was covered with splotches of white sun lotion. His oversized Tommy Bahama shorts nearly reached his calves, leaving only a short stretch of skin exposed on the way down to his delicate and blue aquatic slippers. A remote phone was resting on his lap; the wire earpiece was firmly planted in his ear.

Sean slid the ceiling-to-floor screen door to one side. Once outside, he sauntered across the bright green manicured lawn.

"Hey, Barry," Sean shouted.

Barry smiled with his lips together and signaled with his hand to give him another minute, just the one index finger extended to avoid confusion. Sean knew that it could be awhile. Barry never rushed for anyone, unless it was nearing the end of an 'hourly' session.

Once inside the gate-enclosed pool area, Sean stretched out on a chaise lounge, one of several blue, red, and white chairs that lined the perimeter. Barry had recently added these types of patriotic touches after 9/11. Sean took his shirt off and exposed the oversized gold 'chai' chain that he never took off - the Hebrew numerical combination of eighteen for good luck. He had kept it since his days at USC. In those days he had had visions of attending the film school, but opted instead for making money as soon as the first opportunity presented itself.

He kept on his jeans, since his pointy Lucchese lizard boots would have been hard to remove. Barry always had extra bathing suits for both sexes in his cabana. From Barry's point of view, Sean's feet were wide apart, framing the 'chai' in the center of the boots, with Sean's nose providing the centerpiece of an unintentional primitive sculpture.

Barry brushed his mop of medium-length curly hair to one side. Sometimes he wore it in fashionable curly spikes, with the help of a styling gel. A few years ago, he had hair plugs added to his receding hairline, so that he could keep his curls out over his forehead in order to utilize them to fill voids in any direction. He kept himself in decent physical condition, but his body shape always begged to expose a little paunch no matter how hard he dieted. He had resigned himself to either wearing trousers a few inches below his actual waistline, or buying high rise styles to cover the unavoidable midriff expansion.

Sean listened to the remainder of the telephone call.

"If Lycos is on the block again and you think Diller is going to make an offer, then buy another twenty-five thousand shares. Right. But only if Diller is buying," he said. Under those circumstances, Lycos was no longer a tech stock and therefore not included in Barry's "I am not buying into anymore tech stock" statement.

"He's going to buy it," said Sean through cupped hands, making sure that Barry heard him. "It's a done deal!"

"I have a guy here who says it's a done deal," said Barry. "Go ahead. Right. Buy the shares. Now! But wait three days before you tell any other clients. We don't need the SEC up our asses."

Barry picked up the telephone, spotted the button to end the call, and pushed it with authority, proud of his 'insider' stock purchase. He pulled out his earpiece and placed the telephone in a beverage holder on his aqua-ride. He awkwardly maneuvered toward the corner of the pool where the steps were located. He used his hands for oars and paddled his banana express, suddenly possessed by great nautical skill. When he arrived closer the steps, he attempted to lift himself out. After failing on the first two attempts – the banana boat kept shifting awkwardly under his weight - he pulled himself hand-over-hand along the wall until he reached the shallow end of the pool, washing his ship up on the 'dock' and allowing him to step off easily and waddle up and out of the pool.

"Waterproof," said Barry, pointing to the sloshed telephone.

"I wish my carpeting was," said Sean.

"So the house is okay?" Barry said as he grabbed a mauve towel that dwarfed his body. Sticking out from under the wrap, his spindly legs appeared to be artificial.

"Just water damage," said Sean.

"So the firemen did it?" Barry sat on a lounge chair and pulled the towel up around his shoulders. "A case against the city?"

"I don't want to talk about it."

"So you came all the way here to tell me that you don't want to talk about it?"

"Barry. You're such a jerk, sometimes."

"I'm a jerk? I have to get dressed and meet someone in less than an hour. I know you didn't come over here for a little chit-chat."

"I don't think I'm going to make it," said Sean as he moved his lounge chair closer to Barry.

"That's how you start every session. Can you be a little more specific?"

Barry rose abruptly and tiptoed to the pool gate. Sean followed.

"Odezza," yelled Barry. "Get me some more towels, and bring my clothes to the dressing room."

Sean knew that Barry milked these moments for all they were worth. It wasn't as if Barry were mean-spirited; it was more related to his general style of being a shrink. The best description Sean could come up with was "like a strict parent".

Sean spoke rapidly. "I really felt that possibly losing the house was symbolic of my whole life. Everything I have going is like that. It's always all about to burn down, or disappear in a mudslide."

Barry turned around to face him. "So what else is new?" His head bobbled around impatiently. "Odezza. I'm freezing. Where are those towels?"

The therapeutic duo stood at the door to a dressing room that was built into the side of the house. Sean was only a few feet away from Barry, towering over him, as Barry pressed his back on the entrance to the cabana.

"Barry, but this time I really felt like I'm never going to have another decent deal. It's that feeling of completing a movie and finding out that it's worthless. That's how I felt about the house. At first I said to hell with it and then I thought I might be losing the house, and then I found out that it was only water-soaked. That's how I feel, like everything is water-soaked, and I'm constantly bailing to keep going."

Barry smiled. He had to brush against Sean in order to pass him. Sean moved aside. "That's a lovely metaphor, but I didn't tell you to stay in the movie business. That's the way it is." Frustrated, he dropped the towel to the ground and headed for the sliding screen door to the living room.

Sean pursued him. "I've got to find something that can grow. I'm just not growing anymore."

"Sean. We can talk more when you come to the office. I have to get going. Let me know when we can meet at your house. Perhaps the two of us can stare at it and come up with what is

really bothering you." He opened the sliding door. "Odezza.
Never mind the towels. Make me a little breakfast."

Sean grabbed Barry by the arm. "Barry. Wait a minute," said
Sean.

Barry pulled his arm away and disappeared inside the house.
"I'm late."

"Meshuggeneh mamzer !" Sean yelled after him.

"Wait if you want. Have a cup of coffee. I'll be dressed in
ten minutes."

Sean felt like having more coffee, as long as it was decaf,
so he walked to the kitchen where Odezza gave him the proper
coffee and a bran muffin, at his request.

Sean stared at one of Barry's *Saturday Evening Post* posters
- the famous one of the umpires waiting for rain. It reminded
Sean that Barry was a collector of art as well as people. Barry
was about the only person who could make Sean feel lousy about
himself; a diminished view of self that frightened him. He
resented Barry for that. It made it hard for Sean to recognize
the real Barry, someone who underneath all the bullshit
trappings of Hollywood was actually a decent doctor. Or was it
the reverse - the trappings were it, and Barry was only in it
for the money? Sean was never certain.

Sean's cell phone rang, breaking his mildly depressive
moment. He picked it up in one hand, flipped open the case and
put it to his ear.

Barry jogged into the kitchen during the call, dressed in
khaki slacks, Ferragamo loafers, and a pale green Polo golf
shirt, the kind with the crossed flags. He helped himself to a
cup of coffee, picked at the breakfast Odezza had left for him -
a cheese omelet with grape jelly on white toast - and listened
to Sean.

"Yeah...Right. I forgot. Tell him to wait. I know. I know. Gary, just tell him to fucking wait…I don't know. Stall him. I'm on my way." Sean forgot that he had an early appointment – anything before eleven A. M. This one was for ten-thirty, and it was with a legendary comedian, Mal V. Rose. Sean closed the tiny cell phone and unlike Captain Kirk, could not be beamed to his next destination by the ever-faithful Scotty. It was a disappointment for people like Sean who felt that transportation wasted valuable time between things that were much more important. "Barry, I've got to go. I forgot that I had someone coming over." He rose from the table.

"Is it anyone I know?" asked Barry, dying to find out if it was someone even remotely famous.

"Mal V. Rose," Sean said in a voice that could just as well have given Barry the correct time of day. "His son Ricky is with him. He's always with him. The kid is a menace. Nobody likes him."

Barry lit up. "Wow. You're kidding. My parents never missed his show. What is he now, in his eighties?"

"He's ninety-five, going on fifty. I want him to appear in this movie I might do in Vegas."

Barry dropped all demeanor of being a doctor and lapsed quickly into fan mode. "Would you mind very much...? If it's an imposition, I would never ask it..."

Sean smiled at Barry. "You are a pathetic groupie."

Barry's voice took on a pleading quality. "He was a legend in my neighborhood. Some said that he was better than Berle, particularly in drag."

Sean began to leave. "Barry. I don't give a fuck if you come. Just hurry up. He's already there. What happened to your appointment – didn't you have to 'get going' or something?"

"It can wait," said Barry. Nothing stood between him and a good star-fucking.

"It can wait," mimicked Sean, enjoying every moment of the quick shift of power.

Barry continued with his reasons. "My Aunt Vitty knew Mal's sister. They went to the same elementary school in Brooklyn. And my Uncle Larry once did security work for him. You know Larry was a NYC detective."

Within minutes the two were in their own mini-motorcade, whisking along Santa Monica Boulevard on the way to Sean's office building in Century City. During the trip, Barry kept up his reasons via cell phone. Sean hardly paid attention, oblivious to civilians' love for promoting their personal connections to celebrities. Los Angles was a city where people could never get enough of fame, and they did everything they could to promote the stars. Lately, a new concept was taking place, talentless people who were famous for only one thing, being famous.

By the time they arrived and walked from their cars, Barry was on his sixth reason. "I actually had a little crush on Mal, particularly when he did that character that looked like Marilyn Monroe."

Sean only smiled, content to watch Barry grovel. This was their most comfortable role, and the most consistent, despite the years of therapy. Barry wanted Sean's access to all things Hollywood.

Sean's office was in a modest black building that was dwarfed by large towers connected to the ABC Entertainment Center. A series of underground passages and narrow walkways connected the enclave of buildings that ran on both sides of the busy Avenue of the Stars. Century City was rather compact, bordered on the north by Santa Monica Boulevard and extended south to Pico, stopping at the entrance to the fabled Hillcrest Country Club. Fox Studios provided the western border. The entire 'city', including an upscale residential condo section, hotels, and a shopping center was less than a mile in any direction, but despite its size still functioned as a business center for many entertainment companies, including law and accounting firms.

Barry's gait resembled a boy on the way to a candy store. From the end of the hallway he could read some door signs. They appeared new. He had been there a few months ago in order to drop off free Zanax samples rather than inconvenience a big shot with a real prescription, but didn't remember seeing the signs. The other door signs looked new as well, an obvious attempt by the landlord to spruce up the building.

Sean had sublet part of the office to Gary, who had his own small company that did most of its business with Sean. Gary was known in the industry for having made an independent film that had attracted a lot of attention, *Eating Beverly Hills*. It was an out and out theft of the cult hit *Eating Raoul*. Sean wasn't ready to admit that his new idea for a movie might have been derived from Gary's biggest and 'borrowed' success. The office also had an old-time agent named Morris Arnoldson, who was a never-ending source for aspiring actresses. Since the movie *Little Voice* had been released, people in the office teased Morris, claiming that the Michael Caine character was modeled on Morris' career. 'Maury', as he preferred to be called, was rarely around, preferring to play golf at Riviera with actor Peter Falk.

Barry read the new door sign before he entered.

> Sean Daren Films
> Lettuce Alone Films
> Morris Arnoldson Agency

From the hall they could hear Mal screaming in an almost effeminate high pitch. "No. That is not going to happen that way. No cocksucker is going to tell me where to stand in a scene. I don't work that way."

Gary and Bob were trying to hold the fort until Sean arrived, but they had made the mistake of discussing the movie with Mal. Spending time in a room with Mal and Ricky Rose eventually wore down the best in the business. Mal V. Rose had managed to outlive everyone he had worked with, including Burns and Berle.

Sean was hoping that this go 'round would be an exception to the Rose onslaught. When he opened the door, he was all smiles. Barry kept his distance.

It was impossible not to notice the rotund Ricky, particularly juxtaposed to lithe and lanky Mal. It was not so much Ricky's size, but his continual oafish movements that he used with a collection of facial muggings that rivaled Jim Carey. Ricky was about thirty-years-old; a product of Mal's dalliance with Will's mother when she was thirty-seven and when Mal admitted to being sixty-five. They eventually married, only to get divorced when Ricky finished Beverly Hills High. She lived in Scottsdale and New York, continuing as a playwright, something that Mal had stifled while they were still married. She saw Ricky once a year, usually at some charity event that gave her star treatment reserved for "wives of". Ricky acknowledged that his mother was an evil influence, after virtually being brought up by Mal and his misogynist cronies. Ricky would never talk about her, but wouldn't allow anyone to make any reference to her. If anyone crossed Ricky and his rules, vengeance was his reflexive response.

Mal was looking forward to his one hundredth birthday, and was still making appearances with the same zeal he did when he

was twenty. With Milton Berle and George Burns gone, and Bob
Hope relegated to staying at his house, Mal reveled in his last-
one-standing status. Mal was never as smooth as George Burns,
nor as funny as Berle, but he was just as famous. Thanks to the
generous Berle, Mal had his share of appearances on shows
associated with Berle. After the *Texaco Star Theater* went off
the air, Mal worked as a guest on shows with Lucille Ball and
Sid Caesar. The sixties begat a syndicated television show for
children called *Mal's Merry Playhouse*, so campy that college
kids took to watching the show stoned. Mal's clowning around
caused Doodles Weaver to appear as if he had studied with
Stanislavski, while Pinkie Lee was elevated to the stature of
an academy-award-winning actor. Picture Pee Wee Herman in drag,
and that was merry Mal.

Sean knew all about Mal. He had followed every step of his
career in the trade papers and the gossip mill that fueled show
business. Mal had a writing partner named Arnie Baylos, who some
say was more talented than Mal. Mal and Arnie loved getting
their names on credits. They wrote hundreds of sketches that
they claimed were original, and registered for copyrights with
the Library of Congress. In the early days of sketch writing
there were very few lawsuits amongst performers. Occasionally,
something had to be done when the rip-off was blatant. Will
Jordan, an Ed Sullivan impersonator, was ripped off by everyone.
Mal loved to tell the story of how Will should have sued Mal,
but instead sued Jack Carter. Sometimes the defendant would
change in Mal's legal story, and Will sued Jackie Vernon or
Jackie Gayle, neither of whom really never did Sullivan in their
acts.

Mal and Arnie were no angels. They published a book in the
sixties called *It's A Mad World After All,* trading off the
success of the movie *It's A Mad, Mad, Mad, Mad World*, from which

Mal had been unceremoniously cut. They had written about sixty
routines which they stole from everyone, including most of Will
Jordan's material, interspersed with a little Jackie Mason.
Jackie would never appear or even stand in the same room with
Mal, "even if it's a dinner for five-hundred!"

Aside from stealing routines, Mal and Arnie wrote many
corny songs, some strikingly similar to prior hits.
Occasionally, one of the songs would be published as a single –
the most notorious was a Christmas song simply entitled *Merry
Christmas*. Mal's son Ricky immediately recognized the tune from
an old Bing Crosby holiday album. No harm, no foul. The song
disappeared as quickly as it appeared, and the Roses gave away
thousands of CDs of that song and others over the next few years
at charity dinners.

When it came to developing television material or movies,
Mal always insisted upon getting story credit, writing credit,
and "based on an idea by" credit, which made it tough to find
writers willing to work with him, aside from the horrors of the
actual writing and editing process. He also had a mean streak
for creative people, which included making them grovel for their
money. Payday on his show was a circus in need of a big top. Mal
would give the paychecks to then thirteen-year-old Ricky, who
would stand on top of the old NBC building in Burbank and call
out the names on the envelopes with a bullhorn, one at a time.
The envelope would be sent into the prevailing wind, often
sailing out over the street, and sometimes landing in two-way
traffic or a tree. When Ricky was in an even friskier mood, he
would rubber-band a baseball to an envelope and see if he could
make a throw across the street, and into a fountain that he
envisioned as home plate. Mal would often peek outside and laugh
himself silly as he watched his writers scramble all over the
street for their money.

Late at night, Mal would have food brought in from the
Brown Derby or Chasen's. He never offered the writers anything
to eat. The junior writer in the group, Tubby Edwards, would
additionally drive all the way to Schwab's in Hollywood to pick
up a sundae with strawberry topping that Mal expected would be
delivered to his home in Beverly Hills in time for his arrival
after work and before the ice cream had dared melt.

When Barry saw Ricky, their eyes locked for a moment. Barry
hadn't treated him for many years. Ricky quit therapy when he
was about twenty-one. Barry knew Ricky's character disorder
well. In short order, he was a rude, selfish, self-indulgent kid
without his father's talent, and lived uncomfortably with a
borderline nonspecific personality disorder. Barry had helped
him through a phase when he wanted to become a writer. It
required finding writing 'partners' for Ricky, someone to do the
actual writing work, similarly to Mal. However, Ricky would try
to come in at the end of a project and take credit for
everything. He implemented that with Adam Manella, a childhood
friend who was known as a competent screenwriter. Everyone knew
Adam's father, Larry Manella. Larry had won a Tony, an Obie, and
an Oscar. Ricky ultimately used his old-school powerhouse
attorneys to get Adam's name removed from a screenplay that they
had written based on a story by Adam's father - with father and
son named in the lawsuit. Ricky claimed that the entire project
was solely his idea. The case didn't get very far, nor did the
project. Barry knew as well as anyone that Ricky desperately
wanted to be Mal. Barry was sure that it was partly an
unavoidable genetic aberration; repeated for hundreds of years
in the Rose genealogy. Ricky felt that he had been wounded by
his mother, Mal, and all their and his friends. He was owed more
than he had received. Ricky pranced around daring people to be
nice to him. Anyone who made that mistake would be drawn into

his character disorder and vengeful behavior. During therapy, he'd led Barry off the essential topics and never gave him a chance to input very much, plus refusing a variety of medications. He spent the latter part of his treatment constantly distracting Barry with accusations of how Barry had mistreated him. "I am worse off now than when I met you," Ricky said more than once. During one rant, Ricky spilled the remains of his soda in Barry's lap. In most ways, Ricky was a classic Hollywood kid. He had every advantage as a child, and burnt all his bridges growing up. As an adult, he was at odds with everyone he came in contact with, making it virtually impossible for him to succeed at anything. Sadly, Mal fueled Ricky's life by allowing him to continually trade off Mal's fame. People brought Ricky deals of all types, and he had been suckered more than once, or so he claimed.

Worse, Barry knew that Mal simply didn't care all that much for Ricky. Parental love had escaped Mal's repertoire. Mal attended a few therapy sessions and then followed up by privately giving Barry an earful of criticism. Mal was annoyed that Ricky was a little portly, with sloppy hair. Mal hated how Ricky and his "beach-bum" friends would color splatter their hair and give it a "lousy" California streak job. Anytime Barry brought up 'love' he was met by a slow rant. "The little pisher wore those short black stretch bike pants, a dumb choice for a kid with a fat ass and a bulging belly, and those "Mephistowitz" shoes that looked more like they belonged to an Israeli soldier patrolling the new Gaza settlements in Palestine. The plain black socks that barely covered his ankles could have gotten him a job as second banana if vaudeville wasn't dead. I always told him to dress like me. Everything else the little prick wanted to copy, but not the clothes. Of course I like him; he's my son."

At few years ago, Barry ran into Adam Manella at the Emmy
Awards. Adam insisted on talking about Ricky; a way to make
peace, to make certain that he understood things and didn't hold
a personal grudge. "Ricky was Ricky. You never knew what he was
going to do. He was always getting me in trouble. One time I
remember him suggesting that we steal Lucille Ball's garbage
cans. It seemed funny at the time, but when Mal found out what
Ricky had done - Ricky was always the first suspect when stuff
like that happened in the neighborhood - he hit the roof. There
was another time that Ricky insisted on taking apart my new
bicycle. He told me that he had done it before and knew how to
put it back together again. Like a jerk, I let him do it, and
then he walked away laughing with the thing in pieces. That's
when I started to realize that Ricky was not playing with a full
deck. Something was wrong. My father warned me to stay away from
him, but I didn't. So I, like everyone else who knew Ricky,
eventually wound up in some kind of trouble because of him."

That morning in Sean's office, Barry continued to mostly
avoid Ricky. Barry scooted toward Mal, who was oblivious to the
fact - or at least pretended to be - that anyone else had
entered the room.

Mal's rant reverberated throughout the office. Now his
voice took on the range of a light whiskey baritone. "Who the
fuck does this little cocksucker think he is?" Mal surveyed the
room by peering out of the corner of one eye, as if he were
backstage behind a curtain, checking the house before a show.
"The price is going up. Every minute that prick makes us wait is
another thousand. By the time I get through with Sean Daren he's
going to have to change his name to Sean Not So Darin', because
he'll be flat out of luck. Hey, Ricky. That's funny. That's
funny." Mal's voice trailed off and he suddenly appeared tired.

114

His age crept into his face as he melted onto on a plain, mahogany office bench.

Barry had already collapsed against a wall, holding his side and hooting at Mal's every word.

Ricky saw his opening to appear involved and in control. "Gary. What kind of Mickey Mouse show are you running here? Look. I'll give it a few more minutes and then Mal and I are taking a walk. Toches ahfen tish! We're walking." He sang the last words and then glanced at Mal for approval. There was none forthcoming.

Toches ahfen tish, Bob repeated to himself. *If Ricky puts his ass on the table it will cave in.* Bob found the whole scene amusing. His lips were pressed tightly together in order not to laugh. When his eyes met Sean's, a brief guffaw exploded through a space forced open by the sound and escaping air.

Sean chortled. "Sorry. Sorry, Mal." He zoomed in on Mal. "You look great Mal. Who does your hair?"

Mal turned away and announced with a breathiness to his less high-pitched voice, "The big shot is finally here. Let me get up so you can kiss my ass." He rose and began to undo his Navajo turquoise belt buckle. "If you're good to me I'll let you kiss it on Sunday morning in front of Nate 'n Als."

Bob said, "I'd like to see that while I'm having my bagel and coffee."

Sean grabbed Mal around the shoulders. "Mal. It's so good to see you. I'm so glad we could get you. I told Gary that it had to be you; you're the only one who could do this." In the back of his mind, Sean knew that he didn't have the money for the movie, and could never meet all of Mal's demands.

"I'm Ricky Rose," said Ricky, as he tried to position himself between Sean and Mal.

"Yeah, how you doin', Ricky? We've met." Sean shook hands with Ricky while glancing over at Gary for assistance. Gary nodded to let Sean know that he would help with Ricky.

Sean took Mal by the arm. "Mal. Please come into my private office. Can I order some lunch for you? Bob will see to it."

Bob grabbed a pencil, licked the end, and sat up tall in his chair like a fourth grader trying to get the teacher's approval. He took notes while Mal spoke.

Mal stood and faced Bob, and delivered a desperate reading. "Yes. I would like something. Junior's. From Junior's. No place makes it better. Get me the lox, eggs, and onions from Juniors, a Dr. Brown's cream soda and an order of sourdough toast, lightly buttered. I don't like a lot of butter, just enough, not too much, not too little, but I don't like a lot. A lot is no good. Also, no dark brown on the toast. Also a bowl of sour cream with bananas, and make sure that you ask that the sour cream is fresh. I want sugar, real sugar, no Sweet and High, Low or Indifferent. It has to be from Junior's Deli, not Nate 'n Al's or Factors, just Junior's. And don't try anything funny, you little cocksucker. I'll know."

Bob stopped rolling his eyes as Gary turned to confront him, a move intended for Bob to control any further outbursts. Bob smiled and gently waved his hand in order to signal 'not to worry'.

Mal delivered what to him was a mandatory 'punchline'. "If you get me anything from that fakakta Jerry's Deli, I'll have your balls for dessert instead of the bananas!"

Sean laughed. "Mal, you are so funny. Unbelievably funny."

"Who's funny? I'm hungry." Mal slinked toward the inner office.

Barry grabbed his side, still laughing.

"Mal has a very sensitive stomach," said Ricky. He followed Mal.

Sean cocked his head and rolled his eyes at Gary.

Gary grabbed a script and jumped up from the desk. "Ricky, I need someone to check Mal's big monologue."

Ricky rudely grabbed the script, and nodded knowingly. It was as if Henry Kissinger had been asked to review potential attack plans for Iraq. "Okay. I can look at this. But make sure Mal's lunch stops here so I can check it first."

"Shut up, Ricky." Mal turned to face Gary. "God. He's a little annoying prick, isn't he?" He twisted his face into one of his classic poses.

Barry sunk to his knees. "That's the one! That's the one you did on your show!"

"Bob. Make sure Mal gets what he wants," said Sean. Then he turned so that only Bob could see his face, a forced teeth-together smile. "And Ricky, too."

Bob's body language was a scream, perhaps naturally funnier than Mal's. Stooped over his desk, he had a cigarette dangling from his pasty lips. He would smoke any kind of cigarette or cigar. His bangs were always falling in his eyes, and he had a habit of swiping his forehead even when his hair was not in his way. That time he blew air up past his extended lower lip. It made his bangs fly up and fall back down. "Of course. What else would you gentlemen like to eat?" asked Bob, as he extended an open palm in Ricky's direction.

"I want a turkey club sandwich and a chocolate shake," said Ricky, almost copying Mal's rhythm. "I don't like lettuce. I'll send it back if it has lettuce." He stood over Bob, waiting for the slightest bit of confrontation. "No lettuce touches my food."

Bob's voice took on the tone and diction of a New York waiter from Ratner's - a lower east side relic. "You want tomatoes with that; maybe a bissel cottage cheese on the side?"

Mal gave Bob a double take. "And a nice side of potato latkes." Mal paused. "Now that's how you do a Jewish deli accent. You sounded like you were doing Zero Mostel taking a dump!" The reference wasn't lost on this crowd.

Barry gestured with his hand and was about to speak.

Mal did another take aimed at Barry. "And you shut up. Who the fuck are you, anyway? You look familiar…"

Barry gushed with giggles.

Sean studied Ricky up and down as he stood over Bob, daring him to say anything else about his turkey club without lettuce. Bob locked eyes with Sean, and rolled his tongue against the inside of his cheek.

"They have a nice rice pudding. You like rice pudding?" asked Bob in his normal voice, which came off funnier than anything that had preceded.

Sean's eyeballs disappeared inside his skull.

"Yeah, right." Ricky took it as a joke. "Get me some kugel, while you're at it." He paused to think, opening and closing his mouth with deep breaths. "You know what I would really like? I would like a piece of marble halvah. Not the plain white. You know, with the two colors."

"I know what marble means," Bob said quietly.

Sean nudged him in the shoulder, as a gentle reminder to behve.

"Right. Not the plain white, but the marble." Bob began to cough as he wrote down the order. "Tomatoes?"

"No!" Ricky was adamant. "If I wanted tomatoes I would have asked."

"Fine." Bob couldn't control his coughing. "Most places put them on turkey club sandwiches." The last words were nearly lost in an uncontrollable chain of coughs.

Mal burst into song. "When Smoke Gets In Your Eyes."

Bob took a deep drag on his cigarette. "Thanks for the warning. I just had a nodule removed from my right lung about six months ago. You'll be pleased to know that it wasn't invasive." He inhaled deeply. "Kept more than half the lung. I feel…" He drew the last word out for all it was worth. "Won-der-full."

"Thanks for the news. You know they're having a sale on plots over at Hillside. I can get you one not too far from Jolson's," said Mal. "Can you spell 'cancer'?"

Sean intervened. He could see that Bob wasn't able to take much more of the Roses. "Bob. If you want. I'll order the sandwiches once we're inside."

"I think I can do it. I survived hanging around the set of *Goodfellas* for almost a month. I think I can handle lunch for the Rose family."

"Don't be such a smart ass, you Jew cocksucker." Mal spread his hands wide and leaned over Bob's desk.

"Yes, Mr. Rose." Bob smiled. "Lunch, coming right up. Does anyone want a pickle with their lunch?"

"Don't forget the Halvah," said Ricky, deaf to any other part of the ongoing conversation.

Bob rose from his chair and tried to stare down Ricky. Bob held the food order at arm's length. He sounded like Steve Martin, playing a 'dumb' character. "Would that be chocolate coated, vanilla, or do you like your halvah mixed? I forgot. What did you call it, you know, the thing you want, ma-balls?"

Ricky was already busy flipping through the screenplay. Any humor was usually lost on him. "Mixed. You know the kind,

119

without a chocolate coating," he answered without looking up. "It's mixed inside, and there is chocolate on the inside. But not the outside."

Sean could tell that Bob had reached his limit. Bob said, "I'd better call from inside your office, Sean". He moved toward the inner office.

"Sure," said Sean. "We can stay out here for a bit."

Barry remained at a far wall. He approached slowly, wanting to speak, but nothing escaped from his mouth.

Mal stared at Barry and did another classic double take. "Who the fuck is that? Don't tell me you brought an attorney here. If you are an attorney, you need to raise your hourly rates. Where'd you get that outfit - Kmart?"

Barry stepped forward. "It's Barry," he said. "How are you, Mal?" They had met a few times at functions and during Ricky's treatment, where a disgruntled Mal had always cut the sessions short.

For a second Mal appeared puzzled. "Another meshuggeneh fan. Ricky. Get him an eight-by-ten glossy. The Jerrys are everywhere." 'Jerrys' was an unaffectionate term that Mal used to describe his fans.

"Mal. It's the doctor. From Beverly Hills," said Ricky. He appeared uncomfortable, afraid that the conversation might escalate to something personal or critical.

The moment proved awkward for everyone and for a second or two things froze as everybody but the Roses and Barry considered their brush with an alternate reality. Mal automatically launched into one of his doctor routines, pulling everyone in with him. The fear that had shown on all their faces thawed, and any thoughts that Barry's presence would ruin the typical show business encounter with Mal disappeared.

"My doctor told me I only had six months to live. I told him I wasn't going to pay his bill. He said, 'Okay. One year, but that's my best offer'."

Everyone laughed, this time on cue.

"We were at that black tie last year," said Barry. "You know, the one to commemorate your first wife."

Sean knew that Barry said that as a cover. Barry didn't publicly reveal who came to his office. If pressed by Sean, Barry would hint about a megastar patient, or someone who fell into the billionaire category, like a Geffen, Murdoch or Gates. Barry saw nothing wrong in commenting posthumously on a famous patient's life or if someone was no longer in treatment. Others had done it before him, even though it wasn't the norm in his profession and still considered a breach of the patient-doctor relationship.

When Bob returned from Sean's office, the conversation had become heated, but was an expected formality with someone like Mal. Bob returned to his desk.

"One day? One day is going to cost you the same as a week," Mal said with a half-smile. "Is it a day, like in the bible? How many hours are we talking about, anyway?"

"Fine. We just want you to include your act," said Sean. He had no intention of paying Mal any more than Gary had originally allotted before calling Mal's friend Arnie - the best way to contact Mal.

"You know I'm a great director. Who is directing this picture?" asked Mal. He was serious when it came to his perception of his own talents.

"I already have someone. I didn't know you were available," Sean said seriously enough to fool Barry.

Mal went into a higher gear. "Don't bullshit me you little cocksucker. When I do my scenes, I do the lights, the staging, the directing, and the sound. How many people really know how to do sound? Am I right, Ricky? Mal V. Rose is one of the best soundmen in the business. I taught half of the guys on television how to do sound. I do it. Just like I did it on my show. Do we have an understanding?"

"Of course," said Sean. "I'll have you in Vegas in the morning, and out by dinner time. Bob will pick you up at the airport in Vegas. Bob knows Vegas."

Bob rolled his eyes and smirked at Gary.

"Gary will be on the set the whole day," said Sean.

"Is this the final script?" asked Ricky.

Nobody paid any attention to him.

Gary nodded as if he were taking a curtain call.

"And Gary will take care of all your meals for you in Vegas," said Bob, nodding to Gary.

Mal slid spryly over to Gary. "What's the matter? Who do you think you are, Marcel Marceau?" asked Mal.

"Sorry," said Gary. He laughed. "I'll be there to make sure everything is okay." He rarely spoke during these encounters, hardened by years of caring for celebrity pets and parents of nine-year-old former sitcom stars.

"We'll have you back home in Beverly Hills by ten P.M." said Sean. "Any later and I'll pay you for another day."

"Week," said Mal.

"Right," said Sean. It didn't matter; the object was to get the meeting over with.

"That would normally be something that might be okay. I mean, I don't know if that is what you would normally do in a situation like this but Mal and I intended to stay over at least the night," said Ricky. "Probably two."

Sean had anticipated this, and didn't flinch. "No problem. There are a lot of hotel rooms in Vegas. I'm sure Bob can set you up nicely."

"We want the Bellagio, a suite in the tower, two bedrooms, and here is a list of how the room is to be prepared before Mal gets there," said Ricky. He revealed a piece of paper that he had concealed inside the screenplay.

Sean controlled himself. The film had the potential to make him a bundle in the nostalgia rush that enveloped the country after 9/11. He took the paper from Ricky and smiled. "Boychick. I'll take care of it." None of it mattered now, anyway. He had many other stars to line up, and could easily pass on Mal if push came to shove.

"And we don't fly coach," said Ricky.

Bob's head drooped, as Gary's jaw dropped.

"First class," said Mal. "Or a private jet. Your call."

"I don't even fly first class to Vegas. It's such a short flight," said Sean.

"First class," repeated Mal. "You want Mal V. Rose should sit in the back of the plane with the 'Jerrys'?"

"What about a limo, all the way, L.A. to Vegas? It's a nice ride," said Sean. He had a friend who was in the business, and had converted vans and Navigators for luxury hauls.

"A nice limo?" asked Mal. He didn't mind a long car ride.

Ricky appeared shocked. "Mal?"

"Shut up, Ricky." To Sean, "You mean something like a mobile home?"

"I'll get you the best. If you want I'll get you something with a kitchen, leather seats, television, and stock it with Junior's party trays. How's that, Mal? Am I taking care of you?" asked Sean. He did the math; depending upon the airline it might be cheaper to let the Roses fly first class.

"Dad. Don't fall for it. We're flying first class. Come on. I have to get you over to the Friars," said Ricky.

"What about the food from the deli?" Bob sounded desperate.

"You guys have it," said Ricky.

"Don't worry. We can cancel the order," said Sean.

"I'll call." Bob rushed back into Sean's office.

"Got to go," said Mal. "Ricky. A special van thing sounds nice. It's only five hours or so."

"Longer," said Ricky. "Mal. They're waiting at the Friars. Red Buttons is there. You know that S.O.B. will hit the roof if you're late."

"Sorry you have to go so soon. I wanted to swap some of those stories you know about Berle," said Sean.

"Berle. What a miserable sonofabitch. He once did my whole act before I went on, you know, at a celebrity roast. I had to wing it. Lucky thing for me I could work live like that. A lot of guys would fall flat on their tuchus."

Mal and Ricky were gone with minutes.

Barry decided to stay on for lunch. The location was a Chinese restaurant in a mini-mall near the office, a place the producing trio frequented when they didn't have to entertain anyone in the business. The cuisine was ordinary, but Sean had previously declared it sensational, most of all because it was cheap. Despite the fact that Sean did all the ordering, nobody seemed to mind. He essentially knew what everyone liked and even at this local dive, it filled his need to be the boss. They sat sipping iced teas, and nibbled on an assortment of Americanized appetizers, potstickers, egg rolls, and fried wontons.

"He's a troubled kid," said Bob with this mouth full. "Did you see the way his eye twitched when he got excited?"

A server deposited more dishes on the table.

Barry spoke while he chewed on a potsticker. "One of my
other patients went to school with him at Beverly High. He was
always a pain in the ass, but a lot of people were afraid of him
because he was Mal's son. It's hard to make a career out of
being Mal's kid. The teachers let him get away with stuff. He
was kind of mean to a lot of the kids who weren't from Hollywood
backgrounds. I think he had the lowest self-esteem of anyone I
ever met. I saw him a few years ago at a benefit thing at The
Comedy Store in West Hollywood. Then he just seemed like an
egotistic prick. What can I say? He is no longer cute, just an
obnoxious older person. He actually once interrupted Mal when he
was on stage, and went up to do a few jokes with him. Mal seemed
annoyed, but played along. I don't think I've ever heard anyone
say anything nice about Ricky. He has a passion for racecars and
for following around his father. He hangs around with the worst
kind of people, the hustlers, con men, and outright crooks. Mal
was no picnic, but Ricky never did anything to help himself. Now
Mal is washed up and Ricky still tries to get by with his wise
guy antics and clinging to Mal."

Sean added what he knew, between dips of his shumai in hot
and sour sauce. "I've known Ricky since he was born. He has been
nothing but trouble for a lot of people, but I didn't see him as
so bad. When you're young you can get away with being a wiseass,
but now Ricky has grown up to be quite the bastard. You can say
the nicest, most innocent thing, and Ricky will make you feel
bad for living. I remember the time that Ricky blew the deal at
ABC for Mal. Ricky was all over town trying to talk with the
media. After the story died down, Mal and Arnie Baylos
confronted Ricky at home to try to get him to understand. It
seemed like he was going to accept it. I was there for moral
support or something. I don't know why I was there, really. I
guess Ricky always liked me and Mal knew that. Anyway, when it

was all over, Ricky looked Mal in the eye and said, 'but it was good to keep the buzz going.' Mal covered his eyes with his hands and screamed. 'Ricky. I don't want you giving interviews about me. What the fuck is so hard about that?' Arnie tried to calm Mal down, but it didn't work. Mal and Ricky started screaming at each other. I thought Mal was going to have a heart attack. He had a way to make his voice so high, almost like an opera singer. I was scared that one of them was going to hit the other. And then in the middle of the whole thing Ricky yells that he can straighten the whole thing out. 'Mal. After the first of the year, you and I will get on the phone with the guy at ABC. We'll make a plan to do the publicity right.' Mal ran screaming from the room. I can't remember what he said. Arnie was begging Ricky by that point. 'Ricky. Didn't you hear us? Can't you stop? Please assure me that you won't call anyone. Please. Okay? I don't want you to sabotage anything else, okay?' That set Ricky off into a rage. He was like that. If he had an idea, he would never let go of it. It seems like everything he did ended up going sour. I feel sorry for him, but I shouldn't, really. He had every advantage and never got anywhere. People in the business really hate him."

A few dumplings later, Barry revealed the version that he had heard from Arnie Baylos. Arnie had told him, "Ricky was always a P.R. problem. In the early days we had no idea what was happening. The tabloids didn't have a really big circulation. Ed Sullivan still had his column. Somehow Ed found out that Mal was given the contract for a sitcom on ABC. When the young turks at ABC saw the column, it blew their whole promotion strategy. The head of the network pulled the plug, and Mal was out of a job. It took me a while to figure it out, but I was sure it was Ricky. He would take all the Sunday papers and head up into his room. He knew the name of every gossip columnist. Mal and I decided to confront him. Crying, Ricky confessed that it was just a prank, and he would never do it again. It was the only time I ever saw Mal hit Ricky. I think it crushed him, scarred him for life. After that, things were always different for Mal and Ricky. Mal held on to the love and Ricky wanted it. It was a sad thing to watch. Ricky wanted to be closer and closer to Mal, and Mal kept leading him up to the door and then slamming it shut."

Like all Hollywood stories, embellishment was taken for granted, including changing certain details. However, there was no mistaking the overall toxic feeling in town toward Ricky.

A striking blonde woman approached the dim sum boys; her perfectly proportioned figure caught the eyes of nearby lunch gazers.

"It's Heather," said Bob with his mouth still full.

"Hi, boys. Can I sit?" She was all smiles.

Bob waved half-heartedly.

Sean stood up. "Of course. Have you eaten?"

Gary also jumped up and pulled over a chair from an adjoining table.

Heather froze. "No, but they don't have anything here that I eat."

Barry spoke with a direct, calming voice. "They have a Chinese chicken salad."

Heather answered with a child's response to a parent. "That's right. We spoke about it once." She took her place at the table. "So, what are you movers and shakers up to today?"

"We're trashing Ricky Rose," said Bob.

Heather giggled and said, "Wow. This is a sport I know how to play."

"You don't have to," said Sean.

"But, I want to. He's such an ass."

"Let's hear," said Gary. "Come on. You guys love gossip as much as the next guy."

"I need a cigarette," said Bob. He left the table and headed for the outdoor terrace that encircled the frontage and one side of the restaurant.

Heather giggled more as she told her story. Her audience proved to be incredibly attentive . "Ricky used to ride up and down Hollywood Boulevard taunting the hookers. What he didn't know was that some of the same women who were fucking Mal also like worked on the side a little. I spent a few nights with Ricky and some of his friends. These guys were into doing all sorts of group stuff, but they didn't know much about it. I think Ricky was really in over his head. He wasn't good-looking, and he acted like this incredible spoiled brat. If he knew that I was a regular of his father, he'd probably be jealous. I think Mal still likes to do it. Only a few people know this, but when Mal's wife moved out of town, a couple of the girls took over the job of giving Mal his daily enemas."

Sean interrupted. "Waiter. Will you bring a Chinese chicken salad, right away?"

"Anything to drink?" asked Barry.

Heather was quick to answer. "Yes, okay, I want a plain iced tea. No lemon. No nothing."

Barry nodded in approval.

"And a plain iced tea," said Sean.

The waiter nodded and took off.

Bob rejoined them. "I heard something about enemas. Sorry I missed it."

Heather continued, as if she hadn't finished a lecture. "Mal is a very interesting man, a very interesting man." She offered what Sean felt was a knowing smile. "Oh, and not a bad lover. All the girls really liked being with Mal. He was a considerate lover. Oh, I've heard those rumors that the thing about women was all a put on and that Mal was gay or something. I think it's all very funny, the public perception thing. I can tell you this. Mal was probably bisexual, but I think he definitely preferred women." She laughed as if she were withholding something very pertinent. "That's all I really want to say about Mal. When I spent a lot of time with the Friars boys, I worked part-time for a housewife who ran a stable of girls out of her house near Beverly Glen. Ricky and his friends would get all coked up. Ricky loved to get his dick sucked when he did coke. I don't mean a little, I mean until it was shriveled up like a Popsicle that was left out on the beach to melt. It was a joke after a while. I always brought extra ChapStick when Ricky called. If I didn't, my lips would be out of commission for three or four days."

Barry and the production boys burst into uproarious laughter.

Sean banged the table with his hand. "That's so funny."

"And a little pathetic," said Bob.

"Working at all?" asked Gary.

"Yeah. I've got five lines on *Will and Grace*."

"Great," said Gary.

"Did you ever talk to the name I gave you?" asked Sean.

"Yeah, the old guy from *Murder She Wrote*. I think he just wants to get laid."

Sean snorted. "That may be true, but he knows a lot of people."

"Where I have I heard that before?" She batted her eyelashes and winked, holding the pose for effect.

Bob chortled. "That's the damned truth. The casting couch may be gone, but it's been replaced by a Land Rover and a cell phone."

Sean responded. "Bob? Have you ever thought of doing a little writing? That's so creative."

"Creative maybe, but I still don't get it," added Gary.

"Don't pay any attention to them," said Barry.

Heather said, "I think it was creative. Don't let them make fun of you, Bob."

Bob spoke rapidly. "I can take Sean's sarcasm. They can't help it. It's the cheapest hobby they can find. Hey, pass me another one of those enchilada things with shrimp. Heather, thanks for coming to my defense, but I could care less about what these schmucks think."

Barry picked up the plate in order to pass it. "One Chinese enchilada thing with shrimp. Coming right up."

Bob took the plate. "Oh, tank you berry mush, honorable doctor. May your offspring be blessed by a flying Peking duck."

"I don't get it," said Gary. He glanced around for agreement.

Sean laughed. "What's to get?"

"It's called a sense of humor." Bob wolfed down the shrimp. "Some of us are not as droll as you."

Gary asked, "What do you mean by 'droll'?"

Bob smiled. "Forget that. How's 'humorless'?"

The rest of the meal centered around ways to help get Heather more acting work.

After lunch, Sean and Heather escorted Barry to his new white Porsche. Barry enjoyed talking while leaning against his car. He tried to make eye contact with women as they strolled past, an endeavor Sean dismissed as sophomoric 'eye fucking', something he had given up in college.

Sean asked, "Seeing anyone new?"

Heather said, "I've been keeping up with this older guy from Hillcrest who has an ostrich farm."

"No shit."

"No shit."

Barry said, "I'll wait in my car."

Sean walked a few steps with Heather and said, "Let me know how his business is going."

"Sure, but I don't think ostrich farming is for you."

"If I don't find something soon, I might give up."

"You will." Heather gave Sean a peck on the cheek. "Be a good boy. I need to work out." She was off to the Sports Club L.A., a giant gym on Sepulveda where wannabes mixed with people who had already made it in the business. There was the usual sprinkling of ancillary followers who had a few bucks in their pockets and didn't mind spending it on venues that allowed them to rub shoulders with the stars.

"Maybe that's my problem." Sean turned and headed back toward Barry. When he reached the Porsche, he leaned inside the open window and said, "I'm coming to your office later. Don't fuck with me on this, Barry. Okay?"

"Yeah. Fine with me. But you have to come after six," said Barry.

"Fine. Do you have some seltzer there or should I pick some up?

"You pick it up. And for god's sake, it's 'sparkling water'. And you have to buy dinner after the session. Can you get us into Spago?"

"I don't know. Probably. Wolfie still loves me. What's the difference? You always order mundane bullshit that you can get at a salad bar in some dump."

"What? Just because I don't eat raw fish and meat. One day you're going to wake up dead from eating that shit," said Barry. He waved goodbye and closed his window. He paused, opened the window, and yelled back to Sean. "Funny thing…That Mal…"

"What?" said Sean. "I'm busy. I've got calls to make."

"I don't know. You know how I say I can spot someone's sexuality right away?"

"I know how you say it, but you do remember the transsexual you picked up at the AIDS L.A. benefit?"

"I didn't say I'm a hundred per cent accurate," said Barry. "A lot of the time I can tell. This Mal V. Rose. I didn't get any feeling, one way or the other - years ago, the same."

"So? Heather said she always thought he was 'bi'."

Barry looked at Sean and realized the same thing, "You're right. So what?" He shrugged his shoulders in acknowledgement. "Yeah. Forget it."

"Forgotten. Who cares if Mal is gay?" asked Sean.

"Yeah. See you later." Barry rolled up his window.

Sean ended the conversation with a nod and headed toward his office building.

Once inside his inner office, Sean took a bottle of 'seltzer' from a refrigerator hidden by a walnut cabinet door. He waltzed back into Gary and Bob's office, swinging the bottle at his side between his index finger and thumb. He sat in the middle of the room on a deep-cushioned leather chair and made idle conversation with the boys. Bob was a pro at reading screenplays and talking at the same time, while Gary had the same level of expertise at pretending. That's the way it went almost every day between meetings and phone calls - a lot of sitting around waiting for something to happen. Business was back to usual at Sean Daren Productions, although most of Hollywood was still reeling from 9/11.

Sean loved his seltzer. That's what he had always called it. When he had married, his future-former-wife Sarah talked him out of it, but after the divorce he went back to calling it 'seltzer'.

"Sean. It's not seltzer. It's sparkling water," she would say, just like Barry, convinced that the entertainment industry would recognize Sean's background as an ordinary Jew (anyone who didn't keep up with the new pretenses) and dismiss him as a potential super-Jew, the role that all the up and coming Jews coveted and tried to maintain by copying each other's new clothes, cars, and bottled water.

Sean felt that that was Barry's fear, too, that his friend would appear old and out of touch, and sent out to pasture like most people in the industry who had hit fifty - no longer 'cool' enough or the archaic 'hip'.

Many rules kept changing, making it more difficult to stay abreast of the social and political decorum inside the business. His ex-wife Sarah made sure that Sean had learned everything. No more shopping at Ralphs, Pavillions, and Lucky's, the ordinary chain supermarkets. It had to be Gelson's or Bristol Farms, the upscale food emporiums that served everything from café au lait to raw yellow tail, with Bristol Farms parking a new store inside the old Chasen's restaurant façade, including a lunchroom that featured the original red Chasen's booths. Alcoholic gifts couldn't be purchased just anywhere; they had to be sent from special stores like Wally's in Westwood, because the people in Wally's knew who liked what. You couldn't get someone a wine that wasn't his favorite. That would be dumb.

Sean had learned when he was amongst the upper echelon in the business to be sure to ask for sparkling water. He didn't care what brand it was. Usually it was the large bottle of Pellegrino, or Perrier, which seemed to be driven out of fashion in many of the Hollywood restaurants, obviously by aggressive marketing and new distribution deals. The water business in Hollywood was a cottage industry, adding millions to the coffers of eateries and catering businesses. This all took place while

Consumer Reports, year after year, named Los Angeles City tap water as one of the best in the nation.

Sean drank nine or ten bottles of sparkling water a day. He kept a little refrigerator next to his bed at home, filled with Arrowhead sparkling water, a less expensive version that only a select few would be allowed to view. These were sixteen ounce bottles, adding up to an intake of about one hundred and sixty ounces a day.

"This seltzer shit is good for you," Sean said while Bob and Gary looked on, sipping their respective herbal ice tea and coke. Bob was known to drink more Long Island ice teas than non-alcoholic ones.

"What's the matter with iced tea? It's got herbs in it," Bob intoned, as if he was asking the question at a Mayo Clinic seminar.

"Caffeine for starters. This is pure mountain water," Sean continued, stopping between his nutritional dissertation to take large gulps from the fancy little pop-up caps, created for those on the go who obviously wanted to keep the little bottle with them as they climbed the Himalayas or more routinely driving from office to office around Hollywood in all-terrain four-wheel-drive vehicles.

Bob added, "That stuff gives you too much gas. One day all that gas is going to accumulate and your stomach will blow up like a balloon. You'll look like a fuckin' balloon on those skinny stick legs of yours. And then you'll just float away or blow up or something. Or maybe Macy's could use you for the parade."

"Fuck you, Bob. You never did anything healthy in your whole life," said Sean.

Bob smirked, swirled his desk chair around and grabbed a pack of cigarettes. He snagged one in his teeth and whirled the chair back around, facing Sean. His arms waved wildly out of sync like a failed invention designed to lift him off the ground. "Fuckin-A, sonofabitch. I'm gonna die happy, you miserable prick." He practically chewed off the end of the cigarette, and had to reverse it in his mouth in order to light it. Once lit by his cheap bright purple supermarket lighter, he blew the smoke toward Sean.

"Jerk," said Sean. "I'll be in my office." Sean popped up and walked toward his office.

"Right," said Gary.

"If I were you I'd see a gastroenterologist," said Bob. "You've got too many bubbles."

"Fuck off," said Sean. His voice was muffled.

"I don't feel so good myself," said Bob, as he stroked his stomach.

"What's the matter with you?" asked Gary.

"I don't know. I think it's the Chinese."

"How do you know it was the Chinese?"

"I've got a sudden urge to convert my wool sweater into a ball of yarn so I could catch my claws in it".

Gary thought for a few seconds. A laugh reluctantly escaped his mouth and a moment later he was back to stone-faced. "That's funny. A cat joke."

"I wish this screenplay was." Bob closed the cover and tossed the screenplay onto a pile of scripts on the floor. "I gave it every conceivable chance. When did farting become so funny?"

Inside his office, Sean was daydreaming about his past exploits. He usually picked the middle of a Friday afternoon, the quietest period of the day, a time when some movie executives were still finishing lunch at Spago and giving serious thought to not returning to the office. It was a time

for either changing to one of the more secluded banquettes that
were loaded with actresses or instead having Wolfgang Puck come
over and dance around the luncheon table for the guests. Always
charming, Wolfgang would smile and ask in his thick accent, "Did
you enjoy your meal?" He could laugh and joke with the best of
them, never forgetting that he was originally adopted by the
entertainment industry, big time, when his restaurant was on
Sunset and Horn.

Sean had been friendly for years with John Gaines - the
flamboyant owner of the APA Talent Agency. It was one of the
hip, newer agencies on Sunset Boulevard. John would demand a
front view table in the old Spago, up on the rise, and held
court while clients from Morgan Fairchild to Steve Martin would
stop by his table. When it came time for dessert, John would
insist that Wolf bring over everything chocolate, and John would
help himself. He would also grab things from the dessert cart at
La Dome, the nearby celebrity-driven restaurant. It drove the
owners nuts, but they knew how much clout John had. Sean knew
that people in the business could be rude and get away with it.
Acting out in restaurants used to be reserved for actors, but
now everyone did it, right down to people who had the audacity
to call themselves 'facialists', some with zero medical
training. To Sean, it sounded like something from a porno
website. John eventually succumbed to AIDS, and another agency
partner, Marty, dropped dead about the same time. Sean missed
the feeling of the eighties and early nineties, mostly because
he got to rub shoulders with the APA clients, a range that
included one of the Redgraves, along with most of the popular
comedians like John Candy, also gone, and Rick Moranis.

John Gaines had once invited Sean to a Christmas party at
actress Veronica Hamel's house. Most of the cast of *Hill Street
Blues* were in attendance. Veronica was living near Bel-Air and

had rented a bunch of Christmas decorations – with the tags still showing - for the party. When Sean moved past the buffet line he noticed that all the food was Indian. Only moments later he bumped into the Amritraj brothers, famous Indian tennis players turned movie producers. Later, while sitting on the couch with John, former UCLA basketball-player-turned-television-producer Michael Warren appeared with his plate of tandoori chicken and sweets. After a few verbal jabs from John, Michael came out with, "I know what you mean. Last year I was treated to chitlins and fried chicken." The smile on his face clearly conveyed the message.

Sean abandoned his daydreaming and returned to the front office. The office wall was newly decorated with Bob's lung x-rays. A big red bull's-eye outlined the area that his physician had identified as a "possible pathological spot". Bob sat beneath the x-rays, chain smoking while he continued to read another screenplay.

Sean went through his list of callbacks with Gary, part of an end of the week painless ritual.

Gary saved the most innocuous for last. "Did you ever call back that dentist that wants to rent the apartment at Horn-Sunset Towers?"

There was nobody else left to call. "Shit. That's right. Get him." Sean picked up one of phones facing the outside of the desk, generally reserved for guests. "Let's do this on the speaker," he added, nodding to Bob to push his speakerphone button. It was a game they played with 'civilians'.

Bob lowered the screenplay and gingerly pushed the appropriate button, leaning forward to see if the proper light was on. He mumbled, "I hate these twisted mother-fuckers. I miss my rotary phone."

"You got it," said Gary. "Let's try his home number first." After checking the number he added, "Hey, I thought he was in New York." He pushed the button on his main console to allow the call to come through all three telephones in the room.

"Hello." I was sitting on the balcony, facing the beach. That was a true California moment for me, remote phone in hand and barely budging off my chaise lounge. Very few patients liked or were accustomed to late Friday appointments, so I had learned to leave the office early. Health professionals in Beverly Hills were hard to find after 3 P.M. I wasn't sure who trained whom, the doctors or the patients. I settled on both.

"Hi. Sean Daren. Is this Dr. Benjamin?"

"Oh, yeah. Hi. How ya doin'? Thanks for calling back."

"No problem. I like Laurel. Do anything for her. Anything." Sean paced the room as he talked.

"She said you might have an apartment for rent."

"I do. When are you coming out?"

"I'm in Venice. I made arrangements to stay at a friend's place at the beach."

"Venice?"

"Not exactly. The Marina Peninsula."

"It's nice there. Listen. Give me a call when you want to get together. What kind of doctor are you? She didn't say."

"An Endodontist."

"A root canal guy," said Bob in a hushed tone.

"A root canal guy?" bellowed Sean.

"Well…I guess so. Laurel said that you make movies. She said you were the guy who produced *I Spit On Your Pasta*."

"Yep. That's me. Don't tell me. Let me guess. You're an actor, too."

Gary shook his head and mouthed the words "not again". Then he mocked hitting himself in the head with his fists.

"Not exactly. I wrote some plays, and now I'm adapting them for the screen." I had to say it, and I felt like a jerk for saying the phrase "not exactly" more than once in the same conversation. Mentioning my current book idea to this crowd was far from kosher, so I stuck with my past creative endeavors.

"Anything I would know?"

"I don't know. Do you go to the theater in New York?"

"Yeah. Maybe I saw one of them."

Gary gave Sean the signal to wrap it up - his hand rotating at the wrist.

"They were off-off Broadway."

"I go, okay?" I thought that Sean sounded annoyed. "Do you want to tell me a title or would you rather wait until AT & T cuts off our call for going over my long-distance limit?"

My voice grew meek. It happened whenever I spoke about my writing. It was some sort of twisted apology to my family, who thought that my theater activities were frivolous. "I wrote *Small Steaks*."

Sean became animated. "I saw that. Bill Hickey was in that, wasn't he? You know, the old guy from *Prizzi's Honor*, with Jack and Angelica. He was nominated for that - did you know?"

Bob did his best Italian accent and drew out each syllable. "Don Corrado Prizzi".

I became ecstatic. "You saw it! Yeah. Bill did do it. I'm writing a screenplay based on it." I really had planned to, but I was learning a little about taking advantage of any situation in town.

Sean was finished me. "Listen. Give me a call when you get out here, boychick. Send me the screenplay. Hold on. My associate, Bob, will give you my address here." Sean walked toward his office.

I said, "I'm out here now. In the Marina."

Gary was firm and didn't give Bob a chance. "Got to go. Call Sean back, okay?" Gary disconnected the call.

Bob signaled with the universal hand gesture for jerking off. He was glad the call was over.

"Poor schmuck," said Gary. "He's coming out to Hollywood to write."

At least I had made contact. I thought that they came off as rude, but it didn't take long to learn that that was perfectly normal and acceptable in their world. In fact, that dynamic trio would prove much nicer than most.

Before Sean left the office for the day, he remembered that he hadn't called the plumber to fix his sprinkler pipe. He sat at his desk to make the call.

Jack Reilly, Inc. were the plumbers to the stars. Jack had started the Beverly Hills business after learning his plumbing skills during World War II. Jack retired about ten years ago to move to South Beach, Miami, and left his less-than-competent son Charlie to run the business. Charlie had his own way of doing things.

"Yeah. Hello," said the disconnected voice.

"Is this Jack Reilly?"

"Yes. What is it?" Charlie's voice gave away his unhappiness.

"I need someone to come out and repair my sprinkler."

"We don't do that kind of secondary work." Charlie was at once dismissive and condescending.

"I want you guys to do this. You did the outside plumbing on my house."

"Who is speaking?"

"This is Sean Daren."

"It's Charlie." He pretended to be more congenial.

"Charlie. You don't sound so good." Sean thought that he sounded drunk. After all, long Friday lunches were common.

"It's been a rough day."

"When can you get someone out there?"

"Is it a secondary problem?"

"I don't know what the fuck you're talking about. I just want to get a plumber over to the house to fix the leak."

"We don't like to take the time to do a lot of secondary work. Is it still leaking?"

"The damn water is off in the house. What is this, an FBI investigation?"

"Mr. Daren. We have a very busy schedule, with the holidays and all."

"I don't care about your schedule, Charlie."

"We're doing a big job at Brad Lewis' house, the writer. He wrote that book about Milton Berle."

"Charlie. Why are you doing this? It's Sean Daren. You shouldn't fuck with me like this."

Charlie had practiced and honed a relentless form of torturing his clients. "It's my job to first find out if you have a leak in a primary or secondary pipe. If it's secondary, we probably can't get out there for a day or two. We have two other big jobs going on, one in Malibu and the other in Bel-Air."

"Charlie. Your guys put the pipes in," said Sean. "What's the difference?" He was losing his patience.

"We don't put in sprinkler pipe. Well, sometimes we do. Look. I'll put you down for this afternoon, but I can't promise anything. They might get there tomorrow."

"Charlie. It's Sean Daren. The movie producer. Malibu. Remember?"

It finally clicked, and Charlie's tone and demeanor flipped to accommodating. "Oh. Mr. Daren. You know I didn't get your full name at first. Sorry. Look. I'll have them stop by early before they do the other job in Malibu. Is it the front or back of the house?"

"The front. I'll tell the contractor to meet you there. The hook-up to the main water line is a bit unusual."

"Understood," said Charlie.

They both hung up.

The phone call was the finishing touch to the day. Nothing but stress. No firm deal with Mal. No money coming in. Maybe he would make his 'fuck around' calls to friends. He drove to the Bel-Air Hotel, parked his car with the valets, and watched the Golf Channel at the bar while sipping Bloody Marys.

His first thought was to remind himself to stay clear of Ricky. Sean knew Ricky's type well. Hollywood was full of people who seemed to exist in a happier space only when they were leaving someone - a family member or a lover - or a business relationship that they had intentionally propelled themselves away from through varying forms of self-sabotage. Sean made up his own version of their lives - *the grass is always greener the second, third or fourth time around*. For Ricky and others like him it was an endless cycle of movements away from people and deals, and yet that perversely negative approach seemed to survive in Hollywood. New deals always materialized if you or a family member were 'in the loop'.

Sean told himself his own little joke. *Ricky's next business could be called 'Repellants R Us'*. Sean imagined that Ricky could hire himself out to kill other people's relationships and deals. For certain, there would be takers.

Later that evening, Sean's dinner with Barry became one in a long string of events that blended together like the shadows in an aging sepia photograph. By the time Sean arrived home, he could think only in dark shades. Barry had left him more depressed than earlier in the day, not an entirely unusual occurrence.

CHAPTER FOUR
Mal, Ricky
Sean

The Friday luncheon at the Friars had proved reliably
uneventful for Mal and Ricky; they had done it so many times
before. Ricky enjoyed those moments more than Mal. The least
little thing could set Mal off. That day it was a pepper shaker
that didn't exactly match the salt version. "What are those
little Mexican cocksuckers doing in the back with these things?"
Mal held the pepper shaker up to his nose and sniffed it like a
little dog. Things calmed down when someone's luncheon guest -
another unsuspecting 'Jerry' - stopped at the Rose table in
order to fawn over Mal.

The nicely dressed woman kept her distance, both physical
and verbal, and spoke with a jittery cadence. "Mr. Rose. I must
say what a great fan I am of yours."

Mal studied her with a detective's eye. "And I must say
what a great fan I am of anyone who wears Cher's old wigs." The
group at Mal's table cackled on cue, while the 'Jerry' beamed
with delight because her comedy idol Mal V. Rose was paying
attention to her, completely unaware that for the next few
minutes he would continue to make her the butt of his jokes. No
matter what he said, she basked in her idol's starlight,
periodically glancing back for approbation from her peers.

Back at home, the daily routine that followed for Mal was
simple. Nap after lunch in a room darkened except for a
nightlight to the right of the headboard. After the snooze,
Ricky would escort Mal around the block. Mal wore his quilted,
maroon smoking jacket and matching slippers while he waved to
the outlandishly decorated tour buses that drove to the star
homes. The Roses lived quite close to the Beverly Hills Hotel,
prime rubber-necking territory.

That night, Ricky had to shuttle Mal over to UCLA Medical
Center for a benefit. The fundraiser was being run by Mal's
internist, Dr. Leonard Kopplemeyer, and he had asked Mal to
perform as part of the lengthy, rubber-chicken dinner show.

My friend Mickey had his own table that came with his large
donation. I showed up early and sipped cocktails, leaving my
tape recorder on most of the evening. Our table included Ira,
Neil, Les-Lou, a few television actresses that I'd never heard
of, and Mickey's mother, Gloria. Mickey saw to it that she lived
way beyond her means. It made him feel accomplished, and she
certainly had no objections.

By the end of the cocktail session, I had eaten every kind
of appetizer that Wolfgang Puck could provide. To his credit,
the dinner did not come off like so many rubber-chicken slam-
bang-thanks-for-the-donation deals. The food was quite palatable
and I had plenty of decent booze. If this was Hollywood, I could
learn to accept the missing crispness on the outside of a real
New York bagel, as well as moist pastrami on proper fresh rye.

Dr. K., as his friends called him, was known as much for
his star-fucking and high-flying investments as he was for his
medical acumen. He had lost plenty, but also made bundles by
constantly using his patient contacts to find out inside
information about a variety of companies, ranging from the now
defunct Internet stocks back to the old days when he would get a

telephone call from a female attorney at Disney marketing,
Kendra Delray, who advanced Dr. K. the summer release schedule
in time for him to load up on Disney call options. Dr. K. would
contact his broker as early as March to get a jump on the
market. He bought options with strike prices in June and July.
For a number of years, the process was almost a sure thing, with
or without the insider information. In some cases, 'friends'
would give him information that anyone well-connected in any
high-level- business could get, but it kept the relationships
lively, and made Dr. K. secure that he was one of the 'chosen'
insiders. He was quick to publicly condemn Martha Stewart for
her 'insider' trading activities, even though he'd sold stock in
the same company about eighteen hours after she did. By that
time, the SEC had a whole bunch of trades to examine and never
got around to Dr. K.

A lot of people humored Dr. K. socially, particularly his
most wealthy and powerful patients. They counted on him for
extra service, ranging from a never-ending supply of narcotics
to having the plug pulled on an aging relative whose estate
papers were 'kosher', occasionally including the good doctor as
a beneficiary 'for a lifetime of devoted service'.

Through the seventies to nineties, Dr. K. was in the thick
of the Hollywood retread 'sexual revolutions' that ebbed and
flowed with cocaine usage. Hollywood always remained the same
beneath the fluctuating facade, but it was the political mood of
the country and the media reflection that determined how much
attention was given to the excesses. In the seventies,
overindulgence flowed, and was topped off by a stock market
economy that poured money into Hollywood. The eighties would
temper Dr. K.'s public image, but not his personal life. The
eighties had a tremendous impact on his practice, since it was
no longer acceptable to wink at a patient with the excessive

runny nose and send him packing off to the 'allergist', whose own eye was sore from winking. Sexual promiscuity could no longer be overlooked, since several of Dr. K.'s high-profile patients were ill with the 'plague' that took root in the eighties and had to be addressed and taken very seriously in a most professional forum.

Heather knew Dr. K. well, and in her sessions with Barry had revealed a great deal about him without using his name. It gave Barry enough information to know specifically whom she meant. "There was this one Beverly Hills internist. I can't give you his name, but he reminded me of a chubby fish. It's not that he was into water sports or anything. He just had big fish lips. I would see him at least once a month. He was probably my most wild client, but he didn't know it. I remember the time he wanted me to drip hot wax on his dick, but I told him it might be dangerous, so we settled on his ass. He got bored after a few minutes anyway. He was always up to something new. He was never mean to me, and always gave me a generous tip. And it didn't hurt to get my Vicodin for free."

Barry took in information like this from varied sources. For his own sanity, he spoke with his Rabbi, Harvey Ermis. This is how Rabbi Ermis answered Barry's query about how to handle the prevailing changes in town. "I was very much aware of how people's views changed on sex during the eighties. It was a national problem. AIDS was and still is a national problem, but people became very scared in the eighties. The effect on Hollywood was devastating. The typical Hollywood executive had two problems. One was how to handle sex on television and in the movies, and the other was on how to handle his own sex life. Television shows were beginning to include dialogue about condoms and the need to ask someone about his or her sexual history. By the end of the eighties, things had definitely

changed. *Daily Variety*, the famous Hollywood newspaper, was
receiving more than half a dozen death notices a week for people
in the business who had died from AIDS-related illnesses. That
was some wake up call."

For a first-hand view, Barry had many patients with
'lifestyles' like Bob's, who were not shy about discussing the
party scene. "I remember going to a wild party up in the hills.
We stopped at Max Baer's house first, you know, the guy that
played Jethro on *The Beverly Hillbillies*. He was having some
kind of huge party. After we left, we ended up at some doctor's
house. I won't swear it was him, but I think the host was Dr.
K., the guy who is often on *Access Hollywood*, as the 'doctor to
the stars'. It was the wildest party I had ever been to. There
was cocaine in every room. People upstairs were smoking it and
running around the hall stark naked. I don't kiss and tell, but
there were plenty of well-known people blitzed out of their
minds at that party."

Eventually Barry turned to Sean for his take on Dr. K. "Dr.
K. was a good doctor. I don't care about his sex life. It had
nothing to do with mine. I heard the stories, but who cared? We
had our own problems just making movies. In the eighties, I
couldn't make a sex film like I used to. Not unless I wanted to
go to the pure porno mode, and I swore I'd never go back to that
again. When I first did one in college, I didn't even know we
were making porno movies. I was hired as a second unit director,
if you want to call it that. But that's really what I did. I
shot the outside of houses, people in cars, in restaurants.
Nobody told me that the other scenes were all in the sack.
People were so self-conscious then. I remember sitting at a
screening of Coppola's Vietnam movie with James Caan and
Angelica Huston. People didn't like the kissing scenes. The same
thing happened with Molly Ringwald and Robert Downey. It got

cold. Even the James Bond movies were more or less subdued. It
became a one girl per film kind of thing. Single characters on
television all had to confront how they would deal with the new
morality. Show business always complies with what the people
want. Look at the sitcoms today; they reflect how we wish it
could have been then."

Gary would sit on Barry's sofa and spend the whole 'hour'
talking about how things had changed. "I thought it was all a
joke. All the organizations got into this weird thing about
open-mouthed kissing. The Screen Actors Guild put the tongue
kiss into its own kind of special category, sort of like doing
stunt work or a nude scene. They wrote all kinds of ridiculous
rules, like not telling whom the kiss would be with, just
telling the actor that they expected some tongue action. It was
a joke. Depicting safe sex became such a issue/non-issue. I
still find it hard to believe that people watch television shows
or go to the movies because they are interested in receiving
great home medical advice. Sure. If you are doing hard core, why
not wear a condom, those people are the only ones really at
risk. I'm no doctor, but I don't know anyone who got sick from
tongue kissing. They took sexual humor out of the whole thing,
so we can't have that much fun with it, but it's turning around,
slowly but surely, everything will go back to the way it was. It
always does."

Barry saw it as an infantile sexuality. His profession had
come a long way since Freud. Times had really changed the way
that people thought and the way that psychiatrists practiced.
There were still some older conservative doctors in town who
didn't like the changes. They privately clung to old clinical
definitions like treating homosexuality as a curable disease, so
still labeled well into the seventies. The show business
community that Barry knew was generally liberal, or at least

publicly pretended to be. Barry realized that Arnold and Bruce couldn't have been the only practicing conservatives. Nevertheless, Barry played along with the more popular – at least locally - liberal political and social charade.

The fundraiser for UCLA, a raucous black tie affair, was packed to capacity. If a function had any steam, a rapidly increasing buzz would materialize during cocktail hour. By the time the Roses arrived things were going full tilt. Eager inebriated guests ogled the expensive silent auction items, which ranged from a shiny new Harley, to a benefit for the Democrats, featuring Barbra Streisand.

Dr. K. had invited a collection of the Hollywood celebrity doctors, but was initially hanging around the Roses. Sixty-something Dr. K. was always well-dressed and well-groomed. He wore expensive jewelry, including a ruby and gold frog in place of a boutonniere, but nothing else terribly overdone. His hair was retouched to show the proper mix of black streaks in a sea of naturally white hair. His facial skin had been pulled and tucked back behind his ears, just enough to appear younger, without making his pallor blanched and white.

Ricky couldn't tell if Dr. K. was wearing a make-up base. His skin was lightly bronzed, as if he had worked on the tan for months. The truth was that Dr. K. used the entire makeup line by Victoria Principal, suggested to him by a local dermatologist who was married to the actress. Unless Dr. K. went for a swim or was caught up in a southern California downpour, his secret was undetectable. These two watery events were easy to avoid, particularly since 'it never rains in southern California'.

Mal leaned in toward Ricky. "When I first went to see the Doc, he was buying discount suits at Harris and Frank. Now look at him. One of his suits could feed a family in Afghanistan for a year, and they'd have money left over to buy a Subaru."

"And a satellite dish," added Ricky, yucking it up for Mal.

Mal paid no attention to Ricky when he added a 'topper' to one of his jokes. Mal leaned in and took a closer look at Dr. K.'s suit. "Who picked out the pattern, Stevie Wonder?"

"Funny," said Dr. K. He was always polite with show biz royalty.

Ricky left Mal's side and wandered around the nearby auction tables. He trusted the totally beholden Dr. K. to stay with Mal, the former having proved himself through years of unadulterated service. Ricky zoomed straight to the buffet and slowly make his way past every table, spending extra time at the sushi station in order to gorge himself on California roll and yellow tail.

Mal repeated, "It's a Stevie Wonder original."

"No. Ray Charles," said Dr. K. He actually thrived on the attention, and after years of hanging around the business, was quick on the uptake when it came to doing shtick.

"Doc. I work as a single. You want to make jokes? I'll switch with you for a week. Just line up a few of your best looking patients and I'll do the exams. And it won't be like the old doctor sketch from Smith and Dale. I won't be acting."

Dr. K. laughed. He genuinely liked Mal. "No thanks, Mal. Comedy is too hard."

"I know. Look what it's done to me." Mal screwed up his face as it were made of Silly Putty.

"Did you see *The Producers*? It's a wonderful show," said Dr. K. "I knew it would get the Tony when I saw it in previews." He fancied himself an expert on creative taste, but was always careful to only comment on popular frontrunners. He never saw a loser.

"I don't go to see anything having to do with Hitler," said Mal. "You want to see a good show, rent one of my early musicals. Those were good shows and good movies!"

At any of these functions, it didn't take long before the subject would turn to money. Dr. K. always managed to get in one of his favorite expressions. "I can live as a rich man or a poor man. I prefer rich." The other was borrowed more or less from comedian Joe E. Lewis, "Rich or poor, it's nice to have money."

Mal was soon whisked away by a group that included Red Buttons, Jan Murray, and Lorna Adams, Milton Berle's last wife.

A few minutes later Ricky returned to find Dr. K. speaking to a few doctors and their wives. "We're donating a portion of the proceeds tonight to the anatomy department at UCLA. It's sort of an extension of the charity thing we do. We're encouraging donors not only to make a contribution, but to leave their own bodies to science, and we're having a new drive set up to encourage more donors."

The look on the ladies' faces instantly revealed that their interest in being dissected by a bunch of first-year medical students was not very high on their donation lists. Plus, for many there were religious taboos.

Ricky wasn't paying much attention until he heard Dr. K. say that UCLA would take care of all the funeral expenses. Ricky leaned in to get more details. After dissection, the bodies would either be cremated or returned to the family. Ricky was dreading the idea of having to bury Mal, and didn't want to spend a lot of 'Mal's money' on a funeral. As far as memorial parties went, Ricky was sure he could get some charity or organization that Mal had helped in the past to pick up the party expenses.

Dr. K. waltzed slowly to a nearby podium in order to deliver a brief presentation before heading in for dinner.

Not much of anything at the function concerned the Roses. The press would run a story about how altruistic Mal was, with the copy previously written by Mal and Arnie. The dissection idea lingered with Ricky as he listened to Dr. K. - he might be a little bit richer at the end of the impending ordeal of burying Mal. Although Ricky wasn't sure, he felt that Mal was going to leave everything to him, simply because Ricky was the only person who had stuck by Mal, particularly during the last ten years. Ricky glanced over at Mal, who was comfortably holding court with the other comedians.

The cremation idea also clicked, particularly since Mal had always said that he didn't care if he cremated, despite the taboos of the Jewish faith. Ricky needed to find out how to sign Mal up. Ricky darted toward Mal and pulled him away to make sure that he heard the rest of Dr. K.'s presentation.

"A good dead man is hard to find," said Dr. K., just before the part of the presentation that dealt with finding more bodies.

The ones paying attention would learn that competition existed for corpses between UCLA and nearby medical schools like USC. The area around UCLA had a large Jewish population, and it was forbidden by Jewish law to be dissected, so it was unlikely to find many Jewish bodies donated to the medical school chop block.

Dying was still a good business in greater Los Angeles. An extensive array of city associated mortuaries often had unclaimed bodies, something that nobody ever questioned. The local system was supposed to operate simply. If a body was not claimed it was automatically made available to the medical schools. But, like any other government process, this one had its own intrinsic failed network that allowed most of the unclaimed bodies to escape being sent to places like Gross Anatomy at UCLA Medical School.

So the school had to develop its own neighborhood outreach program, a welcoming marketing tool that let nursing homes know that the local friendly medical schools would be happy to take old Uncle Max off his family's hands, and save the tab for a casket and burial. The program provided free pick-up service and did promise to ultimately cremate the body. The service did not appeal only to the financially needy. Many wealthy people were happy to save the money, particularly if they had planned to be cremated anyway. When all else failed, the school had to buy the cadavers from other medical schools, at anywhere from seven to nine-hundred a pop.

Dr. K. continued, "The dissection class is one of the first things a medical student encounters. It produces a wide range of emotions in students, from excitement to fear - by far the two most prevalent. I know that I cringed during the first few weeks of anatomy class. You have to realize that the goal is to meticulously, inch by inch, millimeter by millimeter, artery by artery, nerve by nerve, organ by organ, layer by layer, slowly dissect every part of the human body. The first thing that the student has to do is remove the skin. It's a humbling way to start, and it reminds everyone in the dissection class that this is what they will be doing for many months to follow." Most of the audience appeared stunned. A few perked up and displayed an artificial rapt attention. Others headed to the lounges and restrooms, drinks still in hand.

The school planned to send out a slick video to accompany the promotional material. The remaining cocktail crowd was treated to a briefer preview. The promo was entitled, *The Special Gift*. Mal yelled out an added subtitle, "*A Once In A Lifetime Offer*."

Of course he got laughs from most everyone except Dr. K., who took himself way too seriously when he was pitching something. The video began with a sweeping shot of the UCLA Medical School exteriors and then dissolved to a hospital room with an elderly woman surrounded by her family and an overabundance of floral arrangements.

The video narrator, an older woman with a soothing voice, spoke with delight about eventually having her body dissected by the eager-beaver first-year medical students. "When the day comes and my family sees me for the last time, just waiting there in the neatly arranged hospital bed, I am glad to know that there is a final gesture that I can make to help others."

Mal wished that he could have edited the movie and included the old woman in bed giving everyone 'the finger' at the conclusion.

The video resembled outtakes from *E.R.*, with handsome young actors parading around, preparing to dissect a body. There was no blood, and the bodies were draped in what could have been Ralph Lauren designed tarpaulins.

Despite his inviting enthusiasm for the program, there didn't appear to be a rush of donors. After the video, Dr. K. and his assistants passed out brochures to the reluctant group.

Mal, of course, thought it was all hysterical. He glanced around the room. "They look like they've won raffle tickets for the Titanic."

Dr. K. made a beeline to Mal. "Mal. This is a great idea, isn't it?"

Mal suddenly became direct and momentarily serious. "Gee. Maybe there just isn't anything really appealing about having your body cut into little pieces by first-year medical students who can't wait to go to work for greedy HMOs."

Dr. K. never gave up. "The bodies come from all over the state, sometimes from out of state, when we run short. People like to leave their bodies to science. It's like the 'village' concept that was promoted in the nineties. These people are paying back to the village, to the society that they were a part of. And, some do it just to save on the funeral expenses."

Mal listened as bit more attentively.

"We don't accept automobile accident victims, or people ravaged by extensive disease. The morbidly obese are impossible to dissect, as are the severely jaundiced. There is a short lag time before the bodies are embalmed, and during that period they are stored in the school's morgue area, where they wait before being embalmed and placed in formaldehyde solution. I help to see that the school has a continuous supply of cadavers for dissection. The city morgue eventually gives up its unclaimed bodies for dissection. Even a mid-priced casket and burial can run you over five thousand. In your case, the estate savings could be substantial."

Mal had heard enough. He wasn't totally convinced, but he could be as penurious as anyone, having evolved from abject poverty to enormous wealth. "That's quite a savings." Mal turned toward Ricky, who smiled, pleased to see that his father was interested in saving money.

Within two weeks, Ricky would have Kyle Bixler, their famous entertainment attorney, draw up the papers. In order to dissuade Mal from having any second thoughts, Ricky planned to slip the forms in between a few other papers that needed Mal's signature.

The Roses soon met with Bixler in his office, atop a towering building in Century City. The typical plush attorney's office was overfilled with expensive contemporary art that had once been at the center of a vicious lawsuit. Bixler's former partners had left with half of the valuable collection during a late-night raid, including ski masks. At the end of a long corridor, close to the kitchen, was Bixler's private office.

Inside, Mal and Ricky sat on high back leather chairs, facing Bixler.

Mal fumbled with each set of papers. "What's this one?" he asked, pausing on the set that Ricky had hoped he'd gloss over.

Ricky cleared his throat. "I'm sorry. Didn't I tell you? It's about cremation. Remember what Dr. K. suggested? You always told me you that maybe you wanted to be cremated, so I had Bixler draw up a paper. It just guarantees that you'll be cremated. And the school pays all the costs!"

After a few questions for Bixler, Mal signed the paper. The afterlife meant nothing to him. Dead was dead. Over decades of retooled routines, he had joked about it many times. Mal lived for the moment, and could care less about the details of his cremation. He was interested in larger financial matters, areas where Bixler was instructed to keep Ricky in the dark.

The mood in the room changed dramatically when Mal moved on to another, much thicker, set of papers. When the moment came to sign that document, Mal turned to Ricky and almost whispered. "Ricky, would you mind waiting outside?"

Ricky flinched, even though Mal had always done this to him. Mal always kept something a secret, as if Ricky was an irresponsible child. Parents like Mal were not about to trust their adult-children with the big bucks, particularly if they were as reckless and difficult as Ricky.

"Mal. Come on. I'm not a kid anymore." Ricky looked to Bixler for support.

"Mal. Let the kid watch. He may learn something." Bixler and Mal knew how to play Ricky. The cremation thing was a setup, something to make Ricky feel involved and momentarily important.

Bixler came away from those types of meetings as the good guy. If Ricky disliked any of Mal's business associates, he would spend hours complaining to Mal, and writing the most ridiculous letters and emails, critical of anyone that Mal knew. Mal could not afford for Bixler to become one of Ricky's rant targets.

"Ricky. Come on now. This will only take a minute. I don't know what you're worried about. You're going to be well taken care of when I'm gone. There will be plenty to go around," said Mal.

"I know that, but that's not what I mean. I mean, don't you think I should be part of everything that goes on? I am family."

"Ricky, please," was all Mal said, and he turned his head back to the papers.

Bixler shrugged his shoulders.

Ricky's face flushed. He hustled to the door, stopped to say something to Mal, but changed his mind. He opened the door and slammed it just enough to make more noise than usual.

"He's still a kid," was all Mal said.

Bixler nodded. He had watched Ricky survive in Mal's shadow for decades. The Rose family was not the first one that had set up a layered series of control dynamics for their children. It was Bixler's job to make his client happy, and Mal saw to it that Ricky would never have any financial independence, unless of course he got a real job or won the lottery. As far as Bixler was concerned, sons of clients had no rights, unless the parent chose to delineate certain privileges within the trust documents. It was easy for Bixler to pretend to be Ricky's ally. No harm, no foul. "Don't you smile when you're fucking someone?" was Bixler's defense, part of his polished, manipulative and charming personality.

"About those codicils I wrote," said Mal. He was more lucid once Ricky had left the room, and exhibited a legal acumen that rivaled Bixler's.

"I have them right here." Bixler opened the center drawer in his desk and removed a similar looking file to the others. "This one is already prepared with all the changes we went over."

Business as usual for Mal. No one, especially his son, would know the details of his estate planning, not unlike many parents of means. However, Mal's life would turn out to be filled with more secrets than even Ricky could have imagined.

Sean glanced at the clock. He couldn't see the usually bright blue numbers, but felt that it was exceptionally early, as if he hadn't slept enough. The night before, a few Hispanic workers from the Beverly Hills Tennis Club had helped mop up the remaining interior water. They had left towels over the soaked carpeted areas. One of the workers brought two fans, which ran all night. The plumbers had yet to make final repairs, so there was no filtered tap water available from the sink or built-in unit on the refrigerator door.

Sean felt a pain in side. He told himself to roll over; it must have been the way that he was sleeping. He shifted his weight. The pain remained.

Gas, he thought. *It's gas.* Since there was no water, he drank only bottled sparkling water the night before, perhaps consuming a dozen bottles in total yesterday.

He took a sip of the sparkling water that he kept on his bedside table. The time-tested theory was that this little introduction of gas would force the other gas out.

Sean rolled over again and waited. Nothing. The pain was still there. He put his hands around his stomach.

159

"What the fuck?" he said aloud.

His stomach was as round as a beach ball.

He heard Bob's taunting voice. "Too many bubbles. One day you'll blow up like a balloon."

Sean began to sweat profusely. *I never sweat like this*. He pushed on his stomach thinking that he could force it down. No luck. He pulled off his white Polo shirt, and bolted to the bathroom to stare into the mirror. He appeared grotesque, a six-foot-five man with a beach ball stomach. He grabbed his cell phone and dialed his internist, Dr. K.

"Dial him at home. This is an emergency," said Sean after arguing with the answering service. "Beep him. Find him! Whatever you do, get that sonofabitch on the phone."

The next thing that Sean remembered was being in Dr. K.'s office, sitting with a bare chest on an examination table.

"Sean. You have a rare digestive disorder. Tell me. Do you drink many carbonated beverages?" asked Dr. K.

"What do you mean, carbonated beverages? Do you mean anything with bubbles, like seltzer?"

"Yes. Anything with bubbles. Do you have more than three carbonated drinks per day?"

"I drink seltzer water, but that stuff is good for you."

"Not in large quantities. How many do you have a day?"

"I don't know. Five, maybe," said Sean. as if he were confessing to a crime.

"That's it?"

"Maybe a few more. Dr. K.! What's wrong with me?"

"Come over here and we'll look at your MRI."

Sean stared at the colorful swirls and patterns.

"Do you see this section here?" Dr. K. sounded as if he was doing one of the new medical commercials that intimidated the public.

Sean moved from the examining table to get a closer look. "It looks like a low pressure system on a weather map."

Dr. K. spoke slowly, as if he were delivering a death sentence. "It's the beginning of Hypergastrobubblemia."

"What?"

"Hypergastrobubblemia," Dr. K. repeated. "It's a relatively new disease. What happens is that the body begins to think it needs the bubbles to survive, so it begins to manufacture and store its own gas cells right on the lining of the stomach. Here. Right in this area here." He pointed to a pinkish area on the MRI. "Once it starts, the body stores the gas, just like a fat cell, except inside the stomach and large intestine, say about here." He pointed out the other areas. "What happens is that digestion is slowed down, and there is a level of malnutrition that develops."

"Is there a cure?" Sean wiped his brow with his hand.

"Is there a cure? John Hopkins recently reported on a case of a girl who went out dancing four or five nights per week, and drank nothing but sparkling water." Dr. K. paused.

"What happened to her?"

"She survived the resection of her GI track, but...but."

"What!"

"But, she'll never dance again."

Sean slumped down in a chair next to the examining table. He knew this would happen. That's the way his luck was going.

"I'm sorry, Sean. But we need more research. A group of people from the Hamptons have agreed to take part in a long-term study. They've been drinking sparkling water for almost twenty years now. It's the only place where we could get the kind of data we need for the research."

"The Hamptons? My life depends on people who live in the Hamptons?" asked Sean, still incredulous.

"We could de-gas you, but it's risky," said Dr. K.

Sean grew excited. "Whatever it is, I want to try it. What's the risk?"

"It's just so much gas leaving the body at once. I'm not sure if there will be any tissue damage. Tell me, Sean, are you a decent farter, in general?"

"Okay. I fortz okay, I guess."

"I need to know more. I mean are they long, sustained, loud, ever feel like they weren't going to stop?" Dr. K. was dead serious.

"Sometimes," said Sean. "When I eat whole garlic."

"Good," said Dr. K. He pushed a button on an intercom console, located on the wall. "Sarah, bring in the electronic bellows. We're going to de-gas Sean."

"Sarah. That's my ex-wife's name," said Sean.

In a flash, Sean's ex-wife Sarah was standing over him. "I told you that I like to be referred to as a 'former' wife, you dumb schmuck, putz, dick-head, prick. Now I want you to swallow this pump tube, and the other vacuum tube we'll need to put right in here." She rammed the tube hard into Sean's rectum.

He screamed as some gas roared from his body.

As Sean shot up in his bed, he grabbed his stomach. It was flat as a board - normal. He glanced at the bedside clock and realized that he was late for his yearly physical. His t-shirt was soaked with sweat. *Oy, what a dream!*

Sean recalled that he had left some of the windows opened last night in order to also help dry the carpet. To compensate for the cool air, he had set the thermostat on high, but had forgotten to lower the heat setting before retiring. Out of habit during the night, he had pulled up his thick down comforter. The excessive heat would give him nightmares, something dating back to his childhood.

When he became fully awake, he put another call in to the plumbers. *Hypergastrobubblemia*, he thought. *I like that.*

Unsettling thoughts traveled with Sean the rest of the day. He made a note to remind his daughter that if anything should happen to him that required hospitalization, to be sure that he stayed on the exclusive high floors at Cedars, those reserved for big-time donors and movie producers with connections.

CHAPTER FIVE
Ira, Neil,
Mel

That same morning, the scene at Venice Beach retained its
usual calm amidst the beginning of activity that would continue
through the dark hours. The eclectic little village was as much
a part of Hollywood lore as any distant segment; connected by
car and the invisible thread of the entertainment business. A
meeting ground where the present and past collided, Venice
embodied a little of everything and everyone. The beach stage
was a venue where the world's castoffs could mingle with the
power-hungry elite, while the famous-as-god actors, who wanted
'privacy', walked amongst the throngs unnoticed. Venice fueled
eccentricities and welcomed the unusual, while tolerating people
like Angelica Huston, who complained about her neighbors once
she had settled in, just like inside any other small town.
Dennis Hopper had lived there long before Hollywood had put it
on the chic list.

A beach cruiser cranked slowly along toward the winding
path alongside the 'boardwalk'. Seated on top of the classic
upright bike was Ira, his body seemingly attached to the large,
flat seat. He had a stocky, rugged build with a mop of curly
brown hair. He was never fat, but his nickname in college was
'Descartes a la Carte', because he loved to say "I eat,

164

therefore I am." Ira felt the morning fog tickle his face as he crossed over Washington Boulevard to reenter the bike lane as it turned to become part of the famous Venice Beach frontage.

The sun had been up for almost an hour and no business regulars were yet in sight, one of the best times of the day at the shore. The usual six or seven homeless people sitting near the pier enjoyed their morning coffee, if they had any. For some of the disenfranchised wanderers it was a nightcap, having staggered around the pier area most of the night. Early risers, oblivious to the homeless, jogged or biked by, some also stopping for coffee, creating a frame that encompassed all socioeconomic strata against the backdrop of whitish waves and a pure blue sky. A few inline skaters and a couple of people meditating rounded out the variable portrait.

The robed mystics preferred a closer proximity to the water's edge. On a foggy morning like that one, as the spiritualists neared the shoreline, they almost disappeared, adding to their transcendent aura. In contrasting image and purpose, an older man wearing a yellow rain slicker and matching hat sloshed along the pier with his pail and pole, feeling for the right place to cast his lucky fishing line.

Ira and Neil had known each other since elementary school, but Ira's family moved to New York after fifth grade. The boys stayed in touch, saw each other on occasional family trips, and were eventually reunited in college. This year was to be Ira and Neil's freshman year at UCLA Medical School. Ira's parents were pleased since Neil's father, Larry Hous, could keep his eye on Ira. The apartment the boys had rented near Mickey had originally started out as a summer sublet. Now it was home for at least the next year.

Neil had been previously working as an assistant to a stockbroker - rumored to have been divorced from a Warburg - at the local Dean Witter office on Maple Drive, south of the famous residential area in Beverly Hills. Neil's father Larry was a broker at the company and had insisted that Neil work there as well, bribing him with rent money and a car if he completed the broker-training program. The office was directly across the street from the Beverly Hills Tennis Club, where the Hous family were members. Neil spent most of his time lunching at the club and leaving his office early to play tennis with people in 'the business', mostly producers and aging actors. Neil was constantly hounding people like Wayne Rogers, the well-known television actor, also renowned for his financial acumen inside and outside of the entertainment industry. Wayne was then doing stints as a 'money guy' on FOX.

Neil had quit the Dean Witter job after a few months. He told his father that the brokerage business was just not for him. "There's too much lying, cheating, and deception. I don't want to end up like Jett or those guys who helped Enron or Adelphia," he moaned to his father. The buzz words momentarily gave his father pause. The truth was that Neil wanted to be a movie producer, "someone with some power out here." That's what he had told Ira. Lying, cheating, and deception were okay with Neil, but only if he got his name over the product. He didn't want to be one of the brokers dumping profitable stock into a CEO's account, in exchange for more business from his company. There was little chance of getting a brokerage firm to feature a line of 'T-Bills by Neil', 'Neil Hous Presents Zero Coupon Bonds', 'Neil Teaches How to Skirt SEC Regulations' or 'A New Issue Based On An Idea by Neil Hous'.

"You can't end up like Jett," his father answered with a straight face. "He's black." His father would always taunt Neil whenever he was trying to reveal his true feelings.

Neil would fight back to no avail. "Would you be comfortable if I ended up like Ivan Boesky or the Rigas family – the guys they put in jail from Adelphia – or something?"

"Try Milken. He's still got half his money." His father wouldn't give in. "The idea is to make the money and worry about the legal repercussions later. That's how the game is played."

Larry knew up front that a brokerage job wouldn't work out for his son, but he had promised Neil's enormously wealthy mother (drugstore chain heiress) that he would encourage him to give it a try. Money or not, she wasn't going to 'spoil' Neil by continuing to shell out his eleven-thousand-dollar a year tax-free gifts, which she withheld until December 31st of each year so as not lose any interest on the money. Neil's mother lived alone in the family home on Rexford Drive, where Neil grew up. She had kept the house as part of the divorce settlement. After two years of unnecessary litigation, Larry gave in. "Better this than more panic attacks," he told his attorneys. "She'll never move out of that house. Let's just take the low-ball appraisal for the property and get the fuck out of here." Lately, the elder live-in housekeeper had complained to Larry that she was going to quit unless Mrs. Hous stopped walking around at night turning off all the lights. The maid said that she was afraid someone was going to fall down. Like the darkened home, Mrs. Hous lived in the shadows of her past, unwilling to compromise on anything. The family shrink had once told Larry that his wife was delusional and lived in an alternate reality. "Nothing you can do, Larry." But Larry continually tried, only making his own life unnecessarily painful.

Having a mother develop into a penurious and continually depressed recluse was not part of Neil's life plan. She had taken a half-million out of the estate to give to Bob Barker's animal rights group. "How can you give money to that *Price Is*

Right schmuck and you won't help your own son?" was Larry's
response.

I would learn a little more about Neil from Manfred Safire,
the son of a well-known orthopaedic surgeon. "After I left South
Africa, I took a job working at the Dean Witter office. Neil and
I started hanging out together. He was a hoot. I didn't have two
bob to rub together, but when I got here I met all these Beverly
Hills kids that never worked hard, not a day in their lives.
Neil acted like a big shot because his father had a job there. I
didn't care. I was happy to get out of South Africa and get here
with a little money. Neil wasn't a bad guy, but he really wanted
to skip a few steps. You know what I mean. If ever there was a
shortcut guy it was Neil. His friend Ira was a good guy. I liked
both of them, and basically if they ever needed help with
anything, I wouldn't hesitate. It didn't matter to Neil if he
was making a few bob, he wanted to be rich and powerful, and
tomorrow!"

Despite the fact that Neil would eventually be left some
money, he was challenged by his father to apply to medical
school when they received the news that Ira might be coming to
town if he was accepted at UCLA. "If Ira can get into UCLA
Medical, then why can't you?" He had a point; neither was a top
student.

Neil had very little interest in attending medical school
until his father gave him some more 'friendly persuasion'.
"Neil. If you go to school with Ira, I will pay for the whole
thing. What's more, I will help you start a little surgical
center somewhere when you get out. Who knows? You might build up
your own little HMO. A national company?"

Neil didn't bite until his father came back to him, clearly
changing the stakes of the game. "If you don't apply I'm going
to cut you off. I am also going to call your mother and convince

her to amend her estate plan, and you know how your mother loves to save money." Neil wasn't the first medical student cornered by his father to attend school.

Neil called Ira to talk it over. It was a lengthy conversation. Neil knew that he was trapped. He would do anything to keep up his cash flow. A remark by Ira at the end of the talk made Neil really consider medical school as a viable possibility. "Neil," said Ira. "I'll help you get through."

Ira coached Neil through the remaining basic courses needed to apply, including some not-so-kosher lab reports and test-taking. Neil didn't score well on the national entrance exams, but his father Larry knew enough names-on-the-buildings-philanthropists connected with the school to at least get him on a waiting list. A few months before the first semester, Neil was accepted.

"I'll try it for a while," he told Ira. "If it doesn't work out, I guess I'll have to come up with something else."

Neil insisted that the boys rent on the south side of Washington Boulevard. That was where Dudley Moore used to live during his heyday, while other stars still maintained homes on what was still known as the Peninsula. Despite the upscale beachfront homes, there were plenty of affordable apartments, particularly if shared. Most were a block or two from the sand. Ira and Neil were on the second block off the beach, a little eight-hundred-and-fifty square foot loft with one bathroom. The front window faced the beach and they could see the ocean between two beachfront buildings - California nirvana. Mickey was quick to fill them in on the local folklore, including his display of pictures of himself with celebrities, including one of Mickey and Dudley standing in front of a classic Mercedes outside Dudley's bamboo garage door. At least one morning a week, Ira and Neil would walk past Dudley's old house and

169

imagine his fancy cars, which he always left in the open bamboo
garage that faced Speedway, the little street that ran behind
the first row of houses.

All things were pointing to this being the best summer of
Ira's life. He had finally graduated from undergraduate college
after five years, finishing while Neil was struggling with his
pre-med requirements. Ira wasn't really a bad student. He had an
attention deficit disorder. It wasn't diagnosed properly until
after his third year in high school, and by then his study
habits were already in shambles. At college, Ira was the second
best player on the tennis team. To a southern California medical
school that was a damned good credit - equal to honors in
biology. UCLA considered Ira as an 'all around' student, the
kind they needed in a freshman medical school class to, as the
dean of admissions said, "to round it out". There were always
enough eggheads to go around in any health science program.
Medical schools were changing, standards were lowered, as the
bottom line became staying in business. Ira and Neil would
clearly be in the minority. The days of Jewish and Italian
students predominating medical school classes was over.

While Ira was looking forward to tackling medical school,
Neil still had plenty of doubts. One night while the pair sat on
the sand, Neil blurted it out as if it were a confession.

"Ira. You know I'm just doing this to get the money from my
parents."

"No surprise," said Ira.

"But I'm really afraid of doing that anatomy stuff."

"Me too."

"But you've always been better at that sort of stuff."

"What sort of stuff? I've never done any human dissecting
either," said Ira. "What are you getting at?" Ira knew that Neil
wanted something.

"I've signed us both up for a summer tutorial at the school. If we do well, we can take it for credit. If not, we start all over in September, but at least we will have done some dissecting." Neil always wanted an edge, even a repellant one like an extra dissecting class.

At first Ira thought that the idea of practicing dissection was a good one, but then he backed off. He wanted to party as much as he could before school officially started.

"Come on. We're both partied out." That didn't sound like Neil, but Ira eventually agreed to take the summer Gross Anatomy course.

As things turned out, that decision wouldn't be the only thing to put a damper on their summer action.

That early morning on the beach path, Ira continued to crank the cruiser as he passed the unopened shops that faced the famous walk. He was on his way to see his grandfather. Ira and Neil would often ride their bikes to Venice Beach, where Ira's grandfather kept up his old deli. Mel Packer's place was quite a hangout for residents and tourists. An authentic New York style deli, virtually the same since Eisenhower was president, had a cadre of loyal followers, young and old, to say nothing of throngs of tourists. Nobody made an egg cream like Mel. In fact, nobody made egg creams any longer. Smoothies had taken over the mindset of the obsessed rich and nutrition-conscious locals.

When the unlikely duo visited Mel in the mornings, they would be treated to lox, eggs and onions at the deli counter, "And a fresh bagel mit schmear". They would sit and listen to Mel's endless stories. "Sophie Tucker used to come here," Mel would lament. "Now once in a while Madonna will stop by, but she's no Sophie Tucker."

171

People like Orson Bean, the popular actor and former quiz show guest, could be seen around the area. He would always wave hello to Mel when he passed by the deli.

Regulars hung around the deli, like Donny, an 'artist' who could nurse a cup of coffee for four hours. He seemed to have the best connections of anyone in the area. He knew everyone who was even remotely associated with Venice. Rumor had it that Donny used to deliver cash for the studios. He was always trying to bring people into deals. For quick cash, he sold his 'art' for whatever he could get.

I would learn that it was the same Donny, the guy I had met as a patient. He got away with the 'artist' bit in a beach community like Venice. Nobody could attest to the fact that he ever painted anything. Multiple identities were no stranger to Hollywood and Donny evidently made the most of his skills.

Ira's grandfather was something of a celebrity to anyone in Hollywood over fifty years old. Mel was the 'deli man to the stars', a fitting title for the owner of the only remaining restaurant from the early days of Venice. The walls were filled with black and whites of Mel with movie stars, baseball players, and politicians.

When Mel Packer originally left for California, he was given a variety of information that was supposed to serve as advice. It came from his cousins, both named Samuel.

"There's no real baseball out there," said Sammy Susswein. The Dodgers would eventually prove that Sammy wrong.

The strangest remark of all came from his cousin Sammy Baron, a wheeler-dealer salesman who lived big, and loved his sharkskin suits and Lincoln Continentals, right up to the four-door convertible with suicide doors. After pulling up in his flashy '42 Victoria Coach Maroon Continental, he cornered Mel in front of Nedicks at 42nd Street and Broadway, the now defunct midtown eatery that was famous for its orange drink. The two men stood while they ate their forshpeis (appetizer) of a twenty-five cent grilled hot dog on a toasted bun and a ten-cent fresh orange 'juice'. "Mel. It's not like here. The Jews are eating the Jews in California," said the other Sammy. "There's not enough business to go around." He had always been the most dramatic member of the family. "They will eat you alive."

When I heard that told for the first time, it struck me. Did Sammy mean the infighting in the entertainment business? Did the culture in Los Angeles survive on people climbing up over one another? Perhaps he only meant simply that there wasn't enough business to go around in the early days.

Nothing could stop Mel. Hard work was a given. He argued with Sammy Baron. "You are crazy. You've always been a meshuggeneh mamzer! The movie business is getting bigger and bigger. I will do just fine with a deli, nothing special, just good, plain food."

"I am telling you," said Sammy. "Eating them. They are eating the Jews!"

"Your wife was right. You are drinking too much. A real shicker, you've become! Worse. She told me you smoke funny cigarettes, hemp. You know, that Mary Jane stuff. I know what you've been doing," said Mel. "Like that Robert Mitchum."

Sammy tossed his empty paper cup into a huge wire receptacle. "Now you have offended me. I have warned you. The Jews will eat you alive." He turned his back and disappeared in the downtown crowd on Seventh Avenue."

"Meshuggeneh mamzer," was Mel's goodbye. "You can still hear me…Your car is double-parked!"

Mel loved to tell that story. He would finish by saying, "Well. Nobody ate Mel Packer. I'm still here."

Mel was a sweet man with a big heart. He had been quite wild during his youth, but would never discuss any details with Ira. Mel knew each doorman at every Manhattan hotel that had had single women residents, the nearest dance floor, and where to find a band at all hours. He was a regular at forgotten places like Jimmy Ryan's, Club Carousel, and 3 Deuces.

"He used to run around with them all," said Ira's now deceased grandmother, referring to the ladies. "Oy! You shouldn't know from such a flirt! He married much later than all his friends. I'm surprised his schmekel didn't fall off!"

"A man doesn't talk about those things," said Mel with a wry smile, every time anyone would bring up the subject of his playboy days.

Simon and Schuster once approached Mel to write a book on his experiences in New York and later in Hollywood. They knew that Mel could supply an unbelievable kiss and tell. He had a few meetings on the subject with bigshot editor Michael Korda, but they could never make a deal because Mel wouldn't agree to betray anyone's detailed social secrets. The book publishers were mainly interested in what he knew about Marilyn Monroe's death. "That one I flatly refused at the onset."

Mel had delivered food to Marilyn's house the day before she died. "I always brought her stuff like lamb chops or chicken livers. She loved a good broiled steak. She was way ahead of her time when it came to eating. Lots of carrots and sometimes raw eggs with skim milk in the morning. Other times just egg whites, toast and grapefruit." A lot of people tried to get Mel to reveal his more personal conversations with Marilyn, but he wanted no part of it. That was Mel, and a whole body of people respected him for keeping - what they viewed as - another person's dignity intact.

Ira loved his grandfather dearly. It was if they were the same person. Ira understood him. It amazed him that this man was his father's father. It was as if all the genes had skipped a generation and landed inside Ira. He had his grandfather's body type, and the same toothy grin.

Despite their physical similarities, Ira didn't have Mel's sense of Jewish tradition. That was something that had to be learned, and had not been so important to Ira's parents. The idea of being Jewish like Mel was foreign to Ira. Mel wasn't religious, and only entered a synagogue once in a while, and yet Ira didn't manifest Mel's Jewish sensibilities. Mel's peers were simple and direct. They divided life into the Jews and the goys. "Goyishe kop" was one of Mel's favorite expressions - the non-Jewish 'head'.

Times had changed, and Ira's secular parents hadn't wanted that kind of religious and biased information transferred to their little Prince Ira. They didn't want him to totally assimilate, but Ira's father had made a point about people who appeared 'too Jewish', a form of anti-Semitism amongst Jews. The politics of being Jewish was something that had always confounded Ira, but he tried to understand it as best he could. Lately, it was hard enough to try to filter in the growing anti-Semitism after 9/11, some on famous college campuses, with certain major institutions of higher learning canceling their financial support for Israel or selling investments in companies that did business with Israel, as if that made any sort of logical sense to Ira. And there was talk of an academic boycott. A few Israeli professors had already been fired from certain journals.

Ira was almost at the deli. The more flamboyant roller-bladers were hours away from beginning their seemingly choreographed routines, twisting and turning around tourists and regulars, while never truly paying attention to the crowds. All the bike shops were still closed, with the sturdy rental cruisers chained inside theft-proof sheds.

Ira rode past the famous Muscle Beach section. The outdoor benches and barbell equipment stood frozen in the morning fog, as if painted on the sand, perhaps by Salvatore Dali. Later, dozens of men and women would fill the spaces, some with their midriffs covered by tight supportive belts, now sold in dazzling blues and reds. By noon, the throngs of tourists might form three deep galleries in order to watch the fitness nuts train in the hot sun, while a street juggler challenged gravity behind them on the walk.

Ira passed by the closed shops - the sausage stand, the pizza place, the little combo place whose sign boasted Chinese-Thai-Hamburger-Pastrami. That sign always made Ira chuckle. *Only in Hollywoodland*. Ira slowed as he saw Mel's old sign shifting in the breeze on its ancient wrought iron hinge. The name "Packer's" was almost washed out. A little blue paint was still left in the lettering, but up against the black background the letters appeared more white than blue. Ira slowed his bike as he reached the front plate-glass windows. Those windows displayed the name of the deli in a semicircle of huge block letters, covering more than half the window. Under "Packer's" was the word "Deli" followed in small red letters by "Open Every Day", unlike strict kosher delis that observed the Sabbath, something that had become a rarity in Los Angeles.

Ira turned right into an alley, and rode his bike around to the rear of the restaurant. As he expected, the door to the cellar was open wide. The back door, leading into the storage area and kitchen, was also open. Ira parked his bike next to the cellar door. He chained it to the large, rusted padlock on the door. He could hear his grandfather moving some boxes in the cellar, close to the steps.

Ira leaned over the steps. "Zaydeh. It's me. Ira."

"Good morning. Good morning. God. It's a beautiful day. Isn't it?" shot back the older voice, filled with enthusiasm and vigor.

"You need help?" Ira moved down two steps.

"No way." Mel came into view on the bottom step. He began his ascent.

Mel was a powerful man. Old age had taken a couple of inches off his six-foot plus frame, but he still looked like someone to avoid in a physical confrontation. His thin shock of white hair lifted off his head as the sea breeze met his body. He was tanned; his face filled with dozens of freckles.

Rumor on the Venice Pier had it that Mel once fought off twenty drunken surfer bums who tried to rob his deli during the tumultuous sixties. The fable explained how Mel held them off with his Louisville Slugger, a relic from his youth. In the corner of the kitchen, the bat sat for years in a spot that seemed all its own. The kitchen help were told to never touch it, and they literally obeyed, cleaning around it.

Mel was holding two big cans of oil for the French fries. He changed the oil every day. "Once you get the slightest bit of burnt grease in the batch, it will throw off the taste of the fry." Mel had told Ira all the tricks when he was still a boy. During his recent visits, Ira had received a refresher course, and never tired of one word.

Mel's customers came for the uniqueness and hard-to-duplicate tastes. The same one, every time. Very few restaurants could boast that kind of consistency. Mel loved to tell stories about why he had been so successful for so many years. "It's two things, and that's it. First. You never heat the bread in a

177

plain warmer, and god knows you never toast the damn bread. You put the bread in a steamer. That's right. A steamer. That's the way to do it. And you can't over or under steam the bread. If it gets too moist, the rye seeds will start to disappear in the bread. If it's too dry, you might as well buy some store-bought Levy's to make the sandwich. If you want a good sandwich you must steam the bread a certain way. That's number one. And number two is, of course, my cherry soda. I always made my own cherry soda. I didn't start out that way. The Dr. Brown's guy, who sold me the syrup, saw how business began to pick up after the war. By 1955, there was a ten-minute wait at the counter for lunch. You heard me right. Ten minutes. So the Dr. Brown's guy jacks up the price for the cherry syrup. Ganif S.O.B.! Now he wants nearly a penny more per glass on my end. I'm not cutting into each one of my cherry sodas by a whole cent. No way. So your grandmother and me, we experimented for three months on how to make the syrup ourselves. We ended up with an even sweeter version with a hell of a lot more fizz. I'll give away one secret. We put vanilla in the cherry soda. Everyone else was making cream soda with the vanilla. In nineteen-sixty we invested in a machine that could mix the syrup for us. We never charged more than seventy-five cents for our cherry soda, and we don't jack up the price today either. I still make fifty cents profit on the damned cherry soda. Because I learned to make it myself. Harpo Marx used to order a case of syrup when he had parties. Zanuck tried to buy the recipe for the studio commissary. He offered to pay me five-thousand dollars if I would sell the recipe to the studio. No way. I'd load up the trucks for them with all the cherry syrup and ready-made sodas they wanted. But no deals. I still own it. To this day."

When *The New York Times* ran an article comparing New York delis to their Los Angeles rivals, Mel declined to participate.

"What's to compare?" As far as he was concerned, there was no contest. His deli was as good as or better than anything in New York, and he threw in all of Long Island for good measure.

Despite the colorful and successful history, business was dwindling. The bread steamer hadn't been working properly for years, and the deli was in a general state of disrepair. Worse, an old-fashioned deli just didn't fit in on the Venice Boardwalk. When Ira's grandmother had died over ten years ago, Mel started to work harder by putting in longer hours and always hanging around the deli. He hated to play cards and he didn't play any sports, except for a little handball. The work had become his entire life, and with his wife gone he had little reason to return home at night.

Mel walked up a little step near the back entrance, followed by Ira. Inside, the coffee machines were already operating. Mel put down the oilcans and turned on the grill.

"Fill up the vats with the oil, Ira," said Mel.

"Sure, Zaydeh," answered Ira as he unscrewed the cap on the one of the cans.

Ira loved to help his grandfather. He wished that there was some way he could help his grandfather stay more active outside of the deli. The deli was Mel's only source of activity, and Ira worried that once the deli closed, Mel would not do very well. Ira's mother had asked him several times to bring up the subject of retirement. He told his mother that it wasn't his place to suggest that sort of thing to his grandfather.

"He's getting old," she would say. "How long do you think he can keep lugging those slabs of meat and big pickle jars up and down those steps?

"No. He's not," Ira would answer, knowing how ridiculous he sounded. What he meant to say, but never could get out the right words, was that Mel didn't age like the other men. He always looked the same, particularly to his grandson.

That morning at the deli, after a breakfast of salami and eggs, Mel proposed an unexpected idea to Ira. They were sitting at one of the dining tables, across from a long counter with an expansive glass display window, where varieties of smoked fish glistened every day.

"Ira. You know I'm not getting any younger."

Ira was shocked that this was on Mel's mind, too. Ira tried to come to his grandfather's defense. "Zaydeh. You're in the best shape of anyone around here." At that moment, Ira realized his own state of denial.

Mel took his place as King, behind the counter. "Well. Maybe it's a cliché, but I've got to think about the future. Listen here. My idea is this. I would like you to work in the deli for the rest of the summer. It won't be hard. You came here almost every day when you were a boy." He paused and began one of those sighs that implied emphasis, exhaling while he kept the sound at a constant.

Ira took it to mean disappointment. "I'm sorry. My parents wanted to move to New York. It wasn't my idea."

Mel continued as if he hadn't paused. "Of course, not so much since you went east. Business is very slow, and you know it gets slower every year. A good corned beef sandwich is not as important as it used to be. Tacos. They eat tacos. And sushi. I'm going to fly to Florida. I have no more friends here from the old days. The last few I know from New York are in Boca Ratan. Sammy Susswein is there."

"It's Raton. Boca Raton," Ira corrected politely.

"Okay. Ratan. Roton. It's God's waiting room. The whole area. So it's my turn to maybe get in line. I want to try it for the rest of the summer. If I like it, I will sell the deli and get a little coffin, I mean, condo."

"You have plenty of good years left." Ira joined Mel behind the counter.

Mel began preparing the display case. "Mel Packer has made up his mind. If you don't want to, I understand. You have school coming up. It's okay." He placed four bread slices on a cutting board and began to slice from a chunk of brisket.

"But I'll miss you."

Mel put his arm around Ira. "Listen. I'll be back. Listen. Ira. If you don't want to help, it's okay. I can just close the place down for a few months." He turned away and quickly busied his hands by starting a sandwich. When talking to relatives, unintentionally or not, guilt manifested itself as a mainstay, ingrained into any controversial dialogue.

Ira reflexively picked up thinly sliced tomatoes, lettuce, and pickles to add to the sandwich, and then passed it along the butcher-block surface. "Of course I'll do it."

Mel stared at the ingredients. "What? You think I'm making a Big Mac here? He laughed.

So did Ira. "On the side?"

Mel nodded. "No. No. Forget it. I shouldn't have asked." He deliberately kept his head down while he worked. The less eye contact, the better the manipulation. Grandfathers knew all the tricks.

"I said I want to do it. I'll get Neil to help."

Now Mel looked up. "Neil?"

"He's very resourceful."

"I heard the reason he left his father's company was something to do with 'borrowing' some money from someone's account."

Ira knew about it but didn't want it to be an issue. "I can control Neil. Don't worry. He's changed. You know he's going to medical school with me."

"They're going to give that boy a scalpel?" Mel grinned.

Ira returned the smile.

They both chortled, again. This time, longer and less nervous.

Mel scooted close to Ira and extended his hand.

As they shook, Mel spoke. "Then it's a done deal. I'll pay you a regular salary, and everything extra we make, above and beyond expenses, I'll give you a bonus percentage. Better yet. You keep everything we make. I've got plenty saved. Since your grandmother died I have nobody to spend money on. Certainly not the vilde chayas that hang around Venice!"

"You don't have to pay me anything." Ira knew that Mel did not have a lot of money. Mel once confided in Ira's father that he never expected to live so long, and that he was regularly dipping into his principal in order to make ends meet.

"Mel Packer has spoken, and when Mel Packer has spoken, it's a done deal." He slammed the knife on the cutting board.

Ira hugged his grandfather. Helping his grandfather was something he felt obligated to do. Now his summer was spoken for in spades. He had the anatomy class with Neil, and a summer job.

Ira had no way of knowing, but he had been the subject of a session the preceding week in Barry's office. Mel was not big on psychiatrists, but in the last few years he was persuaded to take Barry up on his offer to talk any time for free. Mel had always catered Barry's brunches at his home after tennis, as well as the late night pool parties.

Mel had told Barry, "Ira was always a good kid. He did whatever his parents asked. I don't think he wants to be a doctor, but he will go just to please his family, particularly

my departed wife, who loved to yenta her way up and down the
boardwalk shouting that her grandson is going to be a doctor –
and that was when he was five! His father worked hard his whole
life. I think Ira has other dreams. But we all had other dreams
at one time or another, and that's the most important thing to
learn in this world, that dreams are dreams and 'what is' is
just 'what is'. The rest is a bunch of – Can I say whatever I
want here?" His generation was not big on cursing in front of
doctors.

Barry smiled. "Say whatever the fuck you want to say with
me."

"The rest is a bunch of 'b.s'. That's a fact. Bottom line
is he came out to go to medical school at UCLA. I need help and
he's the only one I trust. Is that a lot to expect from him? Is
it too much to ask of him?"

Barry cleared his throat. "No. No, Mel." He was moved by
Mel's sensitivity and for a moment was transported back in time
to a much simpler world; one with morals, social responsibility,
and respect for relatives.

Mel dropped a little bomb on Ira. "Donny will look in on
you."

"Donny?" Ira panicked. He had always viewed Donny as an
untrustworthy hustler.

"I know what you're thinking. Don't worry about Donny. He
knows I'd have his ass in a sling if he screwed around with
anything here."

Mel had always helped Donny, from a running tab of unpaid
sodas and pastrami sandwiches, to making contacts for him with
some of the big shots in the movie business.

When Mel had asked him for help, Donny became effusive.
"Ira Packer is the best. He doesn't know from the movies." He
meant that as a slap to his own cronies. "Ira's a nice guy. He

was a nice kid, and it's great to have him back in town. He's so straight. You have to like him for that. He's something you only see on television, the good guy who never could be corrupted. I don't know. I won't be tempted to see what he's really made of, so I would never put any bad shit on a plate in front of Ira. Let's say he bit and he really went for the down and dirty. It would spoil my whole balance in life."

"And then you'd have to answer to me." Mel pointed at his baseball bat.

"And then I'd have to answer to you," Donny repeated. "Mel. Don't worry. I'll see that nothing happens to the prince."

Soon after firming things up with Ira and informing his employees, Mel was off to visit Boca Raton. His plan was to eventually buy a small condominium in one of the senior communities that also provided assisted living for those who were in need. He didn't mention that part to Ira. He felt that his health could become be a factor, and essentially didn't want to be a bother to anyone if he became ill.

Ira had a plan, too. Get Neil involved fast. One morning while Mel was still in town, Ira had revealed the pitch while walking alongside the beach. "Neil. First of all, I'll split the money with you. My grandfather can't pay two full salaries, but I'll give you half of mine, and you don't have to work a full schedule. But you can get a share of the profits, if there are any."

"Profits? Everyone thinks your grandfather loses money every year," said Neil.

"That's because he's never modernized. I have some ideas."

Neil's head began to spin. The word 'opportunity' flashed on and off in his mind like a neon sign. "Do you think he'd let us make some changes?"

"I don't think it would be a problem. He said that he intends to sell it. As long as we run everything by him, I think it will be okay. I mentioned to him about different kinds of coffee, and maybe even some kind of pizza that we could make in a microwave convection oven."

Neil and Ira went over the details of the arrangement. Ira had a vision of a nice new look for the old deli, while Neil was already thinking of a chain the size of McDonalds. *McDeli* he joked to himself.

CHAPTER SIX
Brian, Liz
Brian, Barry
Barry, Sean

Inland and cross-town, the CAA building in Beverly Hills was starting to come alive for another whirlwind day of high-powered deals and mostly waiting around for coffee. The most famous agency of the eighties and nineties had been built into a powerhouse by Mike Ovitz, who took a nosedive after a few failed relationships — first Disney, and then his own management company. He was haunted by his remarks about being a victim of the 'gay mafia', a list of names beginning with don't-fuck-with-me-mogul David Geffen - that and several lawsuits by former employees and investors. If such imagined unilateral power had ever existed based solely on a person's sexuality, Ovitz would not have found many business opportunities to begin with, nor could he look to any future ones.

CAA people didn't lose any houses in the Malibu fire, but rumor had it that one agent at ICM ended up with a scorched roof. Word was passed around early that day that a CAA group would be hitting one of the nearby bars. When people greeted each other in the halls, they would cautiously drop the name of the expected after work rendezvous. Cliquish was an understatement.

"The Pen," was all people said. They were referring to the nearby Peninsula Hotel in Beverly Hills. Certain nights of the week cliques would spill out early into one of the acceptable watering holes. All of the baby agents and their associates learned to hang out wherever the big boys went.

Brian Denkler was sitting at his tiny desk outside the agent's office. A telephone headset made his head appear quite small. The tiny, almost imperceptible mouthpiece, once reserved for sci-fi movies, had become ubiquitous. Any eagerly anticipated technological advance became part of the uniform, like the earpiece and cough-drop-sized microphone used 'on the road'.

The phones were quiet and Brian was staring at a copy of the *Hollywood Reporter*. He had trouble remembering who was doing what, had signed for what, and sometimes the names of the clients at his own agency. He felt stupid. "You have a character disorder that interferes with your ability to remember things." That's what Barry told him. After all, nobody was really stupid, everyone had some form of mental illness.

Brian had been going to Barry for about two years. Brian's insurance would only pay for one visit per week, and up to two years. That was only after Barry practically stated in a letter to the insurance carrier that Brian could no longer function without psychiatric care. Brian was described in the exchange as being one step away from being hospitalized. Barry assured Brian that this was common practice. "The insurance companies make us behave this way. It's not like the doctors woke up one morning and decided to lie about the care of their patients. The insurance companies don't want to pay. I don't like having to lie, but if it's for my patients' own good, what choice do I have in the matter?"

Brian didn't care what Barry wrote as long as he received his care, and in an office like Barry's. Barry was an insider, a shrink who knew the business. How could Brian possibly be helped by a shrink who didn't understand the business? Brian had become aware of Barry some time back, at movie premieres. He always was talking to a movie star or a movie executive.

Years before he actually became Barry's patient, Brian observed Barry talking with Goldie Hawn and Wendy Finerman, a movie producer who won an Academy Award for *Forest Gump*, at the opening of *Extreme Measures*, a bad scalpel adventure. At that point, Brian began to wonder which movie stars were patients of Barry's.

Occasionally, Brian would see someone in the hallway before his appointment. One time a woman brushed by him quickly after leaving through Barry's back door. She looked familiar, but he couldn't figure out who she was. With no make-up, skintight black stretch pants, and a deliberately oversized plain gray sweatshirt, it was impossible to tell. Sharon Stone? Brian dismissed the idea since he couldn't imagine that any famous actress would walk around Beverly Hills looking so ordinary. He wanted to run after her to take a second look, but he quickly changed his mind. What if it really was Sharon Stone? What could he say? "Hi. I'm nobody in the business you would want to have anything to do with, but we do go to the same psychiatrist."

But Brian knew that that would all change. He knew that one day he would get the power that he craved. Barry was helping him. It was going to happen for him, just like it happened for all the baby assistants before him. If it weren't for Barry, he never would have been able to keep his job at the agency. When he had first met Barry, he was still doing jobs on talk shows as a paid liar. He would fill in when the producers needed someone. One time Brian was a reformed junkie. Another time he was someone who had admitted to having incestuous relations with his sister. He was outed once, and a minor scandal broke, but temporary news like that was brief and lasted only until a bigger story came along. Barry intervened with Brian's superiors at the agency, assuring them that Brian would give up his fleeting career of lying on television talk shows.

Liz Roth stuck her head inside the office. "The Pen," she whispered. Liz remained a good friend to Brian, perhaps his only true one at the agency. She recently had convinced Brian to move out of his parents' house and take a tiny apartment in her building on Palm Drive. She often rang his bell in the evening to see if he was okay, usually with a bottle of Stoli and news of an impending Chinese food or pizza delivery.

"Got it," answered Brian. He was pleased to be included. "I'll be there."

"Have you seen the *Igby* movie yet?" Liz asked.

"No," he answered. "But it's on my list."

"Sensational. You'll like it. It could become your life story." She was referring to the latest version of Holden Caulfield, filled with upper crust WASPs as a backdrop for a young man's rude awakening in Manhattan.

Brian reacted quickly to the electronic purr made by the sixteen-button telephone. "Hello, Mark Perry's office." Mark was the son of a Beverly Hills thoracic surgeon. Being Mark's assistant was a natural for Brian. They were both sons of well-known health professionals.

While Brian spoke, Liz communicated an entire paragraph with her hands and facial expressions. What it translated to Brian was "Got to do some more work with the phones, see you there, we can tip a few drinks."

Liz saw to it that Brian was never shut out of anything. In return, Brian slipped Liz information about what Mark was doing.

Things like who came to the office for meetings, and wind of any deals that were about to go down. Brian didn't feel that it mattered, because if Liz didn't get the information from him, she would get it from someone else. Liz was only twenty-one, but behaved as if she was thirty. She smartly had told Brian up front that he was too old for her, even though she already had affairs with thirty-something actors of note. Brian was twenty-six, but he appeared more like one of Liz's contemporaries.

Brian regularly fantasized about Liz. He felt things would be different between them if he got a promotion. That's when everyone would treat him differently, including Liz. In the meantime, he occasionally went out with an actress named Heather, the same one that I met who seemed to know and date everyone. Brain had met Heather when she once appeared for a representation meeting at CAA. She had peeked into his office on the way out of the building, and began asking questions about the agent who had interviewed her.

One of the first things Brian researched when he found out that he was accepted at CAA, was to check out the 'in' doctors, restaurants, and clothiers. He thought that would be a good first step towards becoming part of the inner circle, a sanctum that favored certain vacation locales along with a short list of 'he's-the-best' upscale health professionals. Among the specialists, he found a dentist that everyone adored.

"Dr. A.B. Galin," was the name intoned by many, with the kind of reverence usually reserved for members of the clergy, or a stockbroker who could get new issue shares by twisting and avoiding S.E.C. regulations.

Liz concurred. "He's the best. He treats Dolly, Sean, and Hugh, and a few of the young crowd. I think he has both Bens. And he takes the company insurance as a courtesy to our big bosses."

Before Brian made an appointment with Dr. Galin, he talked it over with Barry. Brian always arrived early for his appointments. The waiting room in Barry's office was small, but comfortable. A CD player sat on one side of the room and Barry encouraged those patients that liked to arrive early to bring their own selections or chose from Barry's varied taste. His collection ranged from Leonard Bernstein to Eminem. He had a few with chants, the kind of music often heard while walking through The Nature Company or The Discovery Channel stores, places that tried to sell anything new age, essentially anything.

During sessions, Brian liked to sit straight up, almost at attention. He brought a little embroidered pillow with him, to bolster his back, enabling him to sit flush up against the sinking leather sofa. He brought the same pillow with him to have his teeth cleaned.

When Barry had first observed the rigid positioning, he remarked that many of his patients like to get comfortable during the sessions.

"I am comfortable," snapped Brian.

Barry noted that he needed more time to learn about Brian's special needs. After several sessions, Barry came to a not-so-hasty but accurate conclusion - Brian suffered from an obsessive disorder. Brian still had a lot of trouble getting himself out the door each morning.

When they had first met, Barry couldn't picture Brian working within the structure of a Hollywood agency. Brian was far from creative, but he was very sociable and likeable, more important attributes to be an agency foot soldier. Barry's first impulse was to discourage him from remaining in the agency business, while at the same time work toward getting him out of his parents' house, which he ultimately did accomplish.

Brian had expressed some ambivalence about the agency business. "It's like being told that pro-wrestling is real, and you have to spend the rest of your life selling the business, knowing that it's all fake. That's how I feel at the agency. Sorry. Some of us don't get it right away. I know I can do it. I have to try harder, that's all."

After getting to know Brian better, Barry took an altogether different tact. He had no choice because Brian truly and ultimately believed that this was the best possible of all careers for him. Barry cut out the idea that Brian's parents had a lot to do with his condition and desires. Rather than try to deprogram all those years of behavior modification, Barry began to work with Brian on how to best accomplish his goals. Barry knew other analysts who would go for the jugular and try to break Brian down to his base components, and then hope that he could discover something new that he had truly wanted to do, even truly loved.

Barry was a realist, but he was short of a Dr. Phil. Brian's personality disorder had to be treated, and not with some quick-fix shouting match on television. If it could be treated within and around what Brian was already doing, then that was what would work best. As Barry learned more about the inner workings of the agency business, he realized that Brian's personality profile might fit in. Brian was a tireless worker, paid excessive attention to detail, and was devoted beyond any employer's expectations. Despite all that, his personality disorder often made him appear stupid or slow. He was neither, but his often-paralyzing fears saturated his every breath with a numbing poison gas, and sometimes left him unconscious in an inarticulate haze. This major drawback could limit him to no more than a mid-level career, frozen forever in a miasma of agency mediocrity.

Brian was fanatic when it came to his personal hygiene. He prided himself on fifteen to twenty hand washings per day. Barry helped reduce that, with allowances for normal bathing and bathroom hygiene, including washing off the 'contaminated' public environment whenever he entered his home. Instead of extra washings, Barry suggested that Brian use the chemically treated hand wipes sold in supermarkets.

Brian kept several different kinds of dental floss in his small leather clutch bag, an item that never left his side. His storehouse contained waxed and un-waxed floss, in string and tape varieties, even tiny sandpaper strips, applied gingerly to any little imperfections that he could detect with his tongue, particularly on the sharp incisal edge of his teeth or the cusps of his back molars. He carried a toothbrush to work, ensuring at least three brushings during the day. Barry reduced that number to only one after lunch, in addition to bedtime. Despite Barry's recommendations, Brian would occasionally floss his teeth after a snack at his computer console. He didn't care if anyone caught him in the act, and it didn't matter to most. Flossing the teeth seemed rather reasonable, compared to some of the habits agents were used to observing after getting to know their clients, particularly at parties or on vacation in remote locales where celebrities pranced about unnoticed.

Brian's previous dentist, Dr. Stanley Vogel, dentist-to-the-stars, stopped practicing several years ago. Brian loved Dr. Vogel. He had a nice hygienist who arranged for Brian to have his own account with the Oral-B Company, one of the premiere manufacturers of toothbrushes recommended by the American Dental Association. After Dr. Vogel's retirement, Brian tried several different dentists, but was never really comfortable in any of the offices. The youngish hygienists changed offices often, forcing Brian to relate to a new one after finally getting adjusted to the old one. Most of the dentists were too busy to talk to Brian about things like the new modifications in the angle of the brushes. Despite all the public relations about how the dentist was purported to be his friend, the bottom line for 'Hollywood' dentists was simply churning out the work, often unnecessary work, in order to pay the rent and keep up the payments on the Land Rover and Mercedes.

Brian read every piece of literature that Oral-B had sent him. He knew what kind of filament made the best brush, the number of bristles per tuft, and the ideal number of rows. Brush head angulations were a very debatable subject and Brian, just like the eager marketing representatives for the major brush companies, was still looking for the ideal products. Brian's approach was to have a variety of brush angles, using the one that felt the most comfortable for the operation he needed to perform. Since he was right handed, he liked a slightly angled brush if he was going to brush the buccal or cheek side on the left of his upper back molars. He had the system worked out quite nicely, allowing himself to apply his knowledge and collection of brushes to maximize his oral hygiene.

As far as paste went, Brian was never satisfied. Toothpaste manufactures were never satisfied either. They kept changing colors, consistencies, and flavors. In order to play it safe Brian had several, including his own homemade mix of mostly peroxide and baking soda. He even kept a tidy collection of pediatric pastes, including his favorite, bubble gum flavored.

Barry and Brian ended up spending an entire session going over Brian's plan to become a new patient of Dr. Galin.

At the first visit to Dr. Galin's Beverly Hills dental office, it was rare for anyone to actually see Dr. Galin. Barry thought it was a good idea for him to call ahead in order to mention directly to Dr. Galin that Brian might be a 'special patient', the code word for a 'pain in the ass'. Beverly Hills doctors were always putting themselves above the patients, often using expressions like 'pain in the ass' or 'another nut job' or, amongst closer colleagues, 'he's a crazy motherfucker', to describe a patient that might be a little more difficult to treat than most. The health professionals were spoiled, worse than their patients. The doctors wanted to get in and out of the office without spilling any blood on their Armani ties.

Brian was escorted into a treatment room where a dental assistant eagerly offered him his choice of beverages - coffee, tea, Pellegrino, or Sparkletts water. The Pellegrino was carbonated and the Sparkletts was non-carbonated. Dr. Galin was a thoughtful man, for a dentist, at least when it came to pampering his patients.

While Brian was filling out the required medical history forms, Dr. Galin poked his head into the room. "Hello, Mr. Denkler. I'm A.B." he said, emphasizing the letters as if he were going to announce the rest of the alphabet out loud. The initials were embroidered onto his white laboratory coat, and he underlined his name with his finger, which was written out in red script.

"Hello, Dr. Galin." Brian's palm had filled with sweat the moment A. B. had entered the room.

"Call me A.B." He pointed to the initials again. "I'll be in to see you after the hygienist gives your teeth a thorough cleaning." He shouted her name into the hall. "Lela."

A beautiful woman in her mid-twenties floated into the room; her hand suddenly entwined inside A.B.'s, as if they were taking their curtain call after performing in a musical.

"Lela. This is Mr. Denkler. He's new here. I want you to take extra special care of him."

"Hi. I'm Lela. It's nice to meet you Mr. Denkler."

Now there could be no confusion as to her identity either.
"Hi," said Brian. "Brian is fine."

"Lela will be happy to answer any questions you might have about your dental care." With that, A.B. sort of pushed Lela forward, as if she was a reluctant date, and he disappeared into the hallway.

The only thing Brian could remember about A.B. was that his blonde hair, too light for a man his age, seemed glued onto his head. Brian couldn't decide if it was a horrible crew cut or a questionable hairpiece. It wasn't so important; he now had to contend with the clearly curvaceous Lela.

"He doesn't do that for most people," said Lela. "You know, he kept Sly Stallone waiting in order to talk to you."

"That's great," Brian answered, but he wasn't listening. He could feel his pulse rise as Lela touched something on the top of a tray that she had placed on the treatment table, a little flat rectangle on a mechanical arm that sat slightly above and forward from Brian. All he could see were dozens of shiny little instruments. He looked away and swallowed hard as Lela began to sharpen one of the offensive weapons by putting a little oil on a white stone, and then scraping the edge of the instrument on the stone.

"Do you have to do that now?" he asked, not knowing how he got the words out of his mouth.

"Makes you a little nervous? I know what you mean," said Lela, exuding a modicum of false compassion. She stopped honing the sickle-shaped dental scaler. "Here," she said, as she placed headphones around Brian's head. "We have movies and concerts," she continued, now in an automated mode that guaranteed that she would keep to her schedule. "Would you like to see the routine that won the Russians an Olympic Medal?"

"I don't know." Brian thought that he sounded morose.

"Okay if I pick something for you?" she asked.

Brian nodded. "Yes. Pick anything. How long will this take?" He was treated to *Little Shop of Horrors*. Lela fast-forwarded the movie so that Brian could see the scenes with the S & M dentist, played by Steve Martin. She had done this before, blind to the sick irony, instead finding only humor for herself. Brian lapsed into a mild shock.

She insisted that he rinse with a red dye solution. "Brian. Look at these dark red spots. You've got three on the most posterior - that means back - molars."

"I know what they're called," he said. Nobody challenged his dental acumen.

When the session was over, Lela gave her gleeful assessment of the movie after telling Brian that Steve Martin came to the office and that he "is a great guy." Then she got right down to business. "Brian. You're not doing such a good job," she said with a tone reminiscent of his fifth grade teacher criticizing his sloppy hand washing after an outdoor gym session.

Brian froze. His terror-stricken body became one tight muscle. His breath grew rapid as he wiped his wet palms on his trousers. He felt his heart pound quickly and there was a twinge of pain in his left arm. *Oh, my god,* he thought. *It's my heart. I'm having a heart attack.*

As soon as he was able to squeeze a word out through his moribund facial muscles, he forgot about his heart.

"Da..Dah...Daaah...Daaah-oc-tor...Gaaalin."

"What? You need to relax a little. Just take a few deep breaths." With that Lela turned her back on him and began to clean up the treatment tray.

There was no way Brian could repeat it. He needed to speak with the doctor. Nobody ever questioned his brushing abilities. He envisioned every one of his teeth launching out from his mouth, lost forever because of his inadequate flossing and brushing.

The hygienist jabbered on - one of the modern miracles of dentistry - with the psychobabble 'I'm-your-friend-but-you've-been-a-bad-boy' theory of helping patients. Brian didn't hear a word. She tried to get his attention. She held up a mirror in front of his mouth.

"You've been missing these areas when you brush. I also found some three-point-five pockets on the back molars in the maxilla, you know, up top. You know anything over three is considered pathologic. We're going to have to do deep curettage on those sections. Before you leave today, I'm going to give you plaque disclosing tablets to use at home. You can check where the bad spots are on your own, so that by the time you come back to see me in three weeks we won't have to talk about this ever again."

Condescending, he thought. *I know what posterior means...I can't believe what she's saying. I can't have pockets.*

Lela was relentless. "You see, Brian. I'm here to help you do a better job. That's all I want you to do. Just do a little better job."

Dr. Galin finally spoke with Brian before he left. "Well, well. So Lela found a few little pockets. You do a little better job brushing and flossing and that should all clear up in no time at all." Brian ended up all smiles. He eventually felt that he was in good hands, and he was going to try harder to maintain his oral hygiene. He knew that Dr. Galin was a prosthodontist, a kind of cosmetic and restorative specialist.

Before he left Dr. Galin dropped a little bomb. "We don't want to have to send you for periodontal surgery, now do we?" he said with a Hollywood grin a mile wide.

"Surgery," was the only word that Brian took away with him. He told himself that he could do better. He would do better. He flew out of the waiting room, hardly noticing Bette Midler.

Brian eventually realized that his former dentists and hygienists probably didn't care about him as much as Dr. Galin. Dr. Galin only wanted the best for him and that's why he had this kind of thorough and somewhat obnoxious hygienist. *She was only being thorough*, he repeated to himself on the way out. It was a reasonable theory, one Brian felt comfortable adopting, although the tiny thought crept in that Dr. Galin was always drumming up surgery of some kind to refer to the local specialists, like a Periodontist, a mutual admiration society and a source of cross-referrals from the other specialists.

Before Brian arrived at the Pen, he stopped at the Rite Aid drug store in order to stock up. He bought three different kinds of floss, a new sturdier floss holder, and several extra toothbrushes. The pharmacy had the prettiest, brightest display of dental aids in town, since the office buildings nearby were packed with every conceivable dental specialty in triplicate.

At the Pen, some people in the group gossiped about Brian before he arrived. The group ranged from age eighteen to twenty-two, and they all were on the fast track from the mailroom to assistant agent.

"It is awkward," said one of his female 'colleagues', referring to having to deal with Brian.

"Why does he still work here?" asked a young man in a dark suit.

"I don't know. Mark said he might still become an agent or something," she answered.

Once he arrived, Brian's mind wandered while he sat listening to the war stories. It didn't matter if they were true in the purist sense of the word, only in the context of the

moment; stories fabricated to fit the business of the day,
forced on the listener as factual.

Brian heard the haunting parental echoes of his father. "Do
you have any idea what they pay a guy like Alan King? Do ya? Do
you have any idea? Huh? What would you guess?" his father would
shout over breakfast as Brian spooned his cardboard-tasting
shredded wheat into his mouth, opened wide to show his
fascination for the big agent bucks.

His mouth never opened that wide for the floating cardboard
alone. Even with the mandatory sea of sugared milk, it was a
mild torture inflicted on children by seemingly well-meaning
parents. Brian hated the cereal and once when he was quite young
had said that it tasted like "shit". He had never used that word
before, anywhere. His father reflexively slapped him across his
face. "You don't hear Robert Redford speak like that. No,
never!"

Brian had committed a great sin. To show his atonement he
made a pact with his father to watch all of Redford's movies
every week on their new Sony Trinitron television with built-in
VCR.

Years ago, at most meals, Brian waited for his father to
continue his lectures. Brian had no real sense of what the
salaries meant, but he knew that money was important and people
in show business had a lot of money.

"You won't believe it when I tell ya," his father said. He
paused and glanced over at Brian's mother for her usual, doting
support.

His mother June had once dreamed of becoming an actress,
and still worked as an extra in television commercials. Years
ago she had one line on the last Red Skelton Show. At parties,
Brian's father encouraged her to re-enact the entire scene,
often repeating her one line a dozen times.

The morning of the lecture on show business income, she stood at the electric range and waited for the answer, along with Brian.

"I hear it's over two hundred thousand for four shows," said Brian's father in a hushed tone. "Alan King makes a lot of money."

"You're kidding," said June. Her face flushed red as if she had heard a dirty joke. "Oh, my," she added as she ran her hands across her cheeks.

Brian let out a slow, monotone "wow".

"And do you know what his agent gets?" his father asked in a direct, stern voice to emphasize what was coming.

All the stories led around to the same thing. "The agents really make all the money. They get a piece off the top. That's before the manager, the gophers, and the opening act. You see, Brian, the agent gets his ten per cent off the top. That's the kind of job I'd like to have. Off the top. That's the ticket. Get yours off the top. This is America my boy and only in America can you get yours off the top. First!"

Brian had heard the story and the reoccurring voice "a million zillion times". He didn't remember when the idea had become appealing to him. It was only when he reached puberty and understood that women flocked to agents' doors did he begin to show some personal interest in the business.

After Brian eventually moved out, his parents had registered nothing but disappointment.

"Hello. We're not here. Leave a message," said June in her cheeriest recorded phone voice.

"Hello. It's Brian. Just checking in - ." He was cut off from the answering machine.

"Brian. Is that you? I've been screening my calls."

"Yes. Hi. Just checking in," he repeated.

"It's Brian. Pick up the extension," shouted June.

Brian heard someone, presumably his father, pick up the extension, but he said nothing. That's the way it always went.

"Your father and I just booked a cruise to Bermuda. We got a great deal through your cousin Bernice, she works for the cruise line, what's it called? What's the name of the cruise line, Alan?"

"How should I know? What am I, fucking Regis Philbin? Why don't you call up Cathy Lee and ask her?" said Brian's father.

"Hi, Dad," said Brian.

His father continued, "She thinks I give a damn about the name of some cruise line."

"I think it sounds like that actor. The one who does the kicking movies," said June.

"Don't bring up movies. You'll start him in on this crazy agent work for free thing," said Brian's father. He was making a twisted reference to Brian's low salary.

"You mean kick boxing, right?" asked Brian, responding only to his mother.

"Kicking boxing. Yeah. That's it. Not the Chinese guy. He's American, I think. But he has an accent."

Brian knew whom she meant. "Van Damme? Is that it?"

"Yes. Johnny Van Damme. That's it," said June.

"You mean Jean-Claude," said Brian.

"Did you ever meet him?" asked June.

"Who gives a rat's ass about some faggot actor," said Brian's father.

"Mom. I haven't met him, but what has this got to do with the cruise?" asked Brian.

"The Veendam. That's the name of the cruise ship," said June.

Brian continued. "Oh. I see. I thought you said 'cruise line'. Are you sure?"

"I think so," said June.

"What's the difference? Are you making any money working with the older agent guy?" asked Brian's father.

"I'm doing fine," said Brian. It was a lie, but he knew better then to engage his father in conversation about his work.

"After you work there for a while, why don't you come back out to the Valley and I'll set you up in a nice little building. You can have your office downstairs, and you can even live upstairs if you don't want to live at home. Either way, the office will get some major tax breaks from the building write-offs," said Brian's father as if he were Alan Greenspan instead of Alan Denkler, and was explaining to the American public how the economy could benefit from the move back home. "You can take some of the big actors with you. Sort of set up your own little management company."

"Dad. There are more opportunities for me at CAA," said Brian. *Big mistake.*

"Fucking what? What did he say, June? He said there are more what, opportunities where? You're crazy. Are you on drugs? That's the only thing it could be, June. He's on drugs. Are you on drugs now?"

"Dad. I wish you wouldn't talk that way to me. It doesn't do anyone any good," said Brian. He felt his pulse in his neck begin to throb.

"It's tough love. That's the way it has to be. I read plenty about this stuff. Your friend Solly Schwartz went through it, and his parents gave him tough love," said Alan. He had always preferred the 'Jewification' of Solar to Solly. After all, how could the local older Jews relate to someone who had been named Solar?

"Solar was smoking coke instead of going to his job on Seinfeld," said Brian.

"You're doing something or you wouldn't have moved to Beverly Hills," said Alan.

"Let's change the subject. How is your friend…uh?" asked June.

"Heather is fine," said Brian.

"It's a front. He doesn't even like girls. If he did he would have married Sherry Lockwood while he had the chance," said Alan.

Brian was hooked and fell into the repetitive trap. "Dad. Will you cut that out? Sherry was a whore. She fucked the whole school and a bunch or mariachis when she went to Acapulco with her parents."

"He's just saying that to cover up. This new girl is a cover. I read about that. They hang around with women so no one is suspicious," said Alan. "She's too old for him, anyhow."

"You know your father and I would like to see you settle down," added June.

"Come on. We're two minutes into the conversation and it comes back to the same old thing. You tell me I'm on drugs and then you question my sexuality. Don't you think this is getting old already?"

"Not if you're a drug-shooting faggot," said Alan.

"That's not funny," said Brian.

"Alan. Shush. Enough," said June.

"Mom. If this keeps up I'm going to hang up," said Brian.

Alan screamed. "Go ahead. I'm not letting her send you another nickel. Forget the twenty grand we gave you last year. That was tax free, you know, and I only did it because I thought you might open an office here. And then you moved out of the house. You fucking moved. You took my twenty-Gs and went to la-la land in Beverly Hills to become a faggot junkie."

"I tried to send you an e-mail," said June, hoping to change the subject. "But, you didn't answer it."

"Did you get a message back telling you why it failed?" asked Brian, trying to control his anger.

"Maybe I should just send you a fax. I got good at sending faxes, or I'll just send you a letter. You do take letters, don't you?" She didn't mean it to be irritating. She had never adjusted to the technology. Brian knew that.

"Stick with the e-mail. At least you can't send money through the e-mail," said Alan.

"That's it. I'm done. I've had enough," said Brian.

"You see. You got him angry. I told you he doesn't think you're being funny." June kept trying.

"What's to be funny? He's a faggot who's pissing away his life out in la-la land."

Brian slammed down the receiver.

His mother checked. "Brian. Brian. Are you there?"

"He's off the line. Isn't that rude, hanging up on your parents? Do you know how much it cost to send him to college? And the money for dates and gas for the cars. Why couldn't he have gone into production with his idiot friend Solly? Solly was always dumber than Brian. Why couldn't Solly's uncle put in a word for Brian? We spent plenty in Solly's father's store. I think he made up the prices as he went along. He was a crook."

"Alan?" asked June. She remained calm, preferring to continue to talk on their respective phones. It was symbolic of their own polarity.

"What? What is it? Brian has fucked up his life, that's all I know," said Alan.

"Alan. You were the one always telling Brian to be an agent. Now you're jealous because Solar Schwartz drives a Porsche and goes to Hawaii every year."

"Brian could have done anything he wanted," said Alan. "Except become a faggot."

"Can we hang up? We're still on the telephone," said June. She heard a grumble and then a click.

After these traumatic calls, Brian tried to see Barry as soon as possible. Barry referred to them as "trigger calls".

The agent Brian worked for, Mark Perry, had access to two secretaries as well as Brian. Brian's job was essentially to make sure there was a constant supply of Evian water in their own refrigerator, answer the telephone anytime everyone was tied up, and take an incredible amount of shit from Charlie Miller, the brash twenty-two-year old agent who did deals with Mark.

Brian had discussed this with Barry. Brian was willing to wait and hold on so long as he was on a track to become an agent. Not necessarily a fast track. Besides, it was too late for that. Any track would do. And he was in line, at least according to Mark. Mark told him that Charlie is moving too fast and that when Mark would "get rid of doing deals with Charlie," there was a good chance that Brian would get a promotion.

The last time that Mark and Brian spoke about the promotion was six months ago. Barry had suggested to Brian that he mention the subject to Mark again. Brian refused, citing how easily people were fired at the agency.

"Those are just rumors," said Barry. "I'm sure a lot of the people leave because they got better jobs or they decided that the agency business just isn't for them."

Brian gave more credence to the rumor mill at the agency than to Barry. Brian kept his mouth shut because that was one of the first things he had learned in his early days the mailroom.

When Mark arrived at the Pen to make a brief appearance, Brian felt that it was the right time to speak up. Now he had to say something. He found out that Charlie had taken a job at Bauer-Benedict, a much smaller, boutique agency. Brian had read about it in the *Hollywood Reporter*. The *Reporter* had been following a minor turmoil at BB and mentioned in the article that new agent Charlie Miller would be working under one of the agency principals. Charlie was stealing several hot television writers that he had personally groomed while working with Mark. The meld was perfect for BB. They got a young, brash, aggressive agent, just like the guys who had propelled the agency forward in the eighties, who ironically then fought over it, almost breaking it up.

Brian had convinced himself to ask Mark. He kept searching for an opening, but never got the chance. He excused himself from the table in order to attend a late appointment with Barry. Barry allowed Brian to have 'emergency' twenty-five minute appointments, so long as he understood that he would have to keep his regular hour-long appointment as well.

Once Brian arrived at Barry's, he didn't have much to say. He repeated his problems about not being an active agent, and worried that his periodontal condition would go downhill and ruin both his professional and social lives. During the session, Brian asked Barry to observe him as he flossed his teeth. Barry reinforced that he thought that Brian was doing everything he could to keep his teeth and gums in good shape, and not to take anything said by the hygienist and new dentist too seriously. "Their job is to read you the tooth riot act. I'm sure she is told to exaggerate the pocket depth numbers."

Brian discussed his anxiety attack while in was in the hygiene chair. He concluded those remarks on what Barry thought was a positive note. "I worked this out on my own. I know I can do a better job, and I will. I will do a better job. It's that simple. That's all I have to do."

Barry reemphasized that the hygienist was just doing her job, and was pleased that the new dentist ordeal was over. He praised Brian for taking the 'bad dental news' so well, and then it was back to the larger problem.

"I don't know if I'm ever going to be able to survive. It's too much of a jungle. I go to work every day expecting to be eaten alive. That's not a good feeling. I can't seem to detach myself from everything. It's too hard. Each day that goes by I feel more and more like I'll never make it. The pattern of business I see is scary. There are no rules and there are no morals. It's beyond anyone's comprehension, and yet it all continues, this controlled kind of chaos, it continues, every day, and people drive in to their offices in hundred-thousand-dollar cars and talk on the telephone all day without reaching a single soul. There isn't one single shred of real communication, not one idea founded in the reality of the human condition. It's the same every day. I don't think I've heard one literary idea since I started working at the agency. I think everyone who works for a movie company, no matter how bright they appear, has given up the right to have ideas, the right to construct a logical story about human beings. Instead they all run around pretending that what each one does is real and significant, but that's not enough for them. No. They deify their work as if they were actually making a contribution to mankind as a whole. It's a fake. It's a sham. I have yet to meet one person at the studios who could connect to an idea based on something real and literary. But, in order to survive, I have to accept what these people say and do. And somehow, and this is a tribute to the stupidity of the American people, all of these fakers make a shitload of money for themselves and the monster corporations. "

"Brian. That's the movie and entertainment business," said Barry, as if it were something that everyone took for granted.

"Is that supposed to make me feel better?"

"No. I mean, I guess not. You need to find things that make you happy, separate and apart from everything that's going on around you. You have to be able to say that all of that is business and it has nothing to do with you personally."

"But it is personal. I am there. How can they not mean it personally if they're talking to me?"

That was the type of question that Barry could not solve right away, perhaps never. He began to think that he should give up his more recent tact and start encouraging Brian to leave the agency business altogether.

On the way out, Brian passed Sean in the hall. They had seen each other before, either in the waiting room, or downstairs in the building lobby. Neither acknowledged the other, since any contact might lead to conversation, ultimately about having the same doctor. Men found it a sticky subject.

Minutes later, Barry lit a cigar, and listened to Sean.

"I don't think I'm going to crawl out of this. I don't want to file bankruptcy again. If I do, I have to make sure my daughter can hide as much of the cash as possible. It seems like I'm in this horrible rut. I don't want to keep making these shitty little movies forever. I need something bigger." Barry had heard this all before, but this time there was a larger hint of desperation in Sean's voice.

Barry leaned back and clenched down on his cigar. He sometimes sat in a swivel rocker that he was able to lock into a reclined position. "Sean. At least you've stopped gambling. You lost what, over a hundred thousand last year between those new issues and your facacta football games." Barry puffed and exhaled quickly.

"Yeah. Keep sucking on that cigar until your larynx ends up in some disposable human waste bin in the back of Cedars."

"I only have a few a week," said Barry with a meeker voice. "And why should you care so much about me? You never listen to my advice."

"Fuck you."

"Nice. Very nice. You want a cigar? They're Montecristos from Havana. You know my patient, the guy that lives in Miami?"

"Yeah. The guy with all the bullshit restaurants."

"Yes. He gave me a box. You want?"

"Sure." Sean extended his hand like a little boy expecting a candy treat.

Barry approached the cigar ritual with a surgical precision and timing. First, he removed a cigar box from a reachable bookshelf, selected a cigar, and then slowly peeled off the cellophane wrapper. With even more control, he neatly snipped the tip off of the cigar with a guillotine cutter. "There. Enjoy yourself, and remember. Sometimes a cigar is just a cigar," he said as he handed Sean the cigar.

Sean shook his head in disgust, then allowed Barry to light the cigar.

For a few moments, the two men ignored one another and puffed away, in testosterone oblivion. The conversation took a detour down a familiar road. *My Big Fat Greek Wedding* did almost sixty thousand on six screens," said Barry.

"Out here?" Sean was impressed. It was his territory, a low budget movie consistently making money.

"New York and L.A. - she was great," added Barry, with all the authority of Roger Ebert. "I hope she wins an award." He was referring to the lead, Nia Vardalos, another stand-up comedian who was able to successfully expand her material into a different medium.

Sean appeared puzzled, as if Barry had said that the building was on fire and that he was really a Martian, spying on mental health issues in Beverly Hills.

Barry asked, "Sean?"

Sean mumbled, "Give me a minute, here…"

The men continued to puff on their cigars.

Sean spoke carefully, "You know how your people used to talk about children developing sexual attraction for one parent or the other…"

"Yes. I've heard about it. What's on your mind?"

"I didn't have anything like that. Nothing at all. Never thought about it once. Not even after seeing my parents fucking one night after a Chanukah party. My mother had a nice body, and some pair of nice, big tits, but I never felt anything. I even saw her snatch, spread open wide one night when she was out cold drunk in her room."

Barry felt obliged to make a contribution. "I saw my mother giving my father a blow job once. I got scared and screamed. She told me she was just giving him a goodnight kiss and when I was older I would get a lot of those kisses from other women," Barry said with a wide smile. "I'm still waiting."

They both giggled like schoolboys.

"This is going to sound weird," continued Sean.

"Shoot. I've been here on North Bedford Drive for twenty-five years. I've heard it all. Twice."

"Well. We had this dog named Blackie. It was a poodle. I used to play with its dick, and then I'd let him lick my dick. It really turned me on," said Sean. He stared at Barry, waiting for a response.

"Balls, too?"

Sean nodded. "Why does that matter?"

"So. You played grab dick with your dog. Next case."

"That's it?"

"What? You don't do it with George Roy, do you?"

"No. But I had a date once that wanted to give him a blowjob. So who was I to interfere? I don't mind watching shit like that."

"I know." Barry pressed his lips into a proper smirk.

"So you don't think anything else about it?"

"What do you think?"

"I asked you first," said Sean, mimicking a child's voice.

"Sean. I have to keep some semblance of order here. What I think doesn't really matter. Why did you tell me this?"

"I don't know. I thought maybe it had something to do with the fact that I never had a good relationship with a woman."

The cigar smoke was beginning to collect above their heads, equidistant from their seats.

Barry shook his head. "Maybe it does, but I can think of probably a hundred other reasons you've given me over the years that can be summarized into four words: 'You didn't want to'."

"Why do you keep saying that?"

"Because you don't want to. If you did, you would. You don't, so you don't want to. Analysis can be very simple. Look. It's late. Let's go eat." Barry stood up.

"Okay. But I still think playing with my dog's dick fucked me up in some way."

"Yeah. When your biography comes out about why you are so fucked up, I promise to write a whole section on you and your poodle's schmekel." Barry began his routine to close up the office. He placed the cigar box back on the shelf, checked his answering machine for messages, and walked toward an ancient freestanding oak closet to get his jacket.

"We'd better get going if we want to get a table. We can finish our cigars on the way," said Sean.

"Right," said Barry. He moved to shut off the coffee machine.

"I'll be in the hall." Sean rose and headed out.

"I'll be a minute." Barry shut the coffee machine and went into the waiting room.

A few minutes later, Barry and Sean puffed away during their short walk on Wilshire Boulevard to dinner.

"I'm not getting a steak," said Barry. "Grill on the Alley or not."

"You always say that and then you do and then you fight with the waiter because the chef won't make it well done, or if he does he finds the worst piece-of-shit cut of meat to burn for you."

"Fuck you," said Barry. "I'm getting chicken. You know what? Let's get one of the cars and drive to Kate Mantilini. I'll get their chicken pot pie."

Sean shook his head and laughed. "And you're the shrink?"

They turned back toward the garage in Barry's building.

Twenty minutes later, in a fabled window booth, Barry closed his menu and stared at Sean.

Sean screeched, "What?"

"I don't want you to say anything when I order."

"Why would I say anything?"

"Well, just don't say anything."

Minutes later, Barry nearly whispered to the waiter, "I'll have the sliced New York steak. Well done."

Sean covered his mouth to stop dribbles of his Bloody Mary from escaping.

The next day, Brian arrived at work quite early. A new agent already sat in Charlie's office chair.

Bradley Lewis

The first time Brian waltzed into Mark's office, Mark held up his hand before Brian could say a word.

"Did I promise you anything?" asked Mark in all sincerity. He looked up from his desk and stared with wide puppy-dog eyes. "Don't look at me like that. I didn't even know Charlie was quitting for sure. Come on. Don't make me a bad guy here. I am just as hurt as you are. The call came from upstairs. I had nothing to do with it. You'll get your shot, not just now." That was the last that was ever mentioned on the subject.

CHAPTER SEVEN
Frank
Mal, Ricky
Brantley, Sean
Brantley, Heather

      Sean lunched fairly regularly, at least twice a month, as a guest at The Hillcrest Country Club. He was one of the 'professional guests', someone who was repeatedly ask to join, but never completed the application process. Having enemies at the club was a given for a movie producer. Sean could think of at least two or three members who might go out of their way to have him blackballed. Once, he almost went through with the application, but he knew that even though it was old business history, people in this small town never forgot the simplest 'fuck off' or the backing of the 'wrong' writer or director for a new project. If you were on the bad side of some of the more powerful people, you remained there for life, despite dozens of years of manufactured martini smiles and second-wives' attempts at social reconciliation. Anyone who felt 'fucked over', for any reason, was someone to stay away from. And that also included local moguls from Tex-Mex fast food chains, designer furniture, celebrity chefs, and banks.

      The Hillcrest club had one of the largest concentrations of wealth in California, or for that matter, anywhere. Most of

the members weren't directly involved in the entertainment
business, but nonetheless maintained strong connections to
anyone with a modicum of power. Sean wisely received much of his
movie financing from Hillcrest members; some who knew the
business, and others who got a thrill out of reaping the party
benefits and all-around star-fuck. Sean would sit and listen to
the endless stories over massive Bar Mitzvah-sized lunches,
making sure to pay homage to his regular, and any potential
investors. The Grill Room was usually filled with octogenarian
storytellers, reminiscing of a time when "this town was great".
It was less formal than the catering-hall-sized dining room, and
had been remodeled a few years ago, due to the usual country
club decorating zealots, who loved to fool around with the
interior and exterior design of the club. Someone new on the
membership roster was always remarried to an 'interior
designer'. So far the pool and cabanas had not materialized, but
the younger members were not giving up. They wanted to redo the
entire property so that it looked and felt more like a Ritz
Carlton or Four Seasons resort. Lately, the vote to pass a
wholesale makeover was getting closer, but there were still
enough older members who were dead set against turning the
venerable club into a flashy waste of money.

The few celebrities who were still members rarely
socialized at the club. Sidney Poitier was easy to spot when he
was in town, since Hillcrest had no other African-American
members. Berry Gordy was up for membership; proposed by mega-
wealthy Marvin Davis. Nobody ever saw Neil Diamond or David
Geffen. When George Burns died in 1996, he just about took all
of old Hollywood with him.

For many years, the roundtable at Hillcrest had seated the
Hollywood elite, including every popular comedian of the day.
The only surviving comedian at Hillcrest was Jan Murray, who

could be seen playing a round of golf upon occasion, or
kibitzing in the Grill Room before lighting at one of the
regular tables.

Now the roundtable functioned more for lunch singles,
mostly businessmen. The only thing that remained the same was
the shape of the table, and it was probably maintained in order
to make sure that no one would complain to any committee people
that "there has to be a roundtable at Hillcrest". Things like
that happened all the time. Any poor fool who begged to get
notoriety at the club by joining a committee, would soon find
that life behind the scenes running the elegant dinosaur was a
somewhat dastardly series of deeds, interrupted occasionally by
offensively large holiday buffet dinners and marginal jazz
quartets.

Perhaps the people who still sat at the roundtable every
day were there because they wanted to feel like they were part
of its history. Some used it as a form of power, including one
doctor who forbade newer and younger members from sitting at the
table - "not just anyone can sit here" - until other members
told them to ignore "the delusional old fart". The fabled table
once served the likes of Jolson, Burns, Benny, and the Ritz and
Marx brothers. That is, when Harpo Marx wasn't playing golf
naked from the waist down. He had been chastised by one of the
members for playing golf with a bare chest on an unseasonably
hot day. He was caught in the act by a rules book-wielding
member of the golf committee and driven off the course while
being duly instructed in the proper dress code. He returned the
next day to play sans trousers, since there was nothing in the
rules about playing a round of golf at Hillcrest with ones
testicles flapping in the breeze.

Frank Ford, one of Sean's investors, would refer to
Hillcrest as "a little city within a city". That was about one

of the only things that Frank was right about. That and golf. Anyone who took the time to spend more than two minutes with Frank would learn, whether they wanted to or not, that he liked to talk almost exclusively about his own golf game, including television caliber play-by-play descriptions and details of his personal shots. If it rained, he would tell anyone about his last round, and acted out 'instant' replays that included watching the imaginary ball in flight, enough to have made Marcel Marceau contemplate suicide.

Frank could be a total bore, particularly with women who didn't even play golf. Some men could relate to Frank's condescending and obnoxious manner, something nurtured and accepted by his family when he was growing up - a type of perverse coddling that took place in upper crust environments. Most of the new, younger members, didn't know anything about Frank, and they didn't care to. The few that crossed his path made little, if anything, out of Frank's social decorum. But the unfortunate few who dealt with him for any length of time came away with one expression to describe him: "bitter, old asshole".

This wasn't entirely his fault. He had his genetic limitations, according to his own father. Sensing that Frank's brother William had a little more to offer in the brains department, old man Ford put Frank to work playing golf in order to drum up business or entertain the client stable. Frank's absence from the main office paid nice dividends in the long run.

Frank's father, Farley, somehow came up with the first three parts for variable speed electronic windshield wipers. The Fords, no relation to Henry, were in the auto parts business. Once Farley got his hands on someone else's invention, it became his. Farley and his competitors made millions each year on

little 'insignificant' automobile parts. The windshield wiper
was one of the many coups - the multiple lawsuits came years
later, and by then Frank's family could afford to hire tons of
lawyers who knew how to arrange reasonable settlements with the
estates of the actual inventors.

Ten years ago, the General Motors Parts Division bought out
Farley Ford Automotive Parts for a whopping six-hundred-eighty
million dollars. Hillcrest members could only guess as to
Frank's personal net worth, somewhere in the fifty-million
dollar range, if he had gotten an equal share. Despite that, he
lived in a little house in Cheviot Hills, the less expensive
section of town, walking distance from the club. He never did
stroll to the club, but instead drove a ten-year-old Buick
Century Station wagon, and parked it alongside the Bentleys,
Rolls, and new Ferraris that packed the club parking lot. His
wardrobe could best be described as early J.C. Penney, with a
few more expensive items bought over twenty years ago from
Abercrombie & Fitch or Brooks Brothers.

"A Brooks Brothers suit can last a lifetime," Frank would
intone at the daily Hillcrest lunch. "That's if you know how to
take care of a suit." If nobody stopped him, he would explain
the process.

"And want to wear the same clothes for the rest of your
life," one of the Hillcrest cronies would usually add.

When it rained at Hillcrest, there wasn't a more miserable,
embittered group of people to be found anywhere. The long faces
scraped along the top of soup bowls, with smiles nothing more
than fleeting memories, as the luckless sports orphans stared
out at the empty golf course. On those dreaded days, it wasn't
unusual for fights to break out in the card room, fueled by
extra booze, extra people, and extra body order. If someone
raised his voice, the rest of the group would shout him down,

and the game would continue. Mild, but not continuums, grumbling was tolerated. One day there was a threat of someone returning with a gun. The man, in his mid-nineties, was suspended for a couple of weeks and advised to watch his language and murderous threats.

The day following a moderate soaking, Frank and the rest of his golf cronies would sit nearby each other and stare out of the massive bay window in the locker room, all dressed for golf, wondering if they should go out and risk soggy play. Reed, the venerable keeper of the greens, would call in early and tell the caddy master Manny whether or not to prohibit the use of electric carts, which would damage the wet terrain. Nobody really liked to walk the course, particularly when the ground was soft. It was a shame that a beautiful course like Hillcrest had such ominous drainage problems. Nobody liked the possibility of hitting into the second cut of rough on a hot summer day, only to find that their ball was plugged in the mud. Worse was hitting a shot that appeared propped up in the grass, only to find that on the downswing the club would get caught up in the watery sludge, sometimes sending a dark spray onto the unprotected face and colorful clothing of the ball striker.

When there were no carts available, the boys adjourned to a newer round table near the outer doors in the Grill Room. Some ordered an early lunch, in case the consensus of the group changed to braving the perils of inclement weather.

"It's just a drizzle. Come on. We can walk a few holes. Let's take the old whiskey route," said Robert Reasoner. He was referring to playing a short version of the course, holes one through four, and then eight and nine. The green on hole four was adjacent to the tee box for hole eight.

Robert Reasoner was the son-in-law of the owner of a chain of low-priced shoe stores that had once owned the Stride Rite corporation. He had worked most of his life for the company and retired with a bad back, huge stomach, and gimpy knees. He still played golf, even after three surgeries - back, bionic knee and hip replacement. Watching him swing a golf club was painful to observe, but he denied ever having any discomfort. Like so many, "My surgeon is a genius. Best in the world. He's famous for knees."

"It's not a drizzle, it's a light rain," said Chuck.

Chuck Stirling was a retired advertising executive who had worked his way down from Foote, Cone, and Belding, and other giants like Grey and Compton to a lesser known local agency called Carson Roberts. Chuck's brother, Dave Stirling, was one of the best known and wealthiest members at Hillcrest.

"It's raining. That's all I know," said Stanley Donner, always trying to make a statement with finality. He was holding a pastrami sandwich on rye, unable to quite decide if he really wanted to eat it.

Stanley was born in New York City at Lenox Hill hospital. His parents were born in Haiti, but they had lived mostly in Paris and New York. Very few people outside of Hillcrest knew that Stanley was Jewish. He was a mulatto, obviously the descendant of Jewish and Haitian ancestors. He would not admit that to anyone, and when asked, always said that he was from Paris.

"It's not a light rain. It's a drizzle, maybe a heavy drizzle," said Robert. He wanted to play, hoping to embarrass the reluctant members into acquiescing. His subtle manipulation and tone had worked in the past.

"What the fuck is the matter with you? Look out the window. It's raining. That's what I call rain," screamed Chuck.

"Is this all you guys want to talk about?" asked Stanley.

"No. Let's talk about how you fixed your lie in the last club tournament," said Robert, alluding to Stanley's reputation as a seasoned golf 'cheat'. He would always tell his caddie to go up ahead, find his ball in the rough, and prop it up a little before anyone else could see what was going on. If Stanley had his back to the group, or was blocked by a tree, he would nudge the ball into a better spot, with his foot or the tip of one of his irons.

"Stanley's got the best foot mashie in the bag," said Chuck.

"I just saw *Chicago*," said Robert. He knew how to change from golf to the only other universal subject - movies. After that, it was money.

"Damn good movie," chimed in Chuck. "I think it'll get all the awards."

"I don't know what the big deal is. It's just another over-inflated self-aggrandizement," said Stanley. His mouth was filled with a gargantuan bite of his pastrami sandwich.

"What are you talking about? Over the last holiday weekend, it did something like twelve million!" said Robert. He appeared annoyed to have to deal with people who didn't know the movie business as well as he assumed that he did.

"That much?" Chuck couldn't have cared less.

"*The Lord of the Rings* movie did double that, but that's a different kind of a movie," said Stanley. He was referring to the latest version.

"I didn't know you knew the difference," said Robert. "You do realize that the movie you mentioned opened on a zillion more screens." His mouth was filled with salad.

Stanley smiled. "Eat your salad, Robert. I told the valet to put some carrots in the front seat of you BMW, in case you get hungry on the way to the office. You need to eat more red meat and stop listening to that quack cardiologist you go to on Camden."

Robert lowered his fork and turned, displaying his most confrontational pose. "I got to tell you, Stanley. Sometimes you are really an asshole."

"Sometimes?" added Chuck. "I couldn't resist." He gave Stanley a playful shove.

Meanwhile, Frank reported his recent golf scores to anyone who would listen, including the bus boy or waiter, or even the seasoned cocktail waitress, who probably paid little or no heed to any golf stories. She had seen and heard everything golf connected and otherwise.

When golf was officially declared off for that day, Frank finally ordered.

Robert was almost finished eating, so after waiting politely to hear Frank's latest golf scores, he excused himself to go back to his office.

"You'll have my check next week," said Robert quietly, avoiding direct eye contact with Frank. Even though he couldn't stand him, Robert couldn't resist any new money-making venture.

"Don't tell it to me," said Stan. "Tell farmer boy, over there." He waved his arm and pointed toward Frank.

Robert ignored Stan and left.

Frank took his cue. "I've been doing my research on the ostrich farm. Looks like I'm going to go through with it." He sipped a tiny spoonful of his steaming Manhattan clam chowder. He either had that or matzo ball soup for lunch, always slipping in a mention of his reputation as a connoisseur of both soups. "I had the chef make some changes…" The irony was lost on Frank, as he had a lifelong reputation of mundane and pedestrian taste. Exotic cuisine for Frank was Chinese chicken salad.

"I think it's nuts," said Stan. "It's just a fad."

223

"You see, that's where you're wrong. Ostrich farming has been going on in South Africa for almost one hundred and fifty years," said Frank.

"And that's where it should stay," said Chuck, glancing around for support.

Chuck and Stan laughed immediately.

"I've ordered the eggs," said Frank.

"You did?" asked Stan, still incredulous.

"Where the hell do you get ostrich eggs, if you don't mind me asking? You'll have to forgive me. I just got off the boat and don't know where to get my ostrich eggs," said Chuck with his mouth full of chicken Caesar salad.

"Okay, wise guys. They start at two-hundred dollars a pop and I get them from a guy in Canada," said Frank.

"Frank's not telling us exactly where because he's afraid we'll race out and buy up all his eggs," said Chuck.

Stan tried to further goad Frank. "Not at two-hundred a pop! My guy has been selling them to me for only one and a quarter."

"Very funny. The last time I heard such funny stuff I had to bring my Edsel in for repair," said Frank.

"I had an Edsel," said Chuck.

"So did I. I wasn't kidding," said Frank. "My brother and I chipped in for one and drove it from the dealership clear across the country to Chicago to visit my uncle. He took one look at it and said, 'boys, you'd better see if you can get your money back on that one'. "

"Oh, so now your Uncle predicted that the Edsel would fail," said Chuck.

"I didn't say that, but you know he knew what he was talking about. Ol' Uncle Perry was one hell of a smart guy. You know if it wasn't for his figuring out how to change our machines over from the single lone run to the compartmentalized system, we'd still be in the dark ages in our first factory. Why after that..."

That was the breaking point when people tuned out Frank, if for no other reason than keeping their own sanity. He was relentless and merciless when he spoke about the past, rambling on as long as the people near him were still breathing. At least his golf stories had an ending, as opposed to other club members who were incapable of talking about anything except themselves, and unwilling to stop.

"Robert is really going in with you? You're really doing this?" asked Stan. His concern was suddenly real, fearful that he would miss out on the next big chain. He had visions of Ost-Burger, small boutique fast-food joints, something along the lines of Burger King, only hipper and fancier.

"Damn right I am. I'm all set up. I took a little trip to one of these ranches and checked out the whole thing. There's a worldwide market for slaughtering. You know there's a science to it, just like chicken farming. We've even got a publisher interested in doing a recipe book if we can get one of them fancy chefs involved, like maybe Emeril or Wolfgang."

A few people at nearby tables with built-in money radar ceased talking. They craned their heads as Frank continued his pitch. "You got to have a good vet. Yessiree. Got to have a good one. The poultry business has got the same deal. Avian influenza. You got to watch out for it. But the business is good. Looks real good. A study at Wake Forest says the demand will go over three-hundred-thousand hides each year, and that's without any imports from South Africa. Hell, we even got a hat guy who wants to bring out a whole line with the plumes made from the feathers."

Hats. Retail. Minds clicked faster than spreadsheets on
Microsoft's Excel.

Frank raised his voice. "You know you can get a hundred and
twenty-five pounds of meat off of one of those birds. And you
can fetch twenty bucks a pound for that," he said, pausing to
let them all do the calculations. "Last chance boys. Any of you
want to get in on it?" He loved being the center of attention,
especially since he sincerely believed that he was going to make
a fortune on this one. "Ground floor…"

"No, thanks. But good luck. Send me a few burgers when
you're ready. I'll try an ostrich cheeseburger. Make mine with
Swiss." Chuck always played it cool. When he returned to his
office, the first call he would make would be to a food and
beverage analyst at Merrill Lynch. He was going to find out what
was going on in the worldwide ostrich market. And if there was a
burgeoning market, he knew how and with whom to invest.
Certainly not Frank.

"Yeah. Put me down for a New York filet of ostrich," said
Stan. "Can you barbecue the meat?"

"Why the hell not?" answered Frank, a tad defensively. What
little sense of humor he had did not apply to any of his
projects.

"How's your love life?" asked Chuck. He was always teasing
Frank. "Let's talk about something important."

Frank measured his life by some of the most hackneyed
standards. "The old soldier stands at attention whenever I play
reveille."

"You sure it's not the *Boogie Woogie Bugle Boy From Company
B*'? That was the last thing Chuck would say during lunch. While
Frank began to extol rambling 'war' stories about his social
escapades, Chuck dosed off at the table. The captains were
properly instructed to gently nudge any member who fell asleep

during lunch. It was a nice courtesy, and also cut down on the club's accident liability, particularly when trying to remove the luncheon dishes. Younger members joked that an announcement should be made during lunch, "Diners please fasten your seat belts. We are serving the soup."

Sean's slam-bang down-and-dirty movie in Vegas went off miraculously without a hitch. Mal performed his gig without any major problems. The Roses were driven to Vegas in a customized van. The project proved to be instant relief for Sean, because it kept him afloat. He was able to sell the foreign rights immediately and felt certain that a U.S. distributor would soon follow.

Mal ended up getting a few extra days in Vegas with Ricky. When they weren't on the set, Mal and Ricky sometimes sat staring at each other in the hotel room. They didn't speak much when they were on the road. Mal enjoyed his privacy. He wanted Ricky to be around just before he began a work day. Only Ricky and Mal's little bear doll. Mal would sit on the bed, clutching *Variety* in one hand and his little bear doll in the other.

The good luck doll had held out all these years, from theater to theater, city to city, never once leaving Mal's side, except for the time one of the hotel housekeepers had taken it down the hall to clean. She had accidentally knocked a glass of ice with remnants of Coke onto the floor. One of the ice cubes ricocheted off the floor and splattered watered-down Coke on the good luck dolly. When Mal returned from the show, he immediately searched for the doll, but to no avail. Several hours later, with hotel security, the manager, local police, and one man from the local FBI office (Mal was on good terms with Hoover), the doll turned up, safe and sound, drying off from a club soda bath, courtesy of one well-meaning, but soon-to-be-fired girl from Guatemala.

Ricky was never permitted to see his father dress. At a show, he was only allowed in the dressing room after Mal was fully clothed and had put on his make-up. Now that Mal was older and needed more help, he would sometimes allow Arnie Baylos inside the dressing room, or Tubby, one of the writers that had stayed on with him since his early days in Vegas and later, Atlantic City.

Lately, the trips blended inside Ricky's head as one big blur.

I kept calling Sean. I wanted to get away from the beach, and after checking out the building with Sean's apartment, it seemed like a great location. I looked at other places, but there was always some hitch. I still had my place in New York, and couldn't afford to spend too much. The apartment in Sean's building was something I could handle.

He finally called me back, and I convinced him that I was ready to move. He agreed to meet with me.

Sean thought that it would be a great intimidation move if he invited me to have a drink at Hillcrest. None of Sean's friends would mind if he brought a guest. I gladly accepted, making myself a 'guest of a guest'. I was told by Sean to use the name Dave Stirling as my host.

As I drove Mickey's Mustang convertible up to the imposing entrance, I had the feeling that my lifelong dream was going to come true. Maybe I would leave the root canal business and write fulltime. What a fantasy! I was driving into one of the bastions of the old entertainment industry. I felt the sweat on my palms as I grasped the steering wheel. I stopped at the security gate,

and cooled my hands in front of one of the air conditioning
vents near the steering wheel.

"Yes, sir?" questioned a guard in a dull security outfit.
He had a white handle bar moustache and thick glasses. Security
was obviously an issue for a nearly all Jewish club,
particularly after 9/11.

After he checked my name on the list, I drove around a
horseshoe driveway toward the ornate porte-cochère. Three valets
scurried about while a fourth was off in wandering the west
parking area searching unsuccessfully for a member's car.

Once I marched through the entrance, I was instantly
impressed. The foyer was filled with deep, dark wood. The
moldings were extensive, but tastefully done. As soon as I could
see into the dining room, all sense of the conservative
disappeared. A gargantuan and grotesque ice sculpture almost hit
the ceiling. Perhaps it was a giant swan in the center of the
food buffet, the likes of which I had never seen before, not
even in the movies. My closest reference was *Goodbye, Columbus*,
but now suddenly magnified by ten. And this was just lunch. No
wedding. No Bar Mitzvah. Just a weekday lunch!

Another Robert, the most popular and venerable maître d',
escorted me inside; an African-American man who moved with a
simple understated elegance, almost a hesitation that belied his
experience. He would retire soon, and the room would lose some
of its historic cachet. He made sure that I quickly and
efficiently found my way to Sean.

Sean was seated at a table filled with some men in business
suits and others in conservative golf attire.

"Sean Daren?" I asked. *The guy from the liquor store*.

"Here," said Sean, as he rose from his chair. "Boys. I'd
like you to meet Dr. Brantley Benjamin. He's a root canal guy
from New York."

"Oh, a specialist," Dave Stirling said with an accompanying reverence still reserved for health professionals, something left over from an older generation.

The rest of the group was merciless. "Another New York Jew." It was Chuck.

Frank hopped on. "Come over here and fix this abscess." He pointed to his rear end.

"What's the matter, couldn't you get into medical school?" asked Stan. He laughed heartily - alone.

One by one, I was introduced to the elite crowd - Dave Stirling, Frank, Chuck, Stan and Robert. By the time I left, I had over twenty names thrown at me. Dave made the biggest impression. It was easy to see why most of the boys were intimidated by him, yet he was friendly to me in a seemingly forthright but yet slightly distant way, as if he was hiding something, and needed to be certain that I wouldn't notice. When I mentioned that I had done some writing, Dave asked several questions.

As soon as we were alone, Sean volunteered his view on Dave. Sean's candor surprised me. "Dave is one of the great bulldogs of all times. If he has an idea for a deal, you don't hear about it once. Dave will work on you incessantly, like a friendly jackhammer. He isn't interested in anything you have to say. His only interest is if you want to hop on his bandwagon. He doesn't have room in his life for anything except his own agenda."

I found that funny, coming from Sean. After being in his company for only a few minutes, I was developing the same impression of him. Every time I tried to bring the conversation around to the apartment, Sean broke it off quickly. Sean and I never got a chance to speak about it. After the group had disbanded, Sean stood to leave.

"Call me. We'll have lunch. Maybe at Juniors, not too far from my office. We can talk about the apartment then."

This was his game, the only way he knew how to play. It was new to me, so I had no choice but to play along. I had a positive feeling, despite not accomplishing anything regarding the apartment.

I walked with Sean out to the valet. While we were waiting for his car, he turned to me. "Can you pay twelve hundred, give me two months in advance, and if you break anything you fix it?"

I was caught off guard. It had all been planned. It was two hundred less than what Laurel had told me. "Yes. Great. Fine. I'll have the money at your office tomorrow."

Sean patted my cheek like Tony Soprano. For a moment I felt made, in a twisted Hollywood way. I had had lunch at one of the most exclusive clubs on the west coast, and now I was moving into a high-rise off of Sunset Boulevard. And Sean was giving me a very decent break on the rent. This was a sick movie moment, one of those out of the body experiences when transplanted New Yorkers start believing that they really have gone through the looking glass.

Once Sean was inside his car, I yelled into the open passenger window. "Can I also drop off a screenplay?" I didn't have one fully written, but that didn't matter.

Sean smiled. "Sure. I don't know when I can read it." He pulled away.

Wow played over in my mind like a broken CD. I must have stood frozen because the moment I became aware of myself I was blocking a car waiting to pull in. They tooted the horn, and I moved out of the way, past the somewhat frantic valets.

My first Sunday at the new apartment building was a picture perfect Hollywood experience. It seemed as if everyone who lived

in the sixties edifice was either out at the pool or would pop
by later for a cocktail, a stop-and-schmooze before sunset.
Trivial Pursuit was the focus of the most inebriated tenants.

With *The New York Times* in hand, I made my way from my
furnished apartment to the glistening elevator. The doors opened
slowly, and I faced a woman wearing a terrycloth wrap, clutching
a large straw bag.

"Hi," she said. She smiled with oversized, stark white
incisors.

"Hi," I said as I walked in.

We waited a few seconds for the doors to close. If I
glanced at the corners of the front mirrors, I could see her
rear in the back mirrors. She was wearing high heels, well
spiked and colored a bright red that seemed almost comical. Two
earrings hung in place, bluish balls with gold lines running
through them like topographical river markings on world globes.
The perfume was apparent, but not overwhelming. Her nail polish
matched the shoes perfectly. But, it was the hat that really
caught my attention. The western style golf hat was complete
with a band that had the Callaway logo; hardly noticeable
against the expansive white brim that left a faint shadow on her
forehead.

"I'm Heather. You're new here, aren't you?" She had an
infectious smile. "Don't you remember me?"

I didn't. Especially not in that outfit. She looked and
acted completely different, something I grew to expect about
people in this town. Within each different venue they had a
suitable personality to match.

I faked it for the moment. "Yeah. Of course. How are you? I
moved in Friday morning."

"You'll like it here. There are tons of nice people. What
floor are you on?" I quickly understood that Heather never

232

waited for an answer. "Did you know that Neil Diamond once kept an apartment here? I think Rod Steiger still has one, and that actress who never won an Emmy, you know, whatshername? A lot of actresses live here. John Belushi died nearby. Have you been to the Chateau? Are you going to the pool? That's where I'm headed. The Jacuzzi is great. Stick around until four and George Romero makes his martini of the week. Do you like martinis? They're soooo gooood. I don't know how he keeps coming up with so many different ingredients."

"I like martinis."

"I knew you did. I can just look at someone and tell everything about them." She turned to face me, and I finally recognized her.

"Okay, shoot."

"You're from New York."

"That's easy. The accent." I was sure that I had told her that when I had met her the second time at the Doheny estate, but that was already in the past. It didn't matter.

She laughed. "It could have been New Jersey."

"Ouch. At least you didn't say Joisey."

She laughed.

The elevator had reached the ground level.

"You can sit with me if you want." Heather burst out of the door ahead of me and performed a decent unintentional parody of Marilyn Monroe, buttocks moving side-to-side in a brisk walk and making sure to click her shoes distinctively on the marble floor.

"Okay. Thanks." I followed, conscious not to copy the sashay.

"Good morning, Heather." It was Sam, the manager. He stood behind an old-fashioned reception desk, replete with mailbox slots for residents.

She said, "Hi, Sam."

Sam waved to me. "Hi, Doc. How's it going?"

Heather froze. "Oh, you're a doctor."

I caught up to her. "An Endodontist - a root canal specialist." I was certain that she had known that, too. It was typical – the fact that people never really connected with each other, no matter how many times they would meet. But why should I have expected her to remember anything I had told her? I was just a local root canal specialist. Maybe she held a grudge from the Jacuzzi scenario.

Heather sounded legitimately impressed. "My gawd. They make a fortune. My sister had a root canal done in Beverly Hills. She paid over a thousand dollars for it. Can you believe that? A thousand dollars. Then she had to have the tooth fixed for another two grand."

I walked alongside Heather to the pool area. We passed the valets - two Ethiopian men dressed in smart beige suits and polished military-styled hats.

Heather spoke to the taller and leaner of the two. "Mike. Can you get gas in my car?"

The tall man answered, "Miss Heather. It would be a pleasure." When he smiled, his solid gold canine tooth sparkled in the sun.

"Thanks. Mike, do you know the doctor?"

"Good morning, sir. Will you be staying with us?

"Yes. I'm in 3G."

He volunteered, "It's quiet in the back. You can't hear the cars at night."

That hadn't occurred to me, but I was glad to know it. I wanted to go to sleep early, establishing some kind of regular schedule. I was determined to keep up my quest for straightening myself out. "Oh, good," I said.

"I'll fill up the tank before noon, Miss Heather. Do you want me to wash it for you?"

"Not today. Thanks, Mike."

"You two have a nice day, now."

I said, "See you later, Mike."

It was a short walk past the huge circular driveway. In the center was a fountain that lit up at night in light greens and yellows, the current choice of the board members. The building had the look and feel of a small hotel. Umbrellas lined the perimeter of the gated pool enclosure. Each umbrella proudly displayed the building logo, the street signs for Horn-Sunset, crossed under what appeared to be a regal crown.

Heather continued talking as we strolled toward the pool. "I'm in 16J. It's a double and I face the city. It's beautiful at night. You must see the view. I can see all the way downtown and to the beach. Do you like the beach? Once a week, I drive to Venice to walk around. Have you ever been to the beach here? Did you move out here recently?"

The remark about the beach - she was either pretending or had no recollection of our episode. I asked, "Do you mean from New York?" I opened the gate and we entered the pool area. She didn't respond.

I decided it was best to answer Heather's last question in her series. "A few months ago."

"You really are new here, aren't you?"

"I'll adjust."

"When I first moved here I didn't know anyone. Everyone here is super friendly. I'll introduce you. Did you say where your office was? Is it nearby? Don't specialists have to study more?"

I continued to chat with Heather as we made camp on two adjacent lounge chairs covered with matching green logo mats. I

was enjoying the new version of Heather. I didn't mind her
incessant chatter, yet I reminded myself that if I had run in to
a similar person in New York, I might not have had the same
favorable reaction. I was already feeling different toward
people. Maybe it was the sunny weather, and the fact that people
lived a vacation life all year 'round. That was it. I felt as if
I was on vacation, even though I had to take my work quite
seriously. Things would take some getting used to, particularly
the frequent sight of bikinis.

CHAPTER EIGHT
Ira, Neil

The first day of the summer anatomy class is referred to as 'simple dissection'. The cadavers are all face down on their respective slabs. Their bodies are covered with material that resembles camping tarpaulins. It's quite a sight for someone who has never been around dead people. Talking in advance to sophomore students never adequately prepared anyone, nor did the abundance of reference material.

For most of the students it is their first exposure. There are few things in life that prepares someone for medical school anatomy, except perhaps working as an apprentice to Hannibal Lecter. There aren't many of those personality types in anatomy class since convicted scalpel murderers, surprisingly, have a hard time getting into a medical school in California. Also, it is highly unlikely that anyone in the room had written or verbalized, "extensive dismembering on the road" in answer to the medical school application or interview question "Is there anything else you'd like to tell us about your extracurricular activities that might have an impact on your application?"

The first human sense to be offended in the ungodly room is smell. Even before the eyes can focus on the dissection tomb, the nose is hit with a powerful, repellant, and pervasive odor.

When Ira and Neil took their places at their assigned cadaver, Ira backed up two steps and rubbed his nose, while Neil covered his mouth with his hand.

The odor of formaldehyde required some adjustments in breathing and most students never got used to it. The chemical would invade clothing, taint the skin, and pervade the hair, even after a rigorous shampoo. Over time, the doctors-to-be would take part of the smell with them every day. The strong stench would become embedded in the pages of the dissection manual. Everywhere it went, the offensive aroma went, too. There was no escape, and it was a constant reminder of the cadaver.

A lecture before the first dissection class had described the required process in detail. The preface of the dissection manual told the whole story. "As originally conceived, this manual was intended to supply the inexperienced dissector with concise, specific directions for dissection procedures."

The first time Ira had read it, he wondered what the author meant by "inexperienced". Were there really experienced dissectors lurking around Hollywood?

The introduction reminded all readers, "After centuries of struggle against the prejudice of the unenlightened, the right to dissect the human body has been won."

Neil thought, *Now there's a victory.*

Once they began the dissection, the expression on Neil's face summed up many students' feelings. His cheeks were pale one moment and flushed the next, while his lips turned into a perpetual frown, despite trying every bad joke he could think of.

"Just read the book," said Ken Weiss, a graduate of Reed College, who took his dissecting and entire life very seriously. To some, this was the pinnacle of achievement after suffering through archaic and rigid basic science programs in college.

The dissection manual wasted no time, and dove right into the first incision. "For the dissection of the back," began Neil, who was the self-appointed reader. This way he had a little more distance between himself and the cadaver. "The body lies prone with a block elevating the thorax and the head hanging freely, so that the back of the neck is stretched. Certain points should be identified before the skin is reflected. In the midline of the base of the skull is the external occipital protuberance."

As Neil read on, the group located the surface points. He told himself that he could handle this. If he held on another hour, he could make it through the semester. At that moment, he knew that even for a con man like himself, this was something he was going to have to reconsider. "When these points have been observed, make the following incisions through the skin: (1) a median longitudinal incision starting at the external occipital protuberance and ending at the tip of the coccyx." Neil continued while Ken enthusiastically did most of the cutting. "The reflection of skin will expose the superficial fascia of the back." Neil froze as he watched the skin peeled neatly away from the body.

"God. His back muscles look just like the corned beef in your grandfather's deli," said Neil.

Moments later Neil would blame the strong odor as he found himself on the floor up against the back of a dissecting stool. He didn't remember leaving the dissecting table.

"Neil. Are you okay?" asked Ira, as he held Neil up by his armpits.

"Get me out of here," was all Neil said. "I just need a little air."

Within moments, the two of them were outside on the plaza, safe in the seemingly ever-present Southern California sun, amidst the usual throngs of campus activity.

"I don't think I can make it," said Neil.

"I'll help you," said Ira. "You'll get through."

"It'll take a lot more than help. It will take a whole lot of cheating."

"What are you going to tell your father?"

That reached him. Neil paused to indicate deliberate reflection. "Okay. I can do this. I know I can do this. It was just the smell. The cutting really didn't bother me." Ira didn't think that Neil sounded sincere, but it didn't matter. Plenty of students forced themselves to continue.

"Let's go back in," said Ira. "You'll get used to it."

As Neil and Ira made their way back to the dissection laboratory, they passed two more students from the class who were hastily on their way outside.

"Fuck this," was all one said, over and over. His shirt was damp with vomit.

The second one looked a little woozy. "Great. We'll be ill for seven years and finally get a chance to go to work for a managed health care facility."

"Fuck it," said the first one. "Fuck this. Just fuck this." He sounded as if he would never return.

Once Neil was back in the dissection room, he appeared more composed. He wove in and out between tables, proud of his return to the bloodless battle. He eventually came to a halt behind Ken, who was crunched over the far end of the cadaver, where the feet were still covered by the ugly tarpaulin.

Neil slapped Ken on the back. "Okay, professor, let's rock n' roll." He kept his hand firmly planted in the center of Ken's back.

Ken jumped backward, startled. "Hey," he garbled, as he turned around. "I'm having my lunch." He turned his head to display a piece of white bread and some dark colored meat dangling from his mouth.

Neil could see half a sandwich on white bread, potato salad, a pickle, and some milky coleslaw, centered on the 'picnic' tarp. "Okaaaay." He did a double take any member of *Saturday Night Live* would have been proud of, slowly turned, and bolted from the room.

When the lab was empty at night, Ira agreed to tutor Neil on the individual dissections. They started out the evening by having dinner at a popular ratskeller on Westwood Boulevard which was usually filled with people from UCLA. The noisy, active hangout was perfect for a light snack before staring down the dead, cut up bodies. Two or three beers with some chips were about all Neil could stomach for cadaver nights. He eventually became a little more comfortable during the dissection sessions, but he clearly was not an ideal candidate for medical school for another reason. He had a horrible memory. Nothing helped. He couldn't even remember the pneumonics that Ira had gotten from previous students, who also supplied old exams and notes.

During one of those evenings, Neil suggested that they stop by to say hello to Chris, an acquaintance who also worked as a handyman/waiter at the Beverly Hills Tennis Club. Chris' night job at the school included 'managing' the cadaver room. He was naturally handy, and Neil suggested to Ira that they enlist Chris to help fix up the deli.

After a few turns through a series of corridors, they found themselves inside the anatomy department's research area. "Holy shit," said Neil. "Take a peek at these babes." Through a window in a laboratory door, they could see the cadavers being readied for the dissection room. Neil knocked on the door.

Dozens of human bodies hung from devices resembling meat hooks, a process that drained them before the preservation stage. Some of the skin still looked normal, while others had already changed color due to the loss of underlying blood and the introduction of the preservatives. A small fluorescent night light illuminated the room from under the cadavers, sending the beam up across the bodies in what appeared to be a deliberate macabre pattern. Horror movie producer Roger Corman could not have done better.

With the pans beneath the bodies filled with ghastly colored liquids, the room took on the look of a movie set. *No one actually did this for real. Right?* That's what Neil was thinking as he was reminded of a scene from the movie *Coma*, which he had enjoyed, and the more recent *Extreme Measures*, which he thought was a bomb. Somebody was always doing an 'original' remake that involved cadavers, walking dead and the like.

"Hey. Look at that poor schmuck," said Neil as he stuck his nose up against the plate glass.

"Wow," was all Ira deemed appropriate. He placed his hand on his stomach as he felt a gurgle of liquids make its way down his intestines.

One of the cadavers was in the process of being drained and had a scrotum the size of a basketball. The liquid filled sac was distended almost to the knee.

"I wonder what that guy's nickname was," said Neil, trying hard to appear unaffected.

"Okay. Come on. Let's get out of here," said Ira. "I don't see anyone."

"What's the matter? Can't take it?" chided Neil. He knocked again on the door.

"Don't give me that shit, Neil. Tell me you like this." He playfully pushed Neil in the shoulder.

"You never could take it. I told you to go to law school." Neil enjoyed milking the momentary juxtaposition of roles.

"I'll get used to it. Come on," said Ira. "This is some switch from the first day of dissection. What were you doing, faking it?"

"I'm fine as long as you don't get me to touch it."

"That's what one of my dates said to me."

"Ha." Neil kept knocking.

Within moments, the door was answered by a slight man with a moustache, wearing a full-length white lab coat. "Doctor. Como está?" He was all smiles.

"Fine, Chris," answered Neil. "How are you doin'? This is my friend Ira."

"Doctor. It is a pleasure to meet you," said Chris. He acted as if he had just met royalty.

"If you need anything having to do with cadavers, Chris runs this whole place," said Neil.

"That's good to know," Ira said with a facetious tone.

"How's your cadaver? If you don't like, Chris will get you a new one." Chris was still holding onto the door.

"Actually, what we need Chris is someone to help with the electric at a place my friend Ira has in Venice."

"The vent on the stove is also out of whack," said Ira. "And the bread steamer is broken."

"Sure. No problem. Let me take a look." Chris was always enthusiastic. "I can come after I work at the tennis club, or if you want, I can come on my next day off, which I think is a Sunday, next week."

"Here's my number. The one on the bottom is the deli," said Neil.

"Deli. You say deli? You know I can cook. I make great tacos, enchiladas, you name it." More work meant more money.

"Well. It's sort of an old-fashioned deli," said Ira.

"Whoops," said Neil. He knew that that would only encourage Chris.

"Are you kidding? I help the chef all the time at the Beverly Hills Tennis Club. I know how to make a good pastrami sandwich, a pot roast, kasha. What? You think it's so hard?"

"No," said Ira. "I just don't think we'll need another cook. We need some help with the wiring, and that vent over the stove, things that are broken."

"Sure. Sure. No problem. Let Chris take care of it for you."

"Call me," said Neil.

"You got it, Doctor. I will call you soon." Chris took the card.

"Nice to meet you," said Ira.

"Yes. My pleasure." Chris was all smiles.

Neil and Ira headed down the hall. Chris followed them into the hallway. Neil waved goodbye again. Chris waved back and said, "You come back anytime. If your friend needs anything, you can always count on Chris."

"Thanks," said Neil. "See you around the club."

The two made their way down the corridor. Neil was not about to let up. "I feel like having a nice bowl of guacamole. With a side of tuna and lots of mayo."

"Fine. That sounds good to me." Ira was firm. "You think you can make me sick. You can't."

"You're right. You already are."

"Let's just hope Chris can do the work."

"He's a pro at hustling gringos." Neil meant it as a comfort to Ira.

244

As they squeezed into Neil's white Rabbit convertible, Ira thought about his grandfather. It was time to put in a call. Ira was worried that he would be too busy to take care of the deli, and didn't know if he could trust Neil to follow through on his promises.

On the way out of the parking structure, Neil slowed the car as they passed the loading areas in back of the medical school. "I guess this is where all the stuff gets delivered," said Neil.

"Huh? Yeah," said Ira. He wasn't paying much attention. He felt his anxiety skyrocket as he pondered the enormous task ahead. He was overwhelmed by the thought of how much work was coming. There was Anatomy, Histology, and Microbiology in September. The list never ended.

"You know what they call a Jew who can't stand the sight of blood?" asked Neil, interrupting Ira's series of anxious thoughts.

"What, Neil?" Ira moaned.

"A lawyer!" exclaimed Neil as if he had just won the first prize as a comedian on *Star Search*.

On the way home they had a huge fight over whether or not Garry Shandling was funny.

"The guy acts mean. It's just not funny," said Ira.

"That's what's funny," said Neil. "Don Rickles could be mean and funny at the same time."

They went back and forth until both were exhausted from the argument.

After that night, Neil became overly interested in helping Ira. He didn't know much about the deli business, but he learned quickly. "Let's do this right. I smell money here," was something that he repeated over and over.

Neil was shocked to find that simple meat made such a good deli sandwich. The first batch that he and Ira concocted was a basic steamed brisket. Ira needed only to copy the steps he had seen performed by Mel.

The responses to the sandwiches were generally mixed. The major criticism was that the sandwich was too dry. Neil enthusiastically went around to all the delis, trying to find out how to make the sandwich moister. Most of the answers centered on the use of condiments.

But it was in the old Langer's restaurant, near downtown Los Angeles, that Neil struck pay dirt. The patriarch of the business was behind the counter when Neil asked how Langer's sandwich stayed so moist.

"We steam the rye bread," Mr. Langer said with confidence and authority. It was the voice of a man whose business had withstood the test of time, changing communities, and a fluctuating client base. It was also one of the things Mel Packer had done until his machine broke. Mr. Langer showed Neil a larger machine than the one in Mel's deli.

Neil 'grilled' Mr. Langer for a half-hour. Neil went away with plenty of Mr. Langer's secrets for the basic sandwich.

Still, Neil had other ideas. He wanted to rename the deli, The Hollywood Deli. Ira wasn't sure at first, but he was delighted that Neil was taking such an interest in the cuisine and did not want to ruin his enthusiasm.

"This is really great of you." said Ira. "I'll run the name by Mel."

Neil answered, "Well. It's just an idea, but I think we can really build this place into something again. We've got the best location. The rest won't be easy, but it is surely possible." He was able to locate a machine like the one in Langer's at a restaurant supply company in Marina Del Rey. While he was there, he bought everything from salt and peppershakers to napkin holders, all in the style of an old fifties deli.

The reserve that Ira's grandfather had left in case of emergency was used to patch the tile floor and the old red leather booths. Eventually, at Donny's suggestion and wherewithal, they decided to sell t-shirts, sweatshirts and hats, a known moneymaker, especially since the success of places like The Hard Rock Cafe, where the markup on clothing was infinitely greater than that of the food and beverages.

Everything was falling into place, everything except the sandwich. Despite the fact that Neil had made it more moist, and the responses were growing more positive, it wasn't selling much more than before. The deli sold all the classic types of sandwiches - brisket, pastrami, corned beef, and roast beef. The answer became apparent once Neil toured the fast-food places. He thought that they should come up with some kind of special sauce, in addition to offering all the basic sandwiches. Since barbecue and salsa were so popular in California, he simply mixed up vats of various combinations of the two, sort of a hot barbecue sauce. People liked it, and the sandwich sales picked up, particularly on Reubens with different dressings.

Ira knew Neil well enough to know that he had to be watched. *What possible harm could come from Neil's enthusiasm?* Instead of calling, Ira wrote Mel about the progress; he liked to receive mail. His grandfather could not have been more pleased.

Despite all that, Ira was still concerned that something was wrong at the deli. One night after work, he tossed and turned and couldn't get back to sleep. He rolled off his bed and pulled on a pair of sweat pants. He slipped his bare feet into already laced basketball sneakers, the same ones that he often wore to work or to shoot hoops on the beach.

Once he arrived at the back of the deli, he knew that his instinct was right. There were sauce spills everywhere, and the door to the cellar was broken open. There was a clear trail of hot sauce leading from the door. Now he knew it. Neil's sauce was dangerous, and had escaped from the deli.

A sheriff pulled up outside the deli in an old black-and-white patrol car. "You the owner?" he said in a gruff voice. He looked like a cross between the late John Candy and Broderick Crawford.

"Yes. What's wrong?" Ira kept his distance.

"You don't know? Your hot sauce escaped and it's ravaging the countryside. Seems anyplace with open water is in danger. That sauce must have been too hot. It's seeking water. It needs water."

"He just mixed some barbecue sauce with some salsa," said Ira.

"Boy. Which is it? Are we looking for a barbecue sauce here or are we looking for salsa?"

"I don't know." Ira felt dizzy.

Like an old country sheriff, the officer talked into his radio's handheld microphone with a twisted cord. "What we got here is an angry hot sauce. I don't know yet if it's a barbecue or a salsa. We have not identified it. We do know one thing - it's hot, and it's after water. It needs water. Put out an all-points bulletin for a, for a, for a killer hot sauce," said the sheriff. "Ten-four."

Ira shot up in bed. He glanced at the clock. *Time to go to work*.

By dusk at the deli, the boys continued their discussions about how to improve business. "The best deli in New York is not the issue. The issue is, what elements from what delis do we want?" asked Ira. "I'm talking only Jewish/Kosher style here. We can't go overboard and try and incorporate Balducci's or Dean and DeLuca here."

"They opened a Carnegie Deli in Beverly Hills and look what happened. Poof! Gone in less than a couple of years," said Neil. "Balducci's took its place and now that's gone too."

"That's the problem," said Ira. "You can't just import a New York name. I don't think people who live in Los Angeles have the same taste buds as a New Yorker."

"That's funny, but what is the real problem?" asked Neil. He emphasized the word 'what'.

"Let me explain."

"Please do. You can't just open a New York style deli here and expect it to succeed."

"Thank you, Mr. Zagat."

"That's funny, too. Mr. Zagat," repeated Neil. "I like that, but don't you see what I'm saying? You can't just open some New York kind of place. You know what I mean?"

"I know what you mean, but do you know what I mean? We're saying the same thing, more or less. God. You're making me sound like Pee-wee Herman," said Ira.

"You don't have the hair, but the voice, maybe," said Neil.

"Are you going to let me explain?"

Neil grabbed a dining chair and turned it around so that he could lean his arms on the back. "Shoot."

Ira took out notes attached to a clipboard filled with yellow and pink receipts that he had placed under the counter. "You actually know what you're talking about, but you don't know why." Ira gestured with his hand to stop when he saw what appeared to be a mounting protest from Neil. "You're right. You can't just open a New York styled deli. It's not enough. The Valley and West L.A. are filled with delis that are okay, but they just have the style, and in some cases, only a little. The

Carnegie Deli that they opened here was a massive restaurant, with a huge menu, and they weren't doing anything close with the meat like Leo Steiner and the others did in New York. They bought the name, but the food was about the same as the deli in Caesar's Palace, Las Vegas. Just okay. And nobody worked a crowd better than Leo."

"You've been doing your homework."

"I didn't want you to show me up."

"Where did you get all this stuff?"

"Most of it I already knew from listening to my grandfather. There are probably four really, really good delis in New York. I'm talking Manhattan here. There's the Carnegie, Katz's, Second Avenue, and the Stage. Some people might throw in Sarge's. There are specialty delis that have huge followings like Fine & Schapiro, the Pastrami King, Russ and Daughters, and Barney Greengrass. Even the Barney Greengrass that they opened in Beverly Hills is nothing like the one in New York. First of all, it's in Barney's, the department store, which is way too much of an upscale store to be associated with 'The Sturgeon King'. I went in there once and stared at chopped liver that had been Hollywoodized with garnish. It was a shame. That's part of the problem with Hollywood. The real thing never seems to be right or enough. It's like how they hire experts to sit and watch while they make movies, but the movie people end up doing whatever they want, even though they hired someone who has authentic information. They did that with the chopped liver at Barney Greengrass. They made a Hollywood movie version. We can't do that. We should have the best, and it should be real. I made a list. Authentic is the key word."

Neil was hypnotized.

Ira referred to his notes as he spoke. "Katz's pastrami sandwich is probably one of the best, if not the best. If we can do that or anything close, we've got it made. For anything else, we can't go wrong by just copying the Carnegie. I'm talking just food now. We should avoid Hollywoodizing our food. We can make the place a little Hollywood, but not too much. We have to shoot for a basic sandwich that is under ten bucks. Whether that will be the actual price is debatable, but we can't go wrong with the basic pastrami on rye," said Ira.

Neil raised his hand as if he were in a classroom.

"Yes," said Ira. "The boy in the front."

"Don't you think we should offer some kind of variation? After all, this is Venice Beach. We agreed we might call it The Hollywood Deli."

"I know what you mean. Sure. As long as we offer the real thing. Did you have something in mind?"

"Keep going, professor," said Neil.

"Okay. I know. We don't have to decide that today." Ira returned to reviewing his notes. "We can have triple-deckers and those giant sandwiches like the old Carnegie Deli double, but remember nobody finishes those, and our waiters will be spending a lot of time wrapping food to go. So the price of this kind of sandwich might push close to twenty bucks."

"Too much," said Neil.

"I know," Ira continued. He took out a blue highlight marker from his pocket and made a mark on his notes. "We don't have to worry about service. Nobody really wants great service in a good deli. It's the food. We have to try to be consistent. That's the major failing of any deli. But here's the thing that I think will make us big."

Neil leaned in closer.

"We should stay open all night," said Ira. "Twenty-four hours. That way will get the club business."

Neil was clearly disappointed with the vision of the work involved, but knew that people would flock to the place, particularly because of the location. "Naw. I don't know. Maybe we can open early and close later or something."

"All night. People will hang out here all night and order breakfast before they go," said Ira. "Donny will watch the place for us."

"Maybe," said Neil. It was sounding better if Ira didn't expect him to baby-sit the place all night.

"Let's see. Those were the major general ideas. I doubt if we can come close to anything New York, but we can try," said Ira. "It's really how the meat tastes. All three major meats come from the same cut - the pastrami, corned beef, and brisket."

"I didn't know that." Neil squirmed in his chair. "Can we have updated celebrity sandwiches, you know, named after famous people who aren't dead?"

"I guess so," said Ira. He hadn't thought about it before. "That's not the key. The meat is the key."

"I know, but it costs so much. Can't we substitute something in the beginning?"

"What do you have in mind?"

"Can't we buy cheaper meat? I'm not talking Spam here, but maybe some already prepared roast beef. You know, the cheap stuff, like they serve in any coffee shop. With the sauce on it, who will know?"

"Come on, Neil. After all the research? You know better than that."

Neil did know better than that, but it bothered him. There was a great opportunity here, and he wanted to be sure that they maximized their profit. He had some other ideas, but he realized at that moment that if he couldn't sell Ira on the idea of the

cheap roast beef, there was no sense talking to him anymore
about cutting corners. Neil knew that Ira didn't have his sense
for business. Neil thought nothing about using shortcuts – of
any kind.

CHAPTER NINE
Brantley
Brantley, Liz

I had written Lilly in New York a longish letter about my dilemma - how I was having trouble adjusting to my new life. She wrote me back more or less an "I told you so" version of her reality. I didn't know which hurt more, the obvious dig about knowing that I wouldn't or couldn't fit in or the fact that in the last paragraph she announced her engagement to Mr. Juice Futures. He had made another killing in orange juice by shorting the unexpected Florida frost, and in an equally chilling fashion dumped his first wife before the new cash windfall materialized.

I made the rounds at the local dental association to ask for leads about additional part-time employment or joining an established practice as an associate. I had been renting space and while I was covering my expenses, it probably was not the best long-term solution. The secretary, someone who looked like she had just stepped out of a suntan oil commercial, supplied me with a list of names of doctors looking for associates. I didn't think I was ready for that, because it would be leading to a permanency I wasn't sure about. Hollywood life and all that went with it wasn't for everyone. She sat at a desk, with a computer at her side.

As I spoke, my eyes dropped to stare at her breasts, a
common misogynistic habit I had yet to lose. People in Hollywood
were much cooler about breasts than New Yorkers. Try walking
past a construction site in Manhattan wearing anything
suggestive. No big deal around Beverly Hills. People were used
to bare navels and jutting breasts.

I stared without trying to conceal my interest. My eyes
caught hers. She looked back at me with total disinterest. For a
second, I thought I knew her, but that was impossible.

"I'm a little new out here. Where does a guy go to have
some fun?" I know it was the schmuck thing of all times to come
out with.

"What?" she asked, trying to appear put off by the change
and nature of the question.

"Hey. I'm Brantley", I said, remembering not to use my last
name. Everyone I met always used first names.

"Laurie," she said. "Where are you from?" Her speech was
cautious.

"New York. The rotten apple." I suddenly knew. The last big
night of debauchery in Manhattan. She was there. *Not possible*, I
thought.

"New York City?" she asked, making the confirmation clear
in her mind.

"Yes. The city."

"I've always wanted to go New York." She sounded insincere.

I wasn't going to spoil it. I know that I was embarrassed.
"Good. We'll go together. Next week. I have to go back to get
some more of my things shipped out here."

She laughed, revealing blinding bright teeth that followed
her lip line forever. Half the people I had met had intimidating
teeth. I thought that they must have all been bonded or bleached

or something. The new thing was to file down the front teeth and paste on teeth that looked exactly like everyone else's.

I persisted, but asked myself if she was the woman from New York why was I continuing on automatic? "So where does a guy go? You're single, right?"

"Yes. But I have a boyfriend...Sort of," said Laurie as she uncrossed her legs and stood up from the desk.

I couldn't see, but a man had entered the room behind me.

"Great. Then why don't you and I have dinner?" I asked.

Laurie extended her hand. "I hope you find someone to hire you," she said without skipping a beat. The dating conversation was inappropriate in front of whoever had entered.

"Good morning, Laurie," said the man as he passed by without slowing down.

Once he walked down the hall and disappeared into another maze of offices Laurie moved closer. "Okay. I'll take a chance. Here's my number. If I'm not there the machine will give you my voice mail and beeper numbers. Call me," she said in an almost dismissive tone.

"Okay. Great. I will." Now I wasn't sure. She did look slightly different. "I'll call you." After my episode with Heather, I was beginning to think that everyone I met was someone I had met before. I was developing a new version of prejudice: *All you Californians look alike.*

"I've got to get back to work," she said with a deliberately coy, seductive smile.

"Okay. Bye. I'll call you." I was becoming a little flustered.

"Okay. You said that." She moved to sit back down at the desk.

"Bye." I turned to leave.

When the night to meet Laurie for dinner had arrived, I readied my apartment for a carefully planned social evening. I thought back to my life in New York. I told myself that I was in control. I was in California now, and things would be different. Like many addictive personalities, I deluded myself with thoughts of self-control, sensitivity, and passion. I still had none of these attributes when it came to women, particularly if Laurie was who I thought she was. What were the chances? Whatever sensitivities I had were usually lost in a haze of intoxication.

My evening with Laurie proved to be a repeat of the past. I told myself that it was a learning curve, like the dips in a stock market graph, or cheating on a diet. The truth of the matter was that I suffered from some kind of social and sexual arrested development, and was a patsy to repeat my mistakes.

Laurie had agreed to meet first at my apartment. "Do you have any vodka?" she asked in response to a drink offer moments after her arrival.

The plan was to have a drink or two, watch the sunset, and then walk along Sunset Boulevard. We would have dinner at one of the great local restaurants.

"Sure," I answered. "Do you want it with orange juice? I can make a great sunrise with vodka. I make it in the blender, with crushed ice."

"Sounds good," she answered. She stood at the big plate glass window overlooking the expansive house lights on the hill behind my apartment building. The foliage was lit in alternating shadows and some bright greens. "It sure is beautiful here."

"It's very convenient to Beverly Hills."

"Have you found a place to move your practice yet?" she asked.

"Not yet, but I have a few leads. I have enough work., so I think I should start working toward getting my own office."

Laurie had done some research on my behalf. "You should call Dr. Harry Pollack. He's really well-known, and he's in Beverly Hills.

"That's a good idea." My mind wasn't on the job.

I reflexively added a chopped up 'Roofie' to the blender. "You're really going to like this." I know, but it was still very popular. I'm confessing to its political incorrectness, although the media-cursed date-rape drug was still the darling of too many health professionals and social acquaintances.

"Would you like one of these?" My conscious would be clear if she accepted.

"What's that?" she asked as she took another pill in her hand.

"Ever seen one before?"

"Never." It lacked any truthful impact.

"I already added one to the drinks." *Ah, a full disclosure.* Laurie shrugged her shoulders. "Okay."

I learned that she worked part-time as a dental hygienist.

After one and one half of the vodka drinks, Laurie slumped down against the sofa. "Boy. I never got this looped before on a few drinks," she said. "I'd better go home and sleep it off. I have to work tomorrow."

"If that's what you would like." I wasn't sure what I wanted to do. I was feeling the concoction myself. "I'll drop you off." I was still using Mickey's loaner.

"No, thanks. It's easy to get a taxi." She picked up her purse.

"Are you sure?"

Then, a familiar discussion.

Laurie rummaged through her purse. "I left my wallet at home."

"I was getting dinner, anyway. Not to worry. I can give you money for a taxi." But that wasn't her concern.

"Oh, great. I wonder if you could help me. I have a check here from an office I work in. It's for eight hundred dollars. Could you cash it?"

That did it. She was definitely the girl from Manhattan or a clone. She had done the same thing in New York. But, what was she doing out here? My cloudy thoughts centered on immediate sex. What was the difference what she was doing here? I knew the routine that was coming as well as the answer to my question, still driven by my same low self-esteem and years of overdoing things. I had always been hustled in New York, and I could not stop myself from sliding backward. "Well. Eight hundred is a lot. How much do you need to hold you over for the weekend?" We settled for a lesser amount, and the business negotiation was over. And Laurie suddenly perked up.

The next morning I felt pretty dumb. Laurie was gone before I woke up. She had taken the remaining vodka, a second bottle in the cabinet, and the plastic bottle of Roofies that I had left on the kitchen counter. I found a note in place of the missing things. "Call me. I had a nice time. Laurie."

I felt like I had been the victim of a 'date rape'. What a reversal of social realities. I tried to make up my mind about Laurie. In New York she was essentially a call girl, while on the west coast she was also a part-time hygienist. Then I recalled that the check she gave me in New York was a dentist's. What a great combo. I thought if I ever saw her again I would try to confirm her unusual but practical dual occupations. Then I told myself that if I ever wanted to straighten out, I should cross Laurie off my social register.

259

I soon got in touch with Dr. Harry Pollack, a
septuagenarian who looked much younger. He was clearly the
Douglas Fairbanks of root canal specialists. We hit it off
instantly, and Dr. Harry, as he liked to be called, made me an
offer on the spot.

"I'll get you started. I'll pay for everything. You get
forty percent. Fair? When you get going we can rethink the whole
thing."

"Yes. It sounds very fair." I thought I should have gotten
a slightly higher percentage, but Dr. Harry seemed like a
straight shooter. He didn't know what to expect either; Beverly
Hills was filled with a revolving door of young associate
doctors.

Sean had sent me an invitation to attend a party at Bvlgari
in Beverly Hills. The card mentioned wine; that was a big enough
hook for me. When I arrived, the store was already crowded with
the regular mix of party hoppers. The outside resembled a mini
movie premiere, with bouncers in dark suits blocking the door
and paparazzi barricaded behind maroon velour ropes.

I couldn't locate Sean anywhere, so I quickly found a
waiter and helped myself to a glass of white wine. I drifted
around the room trying not to stare too much at the celebrities.
I stopped at a vacant corner, and rested against the wall. I
sipped my wine - it was really tart, part of the local
fascination with any kind of chardonnay - and eavesdropped on a
nearby conversation. A handsome man was doing most of the
talking. He looked familiar. He was talking to a woman wearing
jeans with a halter top and a button down sweater.

"I heard that ABC is looking for a local anchor for the
six-thirty," the man informed her.

"That's great Charlie, but what about me?" asked the woman.

"This is about you. If I can get it, I'll make you part of the deal. If I go, you go. That's what I've always promised."

The woman became visibly upset. She moved closer to the man and stared directly into his eyes. She dropped the register of her voice, but I could still hear her speak. It was an annoyed, loud kind of whisper. "Charlie. How the fuck long do you think I can go up in that damn helicopter. I still have to put on a Depends every fucking morning. I am scared of heights. I told you that, and you told me if I took the job, I would get a desk job in a few months. Charlie. It's been almost two years. Two years of Dramamine and diapers."

Charlie smiled.

She kicked him in the shins.

"Hey. Don't get angry with me," said Charlie. "It's better than dragging your portfolio around town trying to get commercials."

This time she threw the last of her chardonnay on his suit, turned, and scurried out of the store.

"Susan. Wait!" Charlie took off in pursuit.

By that time I had figured out that Charlie was one of the anchors on a local station, and that Susan gave the traffic reports from the helicopter.

I turned, to avoid staring at Charlie as he zoomed past.

A well-dressed man, wearing a herringbone blazer and a bright gold vest with a pocket watch chain, caught my eye. He waltzed right up to me and started a conversation, something that reminded me of my New York roots.

"There are only two things that can happen at a party like this," said the man. He wrinkled his lip which moved his graying handlebar moustache from side to side.

"Oh, what's that?"

"Get laid or get loaded."

I chuckled. "That's it, huh?"

He turned to greet a young woman. "Liz. How are you?"

She spoke to him. "Ed. Have you accomplished your party goals yet?" To me, "I'm Liz. What's your name, Scooter? No, wait. You look more like a T. J." She was petite, with shiny blonde hair.

"Brantley."

"God. That's boring," she said. "What are you drinking?"

"Chardonnay, I think. You want a sip - it's god awful!"

"Yuck! No thanks. I didn't know Jews drank that stuff," she said.

"Watch out for her, she's a tricky one," said Ed. He was off into the crowd.

"You know him?"

"Yeah. Everyone knows Ed. He worked in the publicity department for Lou Mayer, Darryl Zanuck and Joe Levine. The Hollywood lore has it that he was standing dick-to-dick at a urinal with Joe and told him to go fuck himself. When Ed got back to his office there was a formal letter telling him to get packing."

I laughed. "What makes you think I'm Jewish?"

"Lucky guess, plus the fact that that lady over there…"

"Where?" I craned to span the room.

"In the corner. See the one in the green sweater. The one who looks like she walked into Neiman's and asked to be personally gift wrapped for Christmas," Liz said, pointing across the room.

"You are cruel, but I like it."

"Come on. She looks like she should be hanging from the Christmas tree at Rockefeller Center."

"Yeah. So what about her?"

262

"I guess you probably would recognize her if you were staring down her tongue."

"What?"

"You're her Endodontist. She told me. So I put two and two together. Beverly Hills, root canal specialist. Prominent Nose. Must be Jewish. It was easy to eliminate the Pacific Rim, and most of the Middle East. In fact, I'd lay odds you were from New York."

"The accent?"

"Three-to-one. Dead giveaway," she said, waving her hand across the front of her body for emphasis.

"You're funny. Can I get you a drink?

"Well, Scooter. That's a fine idea."

We trailed one of the waiters, finally getting his attention.

"Is this a sample or a glass of wine?" Liz asked, eyeing the paltry portion.

"Listen. I don't have any plans tonight. Would you like to go over to Le Dome and have something to eat?" It was worth a try, and I didn't feel that I was up to my old tricks. The show-off in me came out – the fact that I picked such an expensive Hollywood hangout. I had already become Hollywoodized.

Liz set me straight. "Not a chance. I've got to go back to the office. But I will take a rain check. But does it have to be there? I'm tired of all those company hangouts. What are you doing there anyway? Looking for celebrity abscesses or something?"

"No. I just like the food, and they let me smoke a cigar in the front of the restaurant. You know - that little section that they built out in front?"

She mimicked me. "I get it. The front of the restaurant, where they built out a section, in the front. Right."

"Are you making fun of me?"

"Why would I do that? You do it enough on your own."

"I'm not sure how to take you."

"Take me to dinner and find out. Call my office. Just call CAA and ask for Liz Roth. Do you want me to write it down or should I just call you and save you the trouble of trying to remember my name and where I work?"

"No. I can handle it. Are you sure you wouldn't want to meet me later, after you finish your work? I've got some Ecstasy and Roofies in my office bag." *Whoops. Old tricks.*

"Been there. Done that. Nobody takes that stuff anymore. Don't tell me you still take drugs to go get laid. I thought that was a college thing."

"It was a joke." *More or less.*

"No it wasn't. You were doing the test," Liz said, finishing off the rest of her wine.

"The 'test'?"

"Yeah. The I'm-gonna-see-if-she's-a-bimbo test. It's what they used to call the slam-bam-thank-you-ma'am. You know. The Hollywood actress/model/whatever test, 'Like let's go back to my place and smoke something, but first you get undressed while I call my dealer. The next thing you know three days have gone by and you still can't remember the girl's name'."

"That's very funny." *And accurate.*

"I don't know about you. Jewish, Endodontist. I like you Scooter, but you better get the ground rules straight here. If you want to live the wild life, call an escort service. I don't need some sexually immature guy to show up on the third date with a set of handcuffs and a little kit that used to be used to melt wax seals on envelopes. I like my sex the old-fashioned way, devoid of Band-Aids, two-headed vibrators, and spandex. Am I getting through to you?" she asked, exhaling in a way that made the air flip her blonde bangs off her forehead. "If not, I'd like to say that I just had a very pleasant waste of my time." She extended her hand to shake.

I laughed nervously and took her hand. "No. No. That's not me." *What a lie.* "Look. I'll call you. How about a little Japanese place on Third, across from Cedars." I was referring to the massive hospital filled with walls of art and surrounded by streets and buildings named after entertainment celebrities like George Burns and Steven Spielberg.

"You have a deal." Liz zoomed off into the crowd. She turned back to ogle me. She shouted, "You might do. Just might…By the way, the owner, Katsu, is a friend of mine."

I smiling. Liz nodded and waved goodbye with a sweep of her right hand. She turned away and then quickly glanced back. She shook her head, chuckled, and darted out of sight.

Over the next few weeks, I spent a lot of time with Liz. She was bright, funny, and attractive. She had a calming effect on me, and seemed interested in giving me real business advice on writing.

"Content. You make me feel content," I said as I drove her Black Chevy Suburban along Santa Monica Boulevard. She preferred to have me drive when she had a lot of cell phone calls to make.

We were on our way to Morton's, the trendy show biz hangout. Liz had played tennis many times with manager Pam Morton, daughter of Arnie and twin sister to the Hard Rock Café restauranteur and Morton's founder, Peter. Liz could always get a table. She went there mostly for business, but told me that "At least they have good food and a great wine list". We had avoided these types of places up to now.

I was getting used to Liz's direct personality, but I became defensive when she hit me with this. "You've been spending too much time with bimbos."

"What do you mean by….?" I asked, drawing out the words 'mean by' without having to say the word 'bimbos'.

"You just as much told me so yourself," said Liz. "Too many drugged out nights, just about sex. Borrrring!" She sang the last word, twisting it in her breath, and spit it out at me with the accuracy of a laser pointer.

"Okay. You made your point. Where do I turn for Melrose?"

"That's it," she said, pointing.

"Which one?"

"The next one."

"Right."

"Not to be confused with left."

"I meant 'okay'. " We turned onto the beginning of fashionable Melrose.

"I hope this doesn't turn into an Abbott and Costello routine."

"You like them?"

"Not exactly. There's an assistant baby agent at my company, this really obsessive guy named Brian, whose boss has a writer as a client who's like a walking encyclopedia of comedians. He had us over to his house. He was showing a double feature of Abbott and Costello, the one with the French Foreign Legion and other was the Invisible Man.

"That must have been great. I watched them a lot when I was a child."

Liz slowly turned her head and stared. "I don't know about this new development."

"Well not everybody likes them. It's an acquired taste, sort of like drinking Fernet-Branca."

"At least Fernet-Branca can cure an upset stomach instead of giving you one."

"Well, I like them. I think they're funny."

Liz shook her head in mock dismay. "Scooter. You just lost any hope of being totally resurrected by me. There's Morton's. Turn into the lot and give it to the valets."

I had a feeling that she meant it.

Monday night dinner at Morton's was still mostly the real thing. The room was filled with company town regulars, plus insider doctors, lawyers, and accountants. When the room was full, an uneven mix of sound waves reverberated off the ceiling and walls, making it virtually impossible to hear anything, which made a great venue for an actor to scream at a studio head without anyone knowing what they were saying. The pulsating sometimes reached a bad Richter scale reading, creating little quakes for the ears.

We made a beeline for the bar.

A friendly voice shot out. "Hi."

Liz turned to see Godfrey Edwards, the seventy-five-year-old manager of the Beverly Hills Tennis Club. He was beaming as he toasted her with his Scotch and soda.

"Hi," answered Liz.

He had held the job on and off for forty years, and was as much a fixture around the club in the old days as was Walter Matthau, Sinatra, or Kirk Douglas. Then the club's population was more movie stars than lawyers. But times had changed. Younger movie stars didn't relate to the local tennis club scene. The sense that Beverly Hills was Hollywood no longer existed and vice versa. Beverly Hills had become more a small piece of the international film community.

Godfrey had three 'assistant managers' working for him. That kind of cushion allowed him to pursue other interests, particularly in business. He arranged deals for many of the members, often getting a piece of the action for setting things up. He had a very sound knowledge of business structure, and was occasionally hired by small startup companies to initiate and coddle business plans.

Godfrey, at first glance, was a rather elegant, well-dressed polite man. Judging by his appearance, it would have been difficult to guess that he had been married five times, with one children with each wife, plus two children out of wedlock.

"It must have been the drinking," was Godfrey's stock answer.

He was almost tossed out of the tennis club when one disgruntled religious busboy found Godfrey freebasing cocaine in his office. The busboy complained to one of the board members. Godfrey had occasionally dated the executive's former wife, to his constant irritation. The axe-to-grind board member tried to get Godfrey ousted, but it was an impossible task. Godfrey was glued to many members through his business favors and introductions, but for some it was simply arranging 'dates'. During the sixties, Godfrey threw many afterhours parties that began at the club, making sure that none of the wives were close by. When things became too hot, Godfrey moved the party to his apartment, where the expression sex, drugs, and rock and roll seemed polite compared to the actual activities.

"Nice to see you again. You're the agent, right?" asked Godfrey.

"Right. I know you. You're - "

"Godfrey, from the BHTC." He was quick not to embarrass Liz, in case she had forgotten his name.

"This is Dr. Brantley Benjamin," she said.

"Nice to meet you." I shook Godfrey's hand.

"You must be from the East Coast," said Godfrey.

"How can you tell that? I've hardly said anything."

"You shake hands like a man. Most of these guys out here are pulling their hand back before you even touch them. I think they're afraid of picking up bad karma."

"Or a communicable disease," added Liz.

Godfrey laughed. "The fact is, Dr. Benjamin, that it's a power thing. The firm shake is reserved for only those who are important. Most of these guys," he continued, as he surveyed the room, "usually give you the left hand, affectionately nicknamed the Beverly Hills shake."

"I know what you mean. I've come across that."

"You are from New York, right?"

"Right."

"What kind of doctor are you?"

"Don't take him near anyone with a tooth fetish," said Liz.

"Oh, could you do business in this place," said Godfrey. "Let me guess. A young, good-looking guy like you. You're in Beverly Hills. Am I right?"

"Bingo," said Liz. "And he's writing screenplays."

"Why not? You can't just be a doctor in this town. How boring. Can I buy you two a drink?"

"Sure," I said. Godfrey was easy to like.

We sat at the smallish bar.

"So what's new over at the tennis joint?" asked Liz.

"Nothing much. Say. You know, I got the board to start trial memberships. It's really cheap, and there's no obligation. A bunch of agents from Maple Drive have joined. It's fun. And there's more tennis action. Why don't you call me? I'll get you in," answered Godfrey. His promotion came off as a soft sell, only informative, not pushy. South of Santa Monica Boulevard, Maple Drive featured several plush office buildings, including the famous restaurant named after the street. Several movie stars had production offices in the buildings.

"I don't know. The last time I was there, the place was filled with lawyers and land developers," said Liz. "It seemed all about money." The Maple Drive comment was not lost on Liz; she knew the massive office building across from the club.

"It is!" exclaimed Godfrey. "It is, my dear. Isn't everything?"

The conversation was interrupted by the bland, disinterested hostess announcing that our table was ready. After all, who the hell were we?

"Got to go," said Liz.

"Call me about the tennis?" Godfrey asked. He mimed the act of using the telephone, the overused symbol of a telephone society, thumb and pinky pointing out to form the end of the Marcel Marceau phone.

"Is he for real?" I asked as we zigzagged to the table. If she answered "no" I knew that I would be disappointed.

"As real as anyone else in this town. Godfrey is a survivor. He knows how to survive in this town. He's a good guy to know."

"Maybe he can teach me how to survive."

"We all could use a few lessons." She sounded as if she meant it.

The dinner conversation was new to me. Liz had strong opinions on almost every subject. "I am sick of hearing newscasters laugh during the show. What is this new shit? What's next? 'We sent fifty smart bombs into Kabul,' says the handsome talking head dressed in his new Zegna suit. The woman talking head at his side laughs and turns to him as the camera pulls back to go to a commercial. 'That sounds like the shelling you'll get when you get home tonight, Rick.' They laugh at each other as if they were dates at a high school prom. It's that insider's nervous laugh. They can do it on cue. I guess that's why they hire them. While they're laughing, they stick in that little computerized split screen, just a little box of war, and it has Cliff Notes written on the bottom of the screen like something from Sony PlayStation. The camera pulls back and the two jerks keep laughing. I don't know what to look at anymore for the news. Am I supposed to be entertained by these amorphous spirits laughing up the war? And then there's that insert on the screen. It shows the surrealistic fireworks display in Afghanistan with that dull green night scope. It's all very ha-ha-ha. I'm sick of it. I think this is the end of the Walter Cronkite era. For sure."

All I could say was, "you're right," because she had nailed it. We were turning news into only entertainment.

Liz finished the evening on an even stronger note when the waiter said "Let me be honest with you about the desserts." Granted, we had downed a bottle of wine, but I still had to agree with every word she said.

"I can't stand it anymore when people say, 'I've got to be honest with you'. Does it mean everything else they ever told you before was a lie? Why the fuck do people say this? Don't we all know that anyone who says this is chronic liar? But when they have a sense that something is really bad and we might figure it out and be disappointed - like now - so they say it, like they've never lied before, and suddenly they're going to be perfectly honest, which I don't believe either. On the other hand, it could be a total ploy just to upsell us into a more expensive dessert."

As we left the restaurant I asked, "Movie at my place?"

"No thanks, Scooter. It's a school night. I have to be at the office early tomorrow," she said.

"Too bad. I was going to stop at Blockbuster and rent *Abbott and Costello Meet Frankenstein*."

"Rain check. And don't be such a wiseass, Scooter."

I wasn't completely sure about Liz, but I was having a great time.

Liz decided to apply for a trial four-month membership at the Beverly Hills Tennis Club. She was instantly accepted by the board. She was just what they were looking for, a young tennis player who was in the entertainment business, and could afford the monthly dues. Hopefully, if she stayed on after the four months, she could be persuaded to buy one of the expensive 'lifetime' memberships, or a full equity membership in the club.

The club was in the midst of planning a seventy-something anniversary celebration. The literature that Liz was provided pointed out that the club had boasted an impressive membership over the years. Early members were Gilbert Roland, Groucho Marx, and King Vidor. During its heyday, the patio of the Beverly Hills Tennis Club was filled with members like Frank Capra, Billy Wilder, Charlie Chaplin, and Zeppo and Marion Marx. Regulars were Barbara Hutton, Cornelius Vanderbilt, Mrs. Irving Berlin, and Dick and Dorothy Rodgers. And those were just the members. I imagined who those people brought in as guests. In recent years, the club still kept up its power base with Hank Greenberg, Johnny Carson, Neil Simon, Frank Sinatra, Ray Stark, Richard Zanuck, Doris Day, Robert Taylor, Samuel Goldwyn, Jack Warner, William Wyler, John Huston, Lawrence Olivier, Dinah Shore, Walter Matthau, Kirk Douglas, Wayne Rogers, Judge Wapner, and Warren Christopher. The exclusive little group also had some great tennis players, but in Hollywood that didn't seem quite as important. Some of the celebrated tennis names from the Beverly Hills Tennis Club were Perry Jones, Fred Alexander, Ellsworth Vines, Fred Perry, Budge Patty, Frank Parker, Alice Marble, Pauline Betts, Pancho Segura, Arthur Ashe, Jimmy

Connors, and Jonathan Cantor, whose father produced the most recent Tarzan movies. The chic private haven also turned out two great amateur players, Arthur Marx, Groucho's son, and Ronnie Lubin, who won the U.S. Parks Doubles with George Toley. Lubin went on to produce movies and Marx became a writer.

Once Liz was introduced to the members, she quickly became involved in club activities. She ate lunch there at least twice a week, and hung out on the patio on the weekends, where she mingled with most of the active membership. In order to arrange a tennis game, a member only had to call the office, and one of the office staff would set up a game.

Liz suggested that I might try playing in one of the games as her guest. At first I was reticent, but when she said that Wayne Rogers was playing, I accepted. It was shameless, but I was a fan.

"You never know. It won't hurt you to meet people in the business," she said, trying to encourage me. "You have to play the game, and I don't mean tennis."

My tennis game at the Beverly Hills Tennis Club was set up for eight forty-five on a Saturday morning. Liz picked me up at about eight-fifteen, to leave time before the match for coffee at the club.

When we arrived at the club, Liz parallel parked in an alley behind Maple Drive, which adjoined the east end of the courts. The high, green tarpaulin-covered fences were guarded by gargantuan tennis lights, looming over the courts like giant bug eyes. The parking facility for the prestigious club adjoined the garbage bins of the condominium buildings across the alley, an incongruous setting created by onetime loose zoning, the same kind that sometimes sprouted a high-rise building like the Four Seasons Hotel in what otherwise was a peaceful residential community. The alley appeared grimy, with little pieces of

273

windblown garbage dotting the already drab landscape with
freeform colors. As we walked from the middle of one of the
parking lanes to the center of the alley, I counted three Rolls
Royce, six Mercedes, and eight Lexus. The Lexus was the
overwhelming choice of transportation for the mostly Jewish
club, like most of the nearby towns. I wondered if the Japanese
knew when they originally marketed the car that it would become
the status symbol of families from Great Neck, New York to
Beverly Hills. Fifteen years ago the Beverly Hills residential
section known as the 'flats' was dotted with Sevilles or
Lincolns. This hypnotic, collective madness didn't stop at the
cars. Japanese had displaced Chinese as the cuisine of choice.
Families now looked down their surgically-chiseled noses at a
Moo Shoo Pork dinner, opting instead for raw tuna or fake crab
stuffed into the shape of the aptly named American invention -
the California Roll. Dinner at Restaurant Row in Beverly Hills
had become a strange sight. Other than sex, food had become the
new vice. I had witnessed the eager locals valet park their
Lexuses outside pricey Matsuhisa, the hangout for the most
expensive Japanese food anywhere, replete with a full Hollywood
crowd, and backed, no less, by De Niro and Keitel, who took a
liking to the then unknown chef Nobu Matsuhisa. As Liz had said
more than once, "At least the Japanese attempt to take over the
movie business failed, otherwise we might have ended up eating a
hand roll instead of popcorn while watching Kurosawa
retrospectives."

"Buenos Dias," Liz offered to the security guard, who was
already punching an electronic code on a keypad in order to open
the tiny entrance to the back of the club.

As we slipped through the gate, the security guard flashed
us a gratuitous smile. To the right, a nondescript door to the
kitchen had been left wide open. The inside was not surprisingly

antiquated and dirty, as were most older restaurant kitchens in town, while the floor near the entrance was littered with little scraps of paper. Two kitchen workers sat outside on worn fabric folding chairs, eating from paper plates that rested uncomfortably on their laps. Another plate of half-eaten food sat on the ground nearby, obviously abandoned by the security guard in order to open the gate for us.

We continued through a ridiculously narrow path between a tennis court and the main building. I could see people playing through the translucent green tarp. The path led past a concrete stairway and opened onto a little patio, smaller than most of the members' backyards.

"This is it," said Liz. "Let's go in."

We made a right turn and opened an aluminum framed glass door, the entry to a quaint little dining area, complete with a clearly out-of-place giant-screened television. A few members dressed in tennis garb were sipping coffee or juice, while a potpourri of non-tennis playing members was having a full breakfast, with some heads buried in newspapers.

I felt it odd that after we sat down that nobody came to serve us. I glanced around.

"It's more or less like a self-serve, unless you can get one of the guys out of the back," said Liz. She jumped to her feet and made her way over to a little pass-through window that led into the kitchen.

"Hello? Anyone there? Gabino?" she yelled. No response.

Liz moved to her right and pushed a swinging door that obviously led to the kitchen. She disappeared inside and returned with a Starbucks coffee pourer and two cups. She brought it over to the table and placed a cup in front of me.

"Black, right?" she asked as she poured.

"Yes. And I'm not making the obvious joke."

"Why not?"

"It's too early."

Just then, a handsome youngish man made an entrance through the aluminum door.

"Charlie. Get your ass over here. I want you to meet the root canal doctor," Liz said.

Charlie was all smiles as he sat down at the table. He offered his hand to me and said, "I'm Charlie Saffan."

"Brantley Benjamin." We shook hands.

"Charlie's our fourth," she said. "All we need now is Wayne."

"Have you seen him doing that stock stuff on FOX?" asked Charlie.

"Yeah," answered Liz. "I think he's pretty good."

Wayne was known more around the club as a businessman, and his talking-head gig as a stock guru solidified his reputation.

"How does Wayne play?" I asked. It was a long time since I had played regularly and I didn't want to be steamrolled, at least not by an actor.

"Wayne's good. He's got a good solid serve and a strong overhead. He can be tough. How should we play, Liz?" asked Charlie.

"I've already played with Brantley. I'd better play with him," she answered. That told me that Wayne was much better than I was.

"Whoa," laughed Charlie. "I don't think that's much of a compliment."

"I haven't played much, but I'm getting back into it," I said in my defense.

"I checked the 'waiting' cards when I came in. Court three is open. Do you want to hit some balls?" Charlie rose from the table.

"Sure," answered Liz. "Wayne is always on time. I'll get new balls. Brantley, take the coffee with you. I'll meet you on court three," she said.

As we walked toward court three we passed a huge, old-fashioned outdoor pool, complete with a little Jacuzzi. The pool took up most of the patio space, and was surrounded by little tables with umbrellas and lounge chairs reminiscent of mid-level resorts.

Charlie pointed out a little building that housed gym equipment.

"Where are the lockers?" I asked.

"Well, that's the catch. It's up those stairs over the restaurant," said Charlie.

I turned back to the other side of the property. *So much for architectural planning*, I thought. Most of what I had seen in and around Beverly Hills showed little concern for any esthetic or practical continuity.

The tennis game proved unremarkable. Liz was a great player, and could hold her own against most of the male players at the club. Wayne and Charlie did win, but it was close: 6-4, and a 7-3 tiebreaker in the second set.

We all adjourned to an outside patio table for drinks. Charlie ordered a full breakfast of eggs, toast, and bacon. In Beverly Hills, this always came with lettuce and tomato plus a piece of fruit like an orange that tainted the entire flavor of the food.

Wayne was affable, and told a few funny stories.

"You know Brantley is writing screenplays," said Liz.

I choked on my juice.

Wayne's reaction was cautionary, filled with warnings about how tough the business was. He was the first to leave, exiting the club directly from the patio, still in his tennis garb.

277

After Wayne left, the weekend conversation took its usual course.

"*Greek Wedding* did over ten million," said Charlie. "It's been doing great since it opened nationwide."

"I still haven't seen it," said Liz.

"Me either," I said.

I was thinking about the possibility of submitting my screenplay *Small Steaks* to Wayne's production company. I had started working on it after my meeting with Sean. It was almost finished. I didn't know if I should keep asking for Liz's advice; I certainly didn't know how to go about it on my own.

Within minutes, an older man stopped to give Liz a kiss on the cheek.

"Marvin. Meet Dr. Brantley Benjamin."

"Hi. Can I sit?" He already had.

"Please," said Liz.

"Hi Marvin," said Charlie.

"I'm Marvin Kirkwood," he said, staring straight at me. He said it as if I should have recognized his name, like Prince Philip or George Bush.

The conversation became engaging. Marvin spoke about everything from what we should do in Iraq to opera. When Liz sneaked in the fact that I wanted to write, I found Marvin to show detailed, focused interest. And he mostly avoided talking about his career producing movies.

Two weeks later, I was sitting in the Kirkwood's' living room. I had hand delivered my now finished and polished screenplay to Marvin, and he had called within forty-eight hours to schedule a meeting. According to Liz, this was something of a miracle, who said that nobody reads a screenplay that fast, especially for someone that they had just met.

"Maybe he liked what I told him," was my simple answer.

"What did you tell him?"

"Only that it was about first year medical students."

Liz still questioned the situation, but wished me luck nonetheless.

Marvin was married to Rene Kirkwood. She was a pale woman who was deathly and hypochondriacally afraid of the sun, convinced that one sunspot would quickly develop into a full-blown case of basal cell carcinoma, invading her face so fast that doctors would be unable to stop its rapid takeover of her entire body. A lot of people in Hollywoodland were afraid of the sun, but none more convincingly than Rene.

I waited for Marvin in a darkened living room. I didn't know that he was outside playing tennis. The house was deliberately kept dim, and the looming, heavy baroque furniture gave it a Charles Addams touch. As I glanced around the living room, I could only spot a few floor lamps. I sat somewhere between a grandfather clock with roots that appeared to move if I stared, and a candelabra with dark red candles that still had wax drippings filling the base in dizzying patterns. I tried to focus on my conversation with Rene.

"Marvin tells me you wrote a screenplay," she said, sipping her tea in such a way that enabled her to peer over her cup, her eyes firmly fixed on me. The result of her ogling gave me a case of temporary rigor mortis.

"Yes. I did. It's one of the reasons I moved out here, to write." I was beginning to articulate my true motives.

"Aren't you a doctor?"

"Yes. An Endodontist." I was so pleased that she referred to me as a doctor.

"Do you practice anywhere?"

"Yes. In Beverly Hills, on North Bedford Drive."

"I've been a having a problem with a tooth on my right side. Are you familiar with the cold tests?"

"Yes. That's one of the common ones. Sensitivity can be a problem."

She didn't like my answer. "That's the trouble with you doctors. Everything is a problem. More time should be spent on solutions to the problems, and a lot less time making the same mistakes over and over again, and saying things like 'Sensitivity can be a problem'."

Okay, another doctor-hater. There had been plenty in New York. Perhaps she was right, but she caught me off guard and pierced right through my defenses.

Rene placed her cup and saucer back on the coffee table with a calculated show of authority, as if to punctuate her remark.

I tried to explain. "I didn't mean anything…I mean...There are a lot of tests for a proper diagnosis. Have you tried having the bite checked?" I was running through routine things, hoping to show her that I was on her side. I didn't wait for an answer before I asked, "Does it have a crown or an onlay?"

My attempt at mollifying her was lost. "You're Jewish, aren't you?"

"What?"

"Another Jewish Endodontist. Something the world is short of?" She deliberately posed her remark in the form of a question, inflecting a poor New York accent.

I smiled, determined to believe that Rene had a dry sense of humor. "You're right. That's why I want to write. The world doesn't need another root canal specialist."

Then she flipped the conversation elsewhere. "I went to Catholic schools. What a strange experience."

"I'll bet." I was beginning to wonder if this was a set up. I nervously swiveled my head, expecting to see Marvin lurking behind one of the ornate pillars at the entrance to the room. Once Rene had softened me up, he would come in for a kill.

"You have no idea!" she shouted and then leapt to her feet with her arms flailing. "The nuns. The nuns were strict. Sister Mary would check us every morning before school started."

At that moment, Marvin entered the room. He was still in his tennis clothes. His shorts hung well beneath his portly midsection. As he moved toward me, three other tennis players marched silently through the hall behind the living room area, and exited through the front door without one word being uttered or any acknowledgment from Marvin.

"Rene. Thanks for waiting with Brantley" said Marvin. That would be the most upbeat he would appear. He rarely smiled and spoke with an even cadence.

"I was about to tell him about the nuns," said Rene.

"Perhaps another time," said Marvin, in a mildly dismissive tone.

Rene suddenly relaxed, picked up her teacup and saucer, smiled through thin, pale lips, and then exited the room; also in silence. She hardly glanced at Marvin, and he essentially ignored eye contact with her, too.

Marvin extended his hand. "That screenplay was sensational."

I was in shock. Marvin sat with me for over an hour. He had to be one of the brightest men I had come across in Hollywood. Marvin spoke in detail about the characters, and about why the movie seemed like a winner.

I left smiling. In fact, I smiled all the back to my apartment. Who wouldn't? A well-known producer had just told me that he liked my first attempt at writing a full screenplay.

I waited three weeks, but did not hear from Marvin. He was never clear on what the next step would be, or when it would happen. I was in such a daze by the end of the meeting that I wasn't certain what he had said. I know it included something like, "I'll take it from here. I'll be in touch." Still, I felt it would be appropriate to call him. What harm could it do?

"Mr. Kirkwood. It's Brantley. How are you?"

"Fine. I'm busy getting ready for a screening. My documentary on golf caddies was finished," said Marvin. "People are already talking about a nomination. Documentaries are tough, and there's no money in it."

I think I was to take it as a form of altruism.

"Congratulations," was all I could come up with.

"Thanks. Why are you calling?" It seemed like an awfully strange thing to come out with.

"I was…Because…Marvin. I was just wondering about my screenplay." That was about the most aggressive statement I had made since I had hit town.

"I'm not sure I understand," said Marvin.

I forced myself to speak, already sensing that something was terribly wrong. "You had a lot of interest in it. I wanted to know…I wanted to know if you still have interest in doing something with it."

"I told you I think it is absolutely the best screenplay I've read in years. It's one of those great screenplays that just has got to be made," said Marvin.

"What's the next step?" I said, not knowing how I got the words out. By that time I was trembling.

"You know that copies of my documentary go to all the members of the academy, and then they vote on it. I think we've got a good chance, although you never know. The documentary category is unusual. Plus I'm not really known as a documentary producer. I'm not quite sure how all that is going to work out."

"I meant my screenplay. What's the next step with that?"

Dead silence. A few beats. I could hear Marvin breathing. "You're a wonderful writer. I already told you."

"Mr. Kirkwood. Do you have any interest in my screenplay?"

"Of course I do. Did I tell you about my screenplay? It's also about a young couple. Mine is set in a hospital, too." He had a similar project. *Why hadn't he told me?*

My heart sunk to a new low. I didn't know how to react. This was a new kind of disappointment. I would never recall what I said next. I blacked out for a few minutes. When I recovered, I was still standing in the middle of the living room, holding the remote phone, and staring into space.

How can people be like this? How can anyone act this way? Do they spend all their time fucking around with other people, seeing who they can screw out of something, inflict some pain, just for the sport of it? I asked myself over and over if I had misread something. This was new territory for me. I had experienced schadenfreude before, but I had no word for this kind of behavior. In the past, a typical response would be to think that something was missed, a colossal confusion on one side. No. I knew the answer. I was living through my first true Hollywood moment. Things like this really happened, more frequently than I cared to imagine, and not just to neophytes like me. *Welcome to the business, kid.*

CHAPTER TEN
Ira, Neil

    Ira and Neil combed through a list of ridiculous sandwich
names that they had seen in other delis. Some were so over-the-
top that the names became running jokes between them. This was
the tempting way to go, since dignity and respect for the same
'show business' that had greased the town fathers for decades -
whose essential job was to keep the palm trees well-maintained
and the locals quiet - was thrown out the window long ago, along
with any criminal moral code. The darker lineage extended from
Fatty Arbuckle to O.J. and Robert Blake, with lesser offenders
like Winona Ryder and Hugh Grant tossed in to help us keep our
sense of humor. The more innocent celebrities were set up for
slaughter; their only crime was being entertaining and in some
cases too opinionated for the public's taste. Richard Simmons
Tropical Fruit Salad was a plate of cottage cheese, fresh fruit
salad and strawberry Jell-O. Barbra Streisand had her share,
like chopped liver and a hard-boiled egg. Dolly Parton was
usually something with twin rolls or the word 'double'. The
process was just another shameless example of how we paid back
entertainers for keeping us out of shrink's offices or forsaking
all popular culture for an ashram somewhere in the old borscht
belt upstate New York. Little did they know or care, but the
boys were sharing one of the many duplicitous matrices of our

culture, the ability to destroy the idols we had spent so much time and money creating.

Ira exhibited a touch more sensitivity than Neil, if for no other reason than not to offend the targeted celebrity personally. "Let's stay away from the obvious ones. I don't really like these. They're really not so funny. A little too mean spirited."

Neil's bottom-line thinking ran more toward actual liability. To him a lawsuit by a celebrity would be a source of priceless public relations. "Okay, but we've got to come up with something catchy." Neil didn't want to argue about matters like this. He kept his focus on the big picture. He kept thinking Hard Rock Café and Starbucks. However, a good P.R. stunt like a celebrity lawsuit couldn't hurt.

Ira and Neil had everything well-organized, including their basic supply list. New York corned beef, first cut corned beef with less fat, similarly for pastrami, brisket and roast beef, plus turkey breast, tongue, New York style rolled beef, chopped chicken liver and a complete line of Hebrew National products ranging from hot dogs to bologna. They had to continue the fabled dinner plates with braised beef, flanken, chicken-in-the-pot, whole roasted chickens, and stuffed cabbage. They ordered a complete line of Pechter's Jewish Rye, Russian pumpernickel, and onion board, which some people still called pletzel. Tons of salads, from simple coleslaw to Mediterranean, a new and popular variety. Neil suggested that they put a Persian salad on the menu, essentially an extension of the Mediterranean salad. Ira knew that it was pandering to the increasing Iranian population, as so much of Beverly Hills and greater Los Angeles had taken in stride. *Besides, they have their own specialty restaurants,* he thought. The smoked fish section had to be the best, with all kinds of salmon and lox, whitefish, chubbs, kippered salmon, sable, sturgeon, and herrings. The menu needed to mimic a complete New York deli in order to compete with the likes of the closest and oldest competition - Jerry's, Juniors, Nate 'n Al's, and Canters, the latter, furthest away in the Fairfax area. Ira's grandfather, of course, had already laid most of the groundwork, but Ira and Neil wanted an all-inclusive more modern deli menu.

Chris had completed all the repairs to the deli in record time. He bought most of the supplies at Home Depot, a store that sold just about everything related to construction. He kept costs down, greatly impressing Ira. Chris also turned out to be an expert chef, and knew how to prepare foods deli style, as he had previously mentioned. Because of Chris' business and family connections there was now an endless supply of people willing to work for reasonable wages, and all of them had some experience, mostly from working as busboys or waiters at the local clubs.

Business began picking up. They stayed open during the renovation stage and people were beginning to hang out at the deli. It was fascinating to watch, how construction caught people's eye, slowing them down enough to consider stopping. Some people made a point of making sure that the deli was open, and appeared already offended if the answer became 'no'. It was a "How dare you close anything on the walk when I'm here?" kind of attitude that in a perversely logical way was how local residents protected Venice proper from significant change.

During the course of the changeover, Donny began to 'bond' with Neil. It was a perfect match. Donny saw an eager pupil and Neil spotted someone who had done many of the things he had only dreamed about. The first time Donny talked about his movie production experiences, Neil sat fixed on every word, as if the producer Messiah had arrived.

Donny began to show up every day, giving advice, solicited or not, and helping them procure whatever nonfood items Chris couldn't come up with cheap. Ira soon asked Neil not to disclose Donny's sources, not that Donny would be forthcoming about anything that wasn't entirely 'kosher'. A nice little network for a small business had developed part by design and part by happenstance. When tourists would listen, Donny became a free source of entertainment, complete with enough Hollywood folklore to enrapture the eager visitors.

Sometimes Donny could be outrageously funny, but he had to be certain of his audience. "The African Heritage Movie Network? Okay. Okay. But where does it stop? Do we need a Jewish Heritage Movie Network, an Italian, Spanish, you name it? What is with those blacks who want to associate with Africa, anyway? Come on, rich black people born and educated here don't associate with Africa, no more than a third or fourth generation Jew wants to run back to Tel-Aviv every year during the Jewish holidays. Why don't we all just call it a day and start the Neanderthal Heritage Movie Network? At least that way, we'll all be going for the same thing, where it all started, separate and apart from all these recent events." Donny could go on for hours, as long as someone would listen.

Ira grew to completely distrust Donny. It was an easy call for him to make, joining the ranks of many other locals who either had had dealings with him or flew close enough to the flame to only get singed. Ira wondered why, if Donny was such a big shot, why did he find the time to be hanging around such a smallish project?

The meat bills astounded Neil. It was one of their largest and most consistent expenses. He became annoyed that they had to pay so much money, even though it was obvious that the business depended on red meat sandwich sales, including ground beef, despite all the hype about the health conscious in Hollywood. Since 9/11, a lot of people had gone back to eating what they really liked. The newest joints around town were featuring obscenely priced steak, served alongside with snooty hostesses and ass-kissing disingenuous service, like Mastro's in Beverly Hills, and therefore a sure winner.

Neil didn't see how they could make any 'real' money if they had such a high overhead, and not just from the meat bills. He spoke to Donny about it. The blunt answer was simple, "You've got to find another source. Look, I probably shouldn't tell you this but I've been talking to people about this. I've already got some money people who want to invest, but I was first going to tell you that you've got to cut your margins." Donny hadn't talked to anyone, but he meant what he said about the financials.

Neil spent weeks surfing the Internet for suppliers. In the meantime, Mel's old supplier remained the best source. He researched everything he could find, from small businesses to obscure regional meat suppliers. *Who knows what other cuts and kinds of meat might work?* His thoughts ran from *What the hell?* to *Nah, we've got to keep up the quality.* During these late sessions his mind wandered, fantasizing that if he had this same business in China, how easy it might be to substitute other meat sources. How could he keep up the quality, but cut down the costs? He realized that he was in the same situation as everyone, from McDonalds down to the smallest noodle shop in Chinatown. He thought about the old jokes, *I think I heard a cat purring in the kitchen.*

Weeks had passed with no real leads. One night, Neil sat up smoking a joint, staring at his computer. He had just about stopped going to the anatomy class. He had given up there, along with improving the margins at the deli. There were a couple of

wholesale meat distributors that would save them a few bucks,
but a single deli location could not guarantee enough volume to
get the really rock-bottom pricing. *Welcome to a single
proprietorship business.* He began to sing "America, America..."

Neil haphazardly continued and aimlessly skipped from site
to site. He thought back to the first dissection class. Suddenly
he paused, and moved his head slowly to one side, cocking it so
he could look at the screen askew. "No," he said aloud, as a
parent would say to stop a naughty child. Then he smiled. His
whole body came alive as his idea hit him hard a second time.
"Why the fuck not?" He slowly typed in a search phrase on
Google. "Wow!" was all that came out of his mouth when the
reference list of sites filled his screen in less than three
seconds with over one hundred possibilities. "Wow" came out
again, this time oozing with a nervous tremble, as his lips
rounded to form the sounds that stretched the word into a
macabre three-syllable version.

It was a form of divine intervention. Neil was at medical
school for a greater reason, brought on by a series of
fortuitous, yet innocent, connections. Mel Packer left at just
the right time. Ira asked Neil to help. Chris was at UCLA. Donny
unexpectedly made himself available. Neil was the lone common
denominator. He saw himself as the savior who could make them
all rich by knowing how to tie everything together. It was as if
he was being guided by some supernatural force. It was all there
on the Internet, everything he needed to know. The deli god was
speaking to Neil via the Internet.

After a phone call, Neil smoked another joint while he
drove to the UCLA Medical center late that same night. He had
worked out his presentation, his back-up pitch, and a third
method of accomplishing his goal. He didn't know what to expect,

but had no fear of crossing over into uncharted and bizarre territory.

After parking in a handicapped space, he made his way through the deadly silent halls to the cadaver room, and knocked on the door. After waiting for what felt like a long minute, Chris' smiling face appeared at the door.

"Doctor. Comó está?"

"Fine, Chris. Can I come in?"

"Sure." Chris made a grand sweeping gesture with his hand, as if he were indicating a red-carpet path for royalty.

"Can we talk somewhere?" asked Neil nervously.

"Follow me," said Chris.

The unlikely duo made their way past a few hanging cadavers. Inside the preparation area was a small office, set off in the corner.

"The electric job was good, no?" asked Chris. He seemed legitimately concerned about the quality of his work. He pointed to a chair. "You want to sit here?"

"Fine." Neil sat down on a plain, typical university chair, the molded plastic kind found on campuses all over the world.

Chris sat on the edge of a desk that was filled with paperwork. He was trying to keep his smile, but the corners of his mouth were beginning to twitch from holding it so long.

"I can fix the job," said Chris. "The junction box was old."

"The job is fine," said Neil.

"I fire the new guy. He was stealing. I knew it," said Chris. He was covering all bases for a late-night visit from one of his deli bosses.

"No. Everything is fine. No hay problemas."

Chris's face lit up again. "Then why did you want to see Chris? You said it was important."

"I have a little business to discuss with you." Neil spoke calmly and directly, as if he were asking the time of day. "You know after the thoracic section of the bodies are exposed, what do you do with the sections that are cut away at the end of the day, say the area under the first five or so ribs?" Neil had done his research.

Chris leaned his hands further back on the desk for added support.

"We have a company that disposes of them. They probably burn it or something. The guy comes around once or twice a week, and he picks up the stuff." He stopped smiling.

Whoa. All of a sudden he speaks fluent English. "Is it weighed or anything?"

"No. No weighed. Nada,"

Back to the choppy talk with a little Spanish thrown in. "What if I wanted to take some of that material? I don't want to get anyone in trouble or anything. I know how careful the school is when it comes to disposing of cadavers, and if they were donated, getting the bodies back to the families that want them returned for burial. I'm not saying anything about that or the rest of the body, but nobody cares what they look like by then, and nobody cares about the remains for cremation before torching them." He paused to see if Chris had any reaction. He didn't. "I was just wondering if we could get those dissected areas from under the ribs."

"Something like that is going to cost money," said Chris. He quickly returned to Spanish, and offered a different, wry smile. "Mucho. Costo mucho dinero."

"Of course I would pay you."

They both stared at each other for a few seconds. Chris pretended to have no idea what Neil wanted with the cadavers, and wasn't about to ask. Neil didn't know if he wanted to make

Chris openly privy to his plans, but in a few moments realized
that Chris had to have known.

Each one knew what the other was thinking at only one
level. How much does something like this cost? It's not as if
there was a baseline from which they could bargain from, or some
other kind of price history related to human remains.

"You pay me whatever." Chris knew it had to be plenty, but
way less than buying meat from the distributers. He already was
planning to set up the system for delivery so that if anyone got
busted, it was going to be Neil.

"Thank you," said Neil. "I promise nobody will ever know."

"Okay." Chris put out his hand.

They shook hands. The deal was done. Neil had his new meat
source.

Neil made an on-the-spot decision. "It would help if you
knew someone who could prepare the meat." He could see in Chris'
face that he knew exactly what Neil meant.

"The pay has to be great," said Chris. "I will have to take
time away from the club in order to do the work."

"Can you do the pastrami and the corned beef, too?" asked
Neil.

"You worry about the money. Cooking is easy," answered
Chris.

It was that simple. Two unlikely partners had joined in a
business venture without much thought to their intentions.
Somehow they both knew that it would work. It was a rare kind of
fearlessness that accompanies people who cross unheard of legal
and moral boundaries without a second thought. When I eventually
had heard the details I wondered, *Was it the backdrop of the
Hollywood sign, or could this happen anywhere?*

Before he left the building that night, Neil checked the
cadaver room in order to make a quick body count, estimating the

approximate weight of the cuts taken from the rib section. He
would have plenty of beef for brisket. He hoped that Chris
wouldn't give him point cuts, areas with a lot of fat, but it
would have sounded ridiculous for Neil to explain that he wanted
all flat cuts. That could be worked out later.

Later that same week, the deli was in full swing.

Past the dinner rush, Donny was holding court at a corner
table. "Last year was such a strange weather year. The people
don't know what to make of this good weather. The weather people
are out of their fuckin' minds with grief. All the storms are
going north of us, just like before. El Niño was so hyped up a
few years ago. Now nobody has said a word. What? Did it rain
once yet this year?" The earlier storm had escaped Donny's
selective weather memory.

"Ira. Why don't you take off early? I know you want to
study for that anatomy practical that's coming up," said Neil as
he cleared one of the last tables.

"Are you sure?" asked Ira.

"No problem," said Neil. "I'll stay late." They hadn't yet
officially stayed open all night; most of the time they closed
whenever business tapered off.

Neil knew that Chris was coming with the first 'meat'
delivery. Neil wanted to be sure that the place was empty, so he
began serving the remaining customers New York cheesecake bits
with coffee, on the house. The patrons had to settle for
regularly brewed coffee, since Donny hadn't yet secured an
inexpensive enough espresso-cappuccino machine. It wouldn't be
long. A-list restaurants were always going under, and had proved
to be a steady source for some of the equipment. To compensate
for the lack of a fancy machine, Ira had about ten different

flavors to add to the coffee, ranging from hazelnut to
raspberry.

The group began thinning out, all except for Donny. Neil
nervously paced the restaurant. Finally, Donny sat alone,
sipping his coffee, and staring suspiciously at Neil. Donny had
a sixth and seven sense when it came to making money. He knew
that something was up.

"Donny. I'm sorry. I've got to close up," said Neil.

"No problem." Still, Donny took his time leaving. He
strolled through the kitchen and slipped out the back entrance.

Ten minutes later, a torrential downpour came out of
nowhere, sending sheets of rain through the shadows. Donny
watched from under a big palm tree in the back of the parking
lot as a large chrome box was lowered to the ground from the
back of a truck. It was an eerie sight, watching the lines of
rain almost redraw the scene in front of him. The green slickers
worn by Neil and Chris now became army uniforms, and the vehicle
an all-terrain vehicle. With their heads covered by hoods, the
men wheeled the device up a ramp and into the deli. A rare bolt
of lightning lit up the sky over the nearby pier, and then all
went dark.

What are these boys up to? Donny asked himself. He put his
thin khaki Polo golf jacket over his head and trotted back
toward the deli. Inside, the chrome box was open and no one was
around. Donny stopped at the container, but could only make out
thick plastic wrap. He continued to the open kitchen doorway,
where he could see Chris and Neil. Donny watched as they removed
raw meat from one bag and placed it on the counter.

Neil glanced up and saw Donny's figure in the doorway.
"Donny," Neil said, rather calmly.

Donny automatically assumed that the meat was stolen.
"Look. I don't care what you do here. I just want some of the

action. That's all. One thing has got really nothing to do with the other. I didn't see anything." He couldn't resist the opportunity to get something more for himself.

Neil knew that sooner or later he had to make a deal with Donny. "Fine," said Neil. "I'm easy. You work out the details with Ira." Neil waited for Donny to leave.

"Fine," said Donny. I want to hang some expensive art in here, too." Once outside, he ran off into the downpour.

Neil figured that he had gotten off easy. There was no way of knowing how Donny was going to react if he had told him the truth. Neil felt that they were alike when it came to business, but that was only based on observation. He knew that people had mixed moralities, and there is no telling how someone, even with Donny's flexible moral compass, would react to knowing that the deli was going to serve fresh cadaver meat for its specialty sandwiches.

Minutes later, Neil watched as Chris prepared the meat. Neil was thinking ahead, in case Chris became expendable. It only took a few minutes for Neil to realize that he would never touch the meat.

The meat lay on the butcher block counter. It was basically indiscernible from any other cut of meat, only smaller. Neil watched as Chris cut up the meat into its various components.

Chris clearly knew the butcher business. "This cut will make a good brisket. The secret to brisket is that you cook it long and slow. Too fast and it won't come out right."

Neil picked up a strange aura, as if Chris was enjoying the process. He walked through each step as if he had done it before. *Mexican cannibals,* Neil thought, and then dismissed the idea as being preposterous in modern times. This whole thing was beginning to reach him in ways that even made him uncomfortable. He marked off his paranoia to his general increase in marijuana

consumption. He was determined to go ahead with his plan. He had
done the only and right thing. They were nearly out of money.
There was no way they could stay in business if they extended
their credit any further. Initially, Neil had used his entire
credit line to fix up the restaurant. He was already getting
calls from American Express, because he hadn't responded to any
of the overdue letters. On top of that, Ira had borrowed five-
thousand dollars from his parents to upgrade the cooking area.
Ira didn't know much about making money. Neil had convinced
himself, rather easily, that he was doing the right thing for
everyone. He was suddenly very altruistic, rather than perverse.

Neal suggested to Chris, "We'd better find another place to
cut and cure the meat. Maybe a place to store it, too."

Chris responded, clearly understanding his position. He had
his network of relatives that had worked in the clubs and
restaurants in town. "Don't worry. I'll take care of it."

Chris eventually settled on two basic types of preparations
for the meat, convection/microwave and boiling. Both got rid of
a tremendous amount of fat. The cut fat posed a small disposal
problem because of the odor and the consistency.

He didn't want to dispose of the fat in the garbage
dumpster. He didn't want to take a chance on anyone finding this
strange goop in the garbage, or a stray animal somehow exposing
its contents.

The fat was sometimes orange or off-white with yellowish
streaks. It didn't go down the drain easily, so Chris used the
InSinkErator. He added Drano, followed by copious amounts of
water and Lysol disinfectant, usually with a strong flower
scent.

Neil intended this to be a short process, maybe a few
months. Once the deli was on its feet, and the money was pouring
in, they could go back to a more conventional meat source. Even

if he wanted to get away with it on a permanent basis, he had to contend with Ira, who was following their expenses, and would eventually know that something was amiss.

After a few weeks, Ira mentioned to Neil that even though the supplies of meat were running well, there weren't any new invoices from Mel's old meat supplier.

"You know me. I probably threw them away by accident." Neil paused, waiting for Ira to digest the information. "You know me. I lose things. I might have lost them." The repetitive answer seemed reasonable to Ira.

A few weeks later and still no invoices, Ira brought it up again. By that time, Neil had another answer. "I'm hooking us up with Newport. They're a little behind in the paper work." It was one of Southern California's best meat sources.

"Aren't they expensive?"

"Yes. But I got a great deal. Donny helped through Dan, you know, the guy that owns Dan Tana's. They were playing golf, and Dan hooked Donny up. We are sort of piggy-backing Dan's orders."

Soon, Ira finally confronted Neil. "I called over to Newport. We don't have an account." Ira pulled out a bunch of papers from under the counter. "These are our only invoices."

"We don't?" Neil sounded amazed. He mocked looking for the answer in the papers.

"Neil. Don't fuck with me. Where are you getting the meat?"

"It's a new supplier. It's even cheaper than Newport," said Neil.

"Look. First you told me you threw away the invoices, and I believed you because you throw away all your credit slips. Then you tell me that you have a new supplier. You're stealing it, aren't you?"

"No. I'm not stealing it. Come on."

"Okay. So where are the invoices for the new supplier?"

"That part is true. I do have a new supplier."

"Okay. But I'm going to need some accountability."

"Sure. I'll call over to make sure we get the proper papers."

"Don't bullshit me, Neil."

"Come on." Neil sounded legitimately shocked.

Later that night, Neil practiced what he might tell Ira. Neil rehearsed by talking into a mirror. "This is not as bad as all that. People do worse things. It's not quite as bad. I mean, these bodies are already dead. It's not like Sweeny Todd shit at all. It's a better idea, really." He didn't see any conscience in his reflection, although he tried different versions to show some form of contrition, the expected emotion to go with such an outlandish confession.

He knew that he really didn't have to be so concerned. There were no rules in life about getting ahead, and he was only utilizing the available system to achieve his goals. Mixed methods and messages were nothing new. He didn't see it any differently than being Gingrich, Clinton, Bush, or Cheney. They had all been accused of going outside the legal loop in order to achieve their goals. How about those deals at Enron, Adelphia, Global Crossing, and WorldCom? Morality was in the eyes of the beholder, and ultimately it would be up to a jury to decide, unless a plea bargain was arranged that quickly erased or reduced the problem. The ultimate litmus test for morality could be avoided by not getting caught in the first place. If nobody witnesses an immoral act, then it couldn't be immoral. Neil had his role in this deal worked out. It was part of a larger mental imprint to pattern his life. He was prepared to convince Ira to make it all work.

The next week, both Ira and Neil arrived early to open the deli. There was always plenty to do in the morning. Ira thought how lucky he was to have Neil as a friend, someone who was willing to put so much time into what originally had seemed like a losing venture.

Toward the end of the day, Ira asked Neil again. "What happened to the meat orders?" Ira stood on the customer side of the counter, while Neil prepared bread in the steamer.

"Oh. I've been paying cash over at the new place. They're giving me a discount. I have a tally." He knew that he could come up with a list of how much he was paying Chris. "It's a good deal."

"Neil. I hope you're not doing what I think you are."

"I doubt it" This made Neil laugh. "Don't worry about it. I'm taking care of it."

"Neil. You're buying stolen meat. That has to be it."

"No."

"You're lying."

"I am not a liar," said Neil.

"Bill Clinton impersonation. Right?"

"Ira. Look. It's good meat. Let it go."

"Where are you getting the money?" demanded Ira. "You haven't written any checks for a month. You're either stealing the cash or the meat or both. Which is it?"

"Let it go," said Neil. He started to shift his weight, bobbing as he spoke.

Ira leaned in and spoke to him across the counter. "Don't fuck with me, Neil. What's going on here?"

"It's another source. I found something temporary. Just until we can get back on our feet. Besides, everyone loves the food. What's the difference?"

"The difference is my grandfather always bought quality
meat. We didn't buy from any of the lesser places."

"You've seen the meat. It looks great, doesn't it?"

"What are you hiding from me?"

"Okay. It's cadaver meat." He said it with all the
authority of a supermarket butcher identifying his product for a
customer behind the display in the trendy Bristol Farms or
Gelson's.

"That's funny. But now tell me the truth!"

"I meant to do it just one night as a goof. Like some of
the crazy shit the guys at medical school do. You know the
stories."

"Tell the truth."

"That's it. That is the truth."

"That's really not funny." Ira felt his strength drain from
his body.

"I'm not doing funny here. That's the deal. I've enlisted
Chris to supply me with the meat. He is a fucking wiz at
preparing the stuff. Brisket, corned, pastrami. He's got a
backlog now of cured meats."

Ira spoke slowly. "You're serious?"

Neil nodded in the affirmative. He came around the other
side of the counter.

Ira tried to speak slowly and rationally. He continually
wiped his hands on his apron while he spoke. "Let's assume this
were true. It would really be a horrible thing. What am I
saying? Why are we having this conversation?" He began to raise
his voice and placed his hands over his ears. "But I'm not going
to listen to any more of this. This could really be something
very insane, and I can't handle something very insane at this
moment. Let's stop fooling around, and stop talking about
horrible things. Talk about real things."

Neil took Ira's arms and placed them back at his side. Neil spoke calmly, as if he were explaining the global warming problem, with a voice that was part sociologist and part cannibal. "It's not like it's a horrible thing. It's actually a human thing. Eating is human. Eating to survive is human. Eating your own is human. A cousin, is like, nothing. Eating a cousin is nothing. But it's okay to eat anyone. We are not new at it. We didn't invent it. We are just doing something that has always been done, and is still done today. At least our meat is cooked. What about that, we have cooked meat? We are not serving disgusting raw fish for twenty bucks a pop. We are serving the real thing. Meat. Meat. Real fucking meat. Just like our ancestors ate when they were hungry. Think about this. There were no cholesterol problems then. Just the need to survive when the species' own flesh fit the bill. It was leaner than most animals. We're on to something bigger than both of us."

Ira jumped at Neil. Ira's hands grabbed as much of Neil's neck as he could find and felt his fingers tighten mercilessly around the carotid artery. If he couldn't stop the blood supply to Neil's brain, he would continue pressing hard on the Eustachian tube until Neil turned blue.

"Hey! I did it for your grandfather," Neil shouted.

"Bullshit. You did it because…You did it because…" Ira let his hands fall to his side. A sudden calm enveloped Ira as he stood stunned, seeing himself in the moment, as if he were watching from across the room. "Why did you do this?" It was the only reasonable question, and Ira knew that the true answer had nothing to do with Mel.

"It seemed the way to go. All the pieces were there to put into place. I'm only the facilitator."

He really believes what he is saying, thought Ira. Ira still didn't accept what he had heard. He turned and shuffled

301

away, then out the front door of the deli. He kept turning to
look back, hoping Neil would smile and shout, "Trick or treat,"
or something else inane to indicate that it was all a hoax. Ira
slipped further away from the deli. Bewildered, he was faced
with a moral dilemma of epidemic proportions. He concluded that
his closest friend was totally insane, some kind of personality
disorder of biblical scale.

Neil followed Ira for a few steps, trying to rationalize
the unthinkable. "The first time I saw Ken Weiss take out his
lunch during anatomy class, that was it. He was crazy enough to
bring a deli sandwich for lunch and eat the damned thing during
the dissection. The meat on the stiff looked better than the
meat on his sandwich. I thought about it again when I rented a
Sweeney Todd tape. I thought, you know, it's got to be good
quality."

Ira turned back toward him. "Say another word and I'm going
to deck you."

"Sure. I'll be quiet. Just don't jump to any hasty
conclusions. We have a good thing going, and nobody knows about
it except for Chris, and he could care less."

"It has to stop," said Ira. "I know about it."

"I did it one night as a goof. It was a goof. A college
thing. We did worse in college."

"Neil. You did worse in college? What we're talking about
here is cannibalism," said Ira, as if he had just completed a
lecture on aborigine life in the outback.

"It's not like that. There you go labeling things again.
How can you say that? It was a goof, but it turned out to be a
smart thing. Look. The meat is fresh. Probably fresher than
anything we can buy, and Chris used your grandfather's recipes
for the brine. It works. But not a little. It works a lot. Chris
has lined up other sources."

Ira paused for a few seconds, trying desperately to make some sense out of the situation. He didn't know whether to answer Neil or just push his face into the sand.

"Neil. You've been watching too much television."

"What does that mean?"

"You've lost sight of reality. Things that matter. Forget about the lying. So you learned how to communicate like a potential presidential candidate. You're talking about eating people here. I'll just call down to Florida and tell my grandfather that business is picking up and oh, by the way, we're serving human meat."

"You don't have to tell him."

"I wasn't going to tell him."

"Good. I'm glad we'll keep this between ourselves," said Neil with a sigh of relief.

Ira headed back toward the deli. Neil followed closely behind him.

"Neil..." Ira paused.

Once back inside, he didn't know what he wanted to say. He picked up a meat cleaver and slammed it into a cutting board.

"You're angry," said Neil. "I expected that. It's going to take some getting used to. In a few weeks I'll stop, just as soon as business picks up a little more. Even Donny said we have a good sandwich, and if that twisted sonofabitch likes it, we've got a hit on our hands. I can't remember the last time he didn't send back the sandwich because it wasn't lean enough, didn't have enough sauce, was too chewy, whatever. Fucking Donny likes the sandwich."

Ira slowly removed his apron.

"Ira. Where are you going?"

Ira grabbed his blue UCLA sweatshirt and walked out from behind the counter.

"Ira. Hey. Wait a minute. Where are you going?"

Ira hurried out of the deli and made a left on the boardwalk.

"Wait. Wait. Don't go!" Neil followed him outside, realized that he had to shut off the steamer, and bolted back inside.

Ira quickened his pace and disappeared over a sand dune. His mind was racing with the life-incongruous information that Neil had dumped on him. He still hoped that it would all turn out to be a hoax, but he knew Neil and the possibilities of the darkness within him surfacing whenever it came to getting ahead. But, this was way beyond anyone's previous thinking.

A few minutes later, Neil found Ira sitting alone in the sand, not far from the boardwalk path. Neil sat down beside him. Not a word was exchanged for what seemed like a long while. The deli duo remained side by side; neither one willing to take a chance on breaking the ungodly silence that had enveloped them.

Neil's face changed expressions on cue, like a bad actor going through a mock rehearsal of his repertoire, in the off chance that he might be asked to reveal a certain emotional reaction. Ira was reminded of a movie that he had rented starring Oliver Platt and Stanley Tucci, *The Imposters*, in which two out of work actors from old New York grilled each other on their respective rolodex of facial muggings.

Ira was legitimately in shock, so it was easy for him not to show any emotion, his preferred reaction under stress.

"Say something," Neil finally ordered. Using his fingers, he forced the sides of Ira's cheeks to move, lifting the corners of his mouth into an artificial grin.

Ira's lips parted, as if he were going to speak, then he closed them, and pushed them hard together, forming a rounded puffy appearance. He brushed away Neil's hands, jumped up, and rushed away.

"Hey! Hey, Ira. Wait. Where are you going?"

Twilight had begun, but a few people were still lingering on the sand closer to the water. Ira passed a woman with three young children, tired from a day of digging. He looked at them and imagined Neil eyeing each one of them as product. Ira turned back and sent Neil a glare that spoke loudly. Neil shrugged his shoulders, opened the palm of his hands, and shook his head. "No. Don't be ridiculous," he said. He wanted to say more, but he instead ran to catch up with Ira.

Ira moved away at a quickened pace.

Neil caught up to him and held his arm. "Ira. These are cadavers, people who end up on medical school slabs. They're already dead."

"You're out of your mind."

I've got to keep trying. "There is nothing new about this."

"What's that supposed to mean?" answered Ira, his feet now sinking a little deeper with each step in the wet sand.

"Well. It's been going on for millions of years. What about that guy Swift, or somebody, the guy who suggested eating children when there was a famine or something going on somewhere?"

"You're joking with me, right?"

"What?" asked Neil, truly confused.

"That was a satire. That wasn't real."

"It was?" Neil was crushed with the news that his reference would not help his cause.

"What's the difference? This is two thousand and two. It's not done."

Neil was smiling again. "They're eating all the monkeys they can find in Indonesia. The tourists go nuts there for fresh kill monkey brains."

"You're making me sick."

"People eat anything. You think monkeys are very different from us?"

"What are you now, some fucking gastronomical anthropologist?" Ira's voice trembled as he felt his heart race.

Neil gestured with another subtle shrug and a turn of his head, an indication that it wasn't a problem for him.

Ira lunged at him, tackling him around the waist. The two went down hard on the sand. They rolled down an incline and into the water, still grappling.

Neil managed to get on top of Ira for a second. Ira took his free right arm up from the water and punched Neil in the side of the head, just above the ear.

"Owwww!" Neil bellowed.

"Shit!" yelled Ira, feeling the pain in his hand go all the way up his forearm, causing an electric jolt that reached the inside of his neck.

Neil rolled off Ira and splashed into the shallow finish of a wave on its way to the shore. His hair was instantly filled with wet sand. "What the fuck did you do that for?" asked Neil, as he righted himself in order to sit in the water.

"Because you're crazy. You've always been crazy. I don't know you anymore," Ira got up and headed for the boardwalk.

"Well, you didn't have to hit me. You don't hit friends. I'm still your friend. Right?" Neil touched the side of his head, which already had begun to swell in the area where he had been struck.

When the woman saw Ira approaching, she gathered up her children and hurried them off the beach.

"Mommy. What kind of game were those men playing?" asked one of the children.

"I'm not sure," said the mother.

Ira wanted to say that he was sorry if she or the children were frightened. He decided to keep moving. He didn't need any trouble with the Venice police. He wondered how many of them had already accepted free sandwiches from Neil.

By the time Neil returned to the boardwalk, Ira was nowhere in sight. He wasn't in the deli. Only a few possibilities existed as to where to find him. Neil drove to the apartment first. No luck. Then he drove to a local bar called Chez Jays. *Bingo*, he thought as he glanced through the open top half of a stable door.

Ira was ensconced at the bar and staring at the floor. A half-filled martini glass was to his right.

Neil slid in and stood behind him. "You can't do this to yourself," said Neil. *Maybe if I show some concern for how he might be feeling. Nothing else has worked.*

Ira turned to face Neil. Ira waved his arm in what Neil thought was a threatening gesture. Ira almost fell off the stool. "Go away. Get Jay down here. Tell him there's going to be a homicide in a few minutes. Tell him to practice dialing '911' until I figure out how I'm going to do this."

Neil grabbed Ira by the shoulders to steady him. "Ira. I'm your friend. How many of those did you have?"

"Seven. No. Eight. No, seven."

"I did it for your grandfather." This time Neil said it with a new conviction.

"That's the worst thing you've said so far." Ira pushed Neil away.

"Okay. Okay. So I'm a real shit."

Ira locked eyes with Neil. "Keep going. Real shit is nothing. You're a psychopath. What are they calling it, Borderline Personality Disorder or something?"

"That's not me. But I don't see what's wrong with my plan. I really don't."

"I know."

"I won't do it again, if that's what you want."

"How do I know you mean it?"

"I do," said Neil. "Just let me use up what we already have."

Ira laughed through a low mumble that arose from his midsection. Then he howled a forced laugh, as if he had heard a bad joke.

"Ira? You okay?"

"I'm going to let you do it. Look at me Neil." He grabbed Neil with two hands by the collar. "Look at me. What do you see?"

"I don't know," said Neil. *He looks scary.*

"What do you see?"

"You?" asked Neil, hoping to get the right answer.

"Wrong. Do not pass 'Go'. Do not collect two-hundred dollars. I am like you, no better, no worse. I just spend more of my time fighting against who I really am. I am just like you. I always wanted to pretend to be the moral one, the more righteous one. And it was so easy. Do you know why?"

"Because I'm such a shit?"

"You didn't have to answer. It was a rhetorical question."

"Right. I won't do that again. Can you let go of my shirt now?"

Ira loosened his grip, but held on with one hand and sipped his martini with the other. "I am going to let you win for one reason. I want the money. Just like you, but I want it for my grandfather, and frankly I've given up caring about how I get it. I want him to live out his life in a little luxury. It's the least I can do. He was always good to my mother and me, and now

I want to give something back. So if you think you can pull this off, then do it. I don't want to know any of the details. Nothing."

"Nothing. Come on. I'm getting collar burn here." Neil tried to wrestle free.

Ira tightened his grip. "Nothing! I don't want to know!'

"I got it," said Neil. He used both hands in order to pry himself loose.

Ira locked eyes with Neil for a final moment, and then pushed him away.

The bartender glanced over at Neil.

"No problem here," said Neil. "He said his drink was a little too dry. Got him agitated when I told him Jay always serves perfect martinis."

Ira staggered from the barstool and tottered out the front door. Once outside he turned toward the parking lot in time to watch the contents of his stomach explode onto the pavement. The wind and his tipsy equilibrium compromised his aim, and part of his regurgitation ended up on the shiny chrome wheel and bumper of a 600 SEL white Mercedes that had just pulled into the lot. The owner of the vehicle got out of his car in time to see the eclectic decoration on his fender.

"I just had it washed," said the burly man. He was elegantly dressed in a double-breasted pinstripe suit. He chortled. "Damn. That's what I should expect from this joint!"

Neil rushed out of Chez Jay's. "He'll get your car cleaned."

"Sorry," said Ira. "I'm really sorry." He wiped his mouth on his sleeve.

"Forget it, boys. I've been there. I've seen you guys in here before. You're the deli guys. You once brought Jay a sandwich. Right? Kyle Bixler never forgets a face."

"That's right," said Neil. "You're that entertainment lawyer from Century City…Listen. We'll take it to be washed now."

"Forget it. I'll have one of the kitchen guys hose it off," said Bixler. "We've all been there at one time or another." When he chortled again, his whole body shook like Jell-O.

"Not me," said Ira. "My first time. Must have been something I ate, or didn't eat."

"Thanks," said Neil. "Thanks for being so understanding."

"Here, boys. Take my card. If you need any help with the business, give me a call. Ask Jay for my references. If you have any problems, I know a lot of people in Venice." Bixler opened a Gucci leather portfolio and removed one of his business cards.

Neil took the card, and glanced at it quickly. "Thanks."

"Thanks," said Ira. "I'm really sorry."

"You'd better get your friend home," said Bixler. He disappeared into the bar.

"Nice guy," said Neil.

"Oh, god. I've got more," said Ira.

"At least get away from his car," said Neil. He pulled Ira to the side of the lot.

Moments later, when Ira righted himself, he said, "Look it, Neil. You have to agree to certain ground rules here." He still did not believe the words that were coming out of his mouth. He knew that he was flawed, but never thought to this extent.

"Okay. Shoot," said Neil.

"We're not using the brains. We're not going into the delicacy business. Just meat. Just what you've been doing. No other organs. No sweetbreads or any of that stuff. We have a good source for chopped liver."

"Of course not. Never gave it a thought," said Neil. He was lying, having just been reintroduced to what now seemed like a brilliant idea, one he had had before.

"And you quit as soon as we're making good money or I'll expose the whole thing."

"Okay," said Neil. "Come on. Let's go home." He didn't believe that Ira would ever turn him in.

Neil put his arm around Ira as they lumbered toward their cars. Both of them were relieved to have resolved the episode, but for decidedly different reasons. Neither could deny the underlying childhood bond that served as the glue for a new, perverse adult friendship. Neil always brought out the best and worst in Ira, and now had created something so unchartered that even he could not fathom the magnitude of what they were doing.

CHAPTER ELEVEN
Brantley
Sean, Ira, Neil
Mal, Ricky

Liz had invited me to spend an evening at the Beverly Hills Tennis Club, which included a culinary presentation by one of its popular members. We sat at rectangular dining tables, all positioned to face one side of the room, where a display had been set up for the affair. From our vantage point, I could see Neil and his father.

The head of the food and beverage committee was Gibby Richards, a multiple face-lifted survivor of old Hollywood. He was a raconteur of unmatched skill; at least as far as the tennis club members were concerned. In his younger days he led a rather flamboyant life, jet-setting around the world with the likes of Liz and Dick, while lighting on spots in Marbella and Monaco. He was sometimes mentioned and photographed in gossip columns like *Page Six*, always on the arm of a famous actress, heiress, or royal. Gibby had slowed down in recent years, or as Godfrey said, "he simply ran out of money." As a necessary consequence, he begrudgingly married one of the divorced women in town who still had enough in the coffers for someone with Gibby's zest for life.

"No more Paris for Gibby. Now it's Aspen, Hawaii, and occasionally, if he's lucky, Palm Beach. But it's more likely to be Palm Springs." Godfrey would often tease Gibby to get his goat, and usually succeeded.

Essentially true, Gibby had given up the international scene for what could be best described as the West Coast Jewish Jet Set, a rather limited and insular group of rich people who stuck to the same vacation spots every year, while buying property in places with strikingly similar climates.

That night, to the delight of the partisan group, Gibby was hosting a pastrami extravaganza. Pastrami was one of Hollywoodland's prized offerings, and this was one of the few areas in the country where the meat was popularized on subs, making it one of the regional cross-over foods that broke ethnic barriers. Everyone ate pastrami, but not only on rye.

While Gibby coolly went through his presentation, the waiters brought around little pastrami sandwich appetizers on a variety of dark and light breads, with many different mustard dips, ranging from the popular French style to the 'authentic' deli mustard.

"The idea of Romanian pastrami in this country is unlike anything they ever had in Romania. The main difference, and let me tell you, this is a big difference, they didn't use beef. They used goat meat." He paused, waiting for the audience to respond.

He had Neil's full attention.

Gibby continued. "In Romania, pastrami is more a verb than it is a noun or a thing. The process of making something, using a pastrami process is what it is all about, not the product. Any kind of meat can be 'pastramied', so to speak. The process is simple; you can ask any old deli owner. The meat has to be cured, injected with the secret spices and garlic, and then there is salt, and many say the salting is what makes the difference. The dearly departed owner, Leo Steiner, of the Carnegie Deli in New York, told me on many occasions about the brining process that he used on his pastrami. Getting back to Romanians, they would make it from goose, pork, and goat, sometimes using wine grapes to flavor the mix. The stuff we eat here is truly Americanized, which is what we do to most foods. We put our stamp on it, change it, make it a success, and then export it to Japan. Look what we've done to the hamburger. Unrecognizable from what I had as a child."

Gibby knew that he had better get to the main meal part of the evening. This crowd hadn't come to see him, they were here to eat. The appetizers were gone quicker than the audience's popcorn at a Hannibal Lecter flick or the human delicacies he was reported to have devoured.

"The American pastrami is more or less a little like Romanian, but Americans rarely smoke their meat the way they did in the old country. We use spices and very little garlic. The best meat from pastrami comes from steer beef, and not cows. And a good cut of pastrami is always made from the bottom of the brisket. It's really a corned beef that is treated with the spices. Here. If you follow along on the little papers I've left on the tables, you'll see what I mean."

Liz and I picked up the colorful leaflets. Neil rose and slipped into a seat closer to Gibby. Neil made notes on his handout. The chefs, waiters, and busboys had come out of the kitchen in order to stand in the back and listen to the presentation. Gibby glanced at Chris and the employee entourage.

Gibby spoke with delight, legitimately excited about food. "You can see. You have garlic, coriander, peppercorns, and of course, salt. Don't laugh, but a good classic Jewish pastrami has saltpeter to keep the meat pink. I like to work with at

least three pounds of brisket, but leave a little fat on top.
Okay, then some vegetable oil, a little brown sugar, white
vinegar, allspice, and then a full cup of that brown sugar for
the smoke process. It's simple. The garlic, coriander,
peppercorns, all get crushed together and worked into the hunk
of brisket. Let it sit in this stuff for a day or a little
longer, but keep it in the refrigerator. In a bowl, the little
brown sugar, vinegar and spice are added to the meat. Then back
in the old icebox for another day. It's ready to go. The meat
should be steamed, almost covering the bowl. It takes a few
hours, usually between two and three. That's it. After it's
steamed, you're all set. Put the meat in the steamer pot once
the pot is cleaned out and lined with foil. If you want, you can
use another kind of pan. Put in the whole cup of sugar around
the foil. Put the tray back on with the heat, now more on
medium. You'll know when this is going right. The brown sugar
will start to smoke, so you have to cut the heat so that it
doesn't burn. The smoking part needs only fifteen minutes.
That's it. That's it! Get out your favorite bread. Mine is thick
corn rye with real deli mustard. I've included a little recipe
to make your own deli mustard at home. And now here's Chris with
the dinner sandwiches. Bon appetite!"

The waiters moved en masse to serve from large chrome
platters, piled high with sandwiches. Classic side dishes,
including potato salad, cole slaw, and different gradients of
garlic sour pickles were wheeled around on a cart.

After dinner, Neil cornered Gibby, trying to find out more.

Neil soon asked, "Do you always used the short recipe?"

"No. I don't follow that recipe," said Gibby. "I actually
pickle the meat for a week or too, and then smoke it for two or
three hours. That's what I think you should be doing if you want
that really special flavor."

"Why don't you come by and make a batch for us in Venice?" asked Neil. He knew that Gibby was a great promoter, and could only be a plus in the burgeoning equation.

"I'd love to," said Gibby. "Oh, sounds like great fun. I can kibitz with your customers."

He sounds thrilled, thought Neil.

Within weeks, Gibby was sometimes helping them prepare the pastrami for the deli. He commented early on that "the cuts of meat you're getting are excellent. Where do you get them?"

"Secret source," was Neil's only answer.

Gibby took some of the burden off of Chris, who gladly focused on the deli meats that required less preparation.

One sunny day, Sean's plan was to ride his bike from Venice to Marina Del Rey. That would help him think. Sometimes he locked up the bike and jogged along the sand next to the Marina Peninsula. George Roy would run alongside and both of them would get a good workout. Sean especially enjoyed the Venice bike path when it was early and it would be clear sailing all the way.

He parked his car in one of the many beach lots. He left his lizard skin Lucchese boots in the trunk, and substituted a pair of colorful Nike all-purpose 'training' shoes that he had purchased in the Beverly Hills Nike store. Once his shoes were in place, he began the pleasant beachfront ride.

Sean needed to get another project started soon. He didn't want to partner anymore with people like the Indian. He knew that if he didn't come up with something, he would likely spend the rest of his life in movie mediocrity. He had made notes on *Beverly Hills Cannibals*, which for him was a huge step into his creative process. *No need to shoot that in town*. He would use the famous street signs, stores and hotels, and shoot it someplace on the cheap. And then tie it all together somehow

316

with cannibalism. He was searching for the connecting thread, the single plot point that would give him his 'log line', the movie parlance one sentence description of two hours of entertainment.

Maybe one more blockbuster. *That would do it for me*, he thought. *Otherwise, I might be better off in another business*.

As he rode through the section of Venice Beach restaurants, he saw a young man putting up a sign. Neil had agreed to use Donny's idea for a promotion.

The sign read:

HOLLYWOOD DELI

Old-Fashioned Pastrami On Rye

w/Dr. Brown's Soda

Re-Opening Special 1951 Prices

One To A Customer

Sean stopped. He was taken by the sign. '1951' was the year that he was born. He paused for a moment, and said the name over a few times to himself. *The Hollywood Deli*. He liked the sound. He liked the concept. He envisioned the building fully modernized, with umbrella tables outside. He saw a national chain of them, an empire that also sold its frozen products in grocery stores. Perhaps this was the something he could build on. Maybe this was an augury that it was time to leave the movie business. He got off his bike and held it by the handlebars. George Roy was at his side.

"Hey. 1951. That was the year I was born," yelled Sean. "I used to drink Dr. Brown's Cel-Ray when I was a kid. You know it used to be called tonic and not soda."

It didn't matter to Neil. "Great. That's great. Come back for lunch. It's the best deal in town!" shouted back Neil. "Such a deal."

"I just might do that. Hey. Sounds great." It was a long time since Sean had seen a young man, perhaps Jewish, starting out in the deli business. Most small start-ups, deli or otherwise, were relegated to Koreans, particularly in New York. "What the hell are you doing in the deli business?"

"Don't ask! It just happened. We also have a great barbecue sauce that we'll put on anything for you," said Neil, hoping to make a future sale.

"Good luck," said Sean. He swung his leg over the bike seat.

"Thanks," said Neil. He finished securing the last corner of the sign with some clear tape.

An hour later, Sean was lying on the beach in the hot sun. George Roy stood guard next to Sean's bike and shirt. Sean was nearly asleep, suspended in a semi-dream state, awake enough to feel the sun beating on his body. His mind wandered, trying to connect thoughts. *Beverly Hills Cannibals*. *I Spit On Your Pasta*. Of course, *BHC* would be a sequel to *ISOYP*! He chuckled at his own genius. Money. Financing. A shell company. He had done it before. He could finance the movie out of the proceeds of an existing company. He needed to find one that he could pry open, or pick up a corporate shell that had some cash flow left. Was he still enough of a salesman to talk his way in with little or no money down? Maybe he could roll some of his film library inside a shell in exchange for stock and enough control. When he opened his eyes, he was hungry. *I could use a good deli sandwich and a Dr. Brown's,* he thought.

Minutes later, Sean changed his shoes at his car. On his drive back toward Malibu, he stopped to try one of the deli sandwiches. *What harm could there be?* He knew the realities of any business, but told himself that this was no accident. He was meant to find this place before anyone else did.

It only took a few bites of the sandwich before Sean said, "This is fucking sensational." He held the balance of his sandwich in his hand. "What is it? It's not like a regular brisket, but it could be. It's more like a really lean corned beef. Which is it?" It didn't matter; his mind was spinning with ideas.

"Brisket," said Ira at the exact same time that Neil said "corned beef."

"It's a secret," said Neil. "It's a cross between brisket and corned beef. We sort of mix it up a little. For argument's sake, let's call it a really fine piece of brisket. Can I get you another sandwich, on the house? You haven't tried the pastrami special. We have an expert, Gibby Richards. He's been all over the world, a real food guy."

"This is sensational. This is great. This is great," Sean muttered as he stuffed his mouth with the oversized deli sandwich. The sauce dripped down the side of his mouth, looking very much like stage blood oozing down the cheek of an overworked actor in a Roger Corman horror movie.

"I told you it was a good sandwich," said Neil, as he grabbed a few extra napkins from the stainless steel and black holder. "Here. You're dripping."

Sean grabbed a handful of napkins, using them all to wipe his mouth. "Yeah. Thanks. It's like the commercial for whatshisname. Shit. You know. The guy who did his own commercials and the stuff drips all over."

"Carl's?" said Neil, posing it as a question.

"Yeah. Carl's Junior. You could be bigger than that. This stuff is great. Do you have any cream soda?" Sean was really enjoying himself.

"Yes," said Ira. "Dr. Brown's. The old-fashioned kind."

"Fantastic. Who owns this place?"

"My grandfather does but - " said Ira.

Neil cut him off. "But we've taken it over. Here. Let me make you one with the pastrami." Neil cleared Sean's plate.

"Naw. I don't have time and I couldn't eat it anyway," said Sean. He hesitated, and then reached for his wallet, which he kept inside the front of his jeans. "Here. Take my card. Give me a call. I think I can do something with this place. This place is going to be big. I know big. Big is my business." Sean's mind was spinning in full gear.

"Big," repeated Ira as he handed Sean the cream soda. Sean reminded him a little of Donny, only slightly more couth.

"Maybe I'll take that pastrami along with me," said Sean. He gulped the soda. "Man. Big. I'm telling you I can make this place big. Bigger than Spago. You know that he only started in one place and the only thing people spoke about, really, was the different pizzas. This place could make a fortune. I want to come back here with a few guys," said Sean.

"The prices will be higher," said Neil.

"What? You think I'm some sort of food ganif?"

"No. Not at all," said Ira.

"I was joking, boys. Come on. Lighten up. The two of you are acting like somebody died or something," said Sean.

"We have put a lot into this place, and we want to see it work," said Neil.

"But this is deli food," said Ira, who tore off a sheet of wax paper to wrap the sandwich. "You're talking some kind of California cuisine."

"He said 'big'," repeated Neil. "He's talking movie people, industry people. There really aren't any hip company delis. There's just Nate 'n Al's, Factors, the Stage in Century City and the Broadway in Santa Monica. None of them are really industry places. Civilians go to all of them."

"That's right. The Valley has a couple of real moneymakers like Art's and Jerry's. How does the Jerry's near the Beverly Center do?" asked Sean.

"I think they overbuilt and the menu is too big," said Neil.

Ira knew that Neil had no idea what he was talking about. One look of daggers from Ira and Neil became silent.

"Didn't they originally have a new issue?" asked Sean. "How did that do?" He didn't wait for an answer. "Not in this market. We raise the money privately if we can. Hold on to the whole thing. Here, call me."

Sean handed Neil the card. "When?" asked Neil.

"When you're serious about making this into a money machine," said Sean. "Hey. I've got to go." He turned and marched away. The heels of his Lucchese cowboy boots came down hard on the old, speckled linoleum floor, clicking authoritatively as he jangled his car keys like an infant in a crib. He turned back and grabbed the wrapped pastrami sandwich.

"Big," was all he said, forcing a smiling that looked more like a snarl. "Bigger than Wolfgang Puck." Sean loved to throw that name around. He was jealous of Wolf's success, of anyone's mega-success. This had to be Sean's time. He knew that this might be reaching, perhaps a sign of desperation, but it made him feel alive. *What do I have to lose?* he thought. He towered over the boys, in business as well as in physical stature.

"I'll call you. Later babe," said Neil.

Sean waved with the back of his hand and disappeared into the eclectic throngs on the boardwalk.

"Later babe?" mimicked Ira.

Neil just shrugged and smiled. "Do you think he's legit?"

"What does it say on the card?" asked Ira.

"Sean Daren Productions. He must be a producer."

"We'll never make a nickel between Donny and this guy. His boots must have cost a thousand."

"It's that kind of thinking that keeps people down. If you want to move ahead you need someone who knows how to vertically integrate a little company so we can move up."

"Neil?"

"Yes."

"You are fucking out of your mind. How long do you think you can keep up your supply of meat?" Ira cleared away the rest of the debris from Sean's table.

"I don't know. I hadn't thought about it."

"Well think about it. What about when people find out what you're doing?" Ira scooted back behind the counter.

"I don't think we have to tell anyone."

"How did I let you do this?' Ira slumped down in a plain folding chair. His head rested on the packaged loaves of bread. "I'm as immoral as you."

"Stop worrying. Things are looking up," said Neil. "Think of the future, not of morality."

Two young women on roller blades skated inside the restaurant.

Neil walked forward to greet them. "Get up. We've got customers," he yelled back to Ira. To the customers, "Sit anywhere you like."

Ira pulled himself up from his chair, and disappeared into the back kitchen.

Neil wasted no time in getting in touch with Sean. He called him that afternoon.

Sean came right to the point. "I'll draw up a business plan. The whole works. You boys will get rich. A metzieh fun a ganef!" Sean didn't know a thing about business plans, and he knew that the guys in his office were best relegated to movie budgets.

Neil wasn't sure what Sean meant by inserting the Yiddish - he didn't need Sean to tell him that it was a 'bargain' or 'a great deal'. But he was eager to see what he would come up with. As far as Neil was concerned, it was a great position to be in. Right now, there was nothing in the works, only Neil's dream of the same things Sean was selling.

A few hours later, Chris arrived with a new shipment of meat. As he unloaded the truck, Ira heard him singing. He moved closer to listen.

Chris sang, "Attend the tale of Sweeney Todd, He served a dark and hungry god, To seek revenge may lead to hell…But everyone does it and seldom as well."

Ira ran inside. "Neil. Neil. Can you stop him?"

Neil put down the menus he was distributing to the tables. "What is it? What's the matter now?"

"Chris is singing the score from *Sweeney Todd*!"

"I'm impressed." Neil thought, *Jeez, so upset over a song.* "Okay. I'll see if he knows anything from *Les Mis*, but I doubt it. I'm beginning to think Chris' repertoire is limited to special areas."

"Fuck this. I have no sense of humor about this. How can you make jokes under the circumstances? That's it. I'm pulling the plug on the whole thing."

Neil took Ira by the arm. "I'll take care of Chris. You're not pulling the plug. Okay?" Neil shook Ira gently.

"Okay." Ira pulled his arm away from Neil. "I don't want to deal with Chris again. Understood?"

"Understood." Neil headed for the back exit in order to confront Chris about his favorite musicals.

Neil set up a meeting at Sean's office with Donny and Sean. When Neil arrived, he was all set to make introductions. Donny was sitting on Bob's desk, while Sean paced the room.

Neil stood at an angle between them. "Sean. I see you already met Donny."

"Met? Do you know how many years we know each other?"

"You guys already know each other?"

"An actress on one of my movies locked herself in her trailer until I promised to get Donny to renegotiate her contract."

Donny laughed. "What a piece of work she was. We went on a few dates, and before I knew it I was managing her career. The whole thing lasted a few weeks."

"And we stayed friends," said Sean. "Who in town doesn't know Donny?"

Neil quietly took a seat across from Sean. "Okay. That's great." *Or maybe it isn't.*

"It's a money maker," said Sean. "We can do the whole thing from food to sweatshirts and hats."

"I like it," said Donny. "I'll have a business plan for you in a week. No more." He envisioned 'points' on both sides of the deal. It was done all the time in Donny's world, and he had no intention of telling Sean of his 'first in' deal with Ira and Neil. At least not yet.

Sean began to behave as if the deal was going through. He arrived one night at the deli with an entourage of people who could fill an evening of cable reruns, like *Nick At Night* or *TV Land*, only in person. It was an impressive array of talent that could star in any Where Are They Now? show.

Sean was dressed all in black. "Feed my friends and we can talk business later," he announced to Ira.

The counter man whispered to Chris, "Esa chica estaba en la *Isla de Gilligan.*"

"Si," answered Chris. "Silencio." Even television actors were royalty and commanded courtesy and respect.

A few minutes later, the group dined unknowingly on other luminaries from the past, perhaps not as famous as those alive at the table.

While they ate, Sean took Neil outside.

"Have you thought about the terms?" Sean knew that he could talk bluntly with Neil.

"What's the bottom line deal?" asked Neil.

"We're all partners. I'll sell off the other fifty per cent for the limited shares. A straight deal. Are you guys the only owners?"

"No. His grandfather is," said Neil, pointing inside to Ira.

"Oh, yeah. That's right. I'll talk to the old man," said Sean.

"No. Let me. I know him and I know Ira. Do you really think this can work?"

"Sean Daren doesn't think. He does." Sean turned and walked toward the deli. He looked back at Neil. "I know what to say to him. I'll take care of it."

Later that night, Ira and Neil sat impassively as Sean mumbled a soliloquy over his third Bloody Mary. Some of his show biz friends had moved to the beach with a few bottles of wine in tow. "I was in love with the beach as a kid. The beach was my outlet, my way to get away from my life. We were hopelessly middle class. You know I live near the beach now, but it's only a house, not a love. The Beach Boys, the sand, the thought of sex, just being there, meant everything to me. I spent endless summers hanging around, waiting for something to happen, and then it hit me. The beach was just my excuse for being a loser, and anyone hanging around the beach was a loser too, because nothing happened there. I never got laid, and I never made any money. I changed. But here I am, back at the beach, but I'm not the same kid. I'm older and smarter, and can see that we are going to make a ton of money with this business. The beach has a future, and I want to bring us all into the Twenty-First Century." Even Sean realized that he might have overdone it.

Ira and Neal glanced at each other, not sure what to say.

"We want to be on the super-highway to the Twenty-First Century," said Neil. "Or shall we take the train?"

"That's funny," said Sean. "You ought to write." He welcomed the comic relief.

"Now *that* is funny. I always thought I'd make a good producer," said Neil.

"Not now, Neil. What's our first step, Sean?" asked Ira.

"You get your grandfather on board and I'll start raising the big money," said Sean. He decided that it was best to let them try to influence a relative. He inhaled deeply as he stared at the beach. He moved out slowly, as if being drawn by some supernatural force.

After Sean left, Ira suggested that they call Kyle Bixler, the attorney they had run into at Chez Jays, after Ira had decorated his car. "We need someone on our side, to look at the contract."

Neil agreed. He knew that he was heading into the big leagues, and treachery was always lurking in the shadows of business propriety. He knew that he could count on Donny only so much, and Sean was a total unknown.

The next morning, Neil called Bixler from the pay phone in the rear of the deli. Donny had given Neil some kind of bootlegged phone card.

"Who's the guy who wants to do the deal?" asked Bixler. He had his feet up on his desk.

"Sean Daren," said Neil.

"Sean Daren? You're lucky to get him." Bixler had known him for years, and recently had to 'sign off' on the legal regarding Mal's Vegas shoot.

"Can you do the legal for us?" asked Neil.

"Do you mind if I call Sean?"

"No. Why?" Before he got the question out, Neil already knew the answer. *Why should Bixler waste his time just representing me, Ira, and Mel? Bixler wants to rep the whole deal, start to finish.*

Neil also put in a call to Manfred Safire, his friend from his days at Dean Witter. Neil wanted to cover all bases. "Who knows? The company might go public one day," was said at the onset of the conversation. Neil tried to learn everything he could, in advance.

The initial business plan called for startup capital of three million dollars. The general partners were Mel Packer, Ira, Neil, and Sean, although 'deals' could be created to give people "points" on both sides – the initial partners or the investors. Donny was quick to solidify his 'side' deal with Mel, Ira, and Neil; he would get a small percentage of everything that they received.

The question of who to turn to for making fund-raising presentations was on the table. A few names were suggested. It became an easy call. Godfrey, from the tennis club, seemed to be the logical proper choice. He knew everyone in town and beyond, and had the business acumen to make the presentations palatable for anyone.

Godfrey began with a cost analysis of everything from the utilities down to the uniforms. He made pretty, colorful pie charts and graphs from the bundled software that came with the tennis club's computers. Some types of information would be mounted on slides, while others were enlarged and placed on an easel. There was talk of a video, but when the group realized that there wasn't much to shoot, the idea was nixed. Colorful photos of the food and staff would suffice.

Godfrey even created an average individual food check calculation, dividing the chart tables into first course, second course, third course, dessert, and non-alcoholic beverages. He prepared a statement of income based on Mel's best years, averaged in with the last three, which were not as good. He also prepared a balance sheet, including future liabilities, which would come in the form of bank notes and loans, assuming the group would someday go that expansion route for new cash. Sean had ideas of continuing to sell stock privately, hopefully at higher increments, a system that increased the value of the original shares as new investors bought in at higher prices.

The business description was clear. "The Hollywood Deli will be a delicatessen type restaurant modeled after New York versions. In addition to the classic Jewish-style foods, it will also have a full modern bar and popular coffee machinery to serve espresso and cappuccino."

Godfrey didn't miss a thing. Marketing strategy, food preparation statements, management team descriptions, objectives of the team, and a complete menu were supplied. He identified the customer base, market growth, and competition. He made it clear that "it will not be a fast food restaurant," and emphasized that the quality of the food will be one of the keys for success. This was important since many investors from all over the world were taking a bath in Planet Hollywood and similar ventures that turned out ordinary, lackluster finger food.

Neil laughed to himself when he read the food preparation process. "As a Jewish-style delicatessen, many of the final menu items will have to be supplied by specialty out-of-the-area food and restaurant suppliers." The list was extensive and mentioned many of the famous ones - Zion-Kosher Company and Hebrew-National Products, both in New York.

Godfrey did a flowery job with the biographies of all the parties. Mel Packer came off looking like the most popular man in Los Angeles restaurant history, and Neil and Ira were depicted as brilliant wunderkind. Sean was an easy rival for Bill Gates and Donny was credited for being some kind of Hollywood creative genius, at least when it came to business.

On paper, everything looked great. Sean knew that what went down on paper had little to do with how things would go. They had to first get enough seed money to get the concept rolling in Venice. If it worked, they would expand immediately, probably trying to get into Beverly Hills, Brentwood, or Santa Monica. The foot traffic at the Santa Monica mall, adjacent to the Third Street Promenade, was as good as or better location than Venice, but the costs to start up in that area had skyrocketed since Third Street had been closed off and turned into the famous Promenade.

Sean contacted Dr. K., someone he knew would be helpful. He jumped at the chance to be involved. Dr. K.'s wife wasted no

329

time setting up a dinner party for prospective investors at
their home. They had a spectacular house on North Alpine Drive,
one block above Sunset, just a few blocks east of the
prestigious Beverly Hills Hotel, across the street from Don
Rickles and a few doors up from Tom Cruise, the latter two more
important to locals and out-of-town investors.

Dr. K.'s wife was an old pro at setting up these dinners as
well as the suckers. The goal was simple. Ply the guests with
fine wine and food and, at the right moment, get the patrons to
empty their pockets for one of the doctor's latest ventures. He
had previously sold everything – from immune power diets and
gastric bubbles to a chain called The Thinking Stores. Before
arranging the dinner, the esteemed Dr. K. made his own side deal
with Sean. The Doctor would get additional percentage points in
'full partner' stock over any amounts he brought in from 'his
people.' Such was standard and all negotiable.

When the night of the dinner arrived, Dr. K. was walking
with a cane. If anyone asked, he told them that it was a skiing
accident. His remarks inspired a lot of winking.

A few weeks earlier, he had called his wife from the
emergency room at Cedars-Sinai Hospital. The Demerol was
starting to take effect, and the pain in his hip had become a
mere dull ache. "Don't get upset. I'm in the emergency room at
Cedars. I tripped on my way to the bathroom after the staff
meeting at the hospital. I think I may have done something to my
hip or foot or both. Tell Susie that I may be a little late to
the graduation...Honey. Can you get me a glass of water?...No. I
was talking to the nurse...Water. I was asking for water. I
know. A hospital like this should be able to get me some water.
Look it. I'll do my best. They're calling me to go for an x-ray.
Okay...Okay...I will...Later...Right...Bye."

Earlier that night, the Doctor had sat alone in the emergency room icing his hip and staring at a swollen foot. By the time the sun rose he was in a hospital bed with a cast on his right foot. About the same time, Heather was already preparing an e-mail that she was going to spread around Hollywood. The first copy was going to Brian at CAA. The second copy was going to the mailroom at William Morris. There, a friend at Morris would see to it that it found its way to the executive offices. Every studio would get a copy.

Her first draft was coming along fine:

Poor Koppy got sloshy,

And wanted to try his luck.

Another of his fancy fucks.

So he put on his rubber (suit),

Slowly, cause of blubber.

I don't know what rhymes with ass,

So I just can tell you that the hoist broke and he fell on it - his ass, that is.

Poor Koppy!

Heather didn't bother to edit it very much. She wanted it to be disjointed. Within a few hours, all the Hollywood insiders knew that it was Dr. K. Many of the rumors about his extracurricular activities that had originally started during his late-night visits to play 'backgammon' with Hef at the Playboy mansion were further solidified as fact.

Dr. K. could have cared less. He was essentially a business animal who believed that all's fair in love and war. Like an old wounded soldier, he trudged forward. There was a new deal on the table, and it meant as much to him today as it would have thirty years ago. What really got him off was the slithering around celebrities and big money people, and not his sexual escapades with Heather or anyone else.

The night of the presentation, the room was filled with Hollywood legends past and present, some with deep pockets, but most with flash, the runner up to first tier invitations. The latter attracted the former, one of the best and consistent examples of symbiosis in Hollywoodland. The backdrop of deals was always painted with people 'in the business'. Dave Stirling sat next to Dr. K. The crowd from Hillcrest was well represented.

After a brief introduction by Neil, Godfrey made a decent presentation. The video effects added by Donny at the last minute were clean and neat, and the money charts based on past performance of known entities tweaked everyone's interest. The examples discussed were Jerry's Deli and Starbuck's coffee. It didn't matter that Donny had come up with the stats and forced them on Godfrey, who reluctantly agreed to use them without checking their authenticity.

A half-million dollar investment could net each partner no less than a market value of five million each, providing the stock in the company eventually went public at ten dollars a share. That was also taking into account an estimated valuation for the initial investment of a dollar per share, something the SEC would have to ultimately agree upon. Each time new money came into the company, the new investor would be 'charged' more for his stock.

Mal and Ricky were on hand, mostly as window dressing. Nobody cared about Ricky, but Mal was still a big ticket, especially with the older crowd.

Ricky pranced around like a child in a candy store. He sensed the excitement. He could see that this was really going to happen. Things like this could snowball. Before the evening was out, Ricky convinced Mal to invest in the deli.

"Look. Mal. Just do it for me."

"Ricky. It's a gamble," said Mal. "I'm not interested in those big number crapshoots."

"Mal. You've gambled every day of your whole life. I don't know, but a good guess is you've pissed away millions playing the commodities markets." Ricky didn't know for certain that it was true, but Mal had trusted too many people in the past and was left only with Bixler.

"Ricky. If you can get them to sell a quarter share or less, I'll think about it. I'm sure that's possible. But you must run it by Bixler." Little did Ricky know that Mal could easily put up the half-million, but he wanted Ricky to think that he was only comfortable investing less. Generally, his favorite number to throw at Ricky - for any reason - was fifty thousand. Mal actually thought that the deli was a good investment - definitely better than a crapshoot in Vegas. He observed the turnout in the room, and a full house was a good sign for an old vaudevillian. Mal knew most of the faces and the history. He would make sure that plenty of heavy hitters would invest first. Then he would 'go in' after speaking privately with Bixler. Mal would never tell Ricky the true amount.

Ricky spent the evening canvassing the room for people who might also be interested in partial shares, while trying to convince others to sell Mal part of their full shares. He was wasting his time, in keeping with most things that he did, this one set up deliberately by Mal. Mal had enough business experience to know that fractional shares would eventually materialize.

Dave Stirling cornered Sean. "Put me down for a full share. Maybe two." He paused to see if Sean was impressed. "Call my office tomorrow. We can play golf and discuss it further." Dave wouldn't stop with that. He already intended to take over as much of the company as possible. He had missed out on the excitement of Marvin Davis' deal to bring the Carnegie Deli to Beverly Hills. Dave was lucky; the restaurant was a bomb. But he was still slightly bitter about some "lightweights" who had gotten in on the ground floor with Wolfgang Puck.

"Great," said Sean. "I'll do that."

Sean was pleased to have Dave aboard. Dave was a tough businessman, but generally a fair one. Dave's money would bring several highly visible followers, the usual money that followed the super-rich. A few of them enjoyed boasting that they were in a deal with the Stirlings, even if their shares was marginal.

Once verbal confirmation buzzed around the room that Dave and Dr. K. were in, Sean acknowledged that it would be possible to buy half and quarter shares. Of course, Sean had visions of getting Barry to kick in a full share at a discount, including extra points. Sean would pitch Barry the next time he was in the office, and by the fervor in the room, he felt that it would be soon.

Ricky made sure to tell everyone that Mal was going to be on the upcoming Emmy show. "I know how to keep the buzz going," he would always say to Arnie. This type of behavior drove Arnie crazy and Mal apoplectic.

"Ricky. Mal doesn't need you to do his publicity," Arnie would intone over and over.

"If it wasn't for me, people would have forgotten Mal a long time ago," was Ricky's stock answer. He truly believed that he was responsible for Mal's longevity in show business.

By the end of the evening, Sean had raised a ton of money. The unlikely partners were on their way. Dave Stirling cornered Bixler before he had left and received a verbal agreement from him that he would make all the financials of everyone involved available to Dave. Nobody had to know, and Dave would "make sure plenty of new business" came Bixler's way. When it came to business, Bixler always identified who the six-hundred pound gorilla was and like the old joke, knew what to say when he walked into the room - nothing! "And what do you allow a six-hundred-pound gorilla to do if he shows up at a meeting?" - "Whatever he wants."

Within days, Sean began feeling apprehensive about the whole project, especially since more money was coming in. He always had self-doubt when something new got off the ground, the dark fear of failure that crept into every business deal. He had the same kind of feeling with every one of his movies. On the first day of principal shooting, he felt as if the project was doomed to failure. In each of those cases, he ran directly from the set to Barry's office. This project was no exception.

Sean had made a late afternoon appointment with Barry. After exchanging pleasantries, the two stared at each other as Barry munched a chicken salad on a croissant. "You want a bite?" Barry finally asked to break the silence. "I can't eat a whole one of these, but I thought I ought to have something because I have late patients."

Sean was preoccupied with his own dilemma. "Barry. You know I don't have it."

"Have what?" Barry knew what Sean meant.

"I don't have the killer instinct to be in this business."

"Oh. That again? I don't know about that. It comes and it goes. Too bad you still have some morals."

"Come on. It's bad enough I still pay you for these visits. Can't you be serious and pretend like you're a real shrink?"

Barry paused for a moment, as if he were having a revelation. His face took on an innocent stare; he was transported to another place. "Oy vey iz mir!"

Sean thought that Barry sounded legitimately annoyed. Barry threw up his hands, holding them still for a few seconds for added dramatic effect. "Maybe I know you too long, too well, to be helpful. Sean, you are basically a decent person, and yes, you probably are not the best equipped for your business. We've been over this. You are not a killer. You have to be a business killer, a business animal to make it and stay on top. You've done okay. I don't know anyone who is more devoted to his daughter than you are. So…You're not on top. So what?" Barry knew that his remark about Katherine wasn't entirely accurate. Sean's emotional absenteeism during his daughter's life was compensated for with money - 'devotion' in Hollywood.

Sean felt his pulse throb in his neck. "So, what? I'll tell you 'so what'! I'm always on the verge of going broke again, and if I don't get another hit soon I don't know how I can go on. I'll be worth more dead to my daughter than alive."

"Don't talk like that. You always bounce back up. You always have things in the fire. You'll do okay. Are you working on anything new?"

Sean was waiting for the conversation to come around to business. He knew that he could set Barry up by softening him first and then hitting him with the idea. "I do have a new idea.

It's really sensational, but I'm too embarrassed to ask you to get involved."

"Good."

"Dave Stirling has already bought in big time."

"I'm not interested." Barry paused and checked his watch. "How much did Dave put in?"

"Big. That's all I can say."

"Well. Good luck to him. That's all I can say."

"I already have over three million." Sean glanced at his watch. "But, I understand. Taking a risk at your age…"

"Three million. Why do you need so much front money?" Barry figured it out fast. "It's not a picture, is it?"

"I'd better not tell you. Forget it. It's too risky."

"Sean. I'm just curious. I'm not interested for me. I'm interested for you. Now tell me. How much are you looking for?" asked Barry in his most demanding tone.

Sean spilled the deal details like someone eager to confess a crime to the overbearing detectives. "There's another five-hundred-thousand left, maybe a million. I can divide that, even if I have to sell you part of mine." It was all bullshit. The final number for the initial capitalization was still in flux. Sean new that Dave was going to redo the whole deal. That was his style.

Barry spoke slowly. "You put your own money in?"

"Five-hundred-thousand cash. If this goes south, I'm done." Both statements were even further from the truth.

"So that's why you keep talking about going broke." Barry knew that 'going broke' was only a euphemism. "Broke is a relative term."

"Yeah, I have those bonds, but I transferred them to my daughter. A little each year. It's better for her to have the interest, and then there won't be any estate tax on it, ever. And the house is worth plenty. Plus my film library."

"So what's the business?"

Sean leaned forward. "A new issue," said Sean in a hushed tone. "Insider stock before it goes public. Could go public at ten to fifty times the initial insider price."

"What's so special about a fucking new issue? Since the tech dive, the new issues market has been really slow."

"It's going to be all ours. I mean. All of the investors. It's a startup company."

"Not high tech, I hope."

"No. Nothing like that."

"What?" Barry stood up. "Are you going to tell me, or what?"

"It's a deli."

Even Barry had to pause. "A deli?" He forced himself to laugh nervously. He retook his seat.

"It's a great idea. Listen to this." Sean mouthed the words slowly. "The Hollywood Deli."

Barry mouthed the words without making a sound. "I like it, but I can't afford it right now. It's hard for me to see the future in a deli. Haven't the delis been in decline for decades?"

Sean had already anticipated the reversal, and explained the plan. "It's going to be big. We can open six new delis right away in California. The first new location is going to be in the Glendale Galleria or Beverly Hills proper. We already have talked to the mall people, and we can get the best terms there. We will also go into the Santa Monica Marketplace Mall or the Third Street Promenade. It's a tossup because the foot traffic is greatest on Third Street, since it's outdoors, but the indoor mall has that great food court on the first floor with doors on

like three sides. We've also lined up a little shop in Beverly
Hills, right in the heart of the business triangle. It's going
to be a big chain. Once these stores get going we'll go into
Vegas. I already talked to people like Gluck and Kerkorian. Who
knows? We may do a casino deal like the Hard Rock. Barry. This
is going to be big. Really big."

"Who did you say is doing the new issue?"

"I don't know yet, but I've been on the phone with a lot of
people. It might be Montgomery in San Francisco. Our stock is
going to be valued at less than a buck - a buck at most. Within
six months they're telling me they can get more private
placement money for five bucks a share. Five bucks a share!
You'll - I mean - anyone involved will have a paper gain of more
than five times their investment, before we even go public. If
you wanted out then, I guarantee I'd sell your shares for the
five bucks. But, that would be dumb. That's only the beginning."

"Let me think about it," said Barry. "I have another
patient." He would have loved to have said 'yes' on the spot,
but didn't want Sean to know how much he wanted in. It was a big
number for him, but he knew the leverage that it could bring.
Ten to one. Maybe more! would echo in his brain the rest of the
day.

"Sure. Sure. I didn't want to pressure you," said Sean,
even though things went exactly as he had planned.

Barry shot up to escort Sean to the rear exit door.

Sean hammered him with his closer. "Barry. I wasn't going
to tell you this, but if in two years if you don't show a profit
I'll buy back whatever you put in dollar-for-dollar myself,
personally."

"A guarantee? With what?"

"I mean it," said Sean.

"I couldn't let you do that."

"I did it with Kopplemeyer. It was the only way I could get him in."

Barry raised his voice, a rare occurrence, particularly around his office. "That's not why you did it. You give me so little credit. I am a shrink. We do know some things. You want to show him that you're a big shot. He's always been throwing it up to you how many great deals he has made. And he lives bigger and travels better than any of us."

Sean didn't have time for any real analysis. "Whatever. I'll give you the same deal."

"Okay. Thanks. Let me think about it."

"Okay. I'll speak to you tomorrow."

"Right. Bye." Barry opened the door by turning the dead bolt to one side and pulled the door open by holding on to the thumb turn.

"See ya," said Sean as he moved swiftly through the doorway. *I can always tell him later that I'll knock down his price a little*, he thought.

Barry locked the door behind him. He stopped in the kitchen area to get an iced tea, before opening the waiting room connecting door for his next patient. He knew too many of the players to back off of the deli deal. He felt his pulse race. For Barry, it was a true Hollywood moment, and he needed to desperately be a part of it.

Sean made his way down the old, worn, marble stairs; he was too impatient to wait for the elevator. He tried to discern how much of his visit with Barry was real and how much was part of the set up to accomplish his goal, to get Barry in on the deal. Did he want Barry only because he wanted the money, or was it all part of the bonding thing with his own shrink, having him available to help stay the course during any storms? By the time Sean reached the bottom step and skipped outside into the cool night air, it didn't matter; none of it mattered. Within Sean's life, just like in his movies, the back story was of no consequence, only the action that furthered the plot.

Getting the cash from Mal proved to be a problem. His first check bounced and Sean screamed at Bixler. "Get me the fucking money or I'll go to the networks on this. You'll never write another contract for anyone."

Bixler knew that it was an idle threat, and wasn't even sure what threat connection Sean was trying to make. Bixler was more secure than Sean, and had dealt with all kinds of Hollywood fights, from people making claims on the Peter Sellers estate to infighting amongst the families of the Three Stooges and Marx Brothers.

Arnie ultimately hand-delivered the money to Sean, but not without a strong reminder. "Remember. Ricky must never know the size of the investment. If you are ever forced to say anything, say it's 'fifty thou'. The kid is used to that number. Mal has always told him everything cost 'fifty thou'. Okay?" Mal and Arnie were also worried - as usual - about Ricky blabbing to the tabloids.

Sean had no feelings for Arnie's remarks, nor for Mal or Ricky. Sean's job was to collect the money, make sure Dave Stirling got his way, and do everything in his power to push the deal into the stratosphere.

CHAPTER TWELVE
Mal, Ricky

    Nothing ever changed at the Rose home; it was the same as
it had been for the last twenty years. About a week after Mal
had made the investment, Ricky waited at the sunlit breakfast
table until Mal danced downstairs and made his entrance. Mal
didn't allow anyone in his bedroom, which he always referred to
as his 'dressing room'. He wore makeup every day, just enough
applied to hide the nicks and dents in an otherwise ageless
face.
    Ricky never ate very much in the morning. Once Mal was
asleep at night, Ricky would eat box after box of Lorna Doones,
colored marshmallows, and an assortment of Hershey chocolate
bars, the mini ones that came in giant bags. He kept them in his
cheeks like a squirrel, letting the chocolate melt inside his
mouth; he'd been doing that since he was a child. Mal insisted
that Ricky buy his munchies in bulk at Costco, the factory-
styled discount store. When Ricky was nearly satiated, he would
have a night cap of Pop Tarts, right out of the box, dipped in
any kind of melted ice cream. Ricky only bought the largest
quantities of off-brand sale ice cream, quantifying the cost by
the pint, and proudly announcing the money he had saved by not
buying Ben & Jerry's or some other popular brand. Mal had Ricky

well-trained, and Ricky was very much afraid of one day being
poor.

Mal ate the same self-indulgent breakfast every day. He
would start with a small orange juice, to which he would add a
spoonful of honey. "It's good for the chords," he would say each
and every time, like a television doctor giving the health
report on the local news. "In the old days, a lot of guys would
take honey before they went on. That might work temporarily, but
you have to coddle your chords every day." He would repeat the
last phrase, raising his voice to his trademark famous high
pitch. "Coddle your chords every day!" Mal was easily a tenor
and the old crowd used to kid him by calling him a soprano.

That morning Ricky watched as Mal buttered his "Wonder
Bread only" white toast. The butter would go on only if it was
already room temperature. It had to be the proper consistency or
Mal would have a fit. He had fired more than one housekeeper for
not having his butter ready when it came time to butter his
toast. He had to be the one to butter it, "because those
wetbacks don't know shit about buttering toast. Where they come
from they soak the damn tortillas in god knows what kind of
shitty grease." He had similar criticisms for Italians – the
calzones - who put too much olive oil on their bread, and the
French – frogs - who overdid the duck fat. Mal would come off
funny when he was out for dinner with his cronies, somewhat the
culinary racist, but at home over time his audience of one had
grown weary.

Once the toast was buttered, Mal would cut two or three
little pieces of garlic, fresh from a clove that sat already
peeled in a small ceramic dish alongside the butter. Buttered
with garlic was the only way that Mal ever ate toast, or any
plain bread for that matter. Ricky remembered the big Sunday
night dinners at Matteo's Restaurant - the Sinatra hangout.

343

Matty, the affable owner and Sinatra pal from the old days in Hoboken, would run back to the kitchen to make sure that someone brought out plain toast, the room temperature butter plate, and a clove of peeled garlic, while making certain that he didn't sit Mal too close to Sinatra, who wasn't that fond of Mal, especially his dinner habits and conversation. When Mal arrived, Matty's brother Mike exploded into his most exuberant greeting, reminiscent of a leading man in a musical doing the 'big number' or an upbeat 'eleven o'clock number'.

Occasionally someone on the staff thought that they were being helpful and prepared Mal's toast in the kitchen. One night, in the company of Lucille Ball and her husband Gary Morton, Mal threw the toast in the waiter's face after he had gleefully exclaimed, "Mr. Rose. I make it just the way you like it."

"What the fuck do you know about anything? I told you what I wanted, the way I wanted it, and you, and you, you little 'shtick dreck', you think you have any idea what you're doing?" Mal would spit the words out without even glancing at the trembling waiter.

The offending waiter slinked back into the kitchen, and then Mal insisted that Matty force the guilty server to bring out the toast set up all over again.

Mal's garlic habit did not make him any less popular with the women, although there was one time when he was shooting a love scene too soon after breakfast. The leading lady threatened to quit if Mal didn't use breath mints. He usually told the story using Lucille Ball or Marilyn Monroe as the leading lady. If he were talking to a really old crowd and didn't mind dating himself, he would say Sarah Bernhardt. Nobody knew if any of Mal's trysts were real or figments of his imagination and the

Hollywood publicity machine. He was never mentioned as a lover in any star's biography.

"Mal. They called again about the Emmy Awards," said Ricky, trying to interject what he felt was an important subject, utilizing the most innocuous way that he could muster.

Mal continued to eat. "Fuck 'em."

Ricky pleaded, "But Mal. These aren't the same people."

"Fuck 'em anyway." Mal dipped his spoon into his Cheerios, and churned the milk over the little 'o's until they were all saturated to his taste. "A good cereal has got to be porous."

"I know you never got over the fact that you were nominated seven times and never won an Emmy. I know that. These people know that, and they want to make it up to you." Ricky really believed that, but in the mercurial world of show business awards he also knew that old wounds never heal. Mal thought that he had been shunned one too many times by people he found lifeless and talentless.

Mal banged his spoon on the flowery plastic tablecloth. "Mal V. Rose is not going to stand up in the audience like some piece-of-dreck politician on the old Ed Sullivan show." He was referring to the 'look at me and take a bow' routine that Sullivan had used to plug different celebrities during his days as the powerful master of television exposure. "Mal V. Rose is a star, a real star, and if they had any sense they'd hire me to host the whole god-dammed show. They know I'm the best, but they are afraid I'll take the job away from whatshisname, Billy 'Cheap' Crystal." Like many older comedians from vaudeville, Mal resented the success of younger acts, "who didn't put the time in honing their skills." Whether or not that was true in Billy's case didn't matter. Mal had a hard-on for Billy, who appeared to be doing some of Mal's old shtick when he had played an aging comedian in *Mr. Saturday Night*. The cigar-under-the-lip could

345

just as easily have been attributed to Milton Berle or Alan
King, but Mal claimed that he was the first one to use the bit
at some obscure theater on the Orpheum circuit.

"Mal. Billy Crystal hosts the Academy Awards," said Ricky.
He had never learned that factual details didn't matter to Mal.

"What the fuck is the difference? I should host that show,
too. That Billy Crystal is okay, particularly when he does all
of my impressions. Where do you think he got those facial moves?
Huh? Those are Mal V. Rose facial moves. Nobody in the business
ever had moves like that. And does he ever mention me? Never.
Because he's afraid that people will put two and two together
and come up with the fact that he stole his act from Mal V.
Rose, just like dozens of other young comics."

A lot of older people in the industry thought that Mal
'stole' his facial contortions from Harry Ritz. Nobody could be
certain that even Harry was the first. Facial expressions, sadly
for Mal, did not fall under intellectual property law.

"Mal. I think you should do it," said Ricky.

"Call my attorney, fat-face Bixler, and have him draft a
letter. I want it to read like this. Get a pen and paper." It
was typical Mal; he had to run the show - any show; any time.

Ricky jumped from his chair and grabbed a yellow, lined,
legal pad that was used for leaving shopping lists for the
housekeeper. There were twenty or so multicolored markers
nearby, "the big fat kind" - the only kind that Mal would touch.
"Ergonomics, Ricky. Mal V. Rose invented ergonomics." In his
nervous haste, Ricky ended up with a red one, but it didn't
matter, so long as he got Mal's wishes down on paper.

Mal cleared his throat and licked another spoon of honey
while he spoke. "Dear Mr. Whatever-the-head-guy's-name-is: My
client, Mal V. Rose, is pleased to have received your offer to
appear on the Emmy Award show. While he would like to do more

for you, he feels it is time to pass the mantel to the younger stars, and would be happy to appear on the show providing the following press release is sent out two weeks before the show…Are you getting this Ricky?"

"Yes, Mal. I've got it. Press release two weeks before the show."

"Right. The release reads this way…'Legendary performer Mal V. Rose turned down the Emmy's request to be a host at this year's Emmy Awards Show. Mr. Rose graciously suggested that 'it's time to give someone else a chance'."

Ricky smiled. "That's great, Mal. Great."

Mal smiled back and took a sip of his cup of 'half decaf, half coffee, and a splash of heavy cream'. "Fucking right you are, Ricky. Now you back up this story and spread it around the Friars how they fucking begged me to do it and I said 'no'. Got it?"

"Got it," said Ricky, who was still writing. "You want *me* to spread this around town?"

"Yes. You're good at keeping the buzz going. Now get that over to fat-face this morning." Mal stood up and stretched his arms out wide.

"But I was going…" Ricky saw the fuse ignite in Mal's eyes. "I can drop it there when his office opens. It will be on his desk before he comes in."

Mal only nodded. "Well, I'm headed over to the Friars. See you later. Pick me up at one-fifteen, or if you want to have lunch, Jan Murray is coming today. If you want to eat with us, come earlier."

"Okay. I was going down to Santa Monica College to see if they will accept my credits from the advanced placement I took at Beverly High." That was something Ricky had been planning for many years.

Mal leaned on the table for emphasis. "What for? College is a waste of time. I keep telling you. Get a job as a page at NBC. That's the way to start a career."

"Mal. I'm way over thirty. Don't you think I'm too old to be a page?" Ricky didn't really want an answer to his question.

"Is this the first time I told you? The first time I told you was when your mother died."

"She's still alive, Mal."

"Dead. She was dead the day she got on that plane for New York."

Ricky said nothing. He had heard it all before and was confused enough by Mal asking him to do P.R. work, something he had always been chastised for in the past.

Mal pushed himself away from the table and without turning shot back a parting remark. "What the hell can you learn in college anyway?"

"I want to take some math. I was good at math. Maybe I can get into a training program as a stockbroker."

"Crooks," Mal mumbled as he sauntered off. "They robbed my mother blind, and they got me for plenty, too."

"You gambled. Those commodities were risky," Ricky said, as his voice trailed off in a faint murmur. "Never mind…"

Mal mumbled something and disappeared past the housekeeper, who was instructed to clear the table the second after he was finished.

About two weeks before the Emmy program, Mal had Arnie call to say that Mal could appear after all, providing he presented an award with one of the cast members from *Will and Grace*. "But not the guy that plays the fag," Mal told Arnie. If he couldn't be linked with one of them, *Friends* was okay. The request was flatly turned down, but since Mal definitely wanted to be on the show, the production people worked out a premium presenter spot for him after a lengthy negotiation with Arnie. They even agreed to let him sing a small solo as part of a larger number.

The night of the Emmy Awards, after reading the winner for best actor on a sitcom, Mal refused to leave the stage, and started doing some of his old shtick. The director was prepared, and the control room was set to cut to a commercial as soon as Mal finished his first joke. When they returned from commercial, Mal was gone. What the television audience didn't see was a screaming and cursing Mal, who threatened to sue everyone including the network sponsors. He was personally 'dragged' off the stage by the director and Tubby, one of the writers who Mal knew and respected from the old days.

"Let go of his arms," shouted Ricky. He tried to get closer to the situation, but a security guard blocked his way. The guard had been told to keep Ricky away from the backstage area, as well as the control booth and any actors. This was nothing new for the Roses.

CHAPTER THIRTEEN
Brantley
Linda, Barry

     I had made plans to send a screenplay based on my play *Small Steaks* to Walter Mirisch. This came about as result of an unexpected meeting with Dave Stirling. After I had initially met him at Hillcrest, his secretary called my office to set up the meeting. Dave Stirling excitedly jumped on the line and interrupted her – "I have a great idea for you" - including some boilerplate about wanting to help a friend of Sean's. I didn't flinch. It didn't matter to me what his motivation was. I knew that he had a single daughter who was sort of involved or had been involved with Sean. Or perhaps Dave Stirling wanted to add me to his personal list of healthcare providers. At that juncture, I responded without giving it much thought. In fact, I went through with the Hollywood moment of thinking that I was somehow on my way. After all, this was better than nothing and the names that Dave Stirling threw around were all well-known and successful.

     Mirisch was best known for his *Pink Panther* cartoons and movies. Peter Sellers appeared in most of the Mirisch versions. I picked up two biographies of Sellers, so that I could be conversant about him. I read about the self-hating Jew, the sadomasochist, and the egomaniacal cheapskate, who one author compared to Adolph Hitler. As I read about the 'funny guy', it didn't take long to realize that Sellers was a living, walking, hell of a human being. After putting down the books for the last time, I decided not to mention Sellers at this anticipated meeting with Mirisch. Sellers once walked out of a screening, with only one parting remark for Mirisch, "You'll be hearing from me." It wasn't an idle threat. Sellers tried to get the movie destroyed.

Once I gave a copy of *Small Steaks* to Dave - he told me to stop calling him Mr. Stirling - his attitude changed abruptly. It was no longer a simple favor. Dave was going to "handle it" for me. It was in keeping with what New York said about the Hollywood crowd - everyone was in the business. Dave was no exception. I had no idea that he loved to pal around with movie people, pretending from time to time that he was genuinely in the loop.

Dave began a series of bizarre phone conversations with me, as if he owned the property. "I should have gotten a production credit on *The Marrying Man*, but I didn't want to get involved legally. Alan King claimed that he gave the idea to Neil Simon, and there already was some sort of litigation. I knew Kim and Alec very well, so I didn't want to cause any additional trouble."

I was in over my head, but the allure was too great to back away from. I had read about the convoluted nature of movie deals, and was in no position to judge Dave's abilities or background. Movie projects had a history of bizarre financial sources, from fertilizer moguls to baseball team owners to people who vaguely referred to their Middle East or Asian money.

"Who do you think we should get to play the lead?" Dave asked during one of his now frequent calls.

I felt odd talking about this between patient appointments. "What about Jason Biggs or Ryan Stiles, the tall guy on *The Drew Carrey Show*?" The characters they were to play in my screenplay were urban New Yorkers, first year medical students at N.Y.U.

"Fucking-A wrong. You don't start out looking for guys like that. That's who you end up with if you can't get a Cruise. Hey, don't get involved in this part. You're the writer. Remember?" I would learn that writers' opinions were solicited only as a formality, in the extreme case like George Bush asking Bill Clinton as a courtesy when to attack Iraq.

I made a note that so many people said things like 'a' Cruise or "a" Costner, which meant 'A' list.

The situation was nothing like I had expected. Dave told me not to call, write, or have anything to do with Mirisch's office. I was to write a letter to Dave, asking for his help in getting a movie deal for *Small Steaks*. The copy would go to Mirisch. Dave would take care of everything. "Don't worry, Brantley. It's a good thing you know someone like me out here. You could really get fucked around."

During the most recent conversation, Dave had made sure to mention that he had just seen Arnold, Goldie, and movie executive Mark Canton, divorced from his producer wife, Wendy. "Wendy won the Academy Award for *Forest Gump*. If Mirisch passes, I'll just bring it to Wendy."

I did one of the dumbest things; I told Sean about what had happened with Dave. "Dave Stirling is an egomaniac. He is only interested in himself. Having dinner with Dave Stirling is like watching *Biography* on the Arts and Entertainment channel. I think he really believes his own hype."

Sean immediately set up a luncheon meeting at Juniors deli with Barry and I. Barry, on cue from Sean, added his opinion of Dave. "I can't comment on him personally. You know a lot of

people think he's a narcissistic bully. I certainly don't know
him that way. He was always very kind to me, and he gave five-
hundred-thousand dollars to psychiatric research at UCLA, just
because I asked him to do it. There is such a thing as a
narcissistic personality disorder, but I can't say definitively
that it's him. It just wouldn't be right. Look. You know these
kinds of guys. When he says 'he's a nice guy', it means someone
he can control. 'He's a good man' is code for someone to do your
corporate bidding. Look. I don't want to get into his personal
life. Okay?"

That was okay with me. I assumed that the purpose of the
meeting was to let Sean do something with *Small Steaks,* instead
of Dave. It was never made clear, but Sean reminded me to send
him a copy. "Sure. Send it care of Bob. Call him at my direct
office number. He'll be in later. He's really good with this
stuff."

When Sean returned to his office after lunch, he casually
mentioned the information to Bob. "The root canal doctor from
New York is going to send you a screenplay."

"That's fantastic," said Bob. "This sounds familiar."

"Alzheimer's?" Sean pointed at Bob.

"Not me." Bob used his thumb to point back at Sean.

"Listen. Remember that idea I told you about?"

"No," said Bob, even though he did. He lit a cigarette.

"Come on. You know. The cannibal thing, sort of a sequel to
I Spit On Your Pasta. I have the name. *Beverly Hills Cannibals.*
If this doctor can write, maybe I can use him to get some story
down for us, for nothing." That was Sean's automatic way of
dealing with new writers in town - getting free work.

Bob went into his "I'm really interested, this sounds
exciting mode", while laughing to himself at the ridiculous
idea. He had heard these ideas many times before. What usually

353

happened would happen again. Bob would begin with a two-page treatment of the idea, written by one of the many writers that hung around the office, while making sure that none of Sean's ideas were changed, even slightly. Sean would spend days calling up people that he knew, thereby guaranteeing some form of interest in the project. The Indian was always first. Sean would later invest about thirty minutes in a meeting with the writer, Gary, and Bob. The writer was made to feel as if he were the most important person on earth, who was about to embark on a writing career to rival two famous Joes, Mankiewicz and Eszterhas, the latter commanding millions of dollars per screenplay for material that the former Joe probably wouldn't have used for kindling.

Part of Sean's pitch always involved his extensive contacts. If the writer had some prior experience, there would be talk of a contract. Sean was always eager to sign any kind of contract the writer wanted; he knew that it didn't matter. These weren't Writer's Guild Contracts. Most of the contracts were worded properly and detailed what the possibilities were, but included two smallish paragraphs that clearly left Sean and his cronies many ways to change the deal or simply dump it and get out.

All of this was designed to accomplish several things. The first and foremost, each and every time, was to keep costs down. In the case of the writer, it meant that he would never see a nickel until some significant money was raised for the movie. Even then Sean would hedge, dividing the already minimal payments into miniscule allotments. The full fee wasn't due until the first day of principal photography, and that could be never. Whenever possible, Sean tried to make the writer a 'partner', designing lavish percentage contracts that Sean knew could not be honored once new players came into the deal. New

money always meant changes, and the writer would often be fired
if he balked about the changes. Writers were the most
dispensable commodities in the movie business. And lately,
writing was achieved more and more by committee. The first
writer was rarely around by the time a project had a greenlight,
the go ahead to make the movie. In Sean's case, it was all about
the money, since he didn't have to deal with a bunch of studio
people with hidden agendas and fear of failure.

Since I didn't know any of that at the time, I was still in
Hollywood heaven. Through Liz, I was starting to make more of
the social rounds. For a former tried and true New Yorker, I was
uncharacteristically quick to succumb. I was recording a lot of
what I heard, trying to keep my distance as an objective
observer, but I obviously failed, since my backstory purpose was
to sell one of my screenplays. Would I have thrown away my notes
on a book if someone had said that it was a contingency for
getting one of my screenplays accepted for production? Uh-huh.
I, nevertheless, kept writing the book, but was worried that it
might appear as if I was trying to break into the business at
the expense of everyone I had met and recorded. But wasn't that
how show business worked? If I wrote myself into the book, my
motives for recognition might appear even more shameless.
Combine that with my former frat boy approach to the opposite
sex, and I would come across as an unsympathetic character. I
didn't think women editors would want anything to do with a
manuscript that included my fluctuating misogynistic point of
view. Who cared if I was trying to reform?

My first real show business dinner party was hosted by an
acquaintance of Liz's. I found myself inside the private Regency
Club, sitting with birthday boy Sydney Guilaroff, the ancient
but fit and handsome hairdresser to the stars. His MGM fame was
legendary, and judging by the guest list, he was much loved. To

355

my left were Zsa Zsa Gabor and her escort. To my right were
Shirley MacLaine and her daughter. Across the table was Sidney,
sitting next to Ann-Margaret and her husband Roger. At the 'B'
table was Roddy McDowall, Esther Williams, and Stefanie Powers.
Some 'B" table!

Over the course of my continued Hollywood education, I
found myself telling celebrity stories at various venues. I was
previously no stranger to the celebrity world, but somehow I
never became comfortable amongst certain famous actors. That
didn't stop me from launching into anecdotes, particularly when
fueled by questions. The 'civilian' population was eager to hear
whatever I knew, while some celebrities seemed as star struck as
anyone when it came to the fabled performers. I thought my
namedropping stories might help ingratiate me with my new
friends.

After one drink I was usually on my way. "President Nixon
came to my office with a full secret service entourage. They
would sweep the office, making sure who we were, including
identification. Nixon insisted that he be the only patient in an
office that could treat seven or eight patients simultaneously.
There were fights amongst the partners as to how much money to
charge Nixon. My senior partner said often that 'he fucked us
when he was President, so it's time to get even'. Spiro Agnew,
on the other hand, arrived on his own, and was sitting on the
floor outside my office early in the morning. I generally
arrived early with one of the other doctors, so we were able to
open the office door for the very early Agnew. He brought a copy
of his autobiography, which ended up on the bookshelf unread.
Famous patients were always bringing us books." In retrospect, I
probably came off as another star-fucking doctor, but it was
hard to tell in this new territory. With my Sinatra story,
people weren't trying to be accommodating. They listened to

every word. "Sinatra would swagger into our kitchen and help himself to a cup of coffee or whatever he wanted from our daily supply of bagels, croissants and other various snack foods. He knew the nurses' names and seemed legitimately interested in their families. When he was in an examination room, he would harmonize with the piped in Muzak."

When pressed I would go on shamelessly relaying stories about television, movie and Broadway names from Larry Kert to Madeline Kahn.

Bob Hope preferred to be announced by the front desk manager when he entered the office, as if an M.C. were introducing him as a Vegas headliner.

I usually finished with, "Henry Kissinger acted as if my office belonged to him. One time after a lengthy procedure, I had intended to adjourn to my private office, down the hall away from the treatment rooms, and adjacent to the kitchen. I grabbed a cup of coffee and with my free hand opened to the door to my office. I was confronted by Kissinger, who wheeled around in my office chair, his hand clinging to my telephone. His expression and body posture were so intimidating that he had me closing the door as quickly as I had opened it. I waited in the kitchen, numbed by his celebrity cold stare, until he finished his call. For all I knew he was making lunch reservations at Lutece. It took me a while to realize that he had displaced me from my own office."

Not only was I making the rounds with Liz, but I would frequently have lunch with Dr. Harry, who I was working with almost three days a week. There were a variety of places where the local Bedford Drive doctors schmoozed, often with a good-looking employee from the front office or a nurse still in the faux hospital garb - a uniform that had become a common sight around the Beverly Hills business triangle. One doctor could be seen regularly chasing a polo ball with a hand mallet, jogging through the city in his green or blue scrubs. A few of the people who wore hospital garb had little or nothing to do with health professions.

Also on hand were famous patients, who would catch a bite to eat with their doctor, pretending to be a close friend, and guaranteeing Vicodin-on-demand prescriptions.

Very few of the doctors opted for expensive lunch fare. Most of the older doctors had been eating in the same places for twenty or thirty years. Some of the medical buildings had quite adequate coffee shops inside, and those shops were the lunchtime home to most of the medical office staffs.

One day when we were leaving the office, Harry yelled down the hall to a tall, good-looking man in his late thirties or early forties, who was standing across from the elevator. He was wearing a white Polo shirt and matching white Polo trousers, the kind with the little Polo patch on the rear end.

"Victor! Hey, Victor!" shouted Harry, as if the two were meeting at Dodger Stadium.

Victor turned and offered a huge, toothy grin, while keeping one hand tucked inside the now opened elevator doors.

"Harry. How are you?" He appeared legitimately pleased to see Harry.

"Fine. Fine. Have you met my protégé, Brantley? Brantley. This is Victor Boyne. He's a podiatric surgeon with bad vision. Stay away from him."

Protégé, I thought. "Hi Victor." I had seen him around before. Many of the doctors in the building occasionally gossiped about Victor, mostly about his celebrity girlfriends.

"Where are you going for lunch, Victor?" asked Dr. Harry.

"I was going to walk over to Barney Greengrass. You know, inside Barneys. They have a huge outdoor roof patio."

"The Sturgeon King?" I asked.

"Yeah. You must be from New York," said Victor. "Me, too."

When the elevator reached the bottom level, we decided to go our separate ways.

Once Victor was out of earshot Dr. Harry said, "Victor has written a few screenplays. He might be someone for you to get to know."

"Okay. Thanks." *How funny*, I thought. *Everyone out here must really, secretly want to be in the movie business.* And I was one of them.

Harry suggested that we go across the street to a little deli. The food was palatable and if we arrived there early enough there were still be a few tiny sidewalk tables available. We could sit there and watch the spring fashion show, which on North Bedford Drive was a sight to behold, unlike any place in the world. A few modeling agencies had offices on the block or nearby. The CAA office was about two blocks away, plus the well-trafficked medical area had all the top plastic surgeons and dermatology groups, some run by doctors who had their own infomercial shows that ran regularly on television.

While the counterman prepared our lunch, Harry spoke with the lady working the cash register. "*Auto Focus* made no money. I'm not going to see it. If nobody likes it, why should I go?"

"I know what you mean," she said. "I'm finally seeing *My Big Fat Greek Wedding* this weekend. It's still a hot movie, grossing in the top five."

We brought our tray lunch outside - tuna salads with herbal iced tea.

Once we were situated, Harry took a big gulp of his tea. "I never used to drink anything but Lipton."

"I know what you mean. Pretty soon someone is going to open a tea house like Starbucks."

"It might work here. Anything's possible. I was at a place the other night with my wife that served mango iced tea." Harry was old-fashioned, even for a local.

"I've heard of that," I said with my mouth full of salad.

Someone shouted from the street. "Harry. Mind if I join you?" Victor had returned.

"What happened to Greengrass today?" asked Harry.

"I got over there and the girl in front told me that I had to wait twenty minutes. Forget that shit," said Victor.

"Come on. Sit down," said Dr. Harry.

"Sure. Let me grab something. I'll be right back." Victor slid past us and into the deli.

"You'll like talking with this guy. A real New York guy. He's a foot man. Damn good at it they say." Harry sometimes repeated himself.

I had no objections. "Okay. He seems very nice."

"He wanted to write screenplays, like you. They were going to use his screenplay for the first *Superman* movie."

"But they didn't?"

"They flew him to London to meet with the people doing the movie. It was a big deal. He was in all the papers. They even let him try out for the part of *Superman*. It looked like he was going to get it for a while, but they ended up giving it to that guy who's crippled now. I forget his name."

"Christopher Reeve?"

"Yeah. Anyway. Here he comes."

"Hi. I'll just squeeze in here," said Victor as he jostled around so that he could sit at the crowded table with his back to the street. He put down a large coffee and a muffin, the latter a mixture of light and dark colors.

"Victor. Meet Brantley Benjamin. Brantley. This is Victor. Victor does feet. Brantley is with me." Harry redid the introductions as if we were all getting ready for the *Kennedy Center Honors* show.

"Harry. You're losing your mind. We already met. How you doin'?" asked Victor.

"I knew that years ago," said Harry. He laughed.

"Fine. It's nice to see you again," I said.

"So it's teeth for you," said Victor.

"And the thrill of victory and the agony of da feet for you." It was dumb, but Victor and Harry laughed.

"'Fraid so," said Victor.

"I'm sorry to hear that. Not that it's just feet - that you have to spend the day talking to people about their problems while you work on them." I meant it.

"It can be a bore," said Harry.

"Bore. It's awful. But I need the money, and it's the only thing I really know how to do," said Victor. "First wife ate up half of it, and then I married her again." He paused as if he was doing a routine. "She told me that she changed," he said as if he were giving an excuse for the second go 'round. "Now she's married to the dermatologist on Wilshire. It's his third marriage. She's in his infomercial on skin care, so I guess she's happy."

"Victor writes screenplays," said Harry. "Brantley is writing screenplays too." Harry loved to talk up anything connected to the movie business.

"Wrote, doctor. Wrote. Past tense. I gave it up. Now when I get the urge to write anything, I lie down until the idea goes away. Sometimes a few drinks help. Then I end up writing my mother in Boca Raton, telling her that I was sorry I ever yelled at her for making me go to podiatry school. 'A foot doctor is good, but a foot surgery specialist is better. That's where the big money is.' She was right about the money part."

"Did you sell anything?" I asked.

"Sure. But only one was made, and it disappeared into video, at a time when it was not fashionable to go directly to video. I think Blockbuster had it in a sale rack once, and then it just plain disappeared. But don't let me discourage you from writing," said Victor. "Just keep the day job."

"I intend to. I guess it's a very competitive business."

Victor jumped on that line. He pulled himself up to his full height and leaned back. "Imagine that everyone in the Writer's Guild wrote a screenplay. Just one a year. We're talking over six thousand screenplays there alone. Plus everyone who is a name gets to write something at some time or another. Every journalist is now a screenwriter, and every news reporter who stopped being on camera is now a journalist. Every famous politician takes a crack at it one way or another, usually by writing a book first, and then demanding story credit on any movie deals. On top of that, add all the college kids who are studying writing. We're talking a lot of material. And don't forget about everyone else who has that great special movie idea, the man at the gas pump outside of Des Moines, the Legal Aid Lawyer from the Bronx, the daycare physician in Tahiti, and the Cuban ice cream vendor from Havana. They all have screenplays, and they all write them, or find someone to write it for them for free. 'On spec' is how most of the writing is done. Only a handful gets paid, and then it becomes a club, where people get paid over and over again, for a scene or two, or a touch-up of some dialogue. It's not like anything else in the world."

Well, that sounded pretty dismal to me. I didn't know if Victor was just bitter - he had a lot to be bitter about - or if it really was that bad. I figured that it had to be a

combination. "Is there anything good about it?" I asked with a
smile and a forced laugh. I didn't expect an answer.

Victor didn't get it. He was intent on doing a monologue
about how bad things were. "There are perks. An agent friend of
mine named John Gaines used to invite me to meet his clients. It
was fun. We would have dinner one night at Spago, and then one
night at Le Dome. I was separated from my wife, and John decided
that he was going to get me laid. One night we were sitting at
Spago and Morgan Fairchild came over to say hello. John
announced that I was single and Morgan lit up and said, "So am
I." It was all fun and games. Another time, he invited me to a
party at Veronica Hamel's house. The entire cast of *Hill Street
Blues* was there. The food was all Indian. Chutney this and
mulligatawny that. It seemed an odd Christmas food. And then it
became clear that Veronica wasn't really terribly interested in
my type. I saw the Amritraj brothers, the tennis guys who went
into the movie business, floating around and I put two and two
together. I spoke with some really interesting people. The older
man, who played the sergeant, I think his name was Prosky. He
was really nice, a charming guy. I was sitting with John, and
get this, Michael Warren shows up, the former UCLA basketball
player. He had a part on the show. I think he produces sitcoms
now. Anyway he comes over to say hello to John. Guess what he
says. 'Indian food! A year ago she served chitlins, fried
chicken, and collard greens'."

I laughed to appear polite. Harry didn't get any of it.

Sean had told me the same story, with not quite the same
exacting details. It was at that moment that I realized
something else about Hollywoodland. People shared stories,
experiences that either were collectively combined or invented
via some perverse form of mass communication hysteria. With the
advent of e-mails, people in town were kept up to date on every

kind of gossip in the business. Raconteurs, whose own gossipy story lines were running thin, could add a fact or two based on someone else's 'first hand' experience. The process was not unlike production credit for a movie. When a movie became successful, more than one person seemed to know how everything was accomplished. *The Santa Clause 2* had a massive list of producers, all probably willing to take credit for its financial success.

Interspersed in the conversations were invaluable bits of local folklore. "Ben Affleck goes to the Coffee Bean, south of Wilshire. Don't confuse it with the one near Nate 'n Al's. Ted Danson goes to that one." Victor said it with an authority associated with ownership. He made sure to let me know that the best restaurants for celebrity sightings in the area were The Grill, Crustacean, Le Dome and Maple Drive.

Victor gave us a little more about Gaines, the agent. "John loved to sit in the front area at Le Dome. He would yell out at the celebrities coming in, to the chagrin of the owners, who tried to run a civil environment. I met Sherry Lansing there when she was still dating Wayne Rogers. It was fun to see people like Cheech Marin dressed up for a dining experience."

Lansing was the head of Paramount, one of only a handful of women to have any power in the business. I would later meet her at a wedding for a wealthy descendant of a Chicago department store, Ted Field, who produced movies with Bud Cort. The entertainment was supplied by Chuck Berry, in a castle-like house formerly owned by silent film star Harold Lloyd. I would learn that celebrities made nice window dressing for the wealthy.

Victor stood. "Well. I've got to go. An actress is coming over on emergency. Another beautiful woman with pus dripping from blisters caused by poorly constructed designer shoes," said Victor as he got up from the table. "Enjoy your lunch!"

"Thanks," said Harry with a sarcastic twinge.

"Yeah," I said. I hoped Victor wasn't a vision of my future, like the ghost of Christmas down-the-road.

Soon after that meeting I received a surprise phone call in my office from Victor. Based on his Hollywoodized demeanor, I expected him to forget me as soon as he had walked across the street after lunch.

Victor spoke rapidly. "Listen. This guy called me about working with him on a screenplay about his father. These are big time guys. It's Mal V. Rose's son. They were patients of mine, and I stayed in touch. I can't write anymore. You interested?"

I was agape as I listened. It sounded too good to be true. If I were willing, Victor would set up an introduction.

What Victor never told me was that he had already tried to write with Ricky about two years ago, and gave up when Ricky threatened him with a gun.

I checked in with Liz. She asked around the agency and gave me a prompt answer. "There's definitely some interest in Mal, but it depends on the story. Are you sure you want to involve Ricky? I think once he's involved it's going to be a negative to sell. At HBO, they said they could see a story about Mal during the seventies, sort of a Rat Pack thing with Cher, The Osmonds, Liberace, Rich Little, and Don Rickles. Make a story about Mal and cameos of those people and I think I could sell it."

I agreed to meet Ricky at a coffee shop in Encino. It was one of those huge road monsters, the kind that looks the same anywhere across America, with leather booths, a long counter, a gum-chewing cashier with teased hair, and a menu that everyone could recite by heart. And great food. I hadn't had a chocolate malted for years.

The meeting went on for hours. Ricky never stopped talking. One thing that he tried to project, and succeeded, was that he was needy. I jumped at the bait, blinded by my own ambition to get a writing credit. Two days later, Liz agreed to draw up a contract and act as our agent, but not without her having to tell Ricky more than once to "fuck off…either you want me to do this or find someone else."

After we had worked together for only three weeks, I was feeling uncomfortable with the way Ricky was treating me. He was generally rude, and thought of me as an employee. To him, if you didn't work in show business you weren't important, and if you didn't have a defined role of importance, then you were beneath Mal and Ricky. During his entire life, Ricky hung around with Mal and his cronies, people who thought nothing of writers, unless the writing credit belonged to Mal and his closest confidant, Arnie. Tubby was even a low man on the creative totem pole.

Ricky really didn't know any other type of behavior. He had gotten away with being a brash, rude, wise-ass kid, which in Hollywood circles passed as an amusement. Even though Ricky learned to tone down his wise cracks, which now came off only as insulting and stupid, he was ill-equipped to deal with people on any level. His brain didn't have any capacity for respecting writers or writing. And his personality disorder was out of control.

Ricky loved e-mail. It must have been a power thing, sitting up to all hours of the morning, and vomiting out little memos to everyone on his e-mail list. I received about twenty e-mails during the first week of the project. They were all essentially self-centered, selfish communications, that said little about the reality outside of Ricky's self-defined world. The last one really annoyed me.

Dear Brantley:

I went to see the movie *Jackass: The Movie* last night. I got in about 4 AM and decided to do a little writing, but a few things came up. You know I do have things I'm responsible for that just have to be done. I'll try to get the material back to you in a few days.

Mal is going to be on the Danny Bonaduce show, so I have to get him ready for that. Also, could you change the spacing on the material you sent me from double space down to one and one half? I've never seen any scripts with double space, so I think we should conform to what's professional. Okay?

Ricky

P.S. You leave two spaces after a period. I think it's a mistake. Most classic writing leaves only one space.

I made the mistake of responding in the form of a complaint, but I checked my spacing.

Dear Ricky:

I am writing to let you know that although we are making progress, I don't feel like you are totally committed to the project.

I know it must be difficult for you, writing about your
family, but there is no reason to make it any harder for me
to get the information down on paper. Like losing the copy
I gave you, and then finally agreeing to let me fax it to
you, only to find out two days later that there was no fax
paper in your machine.

I know we can do better together. Let's try.

Brantley

The next time we spoke was on the telephone, and Ricky was
furious.

"What's going on here?" demanded Ricky.

"What do you mean? Ricky, I'm just trying to get the
material down on paper."

"I don't like your attitude. Maybe it has something to do
with the fact that you're a doctor or something. But I don't
take that kind of shit from anyone, except Mal. I've always
taken it from Mal, but I won't take it from you. You are
autocratic, controlling, and manipulative. I know how to be a
team player, but I know when someone is squeezing my nuts."

It was at that moment that I realized that Ricky was going
to be nothing but trouble. "Ricky. I'm sorry if I have hurt your
feelings in any way. I just want to get the material written.
Did you go over the paragraphs I sent you?"

"Yes. I rewrote them more in my style, so it has my sound.
And I e-mailed you a copy. I was at a friend's house so the
stuff I sent you is in text form, from an old WordStar word-
processing program. You need to download it once you get it, and
then convert it to whatever you are using."

"Ricky. I told you. I'm using Word. It was your idea. I bought it because you suggested that we work with the best. I also bought that screenplay software, Final Draft. I think that was the name."

"No. Nobody's using that anymore."

Ricky's doubletalk was overwhelming, along with his lack of any sense of professional or plain human decency. This guy was worse than his reputation.

Ricky had done it again. The conversation had moved two steps to the side, and I was frustrated. I wondered how I was ever going to write the screenplay. I had to keep going. This was an opportunity that could lead to a lot more work. I knew I could write a good screenplay about Mal and Vegas casinos, and without Ricky. The trick would be to get as much information out of Ricky, while still making him think I was writing the damn thing with him as a character, and make sure that he didn't sabotage the project as we went along. Ricky had made the point more than once that he should have a major character role in the screenplay.

"Ricky. Can you fax me the work? It was only two pages."

"Brantley. Don't use that tone on me or I'll come over there and blow your fuckin' head off. Okay?"

At the time, the gun thing was not real. "Ricky. Don't threaten me."

"I don't know what you mean by threaten. You can't seem to do this without getting upset, and damn it, Brantley, I'm not trying to upset you. I'm only trying to make sure that I'm not taken advantage of. I've always told you about the people who have done bad things to me in the past. I have to protect my interests here, and if telling you how I feel helps the situation, then, god damn it, you're going to hear from me. I'm not going to stand by and watch you steal my life story."

It slipped out. Ricky thought that it was his story that we were writing. I clenched my fist until my hand whitened and the fingertips became bright red. "Ricky. I think I want to get back and do some more work now. You know I have a practice to run in addition to my other writing projects."

Ricky was unable to come to the end of a conversation. "You know that this is the best thing that any of us could ever have. This is going to be one of the greatest screenplays of all times. It will probably win for Best Picture. You know it's great. What am I supposed to do, feel bad that I don't have a practice to run?"

Ricky was the quintessential no win, someone long on wind and about as short as anyone on self-esteem. I would soon learn that nobody, absolutely nobody in town, had anything good to say about Ricky.

Somehow, I told myself, that I would get the screenplay written.

During that period, Ricky went for new sessions with Barry. "Dr. Brantley Benjamin is a typical schmuck doctor. He has this big ego about everything. He thought because he went to so many schools, he must be smart or something. The joke is on him. He's writing for me for virtually free. It's a great deal. I'm already a good writer. People know I can write. Arnie Baylos knows I can write jokes. I wrote plenty for Mal. I am humoring the doctor so he will do the work. As soon as he comes up with a screenplay for me, I'll probably dump him. Hey. Don't tell anyone that, okay?"

Barry gave his stock answer. "I am not permitted, nor would I break any of my patient-doctor confidences." {Without Barry eventually spilling the beans about everyone I knew who was his patient, I could never have written this book.}

Ricky nodded and kept going. He spoke for almost the whole fifty minutes. "I'm too busy with Mal to bother fleshing out a story for a screenplay. That's why I'm using Brantley. Victor, the foot guy, wanted me to pay him more than Writer's Guild Minimum. I told him to forget it and he turned me on to Brantley. It was great. The schmuck works his ass off for me. Do you want me to call you when the screenplay is done? I'll get the buzz going right away. I'm a P.R. expert."

In the interim, Dave Stirling continued to hype the *Small Steaks* screenplay situation for all it was worth. He felt that he could control me, and so far it was working. Sometimes it appeared that being in charge was as important to him as any social or business bonus that could develop from our relationship.

In between patients, I called Dave several times from the office.   "Hi, Dave. How's it going?" I asked at the onset of the latest call.

"I'm getting the script over to Mirisch today." Dave had said that for a period of about two weeks. "That's exciting, isn't it?"

"Yes," I answered.

"Didn't you get what I said? I'm having it sent over today."

"Dave, I know what you said."

"'Know what I said' - what? What?" Dave didn't like the feeling he was getting from me. "I've got a million things to do today, but the script is on its way."

"Wouldn't it be easier if I just hand delivered the script to his office at Universal?"

At first Dave laughed as if he had heard the most hilarious one-line joke. Then he sighed as if someone had called with bad news like his favorite uncle had died. "Brantley. What the fuck do you know? You know teeth. Am I right?"

"Dave. I didn't mean anything..." I tried in vain to mollify the great injustice of second-guessing a mover like Dave.

"Teeth. Stick to teeth. You wrote this fucking script. I told you, it's not bad. But give me a break. Okay? I'm on this. I played golf at Hillcrest the other day with Howard Koch. I mentioned the script to him."

"You did?" I bit once again.

"Yep. And right away. On the second hole. It's a par three. There was a backup because a few of the alta cacas were hitting their third shots, and they still weren't on the green! So I just mentioned that I had this hot property by a new, young writer."

"Is he interested?"

Dave grabbed the mouse that was connected to the computer next to his desk. As soon as the mouse slid, the screen cleared and a version of Microsoft Golf appeared, which was already in place behind Dave's screensaver, a veritable picture of the world's most famous golf courses.

"I've known Howard a long time. Howard is a member at Hillcrest," said Dave as he began to tee off on the computerized golf course. "You know the Douglas family is there too." He was referring to Kirk and Michael.

"Uh-huh," I decided to shut up. Dave was talking about show business royalty.

"They're great guys," said Dave. "I'll introduce you."

There was a momentary silence as Dave set up his next computer shot.

"Well, okay. Thanks," I said, trying to end the conversation. My words came out with an uneven cadence. "Thanks. Thanks a lot."

By then, Dave wasn't paying much attention to me at all. The computer informed him that his ball had hit a tree. "Damn. See ya. I'll be in touch. Oh. I'm sending you an invitation for something." Then he abruptly hung up the telephone.

It turned out that Dave bought a table every year for the annual Fabulous "250" dinner at the Hillcrest Country Club. The event was sponsored by the Jewish Big Brothers of Los Angeles. Dave's secretary made sure that an invitation went out to me. It was one of the high-ticket events of the year. Each seat was nine-hundred dollars. I was to sit at the same table with his daughter Linda. That night Sean would also be Dave's guest. Dave called him personally to make sure that he was coming.

"They give away cars and televisions. It's a great night, although they're getting tamer every year," said Dave.

"Of course I'll be there," said Sean. "Listen. I have some ideas about The Hollywood Deli."

"We'll talk," said Dave.

Dave had insisted that I arrive at the function early. He didn't want to be alone between his round of golf and the event. He had about an hour to kill after showering, so he invited all his guests to arrive before six, for a private pre-cocktail cocktail. Not everyone acquiesced to Dave's every wish. I arrived first, and waited at a table in the elegant Grill Room.

Dave made quite an entrance. He burst into the Grill Room as if he was jumping onto stage.

"Que pasa?" was directed to the bartender, with a wave of a forefinger.

"How are you, Mr. Stirling?" responded the smiling
bartender. Dave always broke the club rules regarding tipping.
He wanted everyone on staff to kiss his ass, and they did.

Dave's skin appeared as if it had been polished. He
certainly never divulged that he saw the dermatologist Dr.
Manciewitz twice a week, in order to get that almost Max Factor
patina on his skin.

Aside from the weekly scrubs, Dave used a little clear
solution that left that 'just showered' glow on his otherwise
pale face. Dave bought his shirts at Ascot Chang, who sold
overpriced dressy garb to many industry people. Dave's suits
were mostly Valentino or Zegna. That night he had on a new
Zegna, a suit that reeked of its obscene cost. Ties were an
incidental. He wore the loudest he could get his hands on, and
smartly avoided pocket squares, unlike some older-but-hip
businessmen. He never really learned anything about shoes, so he
felt safe with anything Gucci. He wore the loafers that featured
the Gucci colors in the cross strap, for fear that someone
wouldn't recognize the value of his purchase. His hair was a
black mop of sculptured perfection, flipping up a bit in the
rear and begging to have the caked hair spray raked out.

At that hour, only about a dozen people sat inside the
Grill, just a couple of slow golfers sipping their martinis and
eating the fresh popcorn from a movie theater-like machine.
Nevertheless, Dave always made an entrance.

Dave nodded his head to the members, his classic-yet-
repulsive way to recognize someone who held little importance in
his life. Tonight, by design, that person was me. I received the
second nod. I smiled as Dave floated toward me. As he got closer
to my table, he turned off and veered in the direction of two
older men in golf clothes. I rose up and followed Dave, like a
faithful lap puppy.

"Frank, you old fart," said Dave. "How's the ostrich business?"

"I think I'm going to make a killing," said Frank. The truth was that he had no idea. Ostrich farming didn't seem to be catching on in Southern California, but there was no way Frank was going to tell anyone at Hillcrest that he was losing money, particularly his crony investors.

We sat at Frank's table. I ordered a Stoli vodka martini. I downed it while eating a small portion of chili and a side of mixed nuts, two other Hillcrest happy hour staples.

I listened as the conversation switched from the air travel business to new houses, and then square footage of shopping centers. I was getting bored. There was no chance I would ever need to concern myself with the cost of prorated private jet services that were booming since 9/11.

"How much can you make nowadays as a root doctor?" asked Frank, not thinking that his question was the least bit intrusive.

"Not much," I answered. It was true, particularly compared to the present company.

"I'm going to get Brantley a screenplay deal," said Dave.

"From your mouth - !" exclaimed Frank.

"Hey, why not?" said Dave. "The comedian's son, whatshisname, you know. He got a million dollars for some piece of shit thing. I went to see it. It starred that Carey guy. The *Cable Delivery Guy* or something like that. I thought it would be funny. You know, the guy wiring your set the wrong way and you only get porno or something. Something funny, like that. Maybe a little tits and ass. That's what I thought. What a gloomy piece of shit. I heard that's why they fired Mark Canton. Over that. That Carey guy got twenty million."

"Why don't you let Mirisch see it?" said Frank. "He's sitting right over there."

I looked across the room and saw another man, perhaps in his seventies, sitting alone. I wondered why Dave didn't go over to talk to him, since Mirisch supposedly had already received a copy of my screenplay, or did he? Maybe Dave didn't want to bring up the project, since Mirisch had already said 'no' and Dave didn't want to tell me that his big contact was a big bust. I still would have liked to have met him. Maybe Dave figured that this wasn't the right time or place. But if I were going to make it as a writer, wouldn't I eventually have to meet 'his' people? Dave's eyes told me that I shouldn't bring up the screenplay. For a second I thought that I would get up and introduce myself to Mirisch. I made a plan. I would have another martini while more guests arrived, and as soon as Dave went table-hopping or to the john, I would go over and say hello.

My chance arrived when they announced that the buffet tables were open for the party. Dave hopped up and escorted another man out of the room, arm in arm, Mafia style. Mirisch was clearly not going to the party. He stood up and headed for the locker room.

"Mr. Mirisch," I said. My voice came out weak and garbled. He turned and faced me with a bland expression.

"I'm Brantley Benjamin." I still didn't sound right.

"Hello. It's nice to meet you," said Mr. Mirisch as if he were stumping for a campaign.

"The writer. Brantley Benjamin. I wrote *Small Steaks*."

"Oh. You wrote a screenplay." He had no idea who I was or what I was talking about. Obviously, people approached him all the time.

"I…Yes...I wrote a screenplay...based on my play..." I was still mumbling and had no idea what to make of the situation.

Maybe I should mention Dave, I thought, but before I could formulate a sentence the brief encounter was over.

"It's a tough business. Good luck with it." Mr. Mirisch was polite, but totally detached. He turned to continue on to the locker room.

And then it hit me hard. This was Hollywood. And I was nobody. And maybe Mirisch never even saw my screenplay. The rest of the evening I tortured myself with various scenarios on what actually happened. Maybe it was all a hoax or maybe Mirisch thought it was so bad that he felt it was better to say nothing. Or maybe he couldn't remember. He probably read a lot of screenplays. Or maybe he didn't read any. I figured that I would never know, the only thing that proved over time to be a reliable reality.

Linda Stirling arrived late, gave polite hellos, and said very little the entire evening. Dave was disappointed, but he never let on that I had been invited for her. He thought Sean was too old for Linda. She knew her father, and let him carry on so long as he didn't make too much of an ass of himself when she was involved. On many levels she knew that her father was a shrewd, talented businessman. His need for control was legion, but he was always cautious when forcing men on Linda.

After seeing Dave in this somewhat restrictive and more human setting, I began to think of him in an even more convoluted manner. He was an even bigger asshole than I could have imagined. He primped and gesticulated on cue, and made sure to leave his seat four or five times, so that the new arrivals in the room could see him.

The next day, Linda called Barry to see if she could move her appointment up to earlier that week. This happened almost every time that she spent an entire evening with her father. While she respected his business acumen, she was usually annoyed by how he behaved socially and grew anxious from his automated infantilizing.

Linda had been a patient of Barry's for almost five years. She originally contacted him when she had moved out of her parents' house in Beverly Hills. It was the most traumatic experience of her life, yet worse for her parents. Dave had hoped to groom Linda in his image and make her into a clone. Moving out put a crimp in his plan, leaving him less time to continue his lifelong lectures on her future, which when broken down to its simplest elements amounted to doing everything that he said, while supporting the notion that he wasn't merely mortal.

"The genetics may not have been there," said Barry at the first session.

"Do you mean I'm different than he is?" asked Linda.

"Linda. The issue is not so much whether you are like your father or not. It is more an issue of why you are moving out, and those things I think we can discuss separately."

Over the course of the therapy, Linda grew to accept Dave for who he really was - a controlling, narcissistic personality, who saw his children as an extension of himself and tried to use them at every turn to further his own thoughts and wishes. This was not an easy concept to accept, and harder to put to use in real life. Linda had experienced over twenty-five years of bullying control, particularly at every level of her teen and young adult life, and now she was faced with the problem of living her own life while still behaving in a manner that would not offend her father. That proved to be a difficult balancing act, which was the main reason that she still spoke with Barry.

Whenever Linda was in Dave's presence for a period of time, she would sink back to her former role, and often need two or three days to begin again behaving and thinking on her own. She was, as described by Barry, "a classic passive-aggressive personality", who also suffered from bouts of depression.

"The thing is to find some control center in all the chaos," Barry mentioned more than once. He had found with Linda that he had to repeat himself because of her general resistance to change of any kind.

"I don't pay attention to him or his deals," said Linda at her current session. "I certainly don't care about his interest in my lack of dating.

"I think that's a mistake," said Barry. "You have to do more, participate more, take a risk once in a while," said Barry.

"I guess I'm very picky," said Linda.

"I didn't mean with men, although that's probably the best place to start. I think you should get more involved in business. You know a great deal about the business world."

Linda had remarked that one of the men at the Hillcrest table seemed interesting. She had known him over the years, but never spent much time in his presence. They had had a few dates, but nothing seemed to click.

"He seems brighter than he lets on," said Linda.

When the session was over, Barry asked the obvious, since he was neither shy nor compelled to follow classic protocol. "So what's his name?"

Linda paused. "Sean Daren."

"I have an idea," continued Barry. *Bingo,* he thought. *Why didn't Sean ever mention that he knew her?* No matter. He would encourage Sean at all costs. In the back of his mind was the trickledown effect of getting Sean closer to Dave's inner circle, and the trickle up effect of more coin in Barry's pockets.

379

CHAPTER FOURTEEN
Sean, Linda

Sean did not enjoy black tie events. He had attended his
share of company parties like the Golden Globe Awards. Most of
the time, when he had been able to secure decent tickets for the
Oscars, he gave them to friends or clients. Sean didn't have the
patience for Oscar night. He always went to the after parties,
and even had been invited a few times to Irving "Swifty" Lazar's
party at Spago. The Golden Globe Awards were easy to maneuver,
since they were held at the Beverly Hilton Hotel, a location
that was accessible from all sides. Ticket holders didn't even
have to park at the Hilton, since the hotel was walking distance
from anywhere in the Beverly Hills business triangle. The hotel
was a short limo ride from all the major hotels. Guests staying
at the Peninsula or Regent Beverly Wilshire could easily walk,
though few did.

The Southern California Counseling Center event was one of
Barry's pet charities, and their yearly event was strictly black
tie. Barry could be very persuasive. His plan was to invite
Linda and Sean to sit at his table. He brought up Linda at
Sean's next session.   "I'm telling you. She's lovely when you
get to know her. I think you haven't given her your full
attention," he told Sean.

"But she's one of your patients. Isn't this unethical or something?"

Barry laughed. "So I bend the rules a little. There wasn't any rule in my residency that said I can't make a shidduch."

"If she's seeing you, she must be fucking nuts. I know it's made me a Loony Tune."

"Now you have a prejudice against therapy?"

"I've always had a prejudice against therapy, particularly yours. Barry…I hate getting dressed up for a lot of people I don't know. And then we sit around eating rubber chicken or shoe-leather swordfish, listening to people make speeches about themselves. And those tireless video and slide shows they put on now. It reminds me of when I used to drop acid. So many swirling lights. Jeez. Plus those endless auctions. Who wants an autographed copy of a script from *Friends*? I mean, who wants to buy one? It's a wonder these charities make any money."

"Then don't bid on anything."

"Very funny."

"She's beautiful and she's different. She's worth millions."

"Is that supposed to be an incentive?"

"Yes," was Barry's curt answer. "It would be for me, and I've got tons more money than you."

"Let me get this straight. My doctor is suggesting that I pursue a woman for her money?"

"Rich or poor it's nice to have money," proclaimed Barry. "Comedian Joe E. Lewis."

"Now you think you're Bartlett's or something. What's that supposed to mean?"

"It means the money couldn't hurt. Sean...Come on. You've been complaining all year that you don't develop feelings for anyone anymore. Give it a chance. One more night. You'll both sit at my table. You can leave whenever you want, and nobody will get offended. Well, maybe!"

The night of the event, when Sean exited his house dressed in his Calvin Klein tuxedo, he turned to witness a geyser of water streaming over his car.

"Oh, shit." He ran to the water main and turned off the water to the house. Mud was all over the driveway, and now burnished his black lizard boots. "Nobody fixes anything once anymore."

Much later, Linda arrived at the event after everyone was already seated. She wore a plain black pants tuxedo with the most exquisite print scarf. A ruby and diamond bar pin was in the lapel of her jacket, and her auburn hair was a sculptured mass of swirls above her head. She had made quite an entrance.

The evening went off without a hitch.

When Linda returned home, she had made an entry in her computer diary, making believe that she had just met Sean for the first time. In many ways, it was true.

"I met a really nice man today. His name is Sean, and he is tall and handsome. I haven't written anything like this since I was twelve. I like him. He thinks he is so macho, but I think he has a softer side. He asked me out….again…"

The next day by telephone, Linda said more to Barry. "When I first met Sean I didn't know why I wasn't so taken by him. Granted, he was handsome, funny, and very bright. I guess I saw the potential there, the potential to be with someone I could tell everything, and he would tell me everything. That's what we all want, isn't it, someone you can be yourself with? I know it's a lot to ask, but that's what I always wanted, and Sean seems for some reason the kind of man who could be himself with me, and I could be myself with him. It might sound unrealistic, because if people actually told their significant other everything that went on, relationships could never work out. Imagine if Bill Clinton first confessed everything to Hillary. I guess there are limits to our romantic dreams, but I still think it's worth trying to find that person you can be whole with."

At the same time, Sean was busy on the telephone with the plumbers.

Charlie spewed some boilerplate. "Some of your sprinkler pipes are old galvanized. Now we did the best we could to patch the part that caused your leak and give up a new shutoff valve, but you have to understand that we don't like to do this kind of work."

Sean became livid. "You sent me a bill for seven hundred dollars, and I paid it."

"Isn't that what I'm supposed to do? You see, we come out and do the work and then I bill you so that we can make a profit."

"Charlie. It's a month or so - I dunno- later and the sprinkler is leaking."

"There are special companies that do sprinklers."

"You guys did the work on my house, and I want you to fix it."

"We could recommend a good sprinkler company. My guys suggest that you put in all new sprinklers, and then you won't have to worry about leaks."

"Get someone out here or I'm calling my attorney," Sean said very quietly.

"You don't have to say that. I want to help you, but I wouldn't throw good money after bad. Dig it all up, and put in new sprinklers and that's it."

"Fix the pipe today!"

It would take three days for the plumbers to get back to Sean's house.

On one of their dates, Sean and Linda brought a pizza and
sub dinner home from Matteo's Little Taste of Hoboken – the
smaller version of the famous restaurant next door - in
Westwood, and watched the daily news roundup of the impending
war with Iraq. Linda didn't speak much and Sean was still in his
impress mode, so there was more eating and watching television
than either one really wanted.

Sean surfed the channels and stopped because Maria Shriver
was interviewing one of the representatives. Sean liked Maria.
Sean's daughter had attended the same private school as Maria
and Arnold's children.

"They're eating each other alive," said the Democratic
representative. His face appeared somber, while his body posture
indicated his fatigue. The Republicans had won back the house
and things were heating up.

The interview was brief, and the representative was excused
in order to cast his own vote. The mood on the television was
lifeless.

"Boring," said Sean. "They can eat each other alive, but
they have never learned how to put on a good show. That's why
they are always looking out here for support. *Wag The Dog* was on
the money. We really run the show."

Linda was pleased to be with Sean. She sensed that he was
showing off for her, and she didn't mind. In fact, she liked it.
It showed that he was interested enough to make an effort to
please her.

At Sean's next session with Barry, he confessed his worse
fear. "Barry. I had this dream twice this week."

"So. You've been dreaming. Tell me."

"My worst fantasy on the outcome of my life is that I'm at the Mauna Lani hotel in Hawaii, and I'm taking an exercise class outdoors in the thick foliage. I'm wearing one of those ugly paisley cabana outfits; something that looks like it should be in Rodney Dangerfield's closet. I'm communing, I'm being one with nature, and the exercise teacher asks us to roll on our stomachs with our legs up in the air, and arms extended out in front of our bodies, and I try it, but my body just won't stretch that way. I'm feeling alone, empty, and lost. I have finally lost out, and I am floating in a sea of glitzy chic travel with a bunch of people who made their money by buying Internet stocks. I scream out 'Oy vey iz mir' but not so much in pain, but to attract the woman to my right, two people removed from my row. She looks familiar. And at that moment she is my savior. I smile at the woman who looks like she's from Long Island. I am desperate. I am old, and I am looking to make contact with a middle-aged Jewish woman from Woodmere, or worse, Great Neck. Then I realize that I'm not that dead yet, and I go out and peddle my wares in town, in the same ugly paisley cabana set that I wore at the hotel."

Barry roared. He held his stomach, unable to stop his convulsive response. He finally rolled onto the floor, still hysterical.

"What?"

"It's funny. You don't think what you said is funny?"

"Barry. You're a putz." Sean got up to leave.

"Sit down."

Sean stood his ground. "No, go fuck yourself."

"Nobody ever said that to me."

"I don't believe that. I must have said it before today."

"Okay. So you're concerned about Linda." Barry returned to his chair.

385

"That's it? What happened to all those years of dream analysis?"

"Come on. It was just a fad. Don't tell me that you bought all that Freudian stuff you read?"

Sean hesitated to answer and then said, "Some of it."

"A lot of research is coming out that says our dreams are simply the way our brain tests itself before we get up. Sort of like the way a computer goes through the ropes when you turn it on or reboot it."

"You mean all those thoughts are meaningless?"

"Let's say that it's somewhere in the middle. I believe you're anxious about Linda, and you're thinking about having a relationship."

Sean sat down. "She's different," he confessed.

"I know. I did good?"

"Yes. You asshole. You did good."

"Got to go," said Barry. "It's already five minutes into my ten minute break." He jumped up.

"Okay. I'll let you know how it goes." Sean rose again, and followed Barry to the back door.

Barry undid the Medico lock, and let Sean out.

In the hallway, Sean thought about what Barry had said. Sean smiled, and felt happy that he was seeing Linda frequently, but wondered why he hadn't understood her in the past. What had changed about him? Was the money part of it?

About a week later, Sean sat alone at his swimming pool, waiting for Linda. They had had three more dates. Nevertheless, he was preoccupied all that day with thoughts about his daughter.

Sean wondered how his life had strayed so far away from that of his parents and his own daughter from his. Didn't his daughter realize how important it was to be Jewish? Family meant something. Sean wasn't very religious, but he was still very active in the entertainment division of the United Jewish Fund. He even spent time on the phones, soliciting donations on Super Sunday, the big one-day yearly drive to raise money for the charity. The activity wasn't a bad deal for him since he spoke to many people in the business, mostly on his level, and a few who had decent jobs within the studio hierarchy. Sometimes renewing an old contact would pay off, like helping get a distribution deal for part of his fifties sci-fi movies library - movies that were literally thrown away dirt cheap by people who didn't realize their future value.

Sean didn't believe that his daughter had any sense of being Jewish. Sean blamed himself and his former wife, who prided herself on a process of assimilation that included becoming a member of Riviera, the famous golf and tennis club.

The last time he had had lunch with his daughter, the conversation had grown complicated. They sat in a booth at the familiar Kate Mantilini, the 'company' restaurant where actors and others in the business could sit undisturbed.

"I learn a lot from you," said Sean.

"I hope so," Katherine answered, but she really didn't know if he was for real. She was forever questioning her father's own morals.

Sean sat quietly as Katherine spoke. "Jean Piaget did these really cool marble experiments, how young children try to copy the older ones, the ones who know the rules about marbles. It's all about how we learn the rules when we're young."

"Yes, I heard about that." He hadn't. "The young ones copy - that's how it's done."

Katherine was never fooled; she smiled and continued to make her point. "So why is it that in Hollywood so many of the adults develop their own set of moral rules?"

387

"Is this going to be another attack? I made a good living all these years so that you and your mother were well taken care of." It was true, but not applicable as far as Katherine was concerned.

"It illustrates one of the underlying reasons why life here is essentially Godless. The end justifies the means. So long as people are making money, they are happy. Everyone here lives by an alternate set of rules, rules that were created without God. That's why it stinks. I think you have to have a god to make it all work. Otherwise, we're all playing with our own personalized set of marbles, and each one of us determines how to win."

Sean answered, "I get it. It's like all the kids growing up to win at their own game. None of us are in this together." He didn't always listen. Years ago, he had been rather harsh in his approach. Katherine will never forget how he had grown angry at the mention of anything that he didn't understand. "I don't want any Zen shit in my house. We're Jewish, and that's it," he would shout, hoping to make his point final.

Katherine had never raised her voice in retaliation, only calmly explained her point of view. "Daddy. First of all, it's not what you think. It's more of a Kevin Costner kind of thing. You know. More like understanding that the Chinese are out there." She kept at it for years, convinced that somehow her father would really 'get it'.

After Linda arrived, she sat at the poolside with Sean. He was on his best behavior with her. He liked her. She was very different than the women that he knew or had known. After about an hour, they went inside for drinks. Sean had the housekeeper leave some covered plates of food from Gelson's on the table. Linda stayed the night.

Soon thereafter, Barry received a full report from Linda. "Sean and I have had many long, sexy afternoons. We often start outdoors, slowing applying sun oil to our bodies, giggling like children playing doctor for the first time. It may have been the drinking. Once inside the house, we would lie naked in bed, surrounded by the Sunday *New York Times* and a pitcher of Bloody Marys. I was thankful for one thing. When Sean had a lot to drink, he didn't change much, or I should say that my perception of him didn't change. He actually became more interesting, like a great burden was lifted off of him. He spoke more freely and even philosophized about politics, religion, and the meaning of life. We kept coming back to that one a lot, 'the meaning of life'. But I'm worried if the whole thing is a creation to please my father. Is my attraction to Sean a function of my relationship with my father? Since we starting dating, Sean and Dave have become inseparable. I can tell you that all of that stuff doesn't make a difference when you're drinking. But I'm worried that the drinking is the meaning of life for us, and all the things we plan to do, all the dreams that we are starting talk to about maybe won't happen."

Barry was bright, but he was out of touch with someone as astute as Linda. She had him over a barrel. He did his best to help her sort out a perspective that fit the situation, but like with so many of his other patients, everything was compromised by his personal hidden agendas.

Other nights with Sean were spent at Linda's, drinking in the living room of her tony condominium. Most of the furnishings were puffy with pastel floral patterns.

"I guess the saddest thing that ever happened to me was my divorce," said Sean. "What about you?"

Linda turned away, rose, and walked toward the terrace. "There's one thing, but I don't know. I guess I know you well enough, but I haven't ever told anyone this, outside of my mother and the vet." Linda turned back to face him, and stepped

closer. She wanted to be certain that he was listening
attentively. Satisfied, she began to speak slowly, if recanting
some horrific and tragic tale. "Last winter, when we had that
very cold weather. You know it was unseasonably cold for
California during that period. People were wearing gloves and
scarves." She paused to let it sink in. From the sound of her
voice she could have been recreating the history of a bloody
pogrom or part of a Dostoevsky novel.

Sean said, "I remember. The farmers lost a billion in
crops." It was too late to take back. As she leaned even closer,
Linda's face told him that it was an insensitive remark.

"I lost something more valuable." She ambled back to the
terrace doors. "Right there, right there in the corner of the
terrace is where Boomer used to sleep."

"I take it Boomer was your dog or cat or something?" asked
Sean, trying to show his knack for instant recognition of pet
names.

"Yes. That's right. How did you know?"

"Boomer sounds like he would have been a pet." He was back
in the ballgame. "A dog?"

"She," corrected Linda, rather harshly.

"Sorry. 'She'."

Linda nodded like a third grade teacher in recognition of
Sean's cooperation. "Boomer slept on the terrace. She liked it
there. It was like her own private home. She had a little door I
bought that allowed her to go in and out if she wanted to, but
she usually stayed outside once I asked her to go to her room
for a while. That strange night, I had to go to a New Year's Eve
party with my family. My father always took a large table at
Hillcrest. They're not bad parties, but I always got bored. I
don't bring a date; usually my friend C. B. The C. B. stands for
Cecilia Bartholomew, so once she was old enough she never really

wanted to hear her real name again, not ever. I can't blame her.
So I sat through the evening listening to C.B. tell us all about
the men she had had flings with all over the world during the
last year. Every time my father left the table and there were no
other men within ear shot, C.B. began a detailed sexual
explanation of why the relationships had failed. She even began
to talk about how this wealthy guy in Hong Kong had a little
black mole on the side of his penis. I never saw my mother so
interested in anything C.B. had said before, but we were all a
little tipsy, and a mole on a penis can go a long way while
listening to *Stardust*. Mother usually starts her drinking at
home. Before I left my condo that evening, I asked Boomer if she
wanted to go outside to her room. She said that she did and was
outside when I left. I yelled goodbye, but she was busy playing
with one of her toys. She had a switch on the floor that turned
on the television in one of the bedrooms, one that has an exit
to the same terrace. Sometimes Boomer would put on cartoons if I
was gone for a long time. All she had to do was step on this
flat button and the television went on. Boomer was very smart."

"I could see that," said Sean. He really didn't want to
hear the end of the story, but couldn't afford to offend Linda.
He was in new territory. He realized that his relationship with
George Roy was nothing like Linda's with Boomer. Up until that
moment, Sean had figured himself to be a pet lover.

"I probably had too much champagne. I was bored, and a
little annoyed at C.B.'s graphic stories. She said she had to
walk around at one point because her lower anatomy was still
sore from this date she had last night, an ear, nose and throat
specialist from Beverly Hills. When C.B. got up from the table,
my mother remarked that there weren't any good looking, eligible
ENT men in town, or my mother would know about it. She said that
C.B. always said it was a doctor or a well-known businessperson.

391

My mother always thought that C.B. was sleeping with young
models from West Hollywood, boys that she would take out to
dinner and probably buy expensive gifts. I think C.B. is
attractive, but my mother thinks she's a mess. When I got home,
I didn't bother to check Boomer. I just flopped in my bed. The
next morning my mother awakened me by calling. She said my
father wasn't feeling well, could I come over to the house. In
my family, the first sign of bad health is always a crisis. I
knew that he wasn't very sick, probably a cold, but I was
conditioned my whole life to snap to attention every time a
Stirling was sick. I didn't even put on makeup. I just got up
out of bed, dressed, and ran out the door. It turned out that
Dr. K. was there pontificating about how my father was only
tired or had some sort of viral problem. That's what Dr. K.
always said, it was a viral problem. 'Maybe some kind of Chronic
Fatigue Syndrome', he said. My father seemed fine to me, but I
stayed to use the bathroom and then my father insisted that
everyone go to the Beverly Hills Hotel for a holiday brunch.
When I got home, I looked outside at Boomer. She looked like she
was sleeping. Once in a while, Boomer would sleep in and have a
late breakfast. I decided I'd better put a blanket on her. I
went outside and put her blanket over her lower body. She didn't
look right. I said her name a few times loudly. I put my hand on
the back of her neck. She was ice cold. I didn't realize how
cold it was until I did that. I was wearing three layers because
I always run cold anyway, so I wasn't sure. I picked her up. She
was nearly frozen solid. Can you believe that?"

"No," was all Sean could say. He was thinking worse. He
felt that she had been negligent. "I mean, that's unbelievable."

"I took her inside. My first thought was to put her in the
microwave for a few seconds, but then I didn't know what number
to put the temperature control on. There is a defrost button,

but that didn't seem right. I wasn't thinking straight. I called
'911' and the operator said that I should call the vet, that
this wasn't part of what they did. I called my vet and there was
no answer. It was then that I realized Boomer wasn't breathing.
I put my compact mirror in front of her nose and there was no
moisture. She was really frozen. I read somewhere that people
can survive once they've been frozen. I told the service
operator for the vet that I was going over to the animal
hospital, that they should tell the vet to meet me there. I knew
if he got the message that he would come. Dr. Silbert was
devoted to his patients. I drove right over there with Boomer
wrapped in blankets. I feared the worst. When I got there I saw
Dr. Silbert's car, and knew that everything would be all right.
I brought Boomer inside and Dr. Silbert grabbed her from me and
took her toward the treatment rooms. 'You can come if you want,'
he said. I sat down in a heap, in one of the plush lounge
waiting room chairs. His office was one of the best decorated
offices in town. That's what I thought about to take my mind off
Boomer. Dr. Silbert came out in about five minutes, but it
seemed like an hour. I could see it in his eyes. They were
filled with tears. We hugged for a moment, and then I broke
down. 'She's on life support, but I don't know for how long'. I
don't remember the rest of the day, or even the week. I was a
mess. I had let Boomer freeze to death. All I do know is that I
gave my permission at some point for Boomer to be taken off life
support. Dr. Silbert brought her back two or three times, but
after the last time he told me that he was sure that she was
brain dead. When I went back home, I checked the little door to
see why she hadn't come inside. It must have been frozen shut.
When the housekeeper watered the outdoor plants, she must have
gotten a lot of water on the outside, and I guess it sort of
froze over the hinges or something. Boomer probably tried to get

in, but couldn't open the door. Can you imagine what she thought
about me leaving her out there? Her final moments must have been
horrible. *How could mommy do this to me?* I don't think I'll ever
get over it." Linda stopped and inhaled deeply, then drew
herself up to her full height and stared directly at Sean. "It
was unseasonably cold," she repeated, emphasizing the word
'unseasonably.' "Unseasonably. I was caught off guard. Boomer
was my whole life. She was everything to me. Now I know what
it's like to lose a child." Linda wiped a tear from below her
right eye.

   "I'm sorry," said Sean. He couldn't relate to any of it,
but felt certain that he was expected to show some sort of
sympathy. Even if he had lost George Roy the night of the fire,
he knows that he wouldn't have gone overboard with sitting shiva
- the usual seven days would have been plenty. On one level he
wanted to laugh, but knew that that would have been a huge
mistake. He believed that there had to have been other health
complications involved, but didn't raise an further questions
about Boomer's cause of death. And he surely didn't believe that
Boomer was frozen solid.

   Sean developed concerns about his relationship with Linda.
He thought that she was right for him. She was likely the nicest
person he had ever met, but he had some doubts, naturally
brought on by the irrational, almost delusional conversations
like the one about Boomer. He knew that that wasn't entirely the
cause of his worries. Sean was accustomed to a lot of people who
clung to eccentric thinking or beliefs, many of whom lived
happily ever after in their alternate realities, including one
movie executive's wife who slept inside a backyard teepee. He
had the feeling like there was something else missing, as if
Linda was guarding something. He marked it off as his usual
paranoia, but couldn't help the creepy thought that Linda might

be part of Dave's leverage package, someone to use to manipulate Sean.

A few weeks later, Sean sat on the sofa while Barry sipped a can of Gatorade through a long colorful straw.

"This new girl, you know, the one whose father is the gantser macher at Hillcrest?"

"Of course. Linda. Why are you acting so nonchalant? Am I supposed to pretend that I didn't introduce you to her?"

"Barry! You know I already knew Linda. Can you just listen without being an asshole?"

"I think so," he answered. He put down his drink and turned to face Sean. "But, not being an asshole will be tough."

Sean continued, "I've already noticed something about her that might be a problem." He leaned back and spread his arms wide atop the back of the sofa. He wanted to be sure that Barry was ready to be attentive.

"Well?"

"She doesn't seem to be responsible for anything."

"What do you mean? Can you be more specific?"

"Well. Do you remember me telling you about how her dog died?"

"Yes. Froze to death."

"Well. There was something she said that keeps sticking in my mind. She said over and over - that it was unseasonably cold."

"That's normal, to defend herself. She didn't want it to seem that she was totally irresponsible, although someone could easily come to that conclusion. In her case, I think she was overwhelmed from having to spend the time with her parents, people who have a tight hold on her life. People who no matter what they say or do remain a toxic, disturbing influence on anyone around them. Their children will never recover from their childhood and adolescent barrage. They should have moved away a long time ago. But, it's not that easy. Just not that easy…"

"That's interesting. I see what you mean, but I get the feeling that she doesn't feel responsible for anything at all. It's always detached from her, whether she forgets to get salt pretzels at the Manhattan Bagel store or the fact that her father controls all of her financial interests."

"Neither one of those are unusual traits in a rich, powerful family, particularly if the daughter was sheltered. I wouldn't worry too much about that."

That troubled Sean. When Barry said not to worry about something it usually turned out to be something to worry about. Sean didn't think that Barry did it on purpose. It was sort of a curse that Barry had going with Sean. Barry had said not to worry a week before Sean's former wife filed for divorce, when Sean's old partners decided to cave in on him and force him to file bankruptcy, and the night Sean's mother died, just after being released by the ICU at Cedars.

"What does Linda tell you?"

"I see you've switched to your firm, demanding voice," said Barry. He turned on his professional mode, at least in the context of his type of practice. "I can't comment on why I am treating any of my patients. But I can tell you that lot of people who live in this town have disorders that can be lumped into different degrees of passive-aggressive personality disorders. These people should not be taken lightly. They are just as strong and as powerful as people who are outwardly extremely aggressive and controlling. The most obvious disorder in town is always someone that suffers from a narcissistic disorder. They need to talk about themselves all the time, and expect everyone in their entourage to be concerned only with their activities, and all the time. This type of disorder eventually takes its toll on anyone close. The same is true for passive-aggressive. People get worn down in environments where their needs are not taken care of, and they constantly have to be on their toes to make sure that someone else's needs are taken care of first. That's basically it on the surface, but it gets more complicated. Both types of disorders get their way; they just appear completely different in how they go about it."

Sean got the message, although he didn't put two and two together. He got the part about Linda, but failed to realize that the other person Barry had in mind was Dave. The combination was a deadly one, two controlling personalities, one passive-aggressive and the other, a hopeless, bullying, narcissist.

"I think the two of you should come in and speak together. If this thing is getting serious, I should deal with the two of you as a couple." He launched into his credentials, having helped a multitude of high-profile clients in romantic flux.

Well, that's a momentary lapse into decency. "Okay. I'll run it by her." Sean was willing to try, but he wasn't sure why. His former wife had filled most of her free time in therapy, with and without him. *And look where it got me,* he thought.

Two weeks later, Linda and Sean were in Barry's office. Linda insisted on reciting a prologue that she had prepared in advance. She brought notes on colored index cards, the same as when she attended college. When she had finished, she packed the cards neatly in her purse, and looked up at Barry for her final grade.

"I know what you mean. It is tough to have a relationship with Hollywood as a backdrop." Barry paused to see if his statement was digested.

Linda smiled and nodded. That had been the thrust of her opening statement.

Barry said, "Sean, you look puzzled."

"I am puzzled. I don't know what you mean. I don't think where we live has anything to do with Hollywood or not Hollywood." *He's already on Linda's side.*

"Sean. You're a little bit in denial here. What do you think, Linda?"

Linda answered cautiously. "I don't know. Neither of us has ever had a good relationship here. I don't know what it is, but I think people have always put the relationship second."

"That's good. What do you mean by 'second'? asked Barry.

"She means 'second'. What is this, a Bill Clinton thing, like what does 'is' mean?"

"Sean. Let her answer. Do you want to answer?"

Linda nodded in the affirmative.

"Please go ahead. Sean…Give her a chance to speak."

Sean bristled and then added, "I'm not stopping her." He turned his head away from Barry's glare, like a pet being punished.

Linda continued. "Second to everything. Business. Money. All that stuff that people want out of life, but don't realize that it's not important." She turned toward Sean.

Barry said, "Sean is not a happy camper."

Sean said, "Linda. That's easy for you to say because you always have had those things."

"Sean. Please. Not an attack route, " Barry pleaded.

"No. You listen. She always has had everything, so she has had the luxury of not striving for any of those things the rest of us want."

"That may be a little true, but I don't see what it has to do with us." Linda turned to Barry to see if her thought was acknowledged.

Barry nodded. "Sean, back off a little. Okay?"

Sean was at once contrite. "I'm sorry. It's just that sometimes I think you don't know how tough it is for the rest of us, people who never know the future."

Linda said, "I don't know the future."

Barry paused, and then asked without any emotion, "Sean. What would you like Linda to think about business?"

"I..." Sean paused. "I don't want to change how she thinks."

"Then don't," Linda added with a smile.

Sean smiled back, but was still squirming. "Isn't the hour up yet?"

Barry continued the session, surmising that the awkward exchange had passed. "Let's get back to the point. Is it possible to have a relationship here? Not 'here' in Hollywood, but 'here', between Sean and Linda. Isn't that it? Isn't that what we're talking about?"

Sean thought, *Boy, is Barry loving himself right now.*

"Yes," said Linda. "I know I'm trying."

She turned toward Sean. He answered on cue. "I am, too."

"Case solved," said Barry.

"I know there are distractions," said Linda. "But I think it is an advantage with me. I'm concentrating on the relationship for both of us."

Sean didn't buy the whole session, but he never did with Barry. Barry was an unknown to Sean, someone who acted like a friend, but withheld enough so that nobody really knew him.

CHAPTER FIFTEEN
Sean, Gary, Bob
Brantley, Sean

A week later, Sean paced the office while Gary and Bob
quietly sipped coffee at their respective desks. This was Sean's
most comfortable position at work - in motion. Bob sucked on a
cigarette with all the passion of a Frenchman waiting to be
executed by a firing squad.

"How was our checkup?" asked Gary.

"I have to go in to have more of my lung taken off," said
Bob, without any concern.

"I meant, Sean," said Gary.

"Nothing wrong," said Sean. "Perfect."

Sean and Gary paused to glance at Bob. Then their eyes met
in the briefest momentary concern.

Sean made a quick disconnect from their concerns about Bob.
"That Indian sonofabitch. He still owes us twelve thousand. Two
years ago he tried to beat us for five thousand. What happened
with that?"

"He paid, and then he folded the company," said Gary.

"That's not like him," said Bob, who offered a forced
cheek-to-cheek grin.

"The only reason he paid is that he's afraid of Sean,"
answered Gary, with a proud bravado.

"Can we get him again?" asked Bob.

Sean spoke. "Not unless we go after him personally. He bought another shell and wrapped it into that chain of hamburger places. You know, Haven Heaven, or some shit like that. The hamburger places are all owned individually, and all he bought was the name, which really doesn't do any business other than the movies he makes, and only when he does. Otherwise there is no money on hand."

"So we're stuck. How can we get him personally?" asked Bob.

"We can't. Unless you want him to spit on you," said Sean.

"What are you talking about?" asked Bob.

Gary began to laugh.

Sean explained, while trying to hold back his laughter. "The Indian got into the same elevator as a guy who had sued him personally. They had just come out of the courtroom downtown. There were security guards in the elevator with both attorneys. The Indian just turns around and spits a load in the guy's face. It was disgusting, but I guess he felt he owed the guy for getting him 'personally'. I guess to be sued personally is a big deal to people like him, who hid behind corporate shells, and were usually not culpable for behavior related to a company. But this guy caught him."

"I read that screenplay by the root canal doctor," said Bob, glancing up from another script while he spoke.

"So?" asked Sean.

"So nothing. He can write, but the screenplay sucked. He thinks he's Woody Allen or something."

Sean rarely answered Bob's remarks on style. "What was it about?

"It was some boring boy meets girl thing in a medical school dorm. They get into all this psychobabble shit. A couple of funny jokes. That's it. It's over there on the floor. It's

the one with the peanut butter and jelly stains on it. I bought
this great jar of natural peanut butter across the street. It
had peanut butter and jelly already in the same jar. Far fucking
out."

"Thanks for the culinary tip," said Sean.

Bob waved his hand in mock gratitude.

Sean nodded to show his acknowledgment. "Bob. Before you
have your whole lung removed, could you do me a favor?

"Sure."

"Give me a one page synopsis of the plot of Dr. Brantley's
screenplay."

"I thought you were going to ask me to stop smoking."

"Why would I do that? You're going to outlive us all."

"That's a fact. I'll do the synopsis later."

"Thanks. You're a sweetheart."

"I love you, too."

Sean marched into the inner office, only to return a few
minutes later. That day, he had little to do but parade around.

The boys spent the rest of the day exchanging story ideas
while Bob continued his reading.

"We should do something with the Lewinsky thing," said
Gary.

"I wouldn't let her do anything to my thing," said Bob.
"Isn't that passé?"

Gary continued. "No. We do it with a Bush-like character.
We flip the story around and make it some guy on the far right
who's screwing all the super religious chicks."

"I like the Bush approach," said Bob. "Are these going to
be well-trimmed?" He stuck out his tongue. "Bush licks bush."

Gary's excitement level entered new heights. "Come on. Why
don't we do a down and dirty version? It's worked before. We get
all no-names for the leads, and fill in the good small character

parts with one-shot-one-day people. We can probably get Robert
Vaughn and Elliot Gould to play the Ken Starr and Ginsberg
roles. I think Gould would make a great Ginsberg type character,
you know, with the bow tie and everything."

"How many times can we show her going down on the President
in the White House?" asked Bob. He was the only one who had plot
concerns, even with the most exploitative stories.

"What's the difference?" asked Sean.

"I don't know, either. We can work it out once we get it
down on paper," said Gary. "What do you think, Sean?"

"It might work, but we would have to shoot the whole thing
in a few weeks. It's got to be a good script. We can't sell a
movie anymore just because there's a blow job or a cigar in it.
Those days are gone. The problem I see here is simple. Why would
anyone under twenty-five care about this movie, or anything
connected with the White House? They're running to *8 Mile* and
anything with Vin Diesel in it."

"If it's the President of the United States," said Gary.
"That's why. Celebrity sells in this country."

"That's about all that sells," added Bob.

Sean never really wanted anything that the boys brought up,
even it were feasible. "I know, but it may not play out any
better than a cheap action thriller, without the special
effects. All we've got is a movie about sex, not even good sex,
mind you, just some little bullshit sex thing. The more I think
about it, the less I like it. The media already took this little
nothing sexual relationship and made it dramatic as hell, but
how do you make it interesting?" He waited for a response.

"We could bring in the family, and make it a *Terms of
Endearment* kind of thing," said Bob. "Like the breakup of the
family."

"But nobody is sick here," said Sean. "The only thing that died in this story was Bill Clinton's dick. He rarely could get it licked, and he never got to put it anywhere but in his own hand, first with Paula Jones and then with Wiley. When you add it all up, the whole thing is like some high school hand job summer movie."

"We could have someone contract AIDS, get sick and die." Bob had said it with a straight face.

Gary turned his head away in disgust. "What if we made it parallel with what's going on in the world?"

"What do you mean?" asked Sean.

"Like the President on the telephone, talking to Major in London, while some chick is parading around in her thong," said Gary. "Just the idea that she is in the office and he is talking about world affairs, attacking Iraq…getting Arafat to a meeting in the U.S." Gary was still hoping that he could arouse Sean's interest.

"Naw. This is a no movie kind of story. Look at the polls. Nobody really cares. Now, if she had sucked Ken Starr's dick too, then we'd have a real story," said Sean.

"Yeah. That would be a hoot, this guy with connections to Pepperdine, and all that Church of Christ shit. That would be funny," said Bob.

"Sure is a big deal about a few blow jobs," said Gary.

Sean spoke, this time more impassioned. "It's not like a big deal now, but it was then. We've never had a President that was such a schmuck. There is nothing in the constitution to deal with schmucks. That's the issue. Unless the house passes an amendment or some other shit to introduce the idea of a schmuck president, they're all stuck, and that's why the pundits-schmundits and all of the other media didn't know what to make of Bill Clinton. The man was simply a schmuck. That's it. Good

night. Close the door. End of story. Problem? Yes. The guy is
not a crook, did absolutely nothing major to hurt the country.
The stupid schmuck ends up making money for everyone, and that's
the end of the story. A schmuck made them money for the first
time in the history of the country, and we don't know what the
fuck to make out of it, so they voted to impeach the poor guy,
and then wonder what we're doing wrong. All we need is to define
'schmuck' so that future presidents can be accused of being one,
end of story, case closed, and we save fifty million dollars,
and a waste of good media time."

"But what about social security, health reform, and all the
other stuff that's been out of the news?" asked Gary.

Bob waved Gary off. "That stuff is boring. Having a schmuck
in the White House. That's exciting news! But Bush only does
little dumb things. You won't find him caught in any
peccadilloes."

When the conversation quieted down, Sean spoke. "What did
the doctor say?"

Bob answered, nonplussed, "Nothing. The lung thing was no
big deal. I told you. They want to take out a little bigger
chunk. He also found a little mass under my tongue. I told him
to let it go. I'd get back to him. There was this other thing,
something about a valve problem. I probably always had it."

"I told him he's crazy," said Gary.

Sean knew that reasoning with Bob about his health was an
impossibility. He changed the subject to sports.

A few days later, I sat alone in a red booth at Junior's
Deli on Westwood Boulevard. While I was waiting for Sean,
Leonard Nimoy, the Star Trek actor famous for playing Mr. Spock,
was eating and chatting a few booths away. I could not help but
notice how thin he was. He was wearing black glasses and a

collegiate outfit consisting of a V-neck sweater and neatly
pressed slacks. He appeared more like an English Literature
professor than an actor, although I confessed to myself that
both fields might attract similar people.

I wondered for a second how people all over the world would
react to seeing Mr. Spock in costume, eating a corned beef
sandwich in Junior's Deli. Maybe it would become a popular
poster. The anxiety was killing me. This was a 'story meeting'.
Liz had primed me that the expression was a euphemism for what I
had already been exposed to, people telling me how they wanted
to change my screenplay. Everyone saw a screenplay as not only a
first draft, but a creative work begging to be altered in some
way by everyone who touched it.

Sean made his usual entrance. He stopped to exchange barbs
with one of the counter men and looked right past me, instead
waving to Leonard Nimoy. When Sean turned in my direction, he
feigned searching for me. When he 'spotted' me, he smiled and
rushed to my booth, where he continued to stand and survey the
room with a hundred and eighty-degree turn, and when he was
satisfied with his surveillance he sat down across from me.

"Hello, Doctor," said Sean.

"Hi, Sean. How's it goin'?"

Sean grabbed a menu. I copied his behavior.

I wondered what Sean was thinking as he skimmed the menu.

"The sandwiches are good here," said Sean. "Deli food is
the best."

I was surprised to see how ordinary Sean sounded when he
was alone. I felt as if Sean was trying to make me feel
comfortable.

"How's the corned beef here?" I asked, trying to make idle
conversation, but not entirely change the subject unless
directed to by Sean.

"Great. I'm having an egg-white omelet," said Sean. "My cholesterol count is too high. This is a no meat day for me."

Oh, I thought. Maybe Sean wanted me to have the same thing. I wanted a sandwich, and aggressively stated my case to the waitress moments later. "Corned beef/pastrami combo on rye."

"And French fries," Sean dictated to her.

"And French fries," I echoed.

I also ordered a Doctor Brown's cream soda at Sean's suggestion. He had an iced tea. The food came out quickly, but Sean still hadn't gotten around to my screenplay.

It didn't take long to realize that I was eating for Sean's vicarious pleasure. This was a new routine for me. I had met dozens of other people that were fucked up beyond repair about their diets. Half of them thought that Dean Ornish was a guru while the other half swore by Atkins, who let his worshipers eat steak after steak with butter, and then whipped cream for dessert.

In Hollywoodland, it was almost impossible to eat any tasty, decently prepared food without someone spoiling it by bringing up the fact that it was either unhealthy or too large of a portion. Restaurant conversation rarely omitted cholesterol counts, food allergies, chemical additives, salt content, or rapid calculations of calories, courtesy of the thousands who had trained themselves to give on-the-spot summations - walking food computers. And almost all the remarks - unsolicited.

"I like your writing," said Sean, after first trashing the New York Yankees. He hated George Steinbrenner. I believed him. Sean would have made a damn good actor. Not only had he never read a word of my screenplay, but when he spoke about Steinbrenner, it might as well have been Saddam Hussein.

"Thanks." I still took the obvious positive comments as compliments.

"We have to make a change. The cruise thing...I want them to do a sail thing in San Francisco rather than a cruise from L.A."

"You want me to make a location change in my screenplay?" The cruise from L.A. was a cheap three day cruise to nowhere, something that medical students could afford. I had written in the Carnival Line because it was known for its steep discounts, cheap booze, and particularly on short trips. But sailing, that was a whole other thing for my characters. My characters didn't sail. Two were transplants from Brooklyn.

"Sure. Why don't we work on it? Get it into shape. Maybe I can do something with it, but it's going to have to be changed." That was a veiled message that he wanted a lot of changes, not only a venue or activity change.

I was overwhelmed because I was actually talking to someone who made movies, and that person wanted to work on my screenplay. I folded quicker than a tailgate at kickoff time. "That's fine. I don't have a problem with that."

"Great. It's really going to be a lot better this way." Sean sliced his omelet into long, narrow strips.

"Are you working on anything now?" I asked, as I stuffed my mouth nervously with my sandwich.

Sean paused and appeared to be in deep thought or at least that was what he wanted me to think. "I like you, so I'm going to tell you. Cannibals." He stopped as if he had just given me the password to break into the Federal Reserve Bank.

I smiled and laughed. The look on Sean's face meant that he could not have been joking. I stopped laughing and began to cough. "Wow. Cannibals. I was laughing because it caught me off guard. It's really a good idea." I almost had really choked on a piece of pastrami.

"You okay?"

"I'm fine." I had no idea what he was talking about, and was stuck in that strange world of not knowing what to say, whether to be myself or prepare my remarks so that Sean would like me. I already felt that I was coming off like a jerk.

Sean leaned closer to me, almost letting his loose fitting Tommy Bahama shirt touch his food. "I'm going to make millions off of this one."

"Do you think I could help with the writing?" I don't know how I got the words out, but I did. It was so unlike me, but I was picking up the local style; when someone gives you an opening of any kind, fearlessly take it.

Sean smiled - the kind of expression a kindly father would give his child who had asked prematurely if he could try the razor. He shook his head 'no'.

I had taken the bait. "Sorry…Sorry. I shouldn't have asked that."

Then he did a passive flip. "We'll see. I'm just formulating the story now. Let's concentrate on what we're doing, see how it goes. I'm not saying definitely 'no', but this is going to be a big one. I might have to go with a bankable A-list writer." Sean couldn't think of the last time that he was involved in a project with a bankable writer, but he had to keep me champing at the bit.

What I didn't know is that Sean had no intention of doing anything with my screenplay. In the first place, he couldn't afford to make more than one or two movies a year, at best. Besides that, it was unlikely that he was going to do something that someone else wrote. Sean received story credit on many of his movies since he believed that all the stories were really based on his ideas, something he forced on all his writers who were willing to let him get away with it. Another thing that Sean would never reveal or even consider was that his latest movie idea was actually a remake of Gary's *Eating Beverly Hills* - that one being a clear title rip-off of the Paul Bartel's movie, *Eating Raoul*. Sean's was going to be a sequel utilizing the same simple plot and named ingeniously *Eating Beverly Hills II,* or so Gary thought after his private meetings with Sean.

Sean didn't want to give Gary a credit or a financial cut, so he would try to convince him that *Beverly Hills Cannibals* was a sequel or prequel to *I Spit On Your Pasta*, and therefore not related in any way to Gary's movie. Sean had trouble admitting that he didn't have any truly original ideas. Elements in Sean's projects were filled with derivations from clearly recognizable classic and popular movies, as well as derivative scenes from his own prior works. When it came to Gary's movies, Sean always felt free to cannibalize them, since hardly any project that Gary had done could be labeled as entirely original either. To sort things out would have been a nightmare for any intellectual property attorney, whose job might be to find out which ideas were truly original. The movie business was always feeding on itself and few lawsuits found their way to a satisfying settlement.

Sean's plan for my future was simple. Set me up for the flurry of disappointments that come in the industry, and then get me to write a movie for him the way that he wanted it, at a time when I had lost all hope of ever selling anything. Of course, it would initially be an 'on spec' deal, and Sean wouldn't have to spend a nickel 'up front' for the screenplay, not until the first day of principal photography, assuming he was able to fund the movie and reach that point.

The next to last part of our conversation was one that I would hear frequently. "Look it. Brantley. This is a tough town. Don't expect anything to happen fast." The advice was given in a paternal manner, to inspire confidence in the fact that Sean was looking out for my creative interests, while at the same time letting me know that little or nothing was going to happen.

"What do you mean when you say 'tough town'?" I asked with my naiveté balanced on the last morsel of corn rye.

"Tough. It's just pretty tough."

"You mean like a mixed morality kind of thing?" I was feeling confident enough to show that I had some understanding of the human condition, even in Hollywood.

Sean shrugged his shoulders. He hesitated. It seemed as if he didn't want to speak, but eventually decided to continue. "This is a town where everyone feeds off everyone else. It's more than just dog eat dog. Anyone will eat anything or anyone. Make no mistake about that. Writers are at the bottom of the food chain here. You've got to accept that if you want to write screenplays. Everyone you come across will want to eat a little piece of you."

"Including you?" I interrupted.

"Including me."

Wow, that was honest. I thought I'd better cover myself. "I meant no offense."

Sean was brighter and more direct than I had anticipated. He was different from the other people that I had come across. I was reminded of the old joke about the scorpion and the frog who agrees to help the scorpion across a pond, and the scorpion stings him on the way across. In explanation the scorpion offers, "I told you that I was a scorpion."

Sean answered, "I took none. These are just the ground rules. You've got to know the ground rules if you are going to play ball in this town. Everyone chews a little on everyone else. The writer sits around all day and stews. That's no joke. They cook themselves a little at a time, taking little bites out of themselves in order to see if they are done yet. It may sound

411

silly to you, but writers take it out on themselves, nibbling away at themselves, spending so much time writing about themselves. I get dozens of childhood scripts every month, writers who stewed over their computers, cooking themselves as they chew up the history of their own lives and families, little by little until they either can't move ahead to another subject, or keep coming back to the table for another bite out of their family history. It's human nature. Once they get the script out, then everyone else takes a little bite out of them. Remember what I said, writers are at the bottom of the food chain in this town."

That was pretty clear, I thought. I stared at Sean for what felt like an eternity, somewhat stunned, not knowing if it was an act; a prepared speech that he had practiced over the years or something that he really felt. Whatever it was, I decided to choose my next few words carefully. "A lot of people have tried to discourage me from writing. I appreciate what you're saying." I meant it.

"Discourage you? No way. I'm giving you sound advice on how to keep going. Keep writing this autobiographical dreck that you sent me and you'll end up eating yourself alive. You can't write that stuff and survive out here. That's all I mean. Look, let's concentrate on what you should be writing, how we can fix up what you've got. That's the purpose of this meeting, so let's get going. Okay?"

"Okay" I felt that it was the only thing I could have said, but was stung by him calling my material 'shit' in Yiddish.

"I've got a few ideas I'd like to run by you."

"Fine."

"Let's get some more pickles," said Sean as he raised the empty pickle dish up in the air for the waitress to see. He was in no mood for more morality tales about the movie business.

"Sure."

"Do you want both kinds?" Sean didn't wait for an answer. "I like to alternate between the half-sour with garlic, and the other."

"You mean 'dill'," I volunteered.

"No. The other kind."

"Dill," I repeated.

"No. It's another name. Whatever." Sean was always right, even about pickles.

Moments later, the waitress returned with a plate piled high with pickles. "Here you are boys. Knock yourselves out."

"We will,'' said Sean, with his mouth already full of a huge half of a pickle. The juice dripped down his hand toward his wrist.

The rest of the meeting proved uneventful. Sean name-dropped casually and slipped into self-aggrandizing descriptions of his political and social contacts.

After the meeting, I decided to send *Small Steaks* to as many people as possible. It was about this time that I became more determined, thinking that I had a chance to succeed as a writer. I fantasized about the day when I would no longer have to put my fingers in peoples' mouths.

The response was beyond disappointing.

MARTIN RANSOHOFF PRODUCTIONS, INC.

Enclosed please find your screenplay, SMALL STEAKS.

I have reviewed the material and determined that it is not   something that we would be interested in pursuing.

Good luck in setting up the project.

Very truly yours,

Ass't to Mr. Ransohoff

During a tennis match at the Beverly Hills Tennis Club I had met Mr. Ransohoff, who had once run a major production company. We played several times before I had suggested sending him a screenplay. Ransohoff, the former founder and chairman of Filmways was responsible for a wide range of movies including *Catch-22, The Cincinnati Kid, Silver Streak, and Jagged Edge.* The assistant who actually signed the letter would receive a single associate producer credit on one of Ransohoff's movies.

Then there were people who had stone walls around their production companies. I soon was staring at the release form sent by Rastar, Ray Stark's office.

"I desire to submit to you for your consideration material (herein called "submitted material") written by me intended to be used by you to evaluate my writing ability. The material submitted is "SMALL STEAKS" (screenplay). I understand that you may submit the submitted material to third parties. I recognize the possibility that the submitted material may be identical with or similar to material that has or may come to you from other sources. Such similarity in the past has given rise to litigation so that unless you can obtain adequate protection in advance, you will refuse to consider the submitted material. The protection for you must be sufficiently broad to protect you, your related corporations, and you and the employees, agents, licensees, and assigns and all parties to whom you submit material. Therefore, all references to you include each and all of the foregoing...I acknowledge that the submitted material is submitted by me voluntarily...shall be deemed to place you in any different position from any other member of the public...I agree that no obligation of any kind...If there is any dispute…you should determine that you have the independent legal right to use material containing features or elements similar or identical to those contained in the submitted material without entering into a written agreement for compensation to me, and if you proceed to use the same and if I disagree with your determination, the dispute between us shall be submitted to arbitration in Los Angeles, California, before an arbiter mutually selected by us who is experienced in the field…I assume full responsibility for any loss of the submitted material…I hereby release you of and from any and all claims…You may freely assign your rights under this agreement..."

If I sign this I am giving them the right to steal it, I thought. If I don't sign it, they won't read it. If I get it submitted without the agreement they might steal it anyway. What's the difference?

Ray Stark's movies included *Funny Lady, Night of the Iguana, Sunshine Boys, Annie, The Way We Were, and The President's Analyst.* Years back, Stark had married Fanny Brice's daughter. He also did quite well will his shares of Columbia and Coke stock.

I picked up another letter, from the producer Howard Koch. Koch was well-known in Hollywood. He outlived most of his contemporaries, and managed to keep a permanent spot at Paramount. I eventually played a round of golf with Koch. Howard could not have been more affable. He was friendly, down to earth, and very funny. I thought he sounded anxious to see the screenplay. Some of his many features were *The Odd Couple, The Manchurian Candidate, Plaza Suite, Gorky Park, Ghost,* and *Losing Isaiah.*

The letter came two days after I sent him the screenplay.
Dear Dr. Benjamin :

Reference is made to your letter of August 23rd,

relating to the above screenplay.

Unfortunately, the subject matter of your screenplay
is not the type of material in today's film market.

I, am, therefore, returning same to you.

Sincerely,

Howard W. Koch

HWK/k

DICTATED BUT NOT READ

"Dictated, but not read," I screamed. It was my first
'dictated but not read' letter. *What a joke, the guy had to make
clear that he didn't have time to read it or he didn't care what
the letter said.*
I was beginning to get the idea. There were codes, methods,
and unwritten modes of conduct that were beyond my
comprehension. Hollywood had its own set of variable rules,
with its own secret language. I, like countless thousands, were
disposable jerks, including some of our literary treasures.

CHAPTER SIXTEEN
Frank
Brantley, Liz
Brian

Frank from Hillcrest was no longer happy with the state of his erection. His barometer for sexual omnipotence meant making twice-monthly visits to a friend's condo on Maple Drive to 'shtup' his most recent mistress, Heather. Since his wife never ventured to the ostrich farm, that's where Frank spent most of his prolonged dates with Heather.

He had postponed several dates with Heather because of his reduced potency. He couldn't take another chance. After it had happened a few times, Heather accommodated him with a new found desperation, and he did get it up. The last few weeks he had tried looking at some soft porn on the Internet, but he wasn't getting the desired results.

The lifelong dalliance rumors didn't matter to Frank's wife, since there was never much of a spark in their sex life, nor did it matter at the inception of his courtship. His marriage was a business one, founded mainly in concerns about money and power, with consistent country club social acceptability, the later having only to do with the money and power. Certainly, in the segregated card room rumors flowed, particularly during the women's bridge game. Frank was comfortable in only one role, that of the conquering sexual hero, and his wife had played her part for years, an acquiescence with his extracurricular shenanigans that was not uncommon for her generation. When Frank took his conquering hero sex show on the road his wife experienced a silent sense of relief. She became happier when he was out of town.

Frank decided to make an appointment with the popular Hollywood urologist, Dr. Marvin Dooley, a well-trusted crony of the wealthy locals, who were comfortable in his often clammy hands. Marvin was a medical insider, someone who took the doctor-patient privilege to a higher level, often preventing legal interrogatories from exacting any medical truths from him when it came to his patients.

The names Max Factor, Spielberg, and Davis adorned some of the buildings at the Cedars complex where Marvin worked. Gracie Allen and George Burns were the names on streets that ran through the impressive enclave. The hallways in the hospital were adorned with such lavish art that first-time visitors had the impression that they were in the executive wing of a major global corporation.

Marvin's office had a waiting room that could hold thirty patients. There were seven names on the door under the heading Beverly Urology, the corporate umbrella that 'owned' all the doctors. Beverly Urology was run by an even larger national corporation, already in twenty-four states, grossing hundreds of millions of dollars per year by running the doctors' practices.

At least in Marvin's office, people were still being treated like patients. The day of Frank's appointment he waited the basic twenty minutes past his scheduled time. He had refused to tell the front office girls anything except that he wanted a routine exam.

"But you just had one three months ago," said one of the office managers.

"Never you mind. Just put me in the book," was Frank's answer. "I've been coming to the office for twenty years. You just put me in Dr. Dooley's book. Dr. Dooley's and nobody else. Got me?"

The girls giggled behind Frank's back. They put up one dollar each for a winner-take-all lunchtime pool. From a hat, each one drew little slips of paper that contained things like kidney stone, can't pee, impotence, and HIV paranoia. Those days, the odds were in favor of impotence and HIV paranoia. After a scandalous night that sometimes involved hookers, guilt-ridden and health-conscious patients would review their lascivious activities with Marvin in order to make sure that they weren't exposed to the HIV virus. There was a marked increase in requests for information on contact routes after Magic Johnson had admitted that he was HIV positive, following years of promiscuous heterosexual contact. Of course, Viagra was in big demand, and whoever picked it from the hat would have a good chance for success.

Once inside the treatment room, Marvin knew what was up by the way Frank smiled. It was forced, the first uncomfortable sign given by men who were slowing down below the waist.

"Frank. How's the golf game?" Marvin asked. He was standing across from Frank, who was already sitting on the treatment table, with his legs dangling like a schoolboy passing time.

"Fine. Shot my age again Thursday."

Marvin was a pro at appearing friendly, but not patronizing. "Hell. That's great. You really are great. So…What can I do for you?

"It's not for me," Frank said with a tone that gave away his ruse.

Marvin wasn't surprised. Advice for a friend was one of the oldest patient cons when it came to the urogenital system. "Oh. Who is it?"

"It's Stan. He is having trouble, you know. The little boy won't salute for him anymore. He begged me to come in and ask you about getting him some of those Niagara things."

"Viagra," said Marvin.

"Right," said Frank.

"But you know I can't just give it out without an exam," said Marvin.

Frank slid forward and dropped to the ground. He was a full head taller than Marvin. Frank moved closer. "Say. Listen Marvin." Frank was intent on carrying the helpful friend routine to new limits.

Marvin didn't want to play games. He knew what was coming from a mile away. "Frank. Don't ask me - "

Frank cut him off. "Marvin. I want you to do this, okay? No questions about it. That's the way it's got to be. Got to be just like that. That's the way. No other. Be a good ol' boy and do what I say now, and I'll be on my way."

Marvin inhaled. This territory went with the trappings of being a popular doctor. A rich, powerful patient was always asking him to bend the rules. He knew that people could buy Viagra on the Internet. It wasn't such a breach of medical ethics. "You and Stan do enjoy about the same good health. I'll have to make the prescription out to you. That is okay with you, isn't it?"

"Fine. But I don't want it in my records. Got me?"

Marvin nodded.

Frank soon left the office with a prescription for Viagra.

That weekend, Liz insisted that I attend a lecture. It was
given by Rabbi Ermis, a popular local and somewhat national
leader. The title of the lecture was "Morality, Jews, and Making
Movies". Liz was sympathetic toward my complaints about my
recent screenplay experiences, and was doing whatever she could
to broaden my understanding of Hollywood business.

The Burton Way Synagogue was founded about forty years ago
through the efforts of Rabbi Ermis and about two dozen people
with disposable funds, mostly from the entertainment industry.
The idea was to start a progressive, reformed synagogue further
west than the famous Wilshire Boulevard Temple. Over the years,
the new synagogue had grown while the residential power base
moved out of old Hollywood to points west like Beverly Hills.

I sat stunned inside the elegant, but tasteful, house of
worship as I listened to the Rabbi's impressive presentation.

The Rabbi's stentorian voice lent itself easily to public
speaking. "The idea that Jews were entirely responsible for
movies is a silly one. There is no question that Catholics and
Jews sit on entirely different sides of the Judeo-Christian
road, but don't mistake those differences as the basis for
polarity in the movies. On the contrary, movies are just another
type of pageant, a pageant all of us moviegoers love to feast
our eyes on. For some, it's the spectacle itself, the costuming,
or the set, but those of us who enjoy that spectacle on the
screen may find that we are also equally interested in the
spectacle of our own liturgical pageantry. Most of us, if you
are like me, find that we are attracted to both. I myself must
confess that I sneaked into a movie theater one afternoon to
catch a matinee. No. It wasn't Shabbos, although I always
thought of the early Saturday matinee as odd time to run a
double feature since most of the Jews were still davening." He
paused and delivered the next line as a hushed confession. "It

was during the High Holy Days, and I just had to go. I was drawn
to the movie like I've been drawn to everyone and everything
else in life that I love. It was toward the end of the holiday,
but still part of the holiday."

"This guy is good," I said.

"Quiet," demanded Liz.

The Rabbi continued, awkwardly returning to his opening
statement. "It was the Catholics that forced the Production Code
on the industry. You must realize how odd this must have been
for the Jews who founded the industry. Here they had this great
money-making product, started from nothing, and now they would
have to make some sort of partnership with the Catholics. It was
a beginning of a tension between the Catholics and movies that
originated with the nickelodeon and continues today in the era
of our giant screen multiplex theaters. Think about this, and I
find it a funny concept. On one side you had the Jews; most of
the owners were from poor, immigrant backgrounds. They had
worked their way up in a variety of businesses, many of them
coming direct from nickelodeons or ownership of one or two local
theaters. They sat down to make a Production Code, a document
really about morality. And who was it for? It wasn't for them.
It was for the Protestants!"

He paused for the expected laugh, and he received it.

"That's where all the moralizing about movies had its
beginnings. What's not so nice about the whole process is that
one man really got control of the system. Joseph I. Breen was an
anti-Semite who practically set up the moral structure for
movies. Yes, another anti-Semite."

He wasn't sure if he should pause there but he did, and got
a muffled kind of nervous laugh and a few snickers. He moved
ahead quickly.

"He was quoted as saying 'These Jews seem to think of nothing but money-making and sexual indulgence.' He had said some worse things, but I'll spare you. It was the usual stuff of the thirties and forties. Breen used anti-Semitism to help shape what went into movies. Strange, isn't it? In a world run by mixtures of morality, we have a man who clearly was against the Jews, telling them how to make their product, how to tell stories, how to make the movie that made them the money. Needless to say, when Breen died in 1965 there wasn't a single Hollywood executive at the funeral. There were problems with the type of mixed morality forced on the movie business. It often became confusing for the intelligent child. When Betty Hutton gave birth to sextuplets in *The Miracle of Morgan's Creek*, it was interpreted that she must have slept with six different men in one night."

Another pause. Another laugh.

"What I'm getting at is simple. When we try to apply moral codes to our system of entertainment we may be making a mistake. In many instances, the cure is worse than the disease. There is always a danger when we try to force morality on creative works that are better governed by only free expression. Movies have been blamed over the years for just about every ill of our society. Jane Addams had said early on that movies were unhealthy for children. The Payne Fund came up with the idea that juvenile delinquency was caused by the movies. While moviemakers today have a greater freedom than their predecessors, the controversy of morality in the movies will not go away. The industry is popularizing sex and violence more than ever. We don't have to contend with only movies, we also must consider computer games, and the newest kid on the block, the Internet. So let's get down to the meat of my talk. What moral responsibilities do we have in the entertainment business? Has that morality diminished? Are we heading into the abyss, or is it business as usual?"

One of the more interesting sections came toward the end. "The question I've had to deal with more than once is 'How do you justify the existence of God in the movie business, if there is so much evil?' It's a common paradox. Here you have a predominately male Jewish group, who make a product that uses violence, promiscuity, a diminished view of the value of life, and an endless reproduction of action-adventure movies. It's hard to reconcile, even on my end. How can you reconcile the existence of God when you are watching a trailer promoting another action-adventure movie with Arnold? If you are in the business, and you have thought about God, you must ask yourself, 'How can God allow such a thing to take place?' It makes a good argument for the other side, that there is no God if evil can exist the way that it does. Or you can make a new argument, that movies are a new evil, a new higher level of evilness, something that God is still working on. After all, if you subscribe to the theory that each day in creation may have been millions of years, the movie business is still a nothing for God, a minuscule and relatively unimportant work in progress."

His concluding remarks were direct. "It's always going to be controversial. People always want to know where God is when something evil is going on, and the movie business is no exception."

After the lecture we bumped into Dave Stirling. He was sitting in the back row with his daughter Linda.

"Great lecture," said Dave. "Rabbi Ermis is the best."

I introduced Liz to Linda. They seemed to hit it off instantly.

"Where's Sean?" I asked.

"Whoops," said Linda. She blushed. She had made a point of keeping Dave and Sean apart, at least when she was around.

"I get it. You think I don't know what goes on in this town," said Dave. He pretended that he wasn't spending any time with Sean. "How is Sean, Linda?"

"Let's drop it," said Linda, with a playful smile.

We chatted for a few minutes and then disappeared into a crowd of baby agents that included Brian. Liz mentioned that Brian seemed more depressed than usual.

Dave and Linda mingled with some of the big shots. Her father suddenly propped himself up against a wall for support.

"Dad. You look a little pale," said Linda.

"It's nothing. Dr. K. is on it," said Dave. "He found out I had blastocysts in my blood. It's rare. Lucky he found it. He's a good man."

"Dad. He's always treating you for something," said Linda. "What happened to that Chronic Fatigue stuff?"

Dave offered a knowing smile, meant to convey that he knew more than Linda when it came to his health.

We bounced back into the Stirlings on the way out. Dave talked up the Hollywood Deli. "It's going to be bigger than McDonalds."

Liz suggested that we double date with Linda and Sean. Linda was all smiles.

Later that day, Brian sat in Barry's waiting room, reading a copy of his dental records. He had insisted that his dentist, Dr. Galin, give him a duplicate set. He was still having trouble brushing the distal or back part of his lower molars.

After exchanging pleasantries, Brian launched into his oral healthcare dilemma. "Barry. I can't seem to learn how to do this. It's driving me nuts. I sit at meetings with Dustin

Hoffman, and all I can think about is if he knows that I can't even brush my fucking teeth. He thinks I'm a loser. A nothing. He's going to walk out of the deal or get me thrown off the package. I'll be gone and Mark will take my place and all the credit for setting up the package." Brian slammed his head back on the fluffy old couch.

Barry tilted his swivel rocker forward. "Is there anything else you want to talk about?" he asked calmly, sipping on a Starbucks iced mocha drink.

"No. I told you. It's my teeth. I still can't clean my teeth. The hygienist says I'm still not cleaning the back of my molars." Brian had become frantic.

Barry became even calmer. "Well. We discussed the different types of brushes. You know, a lot of people have trouble with the same problem. I don't clean the back of my molars any better than you. I have my teeth cleaned four times a year. It's not really a bad thing to let the hygienist clean the backs of the molars. I'm sure a lot of people think the way that I do, to let them do it, particularly because we do pay for the service." His monotone sounded ideal for a public service message from the American Dental Association.

"Oh, great. I come here for help and you tell me...You tell me...You tell me not to come for this sort of help. I don't get what you expect me to do."

"It's not like the time we went to the gas station so I could show you how to pump your own gas. Pumping gas is a good thing to know. You already know how to floss and brush your teeth. It's enough already."

"I want to do a good job. Okay. I want to do a perfect job. For once I want to follow through until one day I can walk into Dr. Galin's office and have the hygienist tell me that I did a good job." Brian reclined fully on the sofa with his legs propped up with one of the back cushions.

"Oh, that's good for your back," said Barry.

"It was your idea...Last year when I was seeing the orthopedist and I couldn't sleep."

"Right. Right. I recommend it to all my patients."

"What do you recommend to all your patients who have dental cleaning problems like me?"

"Brian. You sound angry at me…Most anyone would be satisfied with how you clean your teeth. Your flossing has gotten much better. Much better." Barry rose and walked toward his little kitchenette. "Would you like a soda or water?"

"No thanks. But you're avoiding my question. I want to know what you tell patients who have this kind of problem."

Barry turned back to face Brian. "Brian. I don't have - " He stopped himself. "What I mean is that I don't consider your problem a pathology. It's perfectly reasonable to clean your teeth at the level that you do. It's the underlying personality problem that we have to deal with, not the tooth cleaning."

"I disagree." Brian grabbed another ancient pillow and held it close to his chest.

The conversation never progressed to any positive outcome. Brian left the session confused. He just wanted to clean his teeth a little better. That was all. Why was this so hard to get across to Barry?

Brian walked the streets of Beverly Hills for the next hour, blinded by a growing feeling of not belonging. He was supposed to go with Liz for a drink at the Beverly Hills Tennis Club a few hours later. She would pick him up at his apartment. He wandered aimlessly, stopping to peer into the Radio Shack window, wondering if he would ever find joy again inside the store. He hadn't touched the remote control vehicle he had bought for himself on his twenty-sixth birthday. He waltzed right past the Sharper Image store. He had hit rock bottom. With everyone getting promoted over him, he was doomed to agency hell, the slow track that prevented anyone from getting close to the level of an Ovitz or Meyer. He would be happy with much less.

The aggressive street aroma of Starbucks awakened his blank mind. It beckoned him to come to it, like so many times before. That day Brian wanted it all to come to a close, his endless frustration with work and his damned dental hygiene problems, which bore the brunt of his obsessive focus to succeed. Why couldn't he have had perfect teeth and gums like Liz? Maybe his teeth and gums had something to do with his failure. He thought that if he were his own boss and he and someone else were exactly tied in every category like cloned workers, he would have to promote the other person for only one reason - his own dental hygiene wasn't getting any better.

Instead of stopping, he headed to RiteAid via little Santa Monica Boulevard. If there was one thing he was going to do, it was to get rid of his periodontal pockets, halitosis, and receding gum line. He was going to do everything in his power to make himself as dentally healthy as possible. Once he got past that, who knows what opportunities might open up for him? At least he would have eliminated the one thing that he was convinced was holding him back. If he couldn't get rid of his dental pockets, how could he expect to succeed as an agent?

Once inside the store, Brian heard the sound of his name. It happened more than once, but to him it was all one horrible muffled cacophony, like when the sound is distorted in a movie running too slow. Everyone in the store knew him by name. It wasn't unusual for a few people to say hello as he made his way

back to the pristine dental hygiene section. That day, he bought
extras of everything, with enough floss to knit a blanket.

About an hour before Liz was to pick him up, Brian sat
naked in the middle of his living room. He couldn't focus on
anything except his teeth. His tongue kept running furiously
over the junction of the gum tissue and his teeth. Back and
forth, back and forth. He didn't like the way his gums felt. He
wanted it to be smoother, if only it was a little smoother,
things would be better. He couldn't think about leaving for a
drink, not until he could smooth out some of the rough spots.
"Damn her," he said, cursing the hygienist. "She did this. She
always does this. I try to clean them, make them smooth, and
then she is careless. She tears the damn gum tissue. Why the
fuck should I try so hard if she ruins it?"

He wasn't sure if he was shifting the blame off his own
shoulders. If he did a better job with his home care, then she
wouldn't need to clean so hard, and she wouldn't tear any
tissue. He knew that he was right; it was all his fault. He was
the blame for everything.

He didn't know why. He just did it. He dissolved dozens of
the colored plaque disclosing tablets in his bathtub. He wrapped
his arms and legs with dental floss until he felt the pulse in
all his limbs. He submerged himself in the tub, and felt his
mind wander. He didn't know why he was there or what he was
going to do. In his stupor, he didn't notice that the colored
red water was overflowing.

Minutes later, Liz parked her vehicle outside the white
apartment building on Palm Drive. She used the outside telephone
system to ring Brian's apartment. There was no answer. She tried
a second time, and then a third. Her instincts told her to think
the worst. She had heard all the horror stories about people in
her industry; accidental and deliberate overdose, alcohol abuse,

depression. Many were victims of a world where the golden rules of childhood melted away in an acidic haze. Brian was one of the fragile ones. Finally, she rang the manager's unit, and he buzzed her in, after saying that he would meet her outside Brian's apartment.

Liz knocked on the door of Brian's apartment, but there was no answer. She wrote a note and slid it under the door. The manager hadn't arrived there yet, so she went downstairs to get him.

About ten minutes later, after convincing the manger to help here, she knocked loudly on the door. "Brian. Open the door. It's Liz Roth." The manager kept his distance.

There was no answer. Liz told the ambivalent man to open the door to the apartment, convincing him that perhaps they were interceding in a medical emergency. "If you don't open it and something is wrong, I guarantee you that the family is going to sue your ass and the owner of building."

Once inside the room, Liz followed the trail of red colored water to the bathroom. "Call '911'. Oh, my god. He's killed himself," Liz screamed back to the manager, who now appeared even more inclined to leave.

Just as she finished her sentence she was inside the bathroom, and Brian's head popped up from under yards of dental floss.

"Not yet," he said.

"Brian! You're okay! What the fuck are you doing?"

"I don't know." He lifted up his arms, which had turned the bright red color of the disclosing tablets.

The following day, Brian took a leave of absence from the office. He made arrangements to see Barry every day, sometimes twice a day. Barry was more than generous with his time, particularly since he was caught off guard, having missed the

severity of Brian's condition. Barry knew that his unorthodox
practice methods could make him lax on occasion. Now he made
more of an effort to be more careful and not go overboard in his
casual, non-clinical attitude toward his practice. Up until
then, Barry had been lucky. Certainly in Brian's case, Barry
felt that they all had been lucky. The episode could have easily
ended in a tragedy.

CHAPTER SEVENTEEN
Sean, Bob
Brantley
Liz, Brantley
Sean, Brantley

The usual story meetings with Sean continued. The boys in the office now maintained a serious schedule of at least once every two weeks, something that usually was an indication that they might just end up making a movie. Sean would generally arrive late, leaving Gary to develop the story with me, knowing full well that anything we put down together could be vetoed by Sean, and usually was. Occasionally Sean wouldn't show up at all, and Gary would have notes that Sean left "because Sean wanted to be sure you had his input". The excuses were always work related, and had to be accepted as reasonable protocol. In the back of my mind I was beginning to realize that there was very little chance that *Small Steaks* was going to be made by Sean Daren Films, or anyone else. As it turned out it was an important juncture, a time when a writer learns that a large part of getting a screenplay accepted, bought, and produced is wasted energy. In this case, it was mostly a creative waste, since it made no sense to continually change a script so often and in such drastic ways, before even having a run through with actors.

The reasons for accepting the worst were simple. With the plot growing so complicated, the budget for the picture had probably swollen to over twenty million dollars. If a major studio were to do all the special effects that were written into the script, it would likely cost in the hundred million range. It didn't take a film degree from USC to figure that out. Sean had turned my romantic medical school comedy into an action-adventure - something more suitable for Sly, Arnold, Bruce, or Steven. There was no way that Sean could get financing for an action-adventure movie. Sean knew that, but he didn't see anything wrong with going through the motions. He had other ideas about how to use my talent.

In contrast to Sean and Gary, Bob had a shred of compassion for young, would-be writers, at least when I wasn't around. "Why don't you tell the kid that *Small Steaks* is going no place fast?" he asked matter-of-factly to Sean, without raising his head from a screenplay that sat on his lap. "Why jerk him off?" He reached for one of his chocolate donuts and began to nibble it slowly while he listened.

"He's learning how to write screenplays," said Sean. "This is the best hands on course in the business. Forget Sid and Truby." Sean was referring to popular gurus who 'taught' people how to write screenplays, a subsidiary business in the industry, built for people who believed in the miracle of a writing education as a key to success.

"That's just plain horse shit. What is this place now, a screenwriting school? All he's learning is how to rewrite your ideas," said Bob, fumbling for a cigarette.

"Isn't that what it is? Someone has an idea, and someone writes it down. Are you going to tell me that it's something else?"

433

"If I had the inclination I would, and seeing that I have the time, I'm already half way there, but let me say it this way. He can write, and you can't. I guess that about sums it up." Bob spread his hands and opened his palms.

"You think you're so smart."

"No. You're the smart one. You've got all the money. Isn't that the way it is, the smart one gets to the top, and the one with the twisted Hollywood morals, at least by your standard, ends up working his creative ass off until there is nothing left to steal, and then a new kid comes along, and the old guy is pushed out into the Valley and spends the rest of his life sitting in Art's Deli talking about what was to a bunch of alta cacas who either don't care or are going deaf?"

"Nobody's kicking you out."

"I wasn't talking about me, in particular." Bob took a deep drag on his cigarette. "I'd never live in the Valley, no matter how broke I got."

"Maybe you can go further north."

"How far?"

"Like I don't know, past Encino."

"How about like past Portland?"

Sean laughed as if Bob had told the joke of the year.

"You find that funny?"

"You're a funny guy, a funny, funny guy."

"Yeah. I'm a funny guy," Bob mimicked as he turned his head back to the script.

"Why don't you call our young root canal guy and tell him to quit working on *Small Steaks*? No. Better yet, tell him it's ready, and he should start sending it out on his own, even while I try to raise the money." Sean and Bob were unaware that I had already tried that.

Bob spoke without looking up. "Nobody is going to buy it with your rewrites."

"Okay, just call the kid and tell him."

"No problem," said Bob. "I'll take care of it."

"Tell him I have another idea."

"Why did I know that?"

"What does that mean?"

"Which word didn't you understand, the 'I', the 'know', or the 'that'?" Bob said, this time facing Sean. He wasn't in any mood for what he considered Sean's typical bullshit.

"Well, it's a great idea. I thought about it the other day. It's sort of a comedy, but a little dark, sort of like *Down And Out In Beverly Hills* meets *Eating Raoul*." It was something Sean always did, representing the same movie idea over and over with a slightly different title or logline.

Sean paused, something out of habit, as if his whole body had suddenly been taken over by a divine spirit of movie ideas, the one pure deity that inhabited the inner sanctum of sacred creative thoughts. Nobody ever knew if Sean believed his own bullshit, but it didn't matter. Either you went along with it or not. There was always the possibility of a real moneymaker lurking beyond the early stages, off in the fog that permeated hopeful imaginations.

"Sounds interesting. Do you have a title yet?" Bob didn't want to bother telling Sean that he had been talking about that for some time, including the similar titles.

"Yes. But I might change it." He strolled to the window and stared out over the traffic, his eyes only seeing the type on a blank page. "*Hollywood Cannibals*," he said slowly. "*Hollywood Cannibals*," he repeated, this time a few beats faster and with the assured tones that only a producer could invoke before one word had appeared on a page.

435

"I thought you're calling it *Beverly Hills Cannibals*." Bob couldn't resist.

"Save your sarcasm. Right. That's right," said Sean. "I'll decide which title is best."

"Do you want me to tell the kid?"

"What do you think?"

"Of what?"

"Of my idea."

Bob looked up from the script and stared at Sean. It was Bob's blank expression, reserved only for people that he was certain were intellectually inferior.

"Do you like it or not?" pressed Sean.

"You don't really want me to answer," said Bob.

"Go fuck yourself. You wouldn't know an idea if it fell on your head on the corner of Wilshire and Rodeo. I don't know why I bother telling you anything."

"Because you're basically insecure, and inside your mind and body is a scared little child."

"You know, I don't have to put up with this shit."

"Right. Do you want me to tell him? That's what we've sort of decided. Right?"

Sean paused for a moment, smiled, and grabbed one of Bob's chocolate donuts.

"That'll cost you a pack of cigarettes," said Bob.

"I just got you two packs."

"History." Bob put his nose back into the screenplay.

"Tell the kid to come in next week, for a story meeting," said Sean. "Maybe tell him to write something. You know how to do it."

"Okay." Bob was through. The telephone rang. "Production," he said. "No. He went out."

Sean pointed at himself and indicated with a wave of his hand that he was not in either.

"No," continued Bob. "Sean is with Gary. Right. I'll have them call you either late today or tomorrow," said Bob. "Right." He hung up.

"The Indian?"

"Right," said Bob.

"Okay. I'm going to lunch," said Sean.

"Bring me back those dumplings from the dragon lady."

"You want the sauce she puts on or should I bring you the little soy sauce deals in the foil?"

"Yeah, and the Chinese mustard."

Sean extended an open palm and stood over Bob's desk.

Bob stood up and slowly removed three wrinkled one-dollar bills from his pocket.

"Do you expect me to pay the tax?"

"Prick," muttered Bob as he scoured the inside of his pants for some change. All he could come up with was a quarter.

Sean took the money and headed out of the room. "You must be into me for a few thousand bucks by now," he said without looking back.

"You'll know when you'll see that - when they make peace with Palestine."

Sean kept walking.

The telephone rang again. "Production. Yes we do. Just make sure you include a self-addressed return envelope with proper postage. Don't call us. Give it about three months and someone will read it. Right. We have an excellent staff of readers here. You're welcome." Bob hung the telephone and continued to read the screenplay. "I love show business," he said out loud. Smiling, he put his hands over his eyes for a moment and rubbed his face. When his hands slid down below his chin, his face had changed from a wry smile to obvious distress. "Gevalt! Gevalt!" He sighed and shook his head. "Jesus. I can't read any more of this." He took the screenplay and tossed it across the room. It landed precariously on a pile of screenplays next to a bookcase, also filled with scripts. The names of the screenplays were written in various colors across the binding formed by the edges of the papers.

Bob lit a cigarette, took a few drags, and then opened a new eleven by fourteen manila envelope. He wrestled with it for a moment, and then the screenplay slid out, a process he had done a hundred times every year, for longer than he cared to recall. He glanced quickly at the cover note, which was handwritten. He began to read a few scenes, flipping through the screenplay. Within minutes, he settled back into an old swivel desk chair, and continued, with all the excitement of the first time.

I could not have been more excited when the telephone call came from Bob. "Brantley. It's Bob. I've got some good news. Sean has given me a go on *Beverly Hills Cannibals* and you're in as the writer." Bob had to control his cynical laughter.

Bob explained that he needed about ten pages of "opening stuff" to set up the story. When Bob broke the bad news about *Small Steaks*, I took it in stride. I was ready to try anything and I knew that Sean would sooner raise money for a movie that was based on his own idea.

I had the pages in Bob's hand in only four days. It wasn't that I was particularly talented; I was desperate.

The first thing that I did was to find out as much as I could about cannibals. That was easy. The Internet was a great source of recently published information. On one of the available magazine databases I was able to find articles like

"Cannibal Lecture: How Could a Culture So Apparently Boring As Ours Have Embraced the Flesh-devouring Wendigo? (cannibals in Canadian literature), (excerpt from *Strange Things: The Malevolent North in Canadian Literature*). The Cannibal Lecture article appeared in *Saturday Night* and spoke about the giant spirit-creature, perhaps with feet of fire, sometimes so large that it left tracks like snowshoes. Most importantly, the being ate human beings, an attempt to satisfy a ravenous hunger for human flesh. The idea of eating man was no stranger to literature. The one-eyed Polyphemus of the Odyssey, as well as some of the big boys in Grimm's fairy tales wouldn't have minded getting their hands on a nice, plump, Beverly Hills accountant. As folklore would have it, once a human being was transformed into a Wendigo, it could be killed in most of the usual ways, but it was well-advised to make sure to remove and burn its new heart of ice.

The idea that a psychosis actually existed that described the compulsion to eat human flesh seemed like an appealing story line. The only way to satisfy such a compulsion was through cannibal acts. Analysts point out that the first attempts to feed that demon were directed at the cannibal's immediate family. I thought that would be a good plot point, having the cannibalism in Beverly Hills begin inside one family.

INT. EXPENSIVE HOME. BEVERLY HILLS FLATS. NIGHT

The DADDY of the house is sitting with his feet up on his elegant recliner, his eyes fixed on a flat-screened television that fills one wall of the room. His oldest daughter, SUSIE,   thirteen, runs down the spiral staircase.

                    SUSIE
        Daddy. You won't believe what Barb is doing to little
        Harry.

                    DADDY
        Every time she starts in on your little brother it
        usually ends up costing me an arm and a leg.

                    SUSIE
        Not this time Daddy. It's Harry's arm and leg!

    Aside from the numerous classical references to
cannibalism, I had several other stories to 'borrow from'. There
was new information that Indians who had lived in Arizona could
have supplied the television chef Emeril with another version of
his Cajun dishes. New fossil records appeared that indicated
that the Anasazi Indians, once thought to be peace-loving
ancestors of the Pueblos, took part in cannibalistic feasts.
    Cannibalism existed as an adaptive strategy. Many other
species eat or ate their own, and at times our ancestors took a
little bite out of each other in order to scare the neighbors,
cut down on overpopulation (maybe Swift wasn't kidding), or for
medical or religious reasons.
    References existed regarding cannibal tribes in various
parts of the world. Flesh was cooked and its taste well-
documented. I read through about a half-dozen articles before
feeling qualified to begin the screenplay. I certainly wouldn't
have any trouble with the first ten pages. That section would
essentially be about what life was like in town before the
Cannibalism began. I had the unoriginal idea to make the cause
of the situation an earthquake, but additionally compounded by a
terrorist anthrax attack. The government would be forced to

quarantine Beverly Hills, something that more or less always had existed, at least metaphorically. Nothing in. Nothing out. A food shortage would already exist because of the earthquake, the water tainted, all the restaurants closed, and local supplies of Prozac and Zoloft dwindling down to a dangerous level. Beverly Hills had become an Orange Alert zone.

EXT. RODEO DRIVE. DUSK

A MAN is desperately searching the streets for an open restaurant. A POLICEMAN pulls up on a motorcycle.

        POLICEMAN
Everything is closed. Go home.

        MAN
Even Spago?

        POLICEMAN
They were the first to close. Wolf flew the entire staff to Las Vegas.

        MAN
This is awful. You mean we have to eat at home? I'm going to call my Congressman. Your chief is going to hear about this!

When I told Liz what I was doing, she informed me about a unique lecture coming up at one of the film schools. Lou Bradley, whose first job had been for Sean Daren Films, was the lecturer.

441

I was definitely game since the subject was "Cannibals in
Cinema". By the time we arrived, the hall was almost filled. We
quickly picked up a few handouts that were on a table in back of
the auditorium and slid into a pair of seats in the last row.

Lou had already begun his presentation. "This is one of my
favorites. It was shot in 1980 in Atlanta, and had an all-star
cast. Just listen to this - John Saxon, Elizabeth Turner, plus
some very well-known Italian and Spanish actors. If you look at
the credit sheet you'll see director Antonio Margheriti.
Everyone in the movie was dubbed except for Saxon and Morghen. I
love to say the title, *Cannibal Apocalypse*. Doesn't it make your
mouth water?"

Lou paused and waited for the laugh he was looking for. It
came slowly; the audience's anxious chortle built as more people
became comfortable with the subject matter, which to many
sounded more like a dark comedy.

"This guy is funny," I said.

"He can be," said Liz.

Lou continued. "This is one of the great openings in movie
history. John Morghen, really Giovanni Lombardo Radice, plays a
prisoner of war named Charlie Bukowski. Literary
reference?...He's not very happy, because he has some kind of
strange virus, a cannibal virus. He bites John Saxon and that,
of course, makes John very unhappy, too. But wait, it was a
dream. But not really a dream, because even though Saxon was
dreaming, he was dreaming about a real event. Morghen comes back
into Saxon's life, probably wanting to rekindle their kinky
relationship. Saxon is not interested. You know, once bitten.
When Morghen can't sink his teeth back into Saxon, he bites one
of the local ladies, just a little neck nibble. He gets in a
little trouble, so he takes over a department store, probably
figuring if he decides to bite anyone else, it should be an

artificial person, like one of the mannequins in the dress department. Eventually this becomes a typical sci-fi plot, with Saxon ultimately helping the veterans Morghen and Tony King, and joined by a sexy female doctor. The reason I like to start with this one is because it is the first entertaining cannibal movie that doesn't have a bunch of zombies running around like in a Roger Corman fifties flick. The common type always has cannibals jumping around in tribes, which is probably true from an anthropological standpoint, but isn't symbolic of what goes on in our own culture. I like the idea that the people in *Cannibal Apocalypse* act just like normal people. It seems a little more true to life, wouldn't you say?"

"He's not funny. He's nuts," I said. 'Normal people' registered a second time. Yet, it was a good idea for any cannibal movie.

Liz hit me playfully on the arm. "Be quiet!"

Lou, in love with himself as much as his lecture, continued. "I know most of you feel *Cannibal Holocaust* is the best cannibal film ever made. Well, it probably is, but for a different set of reasons. Ruggero Deodato tried this out once before, but he didn't quite get the feel for the story we see in *Cannibal Holocaust*. His first attempt was released as *Cannibal* as well as *Jungle Holocaust*. It wasn't bad, but *Cannibal Holocaust* went all the way. There are some really disgusting animal killings early on in that movie. It sort of paves the way for what's yet to come. What this movie does is set up the classic argument in favor of the cannibals. Simply put, cannibals get hungry and go out to kill in order to feed themselves. That sets them apart from the rest of human race, who usually don't kill for food, they have someone else do the killing for them, at least when it comes to basic consumption. And we try to disguise the presentation so that the food does

443

not resemble the source. But murder isn't totally out of the question for non-cannibals; they just don't eat their victims. Although torture and violent death is not unheard of. I'll get back to that later on. The other classic part of this story is that the civilized people in the movie come off looking a lot worse than the cannibals. The classic line is given at the end of the movie by the main character, a guy named Robert Kermen, 'I wonder who the real cannibals are.' And that will be the ultimate point of this lecture, once I finish my comments on the movie. You can save your own answers to which people in this town fit the definition of real cannibals. By the way, you can see in your notes that this story was borrowed a few times down the road. Let's see, and you can follow along in my notes, *Make Them Die Slowly*, *Eaten Alive By Cannibals*, *Man From Deep River*, *Trap Them* and *Kill Them*. Now that's what I really call cannibalizing a story!"

Lou paused again for the laugh. I was reminded for a moment of Rabbi Ermis; both used the same speaking style. Perhaps it was endemic to Hollywood.

I shook my head in disbelief. I knew I was in for a long evening. I slumped down in my seat and put my head against the back top portion of the chair. I still didn't get it. I was part of what Lou was talking about. I was about to take part in a project that had been done a million times before. But that was the movie business, everything old is new again. And why shouldn't it be? Every time someone does Hamlet, nobody stands up and yells that it was done before. Should they?

My mind shut down. I found that I really didn't care. In a short period of time, I was totally indoctrinated. I was ready to write any kind of screenplay for anyone, for any amount of time or money.

Liz nudged me. "Here's the one by those South Park guys, Trey Parker and Matt Stone."

I pretended to be interested. Animal killing, torture, castration, and rape had been enough. Now I listened to the story about miners who sing and dance and eventually eat their dead, but not before making every bad joke ever heard, including scenes with flatulent horses. Lou predicted that the cult following would grow as large as *The Rocky Horror Picture Show*.

After the lecture, Liz and I adjourned to Hamlet Gardens, the trendy restaurant in Westwood owned by Marilyn and Harry Lewis, the famous local couple who had made their name with a chain of Hamburger Hamlet restaurants.

"Why did you like the lecture so much?" I asked, once Liz had her second glass of Merlot in hand.

"It's a taboo subject. It's one of those things that we don't do," she answered.

"You mean like watching Jerry Springer or something."

She laughed. "Always the wiseass. Yeah. I wouldn't want anyone else to know that I did that either, and by the way I do," she added. "Let's get drunk. This wine is fucking great!"

"No problem here. Should we get another bottle? That's another two glasses each, but who's going to drive?"

"I will. I've driven on four glasses of wine before. I had my first one over an hour ago. Don't worry about it."

"Okay. I just don't want end up as road kill. Maybe someone will find us and eat the remains…Waiter!" I shouted as the young man went past us in a flurry of embellished activity. "We want another bottle."

The waiter signaled that he understood and hurried to his appointed rounds. One of the things that took some getting used to in Hollywoodland was that customer service in restaurants remained a distant cousin to most establishments in the east, regardless of reputation and cost.

"You joke, but a lot of cannibals believe there is something biologically sound about eating your own species. Like when an elder dies, eating a little bit of him to see if you get any of the wisdom."

Liz shocked me with that one. I thought that I was the cannibal expert. "Wow," I said. "So, you know about this stuff."

The waiter brought the wine with the bottle already opened.

"Shall I pour?" he asked as if we were annoying him.

"Same glasses?" he posited, but not so much as a question, but rather a suggestion.

Liz glanced at me for approval.

"Sure," I said.

The waiter's eyes widened as Liz continued. "Didn't you ever hear about the worms they chopped up who were smarter than the dumb worms? So they fed the smart worms to the dumb worms and then the ones that were dumb were able to get through the smart maze?"

"I actually did, years ago in Bio 101," I said. "It's probably biologically sound, so long as the animal isn't sick in any way."

"Could you do it?" asked Liz.

"Do what?"

"You know. Like you said. A fresh kill, free of any disease, not contaminated in any way, and you had the person's permission before he died. Say it was cooked by some gourmet guy like Puck and it tasted great. Could you do it?"

"I doubt it."

"What if you didn't know?"

She's not giving up. "It's like all the jokes when we used to go to Chinatown in New York. We used to say we could be

eating a cat but who cared, it tasted pretty good with soy
sauce, sesame oil, garlic and broccoli. I know what you mean.
How come you know so much or care about this?"

"Well, Brantley. It's time I told you." She took my hand
and kissed it, and then turned it over as if she was going to
kiss it again. Instead, she gave me a playful bite.

"Very funny." I quickly withdrew my hand.

"You weren't listening to Lou." She nodded as if to say
'shame on you.' "Some people claim it adds to immortality.
That's the part I liked about Lou's lecture. How he linked
cannibal movies to trends in the industry in general."

"I liked that part, too. That's why we have so many
remakes, sequels, and prequels."

"Yeah. It's the fear of losing the past. This way there is
the possibility of making good movies forever. This idea of
cannibalizing everything that's ever been written keeps all the
knowledge intact."

"But it doesn't always work. Look at the crap they make," I
said. *Who was I kidding?* I sipped my wine.

Liz was on a roll. "But the cannibals that make the movies
don't believe that. They believe that they know what the people
want, have discovered it before, and need to keep giving people
more of what they've already consumed. They make them eat it all
over again."

"Great."

"You're the one who wants to be a writer. I wouldn't want
to be part of that for anything."

"In your business they eat each other alive. Just for
sport. Isn't that worse?"

Liz took a long taste from her wine. "Yup." She paused.
"More like the tribes that would eat one of the defeated, not
out of a ritual thing. Agents are not really cannibalistic, not

tribalistic or ritualistic. It's more like a domination thing.
Eating after the kill. Didn't Lou say that it's called
superiority cannibalism? Yeah, right. Look who I'm asking. The
other one, where they eat to get something from deceased
relatives, that's ritual, like in the South Pacific. Besides.
They didn't eat very much meat. It was like a treat or
something, like someone on a low fat diet heading over to
Fatburger once in a while. A good pair of breasts and a big ass
can be a pretty fatty meal. Whew. I think the wine is finally
kicking in."

"Mine too," I said. "I'll get the check." I was pleased
that the conversation was over.

Liz threw a platinum credit card on the table. "Business.
And I expect you to perform."

"It will be my pleasure." I accepted the card and signaled
to the waiter, card in hand.

I left that night feeling clearly overqualified for the
writing job ahead.

The next day at four P.M., I met Sean at The Grill in
Beverly Hills. His idea. By that time the lunch crowd was long
gone and only professional drinkers who were done with work for
the day lingered over coffee (some spiked) and multiple after
lunch beverages in the back booths. There was also one table of
wannabes, people who traveled significant distances in order to
be part of the scene. They intended to be the last ones out,
often leaving at dinner time. Sometimes Mike, the charming and
respectful front man, had to ask for the table and move the
wannabes to the bar for another round on the house.

The Grill was one of the industry restaurants. The daily
lunch crowd read like a who's who in the entertainment business.
Mike's father was one of the actors on *Lost In Space*, the

classic television show, his grandfather was Rogers from Rogers and Cowan, and his step-fathers included movie giant Mike Medavoy. That was certainly a pedigree background to manage a restaurant. Unlike some of the other front men and women in town, Mike pulled off the job while still acting human, leaving out the condescending and patronizing tones that infiltrated many of the top hangouts.

When I arrived, Sean was sitting at the bar with a drink in hand while talking to Mike. After introductions, Mike excused himself, as a perfect host should.

I paused for a second and realized that we weren't going to move to a table. I hopped on the barstool next to Sean. Perhaps we were going to have a drink or two, and then an early dinner.

"What did you think of that Hitler movie thing?" asked Sean.

I was impressed that Sean was concerned about a television movie in the works by a Canadian company called Alliance-Atlantis. "I think it's a bad idea," I concluded, after hearing more about the project from Sean.

He seemed neutral and then he flipped. "They're entitled to make a buck."

I thought that he was testing me. To Sean's left was a copy of *The Hollywood Reporter*. He'd probably had just read an article about the movie. I decided not to pursue it, I didn't want to conflict with him before he gave me notes on the cannibal pages that I had already submitted.

I ordered a drink, a double vodka gimlet. After a few minutes of talk about the food at the Grill, Sean was ready. "This is sci-fi. It's not Neil Simon. Not that you're a Neil Simon. There's only one Doc Simon. We're not writing this so that some people on Park Avenue will come back to see it two or three times. We are writing for a kid in high school, maybe

fourteen, even less. That's your audience. Who cares if a guy
has trouble getting a dinner reservation? The kid you're writing
for is not going to get it. Plain and simple. If we keep the
early restaurant scene, the girl up front has got a lot of
cleavage and the guy waiting for his table is staring at her
tits. His wife says something to him like, 'you never stare at
mine that way.' Even that's a little too heady, but closer to
what sells."

I didn't know it at the time, but Sean had given me what
would turn out to be perhaps the best lesson on screenwriting I
would ever receive. At that moment, it came off as harsh, anti-
intellectual, and plain stupid. The success of *Jackass*, where
young men tested each other's physical limits of pain while
carrying out bizarre pranks, paid tribute to the lowest common
denominator theory of movie success.

By the time Sean was finished, I had a headache. Basically,
he wanted everything rewritten. Sean dumbed it down by putting
in stupid jokes and copying from prior movies. I still was
having a hard time making the adjustment to his way of thinking.

When the meeting was over, Sean tipped the bartender twenty
dollars. A check never arrived. There had never been any
intention of moving to one of the inside tables. I then
understood how Sean operated. The meeting with me did not
warrant any further attention. I was still impressed, even if I
had to fill up on cocktail nuts.

By that time, we had seen enough of Hollywood's elite to
fill several shows of *Entertainment Tonight* and *Access
Hollywood*. To top it off, on our way out, we walked past Robert
DeNiro. He was sitting with an attractive African-American woman
in a front booth across from the bar.

"The mashed potatoes are better at Tribeca," Sean said to
the couple, referring to DeNiro's downtown New York restaurant.

They both smiled. DeNiro's smile was a little crooked, just like in the movies.

Wow, I thought. *DeNiro.*

Wow.

```
CHAPTER EIGHTEEN
Ira, Neil
Brantley, Liz, Sean, Linda,
Liz, Brantley
Ricky, Brantley
```

Business was booming at The Hollywood Deli. Some days the meat was in short supply. Late in the evening, people were told that the deli was out of certain types of sandwiches. One of the big three - pastrami, brisket, and corned beef - usually ran out; they were all from the same cut of meat.

Late at night, after a busy day, Neil had just finished counting the cash. Ira felt that it was a good time to broach the obvious.

"Great day," said Ira, as he moved about the room, sliding chairs back into their proper positions.

"Un-fucking believable," said Neil. "I'm going to have to tell Chris to really get on the stick." He started to recount the cash, marveling at the sight, as he placed the bills into individual stacks. "I haven't even checked the credit card grosses yet."

"Neil. That's enough," said Ira. "Let's just buy the meat from Newport."

"We can't stop now. We need all the money coming in to expand. Sean says we might be able go public."

"I don't want to expand. I want to make believe this never happened and go back to running the deli, in, in…" He couldn't finish his sentence. "In a human way," finally came out.

"I have another idea. It's just temporary."

"Okay. What is it?" Ira knew that Neil would persist until he revealed his new plan. Ira hoped that it was for some other cheap source of meat - but a regular, common source.

Neil said it without blinking. "Some of the homeless end up on the slabs at school. Why not hasten the process?"

"Neil. I'm going to forget that you said that."

"We'd be cleaning up the streets for the city of Santa Monica."

Ira played along, not really believing that Neil was serious.

"Let the People's Republic of Santa Monica take care of the problem," said Ira. He was referring to one of the many popular phrases for the city that allowed the homeless to live and roam in almost every section of town.

Neil quickly retreated from his remarks. "Ira. Come on. You know me. That was a joke." He grabbed Ira around the shoulders.

"Really?" asked Ira.

"Really," answered Neil. He forced a laugh.

Ira made a decision on the spot. He would go around Neil. He was going to tell Sean about the meat. Sean would put an end to it. Sean and Donny had the responsibility of running the limited partnership, and they had to answer to a lot of investors, particularly Dave Stirling. Ira couldn't think about it anymore.

When Ira had finally called Sean, he was unable to get out the words. Sean said that he was bringing Linda Stirling and two guests to dinner at the deli. He wanted to be sure that Ira would be there. Ira got off the phone without telling Sean about the meat.

I was one of the guests, and Liz was my date.

That night, Ira had picked out a sensational variety of foods. The meal was a hit, like it had been with almost everyone. The accolades rolled off everyone's tongue with the tasty sauces and classic deli garnishes.

"This is interesting. The meat is so moist," said Liz.

"The corned beef tastes almost like roast pork," said Linda. "And I usually don't even like corned beef. This place is going to make a fortune. I'm glad that my father invested in it."

"Is it a public company?" asked Liz. She appeared very interested.

"Not yet," said Sean. "We're on track to expand and open more delis. We're going to be the next hot chain in town. I can feel it."

Linda echoed his remarks. "My father says it's a winner."

Once we were driving home alone, I asked Liz the obvious question. "So? What did you really think?"

"Of what, him or the deli?"

"I meant him, but both. You can answer in any order you wish."

"Thanks. The him part is easy. He's another Jewish producer trying to make a buck anyway he can." Liz stared straight ahead. It was getting dark. She checked to make sure her headlights were set to go on automatically.

"Don't you think that sounds a little anti-Semitic?"

"I gave up Jew-hating as a hobby a few years ago," said Liz, this time cracking a big smile.

"I mean it. Really. Why characterize him that way?"

"Why? I don't know any other way. I've never been called anti-Semitic before." Her tone grew more serious. "I'm not Jewish."

"Very funny."

"No. I'm not. My father was Jewish but I wasn't brought up Jewish. I went to a Catholic elementary school. Why - are you afraid to be out with a shiksa?"

"No. No. Don't be silly."

"Then why are you squirming?"

"Who's squirming? I'm not squirming."

"Are you sure?"

"Yes. I'm sure. I was surprised at the way you characterized him, the fact that you could have said he was just another producer on the make, but you had to say that he was a Jewish producer."

"That may be an oxymoron in this town." Liz wasn't taking what I said very seriously.

I became a little annoyed. "I don't know if you're joking with me or not."

"Brantley. Don't tell me you're another one of these gung ho Jewish guys that gets bent out of shape every time someone refuses to plant another tree in Israel."

"Liz. Why do you talk that way? It doesn't sound right."

"Almost everyone I know is Jewish, so if I have any negative comments to make about them, it's not because they're Jewish, it's because they're the only people I know, so if I say something negative about them, it's because they, the person, is someone I perceive in a negative way, not because they're Jewish, because they are whatever they are."

"I don't buy it."

"Are we having a fight?"

"No. A difference of opinion, but something I think you're wrong about."

"No shit. How can I make you happy on this?"

"You can't. So let's drop it."

We did.

This was new to me, a silent anti-Semitism within the industry itself. The conversation meant very little to Liz. She seemed too flippant about her attitudes, points of view that nonetheless struck a dissonant chord. We would never bring up the subject again. It was one of those things that in her world meant nothing, but I still kept sensitivities that dated back to my childhood and listening to the oral history of anti-Semitism from my Uncle Max from Moscow.

However, this would happen again, sometimes more blatantly. I soon attended a party at songwriter Norman Sach's lavish canyon home in the Hollywood hills. Years back he had created a delightful show that ran in New York, called *My Old Friends*. He and his partner wrote the book, music, and lyrics. The guest list the night of the party included many people in the business, some who had worked with Norman on his recent show, *Jekyll & Hyde*, as well as *My Old Friends*. One woman, who was married to a famous actor and had a daughter on a hit television series, began the night by saying, "Everyone knows that the Jews run Hollywood." Her dialogue escalated and was filled with anti-Semitic clichés. I left after cocktails, not wanting to fuel or be part of the discussion. It went downhill from there, and yet it took three hours before a former advertising executive, Ed Gottlieb, stood up to her. He screamed at her during dessert, and nearly came to blows, flipping his bowl of Häagen-Dazs to the floor. After he left, the actress marked him off as crazy and oversensitive. Nobody argued with her. "Ed was probably

drunk or something", and "everyone knows he's a kook". Her power
base in town was not to be challenged.

I had been in town over a year. The anniversary of 9/11 had
passed. The entertainment industry had gotten over it, and
business was at full throttle.

The cable news networks became free advertisements for
beating the drums of war. Iraq, Iraq, and more Iraq were only
briefly overshadowed by the trial of Hollywood-actress-gone-bad,
Winona Ryder. The nature of the pretrial and trial encapsulated
my experiences to date, forever serving as a metaphor for the
folklore of Hollywood. Her boss on three of her pictures, Peter
Guber, sat on the jury. Go figure. Why the prosecutors went for
the jugular remained open for speculation. The left-wingers
suggested anti-Semitism by the extreme right, having a Jewish
shoplifting actress to bandy about in the news. Those
accusations were always nonsense; more likely another actress
trying to make the most out of free publicity. It would be
impossible for her to get that many microphones thrust her way
even if she had paid a top firm for six months.

It was almost ninety degrees in November, something that
took a little getting used to. I decided to go out for a quick
lunch, to the regular place across from my office. Harry was at
a charity event for the Dodgers, so I was on my own.

I put my lunch on the little table, sesame bagel with cream
cheese, and a cappuccino. When I was about half way through with
lunch, I spotted a familiar figure moving briskly up North
Bedford Drive. He stopped at my table.

"Hey. Screenwriter. How's it goin'?" Victor was always
friendly.

"Pretty good. Do you want to sit down?"

"No. Thanks. I'm on my way to kiss some general practice guy's ass. He keeps trying to do surgeries, then he fucks them up, and then he sends them to me to fix."

"That's what keeps us in business, G.P.s making mistakes." It was true; most of my referrals were the results of work gone sour, attempted by dentists who were in over their heads.

"I know. Imagine if all the surgery you did came from guys who never were trained, and never bothered to find out how to do it. The worst part is this guy down the block tries his luck on only the rich and famous. Then I get stuck with a very unhappy, powerful person, whose business manager calls me up in the middle of night from Paris, screaming about all the trouble I've caused."

"Sorry," I said. It was sounding very much like my life.

"Well. It's my own fault for going into this garbage, cesspool of a profession. I should have kept writing in college instead of taking all that Organic Chemistry. I probably would have gotten laid more too! So, what are you writing?"

"I'm trying to do action-adventure." I really didn't want to talk about *Beverly Hills Cannibals* or Ricky.

"They've got you now." Victor flashed a smile. He appeared amused, something I filed under perverse jealousy.

"What do you mean?" I put down my bagel, keeping my eye on the spot that I intended to bite next.

Victor put his two hands on the outer guardrail, and leaned in to make his point. "Writers only know what they know about. Once you start writing screenplays and start calling them 'action adventure,' or 'buddy movie,' or whatever bullshit-clap-trap-horseshit they call it, you're done. Finished. They'll eat you'll alive. What the hell do you know about what they want, if they don't even know what they want? The only way to beat them is to write about what you know."

"I think I can do it." I was beginning to get annoyed.

"I didn't say you can't do it, but when you're done there won't be any part of you in it. You will have given them what you think they want, a copy of a format you've seen a million times. And then what? They have to decide between your screenplay and the other thousand action-adventure screenplays. I'd say, if you keep this up, you'll become a glorified secretary."

"What about that guy they just paid over a million for an action adventure?"

"I read that, too. I guess for a million I'd become a secretary or whatever else that guy is to the people who put up the money. Listen, Brantley. I'm sorry. Maybe I'm still a little bitter. I'd better shut up."

"No. It's okay. I'll see you."

"Yeah. Take care." Victor straightened up and continued up the street.

I had little appetite left. I rose from my seat and traipsed around the block before going to back to my office. I thought it was weird that Victor never asked about Ricky. Perhaps Ricky was giving him updates, or perhaps Victor didn't care about the outcome.

Victor called as soon as I arrived back at my office. The phone call convinced me that he clearly was bitter, and yet he wanted to help me. It was as if my success would somehow give him some vindication.

"I have someone I want you to meet."

"Who?"

"A producer named Elliott Kastner."

I had no objection. "I don't mind, but you really don't have to keep helping me. I'm meeting people through Harry." I knew the name, perhaps from a reference in the movie *The Player*. That should have been a forewarning.

"I know I'm doing more for you than anyone in town. I don't have to introduce you to anyone. I'm not supposed to nursemaid people; maybe get them through a few doors. Forget Harry. He can't do anything for you. The people he knows haven't made a movie in twenty years. Those guys get off pretending to be working with writers. The thing about this town is that it would take one second for someone to spell things out to you about this guy or that guy, but they don't say a word. They want you to suffer, just like they did. I don't care what people say about Elliott. He's in there. He's making movies. I'm glad I can make the introduction."

It was true. For reasons that were not readily apparent, Victor wanted to be my screenplay guru.

Elliott Kastner turned out to be one of the most magnetic men I had ever met. His tapestry of social charms was hard to rival anywhere on earth. Elliott was bright, witty, and seemed to care a lot about a person when he spoke one on one, although his dialogue quickly grew penetrating, occasionally dripping with sulfuric aphorisms.

I wasn't used to all the personal questions. "Where is your family from? How often did you talk to your mother before she died?" were two questions Elliot asked during our first lunch meeting.

I did my best to answer, even though there were a few moments when I felt a little uncomfortable.

"Why would you want to be a writer when you are already a doctor?" was the gist of many of Elliot's remarks. He made me feel like I was selling out some sacred profession for a lesser one, one very low on the pecking order in the movie business.

Within a short period of time, Elliott suggested that I let him read *Small Steaks*, my original version. Miraculously I received a call within a week and Elliott talked about setting up a deal. At Harry's suggestion, I contacted Kyle Bixler to read the contract. Within an equally short time period, the deal was off. Elliott cited simply, and with an emotional ring, "I'm having problems. I can't do it now. I've got that thing overseas." Welcome to the home of the broken contract. But the overseas comment was true.

Soon after that, Elliott suggested another way to go. That time the contracts were specific to Elliott's design. It involved a ten thousand-dollar payment right away. But, things changed. He waited to ask me personally, inside his Beverly Hills office, under the guise of talking about the project. He even let me listen to several of his argumentative phone calls; some about money.

"I'm a little short this week. I'm in the middle of a few things. Could you make it five thousand, and I'll have it Monday?" asked Elliott.

"That's fine," I answered, eager to get going at any price. I was not in position to negotiate with a man who had made three films with Brando and five with Burton.

Monday passed and I waited. I checked my fax machine, voice mail, e-mail, and old-fashioned snail mail. Nothing.

On Thursday, I called Elliott, but he wasn't there.

George, who worked with Elliott for years, took the call and said something that I couldn't believe. "He's not going to do anything for you," was the only part of the conversation I remembered. Either George had been instructed to get rid of me or it was his way of making a kind gesture. I believed the latter. I liked George. And I still liked Elliott.

I walked around in a daze for about two weeks. I could tell
that my mind and body were not well adapted for the Hollywood
scene. It made me physically ill. I didn't eat well, and had a
chronic upset stomach, which I began to feed occasionally with
Imodium or Pepto Bismol, while adding age-old digestives like
Fernet-Branca to my drinking list.

I was being further destroyed by trying to write with
Ricky. It seemed like anything I said to Ricky would be
misinterpreted. My favorite example was a dialogue I had
manufactured to explain how tough it was working with someone
like Ricky. It wasn't far off from some of our actual exchanges.

"Ricky. I just got up and looked outside. The sky is blue."

"I don't think so," said Ricky.

"It's blue. I just looked outside. The sky is blue."

"Do you mean it's a clear day or are you talking about the
weather in general?"

"I mean in general. What I should have said is every day
when I look outside when the sun is up, the sky is blue. The sky
is blue today, just like yesterday."

"I don't know if the sky is blue."

"Ricky. Take my word for it. I know this for a fact. The
sky is blue. It's just not my opinion. It is the opinion of a
lot of smart, experienced people."

"I don't like that. Just because I'm younger than you I
don't have to accept what you say because you're older and more
experienced."

"Ricky. It has nothing to do with that. The sky is blue.
It's a known fact."

"I can't accept it just because you want me to. Don't you
think we should take some time to do this? I want this project
to be the best it can be, and if I just accept things like this,
it will make the project classless and trashy."

"Ricky. I don't want to make you angry, but what the fuck are you talking about? Can't you see that what you're saying is destructive? You're always trying to stall things, to make a point out of nothing. The only point to that is that you're trying to sabotage yourself and everything around you."

"Look. You've tried to pull that 'sabotage' thing on me before. What do you think I'm going to do, go out and bad mouth my own project?"

"Don't you see? All I said was that 'the sky is blue', and we're all over the map here. I would like you to accept something I say, without some insane diatribe."

"I think it helps us flesh out the best material."

I performed the routine for Liz. She wasn't surprised, but remained amused. "Welcome to the creative side of Hollywood."

These kinds of conversations became routine with Ricky. I concluded that he had the lowest self-esteem of anyone I had ever met. Ricky must have thought that everyone was out to get him, to belittle him, to destroy him, just like his father had been doing to him during his entire life. What Ricky didn't realize was that by over-protecting himself, he had developed mechanisms to destroy each and every thing he ever did, including his relationships. At face value, Ricky was doomed to hopeless failure at every turn. I didn't want to wait around until Ricky self-destructed or destroyed the project.

Without telling Ricky, I completed a first draft of a story for the screenplay. Ricky had written dozens of endless anecdotes about Mal. I decided to focus on one specific time in their lives, the opening of the Resorts Hotel in Atlantic City. It was an exciting time that brought legalized gambling to Atlantic City. The story centered on Mal being invited to perform during the opening week at the hotel. An explosive list of celebrities and politicians filled the guest lists. The more

important part of the story, as told by Ricky, involved his
kidnapping by some lesser level local hoods. They knew that if
they snatched Ricky, Mal would pay up in a flash. They had
additional motivation - Ricky was betting on the ponies every
day. He was into the bookies for over twenty-five thousand.
Since he was Mal's son, everyone looked the other way, until
Ricky opened his mouth to one of the locals.

Ricky let him have it. "Go fuck yourself, you little rat
bastard. Why don't you go back to Little Italy where you belong?
I'm sure you could get your old job back as a waiter at
Umberto's."

The line got a laugh, since it was said in front of a bunch
of wiseguys sitting around the hotel coffee shop at about four
A.M. Even the intended victim belly laughed at Ricky's wise-
mouth crack. That night he asked permission to snatch Ricky.
Nobody cared because nobody really liked Ricky. They had put up
with him for decades because of Mal.

The story grew a little dark. At one point they had planned
to send Mal a jar containing some kind of pig body part,
claiming that it was Ricky's. But before they could decide which
part of the freshly slaughtered pig to send, the guys' wives had
already cooked most of the animal.

Mal was able to make a high level contact with a Tony
Soprano type who quickly brokered Ricky's return in exchange for
paying off most of the gambling debts, and Mal's promise to do a
few weddings and benefits for free on short notice.

I sent the story out to a few people. There wasn't any
initial response. Zilch. Liz suggested that she give it to one
of the agency's clients, Rich Rellenstein, a television producer
who was rumored to be a great-grandson of Adolph Zucker. His
lineage didn't matter. Rich had a track record of soap opera-
styled made-for-TV movies, usually dealing with family dilemmas

ranging from bed wetting to incest. Liz had arranged for Rich to meet me for what seemed like a thirty second meeting. He was a tennis player at the Hillcrest Country Club. The meeting was on the patio, moments before Rich went on court one to play. In Hollywood, people called him "Richie Rich", because his mother's family owned a couple of banks.

"Brantley. I'm going to do something for you that nobody in this town would do. I'm going to read this for you. I like Liz, and she's a friend," was said with all the false sincerity Rich could muster. He was his own hero, in a town filled with heroes.

A day later there was a hitch, told to me on the telephone. "I don't want Ricky. I want the screenplay, and you. I want the brain of the guy who wrote this. Look. I will take this to HBO and CBS."

A week later it was all over, and Rich was no longer my benefactor. "I don't know how to make the Ricky character likeable enough. Plus there are other problems with Mal. I'm not sure where the story is here, plus HBO isn't sure about Mal's demographics. CBS doesn't want any bios right now. But I also ran this by Showtime. The script needs a lot of work. Besides. I don't need you to do a story on Mal V. Rose. Anyone can."

"Are you saying you don't like the material?" I asked with all the naiveté of a freshman creative writing student just scolded by his sadistic professor. I was in shock. In the process of helping me, it sounded like he hastily had the project rejected from just about every major possibility in town.

"That's true. It's really not something for me," said Rich. It came out like I should have known that in the first place. "There are some people in town that this might be good for." He was being helpful again.

It was hard to believe that someone could do a one-eighty in less than a week. The problem was that most people did not want to be associated with anything that had been rejected in any way. Rich was hot only so long as he could get someone else to agree. The moment he found out that perhaps a project would be a hard sell, Rich flipped and became a strong detractor of the same material that he had been trying to sell. He could not see himself losing, which is why a lot of people in town don't want to fight for any material, unless they have a truckload of known cheerleaders backing them up.

I had picked up a little bit more of a Hollywood education, a learning experience that was slowly breaking my spirit, bit by bit. I added the 'Rich' experience to the people who would smile and say "send me a copy", while never having any intention of reading the material or returning my phone calls weeks to months later. The first meeting contrast to New York people was the hardest adjustment. Everyone around Hollywoodland came off as friendly, sometimes making an effort to ingratiate themselves personally, while actually taking the extra time to set up a future fucking.

During this fuzzy period I found myself spending evenings at The Hollywood Deli, where I could make my brisket sandwich last for hours. Ira and Neil could not have been better hosts, often bringing me free rice pudding or a piece of marble halvah – something Ricky always ate - to ease my pain. I got to know them, and found Ira eager to talk about the new business and its leaders.

CHAPTER NINETEEN
Ira, Neil, Sean
Linda, Liz
Ricky, Brantley
Mal, Ricky
Liz, Brantley

Ira decided that the best way to break the macabre meat news was a cold turkey approach. *Oy, cold turkey*, he thought. He had planned to tell Sean the next time he was in the deli. First, he told Neil about his plan. Neil agreed and backed Ira with a false bravado, since Neil felt that nothing would change.

"Fine. I'll show you I'm still on your side. You want to spill the beans. I'm with you. If he wants to stop, we'll stop."

Wisely, they did not set up a plate with fresh sandwiches in advance of Sean's arrival. Instead, they confronted him the moment they saw his tall, lean figure in the doorway. He smiled. The sun shined brightly behind his head. Behind him, the sea glistened in the distance.

Ira conveyed everything in one sentence. "Our primary meat source comes from cadavers."

"What's the joke?" Sean asked. "Hey, I'm hungry."

Neil added, "It's not a joke. We're getting the meat off of stiffs." He laughed. "The price is right and we get no complaints from the donors."

467

"Run that by me again." Sean didn't move an inch from the doorway. His body was angled in such a way that the light formed an eerie patina on his face and arms.

"Our primary meat source comes from cadavers," Ira repeated.

Sean entered, and stood behind the counter. "Let me get this straight," he said, glancing over at the hunks of meat sitting in the counter trays.

"It's not exactly - " Neil tried to say.

Sean cut him off. "I heard you. Now let me sort this out. What you are telling me is that our money-making sandwiches come from the bodies of dead people? Human beings? We have been feeding human flesh to our customers? I ate this?"

Neil was going to speak, but after seeing Sean hold up his hand with the palm facing close to Neil's nose, he decided to wait.

"Say nothing. I'm speaking rhetorically here," said Sean. He inhaled deeply, as if he were in profound thought. He turned around to again look at the containers that had the prepared meat, and then turned back to face Ira and Neil. "Vos macht es mir oys?"

Neil looked over at Ira for a translation.

"He doesn't care," said Ira.

"Why should anyone care? These people are already dead, right?" asked Sean.

This has got to be a setup. It sounds scripted. Neil must have prepped him in advance, Ira thought.

Sean gestured to Neil, who was now smiling ear to ear in response.

"Right. Dead as Clancy's nuts," said Neil. "You know I never said that before. I don't even know what it means."

"Shut up," said Sean. "Let me think, you little tuches-
lecker."

"Ass-licker," Ira translated.

"I know that one," said Neil.

Ira was unwilling to accept Sean's position. "It's okay if
you find this a seriously deranged thing. I would be happy to go
along with anything you really want to do, short of turning us
in to the police."

"Boychick. Don't be scared," said Sean, as he put his hand
on Ira's cheek, as if preparing to pinch it, but never really
squeezing the skin.

The hand felt cold, like stone, and it a sent a chill down
Ira's spine.

Sean smiled, showing his large, pointed canines. He
appeared grotesque; his face split by a thin shadow. "You say
you get all the...product, yes that's what it is, product, from
the medical school?"

At that point Ira knew for sure that Sean and Neil had
spoken long before that day. Nobody had yet mentioned 'medical
school' to Sean, but he knew all about it.

Neil nodded in the affirmative. "When we're short, I have
to buy from a regular source."

"You know we're going to need a lot more of this if we want
to expand." Sean chose only to discuss any possible harm that
could disrupt the business.

"I think the guy who's helping me knows a guy at USC
Medical. That would double our access to product," said Neil,
like a detail man for Xerox. Neil still liked his other plan,
accessing the homeless, but knew better than to mention that,
even to Sean.

"What are you talking about?" asked Ira. He heard them, but
it was becoming harder to believe.

Sean moved on. "Good. We're still in business, boys. I'm going to start selling higher priced shares. This is going to be bigger than Jerry's Deli, bigger than Wolfgang Puck. We're going for it all. First we open new locations, then we have an I.P.O, and then we get into the supermarkets with a smaller microwave version, or some kind of lean cuisine shit. I have to work on that with my guys," he said, lost in his trance of success. "A lot. A fucking fortune. Look boys, I've got to get going. I have to meet someone at the Four Seasons in Beverly Hills in about thirty minutes. I'll just about make it." Ten minutes late in Hollywood was considered on time.

Ira cleared his throat. "All I want is enough money so my grandfather can buy a nice condominium in Boca Raton. Then I want out, and maybe you should buy out my grandfather, too."

"Baby. He'll live like a king," said Sean.

"No. In fact, I want out now," said Ira.

"You don't mean that, Ira. Think it over. Once the big money starts rolling in, you may have a change of heart," said Sean. "This product thing is only temporary. Am I right?"

"Right," said Neil. "Maybe just another month, tops." It was and proved to be a continuous lie.

Sean cleared his throat. "Quitting is death in this town. It's bad enough that most people never make it anywhere in Hollywood; they spend the rest of their lives watching Johnny Grant install another set of hand or footprints on the Hollywood Walk of Fame, and you know what bullshit that is. And you have to pay for your own star, too. I'm going to ignore what's been said here because we're in business together. Where was I? Yes. The fucking death of quitting. You boys have something, something that everyone wants. It's just a beginning. You know the restaurant business is no different than the movie business. Don't you see it? Don't you see what's happening here? You boys are on your way to writing your own ticket, calling your own shots. You want to make movies next, we make movies, you want to act, I put you in. Look at Nobu, the owner of Matsuhisha. He's been in a couple of movies and he got a national commercial for Callaway golf. Doesn't that tell you something?"

Sean attempted his cheek thing again with Ira. "Take it easy, boychick."

This time Ira removed Sean's hand and gently pushed it back toward him.

Sean smiled through his mild disdain. "I'm out of here…Neil. Explain to your friend that this is business, and business is just business. Nifter-shmifter, a leben macht er?"

"What difference does it make, as long as he makes a living?" translated Ira. "I was afraid he was going to say something like that."

"He's right," said Neil. "What he said. He's right. Don't take it personally."

Sean moved toward the rear exit. He walked down the little steps outside the back door before reversing direction in order to deliver what he thought was the quintessential brilliant remark of the evening. "You know, I think there might be a movie in all of this," he whispered in a hushed tone, his eyes bulging out of his head like two bloodshot marbles. "We might work on that idea of yours, Neil."

Ira was stunned. He couldn't believe how casually Sean had responded to the situation. The thing Ira didn't know about Sean was that he would never let on that anything was a problem, even if he thought it was catastrophic. Sean repressed any negative information. He knew that he needed to forge ahead, and that was his focus.

The advertised 'grand' reopening of the deli had arrived. One week to go. Almost every detail was attended to except for the final menu. All of the investors Sean had spoken to had something to say about it. He was able to fend off most of the calls, especially those from significant others who professed 'special knowledge', a newly created culinary cult who had graduated from Julia Child and the long-forgotten James Beard to the over-seasoned "Oh yeah, babe" of Emeril. The dialogue varied, but it was usually about making sure that someone's favorite food would be served. In a pinch, Sean referred some people to Gibby, the food and beverage expert from the tennis club who loved to talk endlessly about food, and could therefore discuss recipe changes, while entertaining variations that didn't conflict with the basic theme – deli. "Thank god it ain't French food," was Donny's solo contribution after fielding so many requests from investors and their relatives.

The remaining menu problem was what to name the sandwiches. Everyone involved suggested his or her own name on a sandwich or salad. Others lobbied heavily for the name of their favorite mogul or movie star. Some even wanted Kyle Bixler to put it in writing. No sandwich naming, no investment. The decision was made to postpone naming the sandwiches after celebrities or investors. Sean wanted to see which investors would actually come up with the big money, and then include their 'pet' celebrities by offering naming rights on the menu once things were more established. Chris had picked up a selection of competitors' menus. The Nate 'n Al's menu had no celebrity names. "You don't need the schmaltz," Sean had told some of the more insistent investors. The Stage Deli in Century City was always changing the names of their sandwiches to cater to whoever was 'in', while dumping the names of those who were around too long to be recognized by succeeding generations. Now they had a Jerry Seinfeld, Shaquille O'Neal, Tiger Woods, Julia Roberts, Denis Franz, and Michael Gelman, the latter someone Sean had never heard of until Regis had made him into a foible. Ten years ago, the names would have been very different. Dolly Parton might have been an 'elder' on the Stage menu. One of the things nobody seemed to know was whether the star involved had agreed to let their name be used. It was a strange kind of 'public domain' issue. To be careful, Sean checked with one of the renowned experts on these issues, Fred Leopold, a famous Hollywood attorney and twice mayor of Beverly Hills who reviewed errors and omissions insurance policies for the giant movie studios and book publishers. Technically, before using a name, the deli should have permission. Sean figured that it would be easy once they increased their celebrity clientele, and made sure to let them know that the star or anyone in his entourage would never have to pick up a check. He wasn't going to worry about the legal details now, particularly since the menus Chris was taking from the Stage Deli showed misspellings like Kevin Costner as "Kevin Kostner," something that didn't seem to disturb the deli or the star. Other names were misspelled, too.

The day before the faux grand reopening, Neil took a final tour of the kitchen area. Chris had done a remarkable job. It was uncanny how many items from the anatomy laboratory seemed like they belonged in a restaurant's kitchen. The extra breads were kept steamed in a second device that was originally manufactured as a dissecting table. It looked just like the steamers that Ira and Neil had seen at Langer's Deli downtown, all stainless steel with two hinged covers. The table was supported by tall legs that sported big four-inch casters that could be locked into position. Chris also 'borrowed' a hydraulic cadaver lift. That device was powered by a twelve-volt battery and was rechargeable. The boys used it for bringing in heavy supplies, particularly items in big bags. It was capable of lifting up to one thousand pounds and also had wheels.

In a short period of time, the little deli that was once part of old Hollywood had been transformed to become part of its future.

The grand opening of the Hollywood Deli became 'an event'. Sean hired old-but-effective Godfrey Edwards to do the publicity. He knew how to publicize any event and fill the room with all kinds of out of work celebrities.

Gibby ran the show. "Gibby's become a poor man's Bert Parks," was how his old friend Godfrey would describe Gibby to his face.

With the restaurant filled for the big night, Gibby took the microphone in hand. "Ladies and gentlemen. You are going to be treated to one of the greatest legends in the history of the business. Here's a man who shared a stage with everyone from Theda Bara and Marilyn Monroe to Cher and Madonna. What else can I say? Ladies and Gentlemen, Mal V. Rose!"

The room ignited into thunderous applause.

I stood in the back with Ricky. We watched Mal sashay onto the small makeshift stage in full drag, with his dark, handlebar mustache leading the way for his rouge-rosy cheeks. His trademark giant pink boa trailed him as if it were alive. Everyone from the old days knew that it was another theft from Harry Ritz.

Mal sauntered to the microphone and puckered his violet painted lips into a suggestive grotesque pose. "Sorry I'm late, but the cleaners mixed up my dress with Michele Pfeiffer's." He mugged, paused, and waited.

Not a great line, but this crowd was loving Mal. It didn't matter what he said or did. He was electrified by the sound of

laughter and applause, shedding twenty years off his life, now
spry once again, and doing the only thing he knew.

It was surprising how many older people showed up to see
Mal. He was someone out of the past, the last memory of a bygone
era for some. The room had more than its share of walkers and
canes that produced rattling noises along with loose dentures.

When he told one of the classic deli jokes of all time, he
brought the house down. "Herb came into work looking a little
farmisht. Leo Steiner, the owner of the Carnegie asks Herb
what's wrong. 'I wake up in the middle of the night. I keep
dreaming about the same thing. I want to put my schlong in the
pickle slicer.' 'Vey iz mir!' shouts Leo. 'You'd better see my
friend the shrink. Here's his card. He's on Park Avenue. I'll
pay the bill. Just go, and don't do anything crazy.' Herb agrees
that maybe the visit to the shrink will help. He has one session
with the doctor. He is to return the next week to tell him how
everything went. The next week, Herb shows up looking even more
farmisht. The doctor asks him what happened. 'I did it. I went
into the deli and put my schlong in the pickle slicer.' 'What
happened?' screamed the shrink. 'Leo fired me,' said Herb. 'He
fired you? That's terrible. Are you okay? Was that the worst of
it?' 'No,' lamented Herb. 'He fired her, too!' "

I watched and thought about my own plight. I had never
written anything like the Rose story before, and now I was
thrown into the center of a Hollywood family battle. So far
there wasn't a soul that I interviewed or read about that had
anything nice to say about Mal. Worse, the same went for Ricky.
Like father like son, each denying guilt in the relationship,
unable to see beyond the delusional design of his own altered
world.

At the affair, Ricky dropped the news to me that he needed cash. "It's not a loan. I own shares in this new company. I'm willing to sell you part of mine."

"I don't know," I said. I actually did know about the company from Ira and Sean, but I didn't want to invest because the price of shares had risen. Bottom line, I was in no position to buy stock.

Ricky became a pit bull when he wanted something. "I got you into a screenplay deal that could make you a million. Think about it. And maybe they'll do a book version of the story, a simultaneous publication when the movie comes out. If the book sells just five hundred thousand copies at say, twenty bucks a pop, that's ten million dollars right there."

"That's a lot of copies," I said. My voice gave away my disinterest, as well as my disbelief.

Ricky launched into his usual diatribe. "Do you mean when you say 'that's a lot of copies', that I'm saying I meant to deceive you? I don't think you meant to accuse me of deceiving you, but if that were the case, I think you would be going over the line here."

"Ricky. What I mean is that books don't sell that many copies anymore. It just doesn't happen that way. I was talking to an agent in New York who knows Liz. He's quite well known. His name is Jack Scovil. He's represented some really famous writers."

"Like who?"

"I think Carl Sagan," I said. "What's the difference? He said that if a book sells between one hundred and two hundred thousand copies that that's really good."

"How do we know the information he gave you is right. We ought to check him out. Did you speak to anyone at the Morris office?" Ricky could best be described at these moments as tiresomely paranoid.

"No. Just this guy, Jack," I said, forever frustrated in trying to explain anything to Ricky. "I think he also worked with Norman Mailer."

"Why don't you see if you can find out anything from the Morris office? They always know what they're doing." Ricky kept repeating those things that Mal had taught him.

"Why are we talking about a book?" I asked. Ricky always dragged me off the track. "Shouldn't we concentrate on the screenplay first?"

"I say we have an expert at the Morris office look over the whole deal," he answered.

"Don't you know anyone there?"

"I used to, but it would be better to wait until we have something fleshed out. I don't want to waste a call, if you know what I mean."

I was beginning to think that Ricky was completely blackballed in every area he had ever touched. It sounded like Ricky was afraid that nobody would take his call. The pattern was becoming apparent, and should have made sense to me earlier. The reason Ricky went along with the idea of working with me, a virtual unknown, was because he had nobody else and no one else would put up with him. Ricky pissed off so many people in town that it was virtually impossible to do anything without someone popping up and bad-mouthing him. Mal had talent and knew how to use it. Ricky had no talent and pretended to be brilliant on every subject from e-mail to changing the brake fluid on a Rolls-Royce.

I told myself to keep going, finish the screenplay, because if I could find a way to get the work done, there had to be some interest in ol' Mal. I felt that if I could get Ricky distracted

from the notion of writing a screenplay by getting him to
concentrate on a book, things might work out better. Surely, I
had enough notes from Ricky and public domain sources to write a
decent screenplay about life in Atlantic City in the late
seventies. I had been there a few times with college buddies,
and still had a sense of the nightlife. There was plenty of
information available on the Osmonds, Cher, Liberace, Steve and
Eydie - all people that Mal had opened for in the casinos.

During the ensuing weeks, Ricky still pressed me for cash,
except he was then willing to sell the shares at the same price
that he had paid. It was sounding better. I spoke to Liz about
it.

"Ricky is willing to sell for less. The newer money is
paying five dollars a share. That's a built-in paper profit for
us."

"For us? You're counting my money?"

"Why not? It's a good deal. Fifty-fifty?"

Liz soon met separately with Linda Stirling to discuss the
possibilities. They had lunch at La Scala in Beverly Hills.

"My father has asked me to get more involved with the new
company," said Linda. "He's been after me for years to become
more active in his work."

"Why don't you do it?" asked Liz.

"I don't know. Maybe because he pushed so much when I was
younger. He's taught me everything he knows. I know the details
of all his deals."

"Don't you want to do it, at some level?"

Linda picked at her pasta primavera. "Maybe. But to answer
what you had said when you called. I don't see any harm in
buying anyone's shares. I ran it by my father. He said you'd be
getting a great deal because the shares are valued higher now.

It's that simple. You're buying into a profit situation. This Ricky Rose must be desperate for the cash, or else he's incredibly stupid. Who's his attorney?"

"He doesn't have separate representation," said Liz. "He uses his father's attorney, Kyle Bixler."

"That explains it. Nobody told him about the next wave of sales," said Linda.

"I think it's more like nobody cares to tell him anything," said Liz.

"I know his father is famous. What does the son do?"

"Not a thing," said Liz. "I have an idea."

"Okay."

"If you get involved, I'd like to help you. I can do your press releases. And I certainly know how to give orders."

"Liz. You're funny. I thought you like being an agent."

"Not as much as I thought I would."

"I'll keep it in mind." Linda glanced at her watch, having already learned how to dismiss her meetings with subtle hints that she had garnered from her father.

The two began to speak regularly. Linda even included Liz in meetings with Dave. It was that simple. Things in town could move that fast.

When It was time for my next story meeting with Ricky, I met him at our usual Encino coffee shop, an old red-booth place with swivel seats at the counter. That day, we went over a few notes. Ricky immediately backed off on a book. He was consistently inconsistent.

Then I got to the important question of the day. "I spoke to a couple of people at Horn-Sunset Towers and they all said the same thing about Mal." I had to convince Ricky that we had to paint an even portrait of Mal, one that showed more of his true character.

Ricky knew from my remark that there weren't many glowing comments about Mal. Godfrey Edwards was the most direct. "Mal V. Rose is the most reprehensible man I ever met. A lot of people I've met say that Mal is gay. Don't get me wrong, but why stay in the closet anymore?"

I didn't want to start up with Ricky, so I kept all the comments to myself. But I wanted to clear up the sexuality issue. It would be hard to write about someone's life without knowing the truth. I didn't want to 'out' Mal, but thought it would be hard to write a movie about a ladies man if none of it were true. *Maybe Mal was bisexual,* I thought. I broached the subject gingerly.

"You can't believe those cocksuckers," said Ricky. He sounded so much like Mal, including his unfortunate choice of words. Ricky even exhaled in a high-pitched wheeze. It was an odd time to have invoked Mal's favorite expression.

"It's probably just a rumor," I said, "But we should have the answer in order to write a good story."

Ricky kept eating his French fries, undaunted by anything I said. "Pass the ketchup," he said.

I reached to my left and handed the ketchup bottle to Ricky. I decided to be direct. "Godfrey is convinced that Mal is gay," I said. "I also asked Gibby, the food maven at the BHTC, and he said he also had heard that about Mal."

Ricky shook his head in disgust. He rolled it side to side as he poured ketchup all over his fries. He glanced around nervously, and found his crumpled napkin, resting under a plate of bacon. He grabbed the napkin and quickly wiped his hands. "What's going on here?" His face flushed quickly, matching the mound of ketchup on his plate.

"Nothing," I said. "I thought we were trying to write about Mal."

"You're one of them. You're one of those cocksucking bastards," said Ricky. "How the fuck can you have the nerve to speak to me like that!"

"Ricky. Take it easy. I'm just reporting what people say. So they're wrong. It's just a rumor. Sorry. It's just one of those things we have to get out of the way."

Ricky threw his napkin down into the pool of ketchup. He shot up from the table.

I stood up, too. "Come on. I said I was sorry."

Ricky grabbed his jacket and flung it over his shoulder. As he made the quick motion, the back of the zipper caught me on the nose.

"Oww!" I screamed as my hand went to my nose. I took my hand away and saw that I was bleeding.

Ricky paused. "You're lucky I don't just take out a gun and blow your fuckin' brains out." He waddled at top speed down the aisle and out the rear exit of the coffee shop.

I slumped back down in the booth and leaned back on the slippery plastic upholstered bench. I asked a visibly concerned waitress for ice. A lot of my thinking leaned toward quitting. Ricky clearly could be violent. Gun threats did not sit well with me. But I would ultimately ignore the warnings to stay away from Ricky, either originating from him or from people in his past. My nearly delusional show business career still beckoned, so I convinced myself that Ricky was only another misunderstood Hollywood child. Yet, beneath it all I knew that I was in danger of turning myself into something similar or worse and become another of the business' many casualties.

Ricky knew the rumors about his father being gay. Hollywood lore had it that Mal preferred the company of men to Ricky's mother. Mal never said anything about it to Ricky, but Ricky had memories from his childhood that confirmed the fact, more or less.

One time when he was fifteen, Ricky remembered entering Mal's unlocked dressing room at the Riviera Hotel in Las Vegas. It was the same year that Mal would last appear as a headliner. The dressing room had two rooms; the second portion disappeared behind racks of clothing. Ricky slid past Mal's chair and makeup case and peered behind the racks. "Mal. Are you there?" he asked, seeing the answer at the same split second that he finished his words.

Mal was down on his knees. His arms were wrapped firmly around another man's hips who was sitting on a Barcalounger, nude from the waist down. Mal's mouth enveloped the man's penis. The man did not see Ricky, and Mal did not hear Ricky's voice above the heavy breathing and grunting supplied in earnest by the pleasured man. Ricky recognized the man as one of Mal's writers, Tubby; who still remained close with the Rose family.

Ricky was out of the dressing room in a flash, his mind trying to erase the vision which was indelibly planted in the recesses of his brain.

That night, I explained the coffee shop meeting to Liz.

She placed a cold pack wrapped in a blue face towel just above my nose, and sat next to me as I stared out over the somewhat tropical foliage on Palm Drive.

"Why don't you drop this guy?" She held her hand on the frozen pack. "Just drop him."

"I think we can get still a movie out of this," I said.

"You really are becoming like one of them."

"Is that bad? Ouch. That's enough ice."

She removed the pack. "I asked around the agency. There still isn't much interest in Mal V. Rose."

"I know there's a good story here."

"You can't trust the little prick."

"You've been out with him?"

"Very funny. Brantley. I don't think you know what you're getting into. This is not the real world. Remember what they said when Clinton was still President - the only place he'll be able to get a job will be here or Wall Street. We've always been a home to the amoral. He just got a hundred thou for one minute's work opposite Bob Dole on *Sixty Minutes*."

"Ricky is still wounded. Underneath. I think he's a good guy."

"When you get that deep, it's going to be too late. The rest of him will have oozed out all over you, and destroyed any sense of reality you had coming in. Drop the guy. He's trouble."

"I don't quit on things."

"Great. You don't quit on things, and the guy pops you in the nose." She held the towel back on my nose.

"It was an accident."

"Maybe next time it won't be an accident. What if he comes at you with a gun?"

I took the towel away from my nose and unrolled it. "Bel-Air Hotel," I said, reading from the towel. "Was it anyone I know?"

"All of you misogynists want all of your women to be whores, but the moment you realize that it might be true, you get bent out of shape. I'm never telling. Maybe I took it from the lobby bathroom."

"I doubt if they have these kinds of towels in the lobby john."

"Do you really care about where I get my towels?"

"No."

She kissed me gently on the nose. "Is the baby feeling better?" she asked, while she ran her hand across the seam of my pants zipper.

"Much better."

"Good. We've discovered a cure for a swollen nose," said Liz, as she undid the top snap on my jeans. "Just transfer the swelling."

"Discovered?" I asked.

"Okay. It's something you learn when you're in training as a fellatio feminist. Men seem to think it's a cure all. It might just well be."

"I'm in no position to argue."

"By the way. I spoke to Linda Stirling. She said that her father thinks we're getting a great deal. So I'm in. We are now partners."

Later, we were lying in bed watching Conan O'Brien, but not hearing all the words. Someone had said something about bad habits.

"What's your worst one?" I asked.

"My worst what?"

"Have any bad habits?"

"I used to chew up my cuticles and eat them. Sort of like a cannibal. What about you?"

I thought for a moment. "I guess overdoing it."

"You're just getting old."

"Maybe, but since I moved here I've been living like a monk. No drugs. No late nights."

"I stick by my first statement. Old age." She propped up the pillows. "I have to be in the office early. Let's say bye-bye to Conan."

I pushed the off button on the remote, and the picture
disappeared into a milky white dot.

My next go 'round with Ricky proved even more challenging.
Ricky had called me early one morning. It was one of his most
obnoxious habits. He would call people whenever he felt like it
and that morning it was at six A.M. I told Liz about his habit
of calling early in the morning, even though I had explained to
him that this was the worst time to call me. It was as if he
were trying to irritate whoever he called, providing himself
with some sort of upper hand. Liz thought I was giving Ricky too
much credit. "Nah. He's not that smart. He ignores most of what
people say. People in the business bring self-involved to a new
meaning."

"Hello?" I asked. I thought it might be an emergency. "This
is Dr. Benjamin."

Ricky took full advantage of the situation and disguised
his voice in a deep baritone.

"Oh. Dr. Benjamin. I was up all night with my roommate
Charlie. About an hour ago we smoked some crack and he asked to
tie me up one last time."

"Who is this? How did you get my number?"

"Isn't this Dr. Benjamin, the Endodontist? My doctor, Dr.
K. told me to call you. It's an emergency."

"Dr. K. referred you to me?"

"Yes. Don't you know him?"

"Yes. Of course. What's wrong?"

"Did I get to the part where Charlie had me bound to the
bedposts?"

"What kind of problem are you having?"

"What kind of doctor are you? Don't you want to hear how I
was injured?"

"Is this a joke or something?"

"No, you dumb motherfucker. My roommate fell on my face. The schmuck tried to stand on the edge of the bed, and he fell on his fat ass, but his fat ass first fell on my face, and it hurts like hell. I think he broke my tooth." By this point Ricky could not control his laughter.

"Ricky? Is that you Ricky?"

"I had you going, didn't I?"

"I guess you did."

"I did the scenes you wanted, the ones about growing up in Beverly Hills."

I knew that I'd better continue with the conversation as if nothing had happened, because there was no telling when I could get Ricky to perform any actual work again.

"Great. So you filled in the stuff about your brother and your mother."

"Most of it," Ricky said sheepishly.

"I do have the answers to things like the relationship between you and your mother, right?"

"My mother is not going to be in the screenplay." Ricky's voice had become flat and direct.

"Come again?"

"You heard me. This is not about my mother. It's about me and Mal. My mother's not going to be in it."

"Ricky. After all our conversations. I can't believe you're saying that. How can I write an accurate scene about your family without some information on your relationship with your mother? I don't think it's possible. Will you reconsider?"

"I can have these scenes over to you by e-mail, if you want them now."

"I'd prefer to get them on paper." I knew that Ricky was deliberately changing the subject. It wasn't the first time that he had insisted on using e-mail.

"All you have to do is download the file and print it out."

The conversation continued for a few minutes, focused on Ricky's technological self-importance, until I gave up trying to reason with him. He would e-mail the material, and there would be no further discussion about his mother. The e-mail came through looking like hieroglyphics, so I would have to negotiate another method for the pages. Dropping off pages seemed outside of Ricky's realm.

I later decided to approach Sean about the project I was doing with Ricky. Sean ran it by Bob and Gary and the response was generally the same as what I had heard from others.

"Sure. If you can tie it up for peanuts, why not take a shot at old Mal," said Bob.

"But really on the cheap," added Gary. "I'll go in on it."

"This could be a real good cable movie deal for us," said Bob.

Sean said, "I think I could go independent. Let's not jump into anything. If I can get the rights, that's the first step. I'm not just buying a screenplay. I want the rights to Mal's story. Once we have that, we can do whatever the fuck we want. We can play Ricky, and in the end just tell him to go fuck himself."

It would be worth one more try to get Ricky to make a deal for the screenplay, which was now based on Mal's last big show in Atlantic City, at the opening of the Resort's Casino. I narrowed the scope of the screenplay down to that one episode. I borrowed heavily from the sentiment in the Louis Malle movie *Atlantic City*, the one with Burt Lancaster and Susan Sarandon. The story for my screenplay paralleled Mal's decaying career

with that of the city. I included the other big headliners at
that time, as well as conflicts with the local mob bosses.

Ricky asked to meet with Sean in the lobby of the Loews
Hotel in Santa Monica, an attractive semi-resort at the shore,
all pastels and floral patterns. Located a block from the beach,
it almost seemed surrealistic in an area of the beachfront that
had seen little renovation since the fifties.

Little wooden shacks with dilapidated storefronts, fish
snack bars, tie dyed t-shirt shops and other beach fare
surrounded the striking hotel. Ancient-but-classic motels still
existed across the street, sprawling one and two-story
structures, typical of those seen in television shows that
wanted to project a Hollywood West Coast image. They conjured up
old images of Efrem Zimbalist, Jr., David Janssen, or James
Garner running up and down the old white wooden steps in pursuit
of the bad guys, hoping to finish the scene in time for lunch.

When Ricky arrived, he drove past the circle driveway in
front of the Loews. He never valet parked his old Ford pickup
truck, something he had learned from Mal. Aside from the lesson
of never paying anything extra for things in life that can be
avoided, Ricky wasn't taking any chances that his truck would
stall while in the hands of the valets. It often did and needed
to be towed, thereby running up even more parking charges while
waiting for the Auto Club to arrive and bring the truck to a
repair shop. One year, at an Academy Awards party inside the
Beverly Hilton Hotel, Mal got stuck with an inflated overnight
parking charge for Ricky's vehicle. Ricky never heard the end of
it.

Ricky knew a little street behind the Loews that ran past
its expansive balconies and restaurants. He found a parking
space on the street, and then quickly stormed up the steep hill
to the front of the building.

I was waiting in the living room styled lobby, an open atrium with a view of the ocean at the far wall.

"Hey. How you doin'?" asked Ricky as he approached. He was winded.

"Hey," was all I intended to say until we were eventually seated elsewhere.

I laughed to myself at Ricky's ridiculous outfit - black spandex pants with a blue stripe running up the side of each pant leg, and a pair of running shoes with glow-in-the-dark designs that glistened as he waddled. He wore a gray sweatshirt from the Greg Norman shark line of golf wear, with a zipper front, opened all the way to expose a completely hairless chest.

Ricky wasn't satisfied and demanded, "How you doin'?"

"I'm fine. Do you want to eat something?" I asked.

"Sure. Do they serve food here?" asked Ricky.

That was a typical Ricky Rose remark, asking something that would be obvious to most people, but posed with all the sincerity of a scientist on a quest for a great Pulitzer discovery.

"Yes. They have a restaurant," I said, standing and pointing to the bar on his right, and then to the opposite end of the room where people were being seated by a young, cheerful, hostess.

"That's the big restaurant there," I said.

"Great. That's fine. Let's go," said Ricky.

Once we were seated, I thought I had spotted Carrie Fisher. "Isn't that - ?"

Before I got my words out Ricky jumped all over me. "Oh, you fucking civilians. Big fucking deal. Forget about movie stars. It's not like that. Wait 'till you find out someone you've always wanted to fuck in your fantasies, someone you jerked off to, likes to sit with an enema tube up their ass while she sucks on someone's respective dick or cunt. Forget it, Brantley. There are no more movie stars; just people with power, people with money, and a pecking order that would make the Roman Empire look like the Boy Scouts." I thought that was pretty well said for Ricky.

I decided not to pursue it, even though I probably agreed with the overall sentiment. Ricky made it clear that he wasn't talking about Carrie. Moments later, Sean appeared. He didn't want to eat. He threw out the deal and Ricky waited for him to leave, afraid to say anything concrete in front of him. Sean had left copies of the deal for each of us. I wondered if his haste was related to not having to buy us lunch.

"How can you expect me to give up my life story for just fifteen-thousand dollars?" asked Ricky. It was all about him; Mal was an incidental.

I flipped through the document. "That's just what he's offering up front. You'll get a great percentage; I think Sean said five percent of the budget. There's a built-in guarantee for something like seventy-five thousand, but we should end up splitting something higher."

"Are you trying to tell me that my life story isn't worth a million dollars?" Ricky didn't wait for an answer. "I spoke to people, writers, experienced writers who told me that this isn't the way things are supposed to be going. I don't want you to think you can take over this thing, because I'm putting an end to it now. It's my life story and I can do what I want with it." His rotund face reddened as he tried to speak with his mouth full of a turkey burger on a thick bun, and French fries. "I also think I'm a better writer than you."

"Ricky. Calm down. Nobody is trying to do anything wrong here." I didn't know how to handle him - not that I ever did.

"I know when my bare ass is being dragged over hot coals,"
said Ricky. "I've been through this before, and I can tell when
it's coming. You tell Sean there is no deal. I can get at least
a quarter of a million for this, and he knows it. I'm not going
to let you steal my life story."

I tried to control myself. "Listen. Please. Ricky. I've
been working on this for free for months now."

"So have I."

"I don't think you understand. Nobody is trying to hurt
you. Nobody is trying to steal anything. This is a good
experience. Sean wants to make the movie. You could end up
making more money when the movie gets made. The contract says
you'll get another twenty-five thousand on the first day of
principal photography. Here. Didn't you see that section?"

"So what?" Ricky shrugged and shook his head. "That's chump
change."

"I don't understand why you think you should get more
money. Nobody has offered us anything for the story, except for
Sean."

"I'm not taking it, and I'm going to do the editing
myself."

"What do you mean?" I asked. I realized that I had raised
my voice.

"I mean that things are going to go the way they should,
and it's my life and my project, so I'm taking over. You've done
some nice things for me and don't think I don't appreciate it,
but I have to take over now."

"So that's it? 'Fuck you! I'm taking over'."

"No. There's no 'fuck you'," said Ricky, without a hint of
remorse or regret. "But I am taking over."

"Look. I got Liz to help us, I wrote a screenplay for you,
and now I have found you a deal, and you want to…you want to…"

I was losing my voice and any form of self-control. "God. Ricky. You destroy people, don't you? You just don't stop. You think the whole world is out to get you, and you're not happy unless there is trouble, unless there is a problem, unless someone is your enemy, and now you're making me your enemy. I haven't done anything but try to help you. How can you do this?"

Ricky stared at his plate. "If I wanted to hurt you, you would know it. I don't want to hurt you. I just want to make sure that this is the best screenplay it can be, and I have to make sure that it turns out that way."

I lost it. "I don't believe this. Well. I have news for you. First of all, you can't write, so editing the script may prove difficult. Second of all, you have about as much business sense as a rug salesman from Iraq trying to sell his wares in the lobby of the King David Hotel in Jerusalem. You couldn't even find a damn book in the library when I asked you to."

Ricky defended himself. "It wasn't there. I asked someone and she told me that it wasn't there."

"Then how come I went there two hours later and found it on the shelf?"

"I don't like what you are saying here. Are you saying I didn't go to the library, because if that is what you're saying I don't like it. I have my self-esteem to think about, and I don't want to let you or anyone do anything that makes me out to be a schmuck. I have Mal to do that for me."

"But you are a schmuck." I knew that I had made a big mistake.

"Great," said Ricky, smirking as if I were taking a cheap shot. He had me where he wanted me, trying to do battle on his murky field.

"Ricky. I mean it. You are the worst kind of loser I have ever come across, and I don't want anything more to do with you or your damned piece of shit screenplay. We're through," I said. "I can't believe you do this to people."

Ricky sat there like a child being scolded. "Wait. We've been through this before. If I were angry at you I'd be at your apartment building with an attack helicopter." That was supposed to console me.

"Fuck you. You are just one rude prick." I threw my napkin on the floor, looked for the quickest route out of the room, and hurried through the restaurant.

"Was everything okay?" asked the hostess as I stormed past her.

"Peachy," I said, and dropped a ten dollar bill on the hostess stand. "Tell the waitress to do me a favor. Bring a whole pie over to that guy's table. It's a surprise."

"What? You want a pie?" The hostess magically made the money disappear into the pocket of her blazer.

"Yeah. See that fat guy. He wants a whole pie." I pointed toward Ricky, who had resumed eating.

"Any kind in particular?" asked the hostess.

"No. Just add some ice cream, and bring a can of whipped cream too. He just loves that stuff. And give him the check for the pie and the lunch. He just loves stuff like this!"

"Okay," said the hostess.

Ricky stared out the window, expressionless, as he continued to munch on the last section of his burger.

A few minutes later, when the waitress brought the pie, Ricky smiled as if he were a celebrity. "How did you know?" he asked.

"Your friend said that you liked pie," said the waitress.

"Great. This is great. Thanks." He consumed most of the pie, trying to belch silently, but to no avail.

When the check came, he asked for a pen, and with a flowing signature signed his name, William V. Rose, and proceeded to walk out. Before he could get to the front of the hotel, he was stopped by a man in a suit.

"Excuse me sir," said the man.

"What's the matter?"

"Sir. You forgot to pay your restaurant bill." The man was polite, but firm.

"I signed for it," said Ricky.

By that time the restaurant manager had caught up with the first man, who was probably part of the ground floor security team.

"We don't have house accounts here. You can pay with cash, credit card, or traveler's check," said the restaurant manager.

"Do you know who I am? Do you know that Mal V. Rose had his eighty-fifth birthday party at this hotel?"

"I helped arranged the party," said the manager. "Yes. I know who Mr. Rose is."

Ricky raised his voice. "Don't you remember me? I'm Ricky. Ricky Rose. I had this place filled with celebrities. Do you remember how much publicity I got for you?"

The manager motioned with his head for the security man to back off.

"Sorry, Mr. Rose," said the security man.

"Okay. I don't remember you, but I don't care to. Don't come here again," said the manager.

The security man stood his ground as Ricky smiled and waltzed out the front door.

A few days later, Ricky received a telephone call from Arnie. "It's Mal. I'm over at Cedars. You'd better come now." Arnie's voice quivered.

Ricky spent the next six hours at the hospital emergency room. Dr. K. arranged for him to come into the emergency room to periodically see Mal. In between visits, Ricky sat outside and listened as Dr. K. explained the situation. "Usually there is a limited amount of time in which to revive someone once their heart has stopped. I think Mal had a heart attack at home. The housekeeper called '911'. According to her it took about twenty minutes before they arrived. The paramedic told me that when they arrived, Mal did not have a heartbeat, but within minutes of their arrival, they restored his pulse. Understand, he's not breathing on his own at this point. On the way over in the ambulance, the paramedics said that they had to revive Mal a second time. What this means is that perhaps Mal's brain was out of oxygen for several minutes, maybe as many as fifteen."

Ricky nodded as if he understood. "Is there someplace to get coffee?"

"Yes. Across the street is the regular cafeteria," said Dr. K. "I'll go for it. What would you like?"

"Just coffee and a bear claw. If they don't have a bear claw I'll take a banana nut muffin."

"I'll take care of it for you," said Dr. K.

"Is your cell phone working?"

"I already called your mother."

"Great. I want to call the Associated Press, UPI and Reuters. Do you think I should give an exclusive to one of the local networks?" Over the next few hours, Ricky took interviews on Dr. K.'s cell phone. Soon, he would have Kyle Bixler negotiate a fee for a television exclusive with *ET* and a separate one for the *Star* tabloid, the latter created by Rupert Murdoch to compete with the *National Enquirer*.

Hours later, Dr. K. came out from the emergency room for the last time. "Ricky. I think we're going to move him upstairs." Ricky knew that it was over. He had accepted earlier that Mal was brain dead when they revived him on the way over to the hospital. Mal hadn't moved for the last six hours and his skin was a little bluish-gray.   By that time, even Ricky had tired of the media. The waiting room was filled with reporters and live television crews. He moved inside to the dismay of the media hoards. Dr. K. gladly took Ricky's place outside and announced that he would soon be making a general statement to the press.

A few minutes later, Ricky was alone in the upstairs room with his father. All the tubes were gone, and Mal lay there at peace, finally. They had kept him 'alive' for a total of six hours, only so that people could stop by the emergency room and see Mal for the last time. Not medically appropriate, but this was Hollywood.

Ricky leaned over to kiss Mal on the cheek, to feel the tickle of his moustache one more time. As he kissed Mal, he felt something strange on the side of his mouth. He put his hand there and felt a soggy, gooey, mess of hair attached to his face. He looked down at Mal. His face was clean shaven. Ricky grabbed the moustache from his own face, and with force placed it back under Mal's nose.

Wow, thought Ricky. Mal's own son did not know that he wore a fake moustache. Ricky felt more estranged than ever before. Another thorn in his side, something else that Mal had hidden from him. A lifetime of deceit.

"Shit," said Ricky aloud. He sighed and kissed Mal again, this time his arm accidentally swept across the hospital gown, exposing Mal's chest. Ricky reached to replace the sheet, but couldn't help notice that Mal was noticeably large in the chest area, something he was previously unaware of, but attributed to old age. *Odd,* thought Ricky. *I always thought that Mal was in*

496

better shape than that. A lot of older men had little, sagging
tits, so it was no big deal.

Ricky didn't know why, but he wanted to take a look at
Mal's dick. There were all those rumors about how big his dick
was, and Ricky wanted to find out if any of it was true.

He lifted the sheet. "What the fuck?" Ricky asked himself
out loud. He stood face to face with a tiny, trim mound of pubic
hair.

No dick. No balls.

"Whoa!" came out of Ricky's mouth, as he leaned over to
take a closer look. Not believing what he saw, he quickly
covered Mal and rushed out of the room.

Later, outside the room, Dr. K. said nothing. It didn't
matter to him whether Ricky found out or not. Mal had always
told Dr. K. to say nothing about it to anyone.

"We'll miss him," said Dr. K.

"Yes," said Ricky. "So, you always knew?"

"I did…I'd like to come to the funeral," said Dr. K.

"Of course," said Ricky, knowing that the Doctor would show
up anyway, like he did routinely at celebrity roasts, weddings,
bar mitzvahs, births, and of course, funerals. Ricky said this
knowing that his brother would only want the immediate family.
He didn't care if it irritated his brother, and hadn't even
fully considered at this point if his brother was actually a
blood relation, something that would be revealed to him down the
road.

Ricky felt somewhat relieved. The rumors weren't true. His
father wasn't a gay man, but rather a woman who was likely
bisexual. That meant that Rickey didn't know his biological
father, and made him consider the obvious, that his mother had a
lesbian relationship all those years with Mal. Maybe Mal was his

real mother and not the other woman who lived with them. Ricky
kept reviewing the possibilities; it was hard to understand.

As he drove past George Burns, another street bordering
Cedars-Sinai Hospital, he thought about his childhood, trying
desperately to put together all the missing pieces of a troubled
puzzle. He had never seen his father naked. Mal had tea in bed
every morning before breakfast. Later, if someone would venture
into his room, Mal would already be fully dressed, sitting up in
bed, sometimes with his blue blazer on. As a child, Ricky
thought nothing of it, but when he became older he realized that
having a father parade around in the privacy of his own bedroom
fully clothed all the time was quite weird.

What about his tits? Ricky thought to himself. He imagined
that Mal always wore some kind of stretch material to flatten
his breasts, probably something like golfers wear under their
shirts to keep their back muscles in place. Then he realized
that Mal knew all the tricks of changing his body to fit a
costume since he had grown up on the road, running with his
mother from burlesque house to burlesque house. Mal probably had
an entire collection of corsets, girdles, flatteners, and
devices Ricky could only imagine, probably including a strap on
dildo, designed to fool anyone fondling Mal's groin. That might
account for all the make out sessions reported in the papers,
like Mal sitting in the Brown Derby hugging it up with Jayne
Mansfield. Maybe he had them fooled, maybe he didn't, but he
sure had his own son fooled.

Imagine that, Ricky thought. *Growing up in a Hollywood
family with a famous father and not knowing your own father's
gender.* Ricky had no idea how common an occurrence it might
actually be, perhaps not to the extreme of being the actual
opposite sex, but Hollywood had its fair share of closeted gay
parents. Today Mal probably would not have had to hide his sex

in order to work, even to have a family, but Mal was from the old school, the very old school, and once he decided to try to get work as a man, he decided to stay with it the rest of his life.

Ricky vowed that he wouldn't rest until he found out the truth about his parents. He wondered about his real father. As far as I would know through my extensive interviews, Rickey would never find out.

Ricky decided that he would not tell me anything about Mal being a woman, because he thought that I would want to include that in the screenplay. Ricky didn't want anyone to know what he had just found out. But he must have known that someone else from the past, perhaps many, knew the history. Very soon Ricky realized that he had to smooth things over with me, because he was in no mood to do any writing work by himself. He soon expressed some willingness to continue.

That vow disappeared quickly as Ricky reminded himself to call Bixler to find out about Mal's estate. Ricky made mental notes to tell Barry about what he had found out, but not until after the funeral. The timing was very important. He first had to get the screenplay on 'his life' with Mal in the hands of a capable producer. It was also time to get rid of me, someone he saw more as a secretarial nuisance rather than a screenwriter, but not until he had convinced me to rewrite and polish the screenplay, so it conformed more to Ricky's version of things. It all had to be handled correctly. Mal's career was an important factor in everything that ever happened to Ricky and he wanted to make the most out of Mal's death.

The Associated Press sent out a hefty release. It would appear in newspapers all over the country. "Legendary comedian and actor, Mal V. Rose, dead at 96. Television pioneer Mal V. Rose died yesterday at Cedars-Sinai hospital in Los Angeles."

That's how it began all over the United States. Ricky loved the attention. He appeared on *Larry King Live* and Conan. Conan did use some drag footage of Mal as an ongoing joke after the interview with Ricky, including a still with moving lips for Mal to carry on a posthumous chat with Conan.

In preparation for the funeral, like so many times before, Arnie Baylos rehearsed Ricky on what he would say. Arnie knew that Ricky was a loose cannon, but he felt that he still owed it to Mal to try to convince Ricky to say simple, civil things.

A fairly significant show business turnout as well as the surrounding community showed up. I came with Dr. Harry. Barry had arrived early. Sean showed up late with Gary. Bob had no interest in "another Hollywood funeral." The old comedy guard from the Friar's crowd showed up in force, with Jack Carter, Jan Murray, Red Buttons, Sid Caesar, and Buddy Hackett leading the way. Jayne Meadows would read quotes about Mal from her late husband Steve Allen.

When we arrived, we walked directly inside. It was a large room. At first glance it could have been a cocktail party, except the drinks and waiters with little food trays were missing. Everyone was milling around aimlessly, hugging, smiling, kissing, just like at any show biz gathering, but once I mingled I picked up an air of sadness. I saw tears. Someone great was gone, and that someone was never known to or understood by Ricky.

Funeral was dress up time. Everyone wore 'show biz funeral chic' - expected dark suits for the men, but with perhaps a more colorful shirt than you would see in middle America, or a flashy pair of sunglasses, tie, or cufflinks, enough to still be fashionable, despite conflicting with the appropriate demeanor for the event. The casual-to-kill dress was the tasteful standard for the ladies, but a few sparkling jewels, watches,

and very expensive scarves were needed and intended for maximum
visibility. Although it was a funeral, it was still a Hollywood
funeral. Anyone who walked in off the street would be certain
that they were at a Hollywoodland function.

When it became time for Rabbi Ermis to speak, I tried to
listen, but didn't hear very much of what he said. It all
sounded rather ordinary, compared to the great speech I had
heard at the Burton Way Synagogue. Rabbi Ermis performed a
somewhat less religious service than would have been expected,
probably in deference to the fact that Mal was far from a
religious Jew. A few of the usual prayers with the requisite
references to God, and that was that.

The Rabbi's part of the ceremony seemed a little short,
maybe because he knew that there were going to be several
eulogies, a couple given by some of the biggest names in show
biz. I made up the mock headline for the story in the *Hollywood
Reporter*. "Rabbi edits God's part out in order to make room for
big name talent".

The obituary that traveled from the *Chicago Tribune* to
Newsday in New York and back out to Hollywood covered a great
deal of Mal's life, some of it boilerplate, before it finally
admitted how important Mal was to Hollywood history. The last
line read, "Mr. Rose is survived by his son Ricky." As always,
Ricky felt cheated. He felt that he should have been mentioned
in more detail. What about the fact that he had schlepped Mal
around for years? Why, without Ricky Mal would have retired, or
so Ricky believed.

I was more struck more by the civility of the whole
memorial service. There were no strained greetings; no bad blood
had come to the surface, yet. That day, I felt totally detached
from Ricky. The exchanges between the immediate family and the
rest of the show biz crowd appeared legitimately emotional. Most

of the gestures from the horde appeared genuine, albeit the inclusion of a little 'love ya babe' Hollywood flavor. It couldn't be helped, that was the way show biz people routinely spoke to one other whether they were sincere or not. They were all awash in nebulous offers to Ricky and his brother, "Just let me know if there's anything I can do, anything at all." Mostly show biz bullshit lip service.

Ricky mingled almost convulsively in order to hear what people were saying. He made a concerted effort to avoid his brother. He hadn't yet come to terms with the fact that Mal was gone. He was still thinking about the money, *I'll find some way to make a bundle on Mal's life story.* He suddenly realized that he didn't have any idea as to how to accomplish that. He had always been taken care of, exalted in the role of a spoiled Beverly Hills brat. He concluded that he could make it without Mal, as long as he had left him enough money.

Ricky really hadn't known Mal, at least not in the emotional terms that would make a son content. For decades, Mal's face was known in every corner of the world that had a television, and Ricky had to live on with the irony of never knowing this 'man' who was so famous and loved by millions of strangers. I was torn between feeling sorry for Ricky and being dismissive of his entire profile, because he had been such trouble to his father all those years and was totally unaware of the continual havoc he had created for Mal along the way.

I eventually cornered Barry on the subject, who was happy to talk. "It was tough knowing both of them the way I did. I don't think I ever helped Ricky. It's okay. I've already given this information to another author who's writing a book on Hollywood. I can't go into the same detail, but I can tell you this about Mal V. Rose. Mal had a classic personality disorder. It is not unusual for people in the entertainment business to fall under any variety of DSM cuckoo categories. Without getting technical on you, he had a narcissistic personality. When you were in his company, he would only talk about himself, and he expected you to share that interest. He could not relate on any level to problems other people were having. He had a 'just get over it' attitude with Ricky, one that obviously damaged his son immensely. In what ways, we can't be sure." Barry knew a lot more about the Rose family dynamic, but even he wasn't going to give up everything he knew for free.

When the service and condolences were over, it took almost an hour to get my car from the valets. Once inside, I called Liz on my cell.

"How did it go?" she asked as soon as she knew that it was me.

"All I said to Ricky was, 'I'm sorry about Mal,' and he hit me on the forehead with the prayer book. Then he said 'We're all even. Let's finish the screenplay'."

"I told you not to go," said Liz.

"I had to go. I want to sell this project."

"You know the routine. Come on over, and I'll pretend I know something about first aid."

"You've cured me before," I said.

"Yeah, yeah, yeah," she said, and then pushed the end button on her cell phone.

Twenty minutes later, I was in Liz's apartment.

"Did you do the sort of Rat Pack thing?" asked Liz, stroking my hair.

"I don't think Ricky will go for it," I said, removing the ice pack from my forehead. "I know it would read better that way, but Ricky wants to be in too many of the scenes, so I've been reworking it."

"Fuck what he cares. If it's any good I can slip it to someone who can get it done. Nobody bit on the story you wrote except Sean. What did you put in the new draft?"

"It's about Ricky growing up in the foothills of Hollywood, you know, with the rich people and the movie stars."

"Who cares about Ricky? Everyone I've ever mentioned him to just rolls his eyes or comes out and says, 'That little prick. Whatever happened to him, anyway'?"

"He is difficult. But I don't even think we have enough to show anyone. I have about ninety pages or so."

"That's plenty. Nobody wants to read more than that. You don't want coverage on this. You just want to see if there is any interest. But from what you said, I don't think anyone is going to be interested in what Ricky has to say about anything. Maybe you can work with him, and convince him to write more about some of Mal's famous friends. I don't know. Wasn't Mal good friends with Bob Hope at one time?"

"Yeah, but they had a falling out. Mal went after one of the actresses on those U.S.O. type shows. I think it was Angie Dickinson, but I'm not sure. Ricky says that Mal didn't know that the girls were dating Bob in order to go on the tour."

"Mal had a reputation of going after everyone. He could care less. How's the nose feel?"

"Horrible."

"Do you really think that this is worth it? This guy is certifiable. He has a criminal record. Do you remember when he pushed that stewardess on a flight from L.A. to New York and the pilot decided to land the plane in Houston?"

"Yeah. Ricky said she had said something about Mal and he had to come to his defense."

"Brantley. Look. We don't know each other a long time, but this guy has a reputation as being so low to the ground you could run a shovel under him and never pick him up."

"Where'd you get that one?"

"I made it up just now. The guy is show business sleaze. He has spent his whole life around the back doors of projects. Everything he ever touched failed. This guy is bad news, and he's already hurt you enough. Drop it. I don't care if you and he have the next *Get Shorty* or *The Player*. Find someone else to work with." She meant it.

"I don't quit on projects or people. I told him I would help him, and that's what I'm going to do."

"Even if it kills you, and with Ricky, you have a fifty-fifty chance."

"I'm going to try to get Ricky to take Sean's deal," I said.

"Brantley. Come on. Haven't you wised up yet? I'm getting a glass of wine. You want?"

"Yes."

We didn't discuss Ricky again that night. Before we called it a night, Liz tried to fortify me with a final thought. "You have enough information to finish your own book. Why not concentrate on that?" She was probably right, but I was either too dumb or too enamored with my sudden rise in the business to concentrate on a book. I had my tapes, notes, and several hundred pages, but I wasn't ready to complete the project. I was being driven by a new force, one that included a healthy dose of masochism. I hadn't had my fill, yet.

The next few days after the funeral, Ricky became preoccupied with his newfound assets. Bixler had approached Ricky after the ceremony to let him know that Mal's body was delivered from Cedars to the UCLA Medical School in accordance with Mal's and Ricky's wishes. In the same conversation, Bixler suggested that Ricky stop by the office in Century City so that they could go over the estate.

Once at the office meeting, Ricky paid little attention to the details until Bixler read the financial specifics.

"Basically, Mal's estate will pay you four thousand dollars a month for life," said Bixler.

Ricky jumped to his feet. "I object. That's it? I can't live on four thousand a month! What about a cost of living increase?"

Bixler cleared his throat. "Certainly you can apply for increases in your benefit. While the trust created does not specifically include the language for a cost of living increase, it clearly states that your needs are to be taken care of. Here is a copy of the will. When you get to the section about you, it states that food, shelter, you know, all the necessities are to be taken care of."

Ricky was no longer listening. "Didn't he leave me anything else? Who got the house? What about the condominium in the desert? The cars. What about all those cars?"

"Mal did leave you one hard asset." Bixler waited.

"He did? What?"

"He left you all the shares in the Hollywood Deli."

Ricky smirked. "Great. I knew that. What's that worth?"

"I don't know exactly. The money Mal put in has no specific value, but I have been using a one-dollar value for SEC purposes, and also for the IRS filing."

Ricky sat down and leaned back in his chair. "But I can sell the rest of them. Right? Isn't the deal still on with Dr. Benjamin and his agent girlfriend?"

"I wouldn't advise following through on that. If this company eventually goes public, your shares could be worth ten times what Mal paid. It depends on the opening share price if and when it goes public."

Ricky quickly did the math. "You mean if it comes out at twenty dollars a share, my share will be worth millions?"

"I wouldn't count on that, but it is certainly a possibility. Mal was willing to let you go ahead and sell half of your shares at the SEC valuation of one dollar. I can't advise you to do that, although even at one dollar you'd be getting more money that Mal paid in."

Bixler could care less if Ricky sold the stock. He knew that Ricky would try to cash out. Bixler was more concerned about his own business liability, so he was giving Ricky normal unadulterated advice. Johnny Carson had sued his own lawyer for bad business activities.

Ricky's face broke into a broad smile. The idea of Mal's wealth had suddenly sunk in. "Son of a bitch. Son of a bitch. I never thought. Whatever. Where are the papers?" Despite his false glee, Ricky still intended to get some extra cash for his stock and over time sue to get more money if not total control of the estate.

Before Ricky even read the new version of my screenplay, a story appeared in the *National Enquirer* about a movie deal surrounding Ricky's life with Mal. I found out about it from Ricky. I was unaware of Ricky's insane hunger for publicity.

"I don't believe these guys. That's the most unflattering thing I've ever read," Ricky began.

I was surprised that Ricky would take the whole thing so seriously. "How did you find out about the article?" I asked.

"One of my friends called me. Do you want me to fax you a copy? I don't know if it will go in one piece. I could cut it in sections, paste it on separate sheets, but then you'd have to be faxed a lot of separate sheets and I don't want to use up the time on your machine or so much fax paper. I could scan the copy and then e-mail it to you."

I had the obvious solution. "I can go to the store and buy a copy."

"I don't want to put you out. Why should you pay anything?"

"It's okay."

"No. It's not okay. I'll get you a copy."

"Just send it." I was trying to avoid one of Ricky's tomes.

"My scanner doesn't work so good all the time. What I think I'll do is scan it into one of the Microsoft Works files for word processing, then I can just change it to a text file and send it to you as an e-mail," he continued.

"Ricky. The files you send never come out formatted that way. I have to retype all of them in my Word software."

Ricky rambled on for about another three minutes. In the end he decided to try faxing, and then never sent it.

I ended up getting the *Enquirer* article at the local Pavilions supermarket. The sad article said that Ricky had been trading on his father's talent his whole life, and now he was trying to capitalize on Mal's death. The writer obviously didn't go for Ricky's point of view.

That week, I ran into Arnie Baylos at the Starbucks in Beverly Hills. Over coffee, Arnie became an incessant talker. "Mal and I gave up trying to stop Ricky from talking to the tabloids. It turned out to work to our benefit, over time. The few months before Mal died he was about as happy as I've seen him in thirty years. The tabloids helped to get his career going again. So in the final scene Ricky was still doing his spoiled

brat shtick, but it ended up being good for Mal. It's been tough
since Mal left us. I wake up in the middle of the night and call
him sometimes, not knowing at first that Mal is gone, and then
dialing him like I did thousands of times to check on him.
Before the house was sold, I called and got a phone answering
machine and heard Ricky's voice on it. Then I knew that Mal was
really gone. Mal would never have a phone machine. I remember
when we were on the road and the hotels started switching to the
touch button kind of phone thing. Mal insisted on having the old
phones in the room. It had something to do with the fear of the
electricity running inside the phone. It took a few years, but
we never totally convinced him he wouldn't get an electric
shock, or worse, electrocuted. He had only the old phones in his
house. When we were on the road, I dialed all of his telephone
calls. He swore to me that in an emergency he would put on the
white gloves he used in his act and dial '911'. God. I miss
him."

CHAPTER TWENTY
Neil, Ira
Ricky, Brantley
Ricky, Barry
Brantley
Sean
Liz, Brian

    Dave Stirling was able to negotiate a lease for the space
in Beverly Hills that had been vacated by the Carnegie Deli of
New York, and afterward occupied very briefly by Balducci's.
Well-known investor Marvin Davis had led a group a few years
back that was determined to bring Leo Steiner's Carnegie Deli to
Beverly Hills. The result was modern and boasted a big menu, but
didn't have the authentic New York deli taste. Despite all the
money, no one had bothered to do the research that Neil and Ira
had done. The Carnegie eventually closed, leaving a premiere
space available.

    The grand opening of The Hollywood Deli in Beverly Hills
proved to be just what everyone had in mind, a raucous, noisy,
food feast. Two large spotlights were positioned on the street,
the same as with movie premieres. Sean had received permission
to erect a tent on the street, only a few steps from the deli.
People milled back and forth from the tent to the interior of
the deli. For the very diet conscious, there were plenty of

'healthy' minded dishes, like carrot and raisin salad, plain salmon plates, and tiny little appetizers that appealed to the strange dietary habits of a lot of people in Hollywood, at least when they were out in public. Inside, it would be strictly the best deli food they could produce, with all the authentic drinks, including a little stand that made the classic egg cream (a drink of milk, seltzer, and U-Bet chocolate syrup). Bars were positioned all over the area, and the alcoholic consumption was surprisingly moderate. The event would cost a ton of money, but Sean already had some upfront cash from his newest investor, Gibby.

The expense was worth it. The place was packed with celebrities.

Judge Wapner was one of the first to arrive. In addition to being a popular television Judge, he was a well-known and respected member of many organizations and charities. Lately, the Judge had another gig acting as a television Judge on an all-animal station, deciding only cases involving animals. He went directly inside the deli to try one of the sandwiches. After a few bites, he wiped his lips carefully with a napkin, and 'judged' it authentic, pronouncing that the boys had a hit on their hands. This was a nice verdict from the famous television Judge.

Gibby was in all his glory. He had his own stall set up inside the tent, where he served his version of chicken livers, the usual source for the popular delicacy served fried with eggs, or chopped. Gibby's booth was instead devoted entirely to foie gras, the more popular-than-ever food made from specially fattened duck liver, a treat for the palates of those accustomed to only the chicken variety. When Gibby had told Neil his idea, they discussed a liver source. The government, after twenty-five years, had lifted the ban on the imports from France. French poultry was now allowed, and the D'Artagnan company was selling its authentic French foie gras at one hundred and twelve dollars for one and one-half pounds, almost thirty-five dollars more than the Hudson Valley product, a staple used at all the great restaurants in New York. After France's politically stinging position on Iraq soured the palates of many Americans, prices were anticipated to drop as talk of boycotting expensive French imports increased, perhaps forcing the amphibian-eating exporters to undersell the Hudson Valley product, like in the days when the poultry import ban was lifted. Not a chance.

Neil had played along. "Which one do you think we should get?"

"I'm used to cooking with the American," said Gibby. "The key to foie gras is a healthy, firm liver, and the American distributors have never let me down."

"Say no more. I have a connection for the American," said Neil. One telephone call to Chris and they would have all the foie gras they could use, 'pre-prepared' to make Gibby's chores easier. Neil made sure to convey to Chris the information regarding quality. That meant a warning about deceased alcoholics. While a fatty liver was more desirable, there were limits to the liver decimation.

And with that, there was never another discussion about where to purchase the liver for foie gras.

Gibby duplicated his own recipe for fried chicken livers. In the center of the booth he had foie gras, eggs and onions, a copy of the deli staple usually done with the chicken livers. His third dish was a mousse of foie gras. Once word spread that there was a foie gras stand, Gibby was in high gear. He lectured as he spooned out the very popular fare to the very eager guests.

The Beverly Hills epicureans ate up his creations and his words. "All the big shots in New York are fighting over whether to use the French or the American. There are differences. You are eating our best American. This foie gras is very flavorful, and a lot of that comes from its fat content. Most of the ducks in our country are hatched by artificial insemination. The ducks are force fed a great deal by hand. They are really fattened up, which determines the shape, texture, and flavor of the liver. In France, they feed the ducks mostly a diet of corn. It makes sense that those livers do taste a little sweeter. Our ducks are eating a lot of cereals, with daily protein additives, getting their nutrition and fattening much the same way we do." If only he had known the truth about his truly American foie gras.

Ricky was present, chatting with me about all the new changes he wanted to make in the screenplay. I got the feeling that he still hadn't read a page since the last go 'round. Ricky conspicuously ate his way through the party. At one point he shouted, "They've got salmon!" and disappeared to refill his empty plate.

Ira hustled back and forth, helping wherever he could. Suddenly, he was struck by the music. He heard the lyrics clearly enough, but couldn't believe his ears.

The woman's voice blasted over the party buzz. "The cauldron was a-bubbling, the flesh was lean, and the women moved forward like piranhas in a stream, they spread themselves before me and offering so sweet, and they beckoned and they beckoned, come on darling eat."

Ira bolted back through the kitchen and found Neil outside in the alley smoking cigars with soon-to-be Guv Arnold and a few of the valets.

"It's great, isn't it?" Neil asked, referring to the party.

"Neil. What kind of music is that?"

"It's great. We're packing them in," said Neil. He took a long draw on the cigar.

"Neil. Did you hear the lyrics to that song?"

Ira pulled Neil over to the open kitchen door, where he could hear the song more clearly.

"Eat the summer cannibals, eat eat eat, you eat the summer cannibals, eat eat eat, you eat the summer cannibals, eat eat eat," continued the song.

"Patti Smith. *Summer Cannibals*," said Neil, as if he had just answered a question on the old show *Name That Tune*.

"Are you nuts? Don't answer. Just change the music. Now! Do it now!"

"Okay. But don't lose your sense of humor," said Neil. He placed his cigar on a concrete ledge. "Don't touch that. It's an eight dollar cigar. Arnold always smokes the best."

"Just change the music," said Ira. "This is becoming a nightmare."

"Okay. How about *I'm Dreaming Of A White Christmas*?"

"Anything. Just take that song off," said Ira.

Moments later, Sean slid over to speak with Ira and Neil. "Well, boychicks. What did I tell ya?"

"Fantastic," said Neil.

A waiter carrying a plate of sandwiches stopped to offer one to Sean. "Which ones are those?" he asked.

"Brisket and corned beef," said the waiter.

Sean said, "No thanks. Send someone over with a turkey or plain chicken, if you see anyone."

The waiter moved on in oblivion, pretending that he hadn't heard anything.

"I guess we can get things back to normal now," said Ira.

"Not yet. I wouldn't change anything. Not just yet," said Sean. His face lit up and he took off after one of the guests.

"Clint! I thought I saw you practicing golf over at Hillcrest. In town for the Golden Globes?"

In the corner of the outdoor tent, Ricky V. Rose helped himself to his third or fourth sandwich, albeit somewhat downsized since everything was free. "This stuff is un-fucking believable."

I agreed. "It does taste pretty good."

Neither Ricky nor I had any idea that he was likely munching on his recently deceased father - exactly what Ricky had been doing in life - and a fitting end to a tortuous relationship. So, in death, it only followed that Ricky would eat up a little more of his deceitful 'father'.

The ending for Mal was in keeping with his disdain for his own fans. Mal despised the people who stopped in front of his house or came at him while he was having his breakfast at Nate 'n Al's deli. Mal must have done thousands of dinner shows where people's gastric juices flowed freely while he sweated on the stage and watched helplessly as they ingested little parts of his soul with their dinner. That's how he felt after every dinner show, as if a little more of him was eaten up by the audience. At the definitive finale, Mal's own flesh would be literally digested by local gastric juices, and little bits of his funny cellular DNA would fuel those same people that he loathed.

It was like the old joke about the cannibal talking to his friend the morning after a small plane with entertainers had crashed on its way to Sun City, South Africa. "Who did you eat?" asked the first. "The comedian," his pal answered. "How'd he taste?" The answer, "A little funny."

Months later, I would get to hear more of Barry's take. "Ricky spent his whole life trying to get Mal's attention. The thing Ricky never understood is that Mal was never going to give him what he wanted. Ricky first wanted to be loved by Mal. Mal couldn't love anyone except himself. I told that to Ricky many times, but it wasn't that simple. It never is. Ricky also wanted to be like Mal. Since he couldn't get Mal's love, he tried to emulate Mal, to show Mal that he could be a, uh, well, this is how Ricky would put it, 'A big shot, so people could kiss my ass.' Ricky was always hungry for a piece of Mal, anything he could get. Ricky loved to arrive early at events, and get the initial attention. Once Mal arrived, nobody would want to talk to Ricky. I tried to get him away from Mal, get him to start his own life. On more than one occasion, I told him that I didn't think I was helping him, and suggested that he see one of my colleagues. He took that as an insult and began to scream. 'Isn't my self-esteem bad enough? Now my shrink is rejecting me.' That's how Ricky took everything. It was a shame, but this was a personality defect I saw often with Hollywood kids."

I was looking forward to having the weekend off. I finished the latest draft of the screenplay about Mal. I decided to give it to Liz first, after having gone through the mill with Ricky, hopefully for one last time. What I never learned was that with Ricky there was no 'last time'. I mailed Ricky a copy, allowing Liz lag time to shop the material without Ricky's intervention. I hand-delivered the screenplay to Liz, who intended to give it to Michael Halpern, a Vice-President at HBO. She was also considering slipping it to someone at a new management company in the Valley who was positioned to get a deal, either by placing it with a star or a famous director. The deal could be packaged completely in house and become an agency project. Liz did prepare me for the possibility that the script would be rejected, just on the basis of Mal's unpopularity within the business.

"But he's dead now. Doesn't that help?" I asked.

"With some. Who knows with Mal? It's hard to find someone in the business to say something nice about him."

"But the story isn't so much about Mal as it is about Atlantic City in seventies," I said. "They can always cut out the stuff I added about Ricky."

"Everyone I spoke to, particularly the people at HBO, sees this as a Mal project, and feels that the demographics they want just don't line up with Mal."

I still didn't get it. It didn't matter what was on the page. It only mattered what was on people's minds. Writing was an idea, not a template for production. Everyone had input, and many believed in predicting success solely based on statistics.

Weeks later, the telephone rang early in the morning.

"Hello," I said in a muffled voice.

"It's William V. Rose," said the enthusiastic voice. He spoke as if the other party was expected to feel grateful for his call.

"Who?" I wasn't quite awake.

"It's Ricky V. Rose. I finally got a chance to read the script for the first time."

"Ricky. Do you know what time it is?"

"No. I just got finished reading the script. I think it's very good, but there are a lot of changes I would like to make. I don't see why we need those scenes with Sonny & Cher, and we certainly don't need the Osmonds popping in and out of Mal's dressing room."

I forced myself to sit up. "Ricky. I edited the screenplay based on my meetings with you. It's at CAA now," I said. "We're done."

"But when are you and I going to sit down and fine tune this? It needs a lot of work."

"Ricky...I'm glad you finally read it, but I gave it to you more than three weeks ago. I sent you two copies by e-mail and the first by regular mail. I called you three times, and each time you made excuses as to why you couldn't read it. You had said that it was better for you to go over each section independently, so I did that with you, particularly the scenes where only you knew what happened in Mal's dressing room."

"Back off. I've just gone through a fucking funeral. My father just died. How was I supposed to do this?"

"Your father died months ago. I'm talking three weeks ago. I told you Liz needed the script. I told it to you each time we spoke. Didn't you get the scripts?"

"I think so, but the one I have is full of spelling errors. We can't have CAA read anything with my name on it if it has spelling errors. Look. I know this business, and I've talked to a lot of people who know, and they say if there are spelling errors in the script it only lessens the literary value of the project."

I wanted to scream. I fervently glanced around the room for something to throw and settled on a pillow. It flew halfway to the television, and landed with a dull thud in the middle of the floor. It wasn't enough, but for the moment, it had to do.

Ricky began screaming. "Don't bring your ego into this again. This is not about your ego. It is about the spelling errors in the screenplay. We have to get it fixed. When can you and I call the people at CAA and let them know that there are spelling errors in the screenplay? Also, you said that you were going to use my e-mails to Mal as I originally wrote them. It looks like you edited one or two words, or maybe that's the computer doing the spellchecker thing."

I couldn't control myself, and was hooked into another
Ricky exchange. "What are you talking about? Why are you
attacking me personally?"

"I'm not attacking you personally. You always misunderstand
these conversations. I need some information, and you feel like
you should take it personally. I don't mean to make it sound
personal, but your ego is not what this project is all about."

I tried the obvious. "Ricky. I've allowed you to drag me
into one of these dumb conversations again."

"Look. We have to get this settled. Why don't we meet this
morning to settle it?"

"This morning?" I wanted no part of it.

"How about the Loews Hotel in Santa Monica?"

"How about tonight instead?"

"Okay. I'll call you later and let you know the best time
for me." He hung up.

I would eventually cancel the meeting. During the week I
was bombarded by threatening phone calls and e-mails from Ricky.
Essentially he was going to pull the plug on the entire project,
but not without warnings about how he had resorted to physical
violence in the past. He felt that it was necessary to describe
those experiences, which included assaulting a teacher at his
high school, and attacking a Friar's Club member who Ricky
claimed had screwed him in yet another Ricky deal gone sour. Mal
had had to pull a lot of strings, because the man Ricky pushed
around was very well connected and respected within the shady
side of show business.

After Mal's death, Ricky had asked Barry if he could come
in on an 'as needed' basis. He cited his quest to find out "who
he really was," and why "Mal kept things from me."

Barry really didn't want to speak to Ricky more than once a
week, but felt obligated to see him. Barry kept repeating

himself until Ricky responded. "You never really knew your
father," was a key expression. Barry was in the dark about the
true Mal.

"I don't know. I don't know. What do you mean I never
really knew him?' whined Ricky.

"Ricky. What is it that you don't understand about what I'm
saying. You never really knew your father." He drew each word
out, slow and deliberate. Barry repeated each word again without
any condescension to make Ricky think about it one more time.
"You never really knew your father."

"What do you mean?" was the continued Ricky response.

"What do you think I mean?" Barry replied to Ricky's ever
more anxious, aggressive, and accusatory style.

"Barry. I think you should explain what you mean," said
Ricky, trying to take control. "Look. I can't ask you to explain
something further? It's not like the rule book says I can't do
that or something."

"Of course. But don't you remember me saying the very same
thing toward the end of last session?"

"What do you mean? I don't know what you mean." Ricky
nervously glanced around. "What are you trying to do here?"

"Last week, toward the end of the session…" said Barry, now
speaking slowly and deliberately with a touch of parental anger.
"Last week I told you the same thing and you said you would
think about it during this week. Did you think about it?"

Ricky hated being confronted by Barry. "Well, er, no. I
don't remember that, and I'm sure if you said something that
important I would remember it."

"Let's discuss it now anyway. I think you never knew your
father. I think you knew only the stage personality that he
used, the same personality that his fans and cronies saw. He
never showed you himself, only what you could see on television,

in the movies, or on the stage in Vegas or Atlantic City. You once told me that you were his biggest fan. Well, I hate to be the one to break this news to you, but I'm afraid that's all you were to him, another fan. I'm not even sure that he liked you. I'm sorry."

Ricky jumped to his feet. "That's a bunch of bullshit!"

"Maybe, but I don't think so," said Barry, as he took the wrapper off one of his Montecristo cigars. "Do you want a cigar today?"

Ricky was happy to have a cigar, and settled back into his seat.

Barry would often leave exhausted from these sessions.

I would soon get more out of Barry. "Ricky finally confirmed my worst suspicions about Mal. It didn't shock me. I think Ricky presented it to me for shock value, but it all made too much sense. Mal was a very funny comedian, but during the era when he was growing up, it was absolutely impossible for a woman to be a headline act. His mother helped him, and created a male performer from a talented little girl. Her goal was simple; to make sure that Mal made some money for the family. It was pure and straightforward, and Mal's mother never gave it another thought. It all fit in; Mal's cross dressing, his alleged homosexuality, and his incredible reputation both privately and publicly as a ladies' man. Mal was probably bisexual, but judging by all of his sexual liaisons with female movie stars I'd have to say old Mal V. Rose was a tried-and-true lesbian. Plain and simple. He probably never had sex with all those male stars."

Despite all the rejections, I was still pathologically determined to get *Small Steaks* sold. Liz said that the original version, the one unadulterated by Sean, was a "funny, romantic

comedy" centered on medical students. I agreed to let Liz send
out the original *Small Steaks* to a few people. She got an
immediate response at Sony. They wanted to see me. I was
delirious.

As I drove south on Motor Avenue, a direction I had taken
many times to go to Venice Beach, I had a hard time convincing
myself that I was not going to turn right onto Washington
Boulevard in order to continue west toward the beach, but
instead stop at Sony Studios, home of Columbia Pictures. I was
told to enter right off of Washington Boulevard and head for the
Thalberg Building, an older, classic building named after the
legendary Irving Thalberg. The low-rise building was restored to
sculptured perfection on the outside, and modernized on the
inside, enough to make the interior offices palatable for the
dozen or so high-ranking production people. Security was
normally tight, even before 9/11, because this was the home of
production for Columbia and Tristar. I was detained at the gate
and even more aggressively in the lobby. The head of both
divisions had offices in the building. The entertainment
industry was high on the list of possible targets after 9/11 and
forced to postpone high visibility gatherings like the Emmy
Awards.

I took the elevator to the third floor, and followed
directions to the office of V.P. Carey Silver. The door was open
to the outer office and a woman in her twenties was busy on the
telephone, while she took handwritten notes. She wore a remote
headset with the little microphone jutting out ever so slightly
in front of her chin.

"Hello. I'm Brantley Benjamin."

"Sit down, please," she said in a perfunctory tone. "Carey
is running late. He should be out of this meeting in a few
minutes."

I sat down at a little table that was set up on the far side of the room. From there I could see the door that connected to what I surmised was Carey's office. The outer office was moderately sized. It made me think that perhaps Carey was pretty high up in the company.

I counted that the woman took about seven telephone calls during a brief period. When she had a free moment, she rose from the chair and approached me. "Would you like something to drink?" she asked with the same tone. She tried to force the corners of her mouth to point upward, but it seemed that her facial muscles were trained to stay rigid.

"Uh," was about all I got out. I could feel the moisture on my palms.

"Water? How's water?"

"Fine. Water is fine."

She turned to leave, raising her voice as it trailed off when she reached the hall. "Please feel free to use the telephone."

I looked down to view the complicated phone at my table. It had six or seven lines. I was surprised that there wasn't any fax machine in the office. There must have been a central area down the hall.

Within a matter of seconds, the woman returned with a little tray on which was a single bottle of designer water. She placed the tray on the adjacent table and quickly went back to her station at the desk.

For a moment I felt very important. There I was in the Thalberg Building, with my own telephone and designer water. So this was what it was like to be a Hollywood screenwriter. *Not bad,* I thought to myself, and then glanced over at the woman as she sat at her desk. *Nice.*

The door to the inner office opened. A medium build, handsome African-American man emerged from the inner office. At first glance, I incorrectly assumed that he was the man leaving Carey Silver's previous meeting.

"Tell Mark I'll be downstairs in about thirty minutes," said the man. He was referring to Mark Canton, the boss.

"Hello. Please come in. I'm Carey," he said, extending his hand and gesturing for me to follow him into the room.

I followed Carey into a slightly larger office. I sat down on a small black leather sofa that faced his desk. Carey did not sit behind the desk, but on a lounge chair juxtaposed to the sofa at about a forty-five degree angle. Carey got right to the point. "When I read *Small Steaks* all I could think of was, 'wow, we have got to make this'."

I felt my pulse rate jump, bulging my neck so fiercely that I could feel the throbbing against my shirt collar. Thirty minutes later, I floated out the back door of Carey's office. I was in Hollywood heaven.

And then it was over. Liz broke the news to me only two weeks later. "Brantley. I'm sorry. I just got off the phone with Carey. They said they're not taking any pitches now. He walked it all the way up the ladder to Mark. They felt it was a pitch because Carey wanted to make too many changes in the ending of your version. So, it wasn't a screenplay, but a pitch."

Nothing. That's what was left. After being built up to believe that I was getting a deal, I was left with nothing, the same nothing that pervades the atmosphere around every writer in Hollywood. I had gotten the full initiation at Columbia, and would now have to wait until the freshly opened chronic wound healed into another creative scar.

Academy Awards night approached, a time when many people in
the business reevaluated their careers, whether they were
directly involved in the awards or not.

For the last few weeks, my mental health had declined. The
events at Sony really took their toll. Nothing in life prepares
someone for that kind of encounter. Liz was more concerned with
getting me a deal, any kind of a deal. "I think a green light
will get you out of the dumps," she told me repeatedly,
referring to the studio expression for a project slated to move
ahead. Yellow would have made me just as happy.

As soon as the Academy Awards show was over, everyone in
Sean's world would head over to Le Dome on Sunset, where he had
his own reserved table for sixteen. This was going to be one of
the greatest nights of his life. He sat in the limo and sipped a
low calorie beer mixed with a little Snapple Lemonade. Since he
had been in high school, he had been drinking a mix of beer and
lemonade. As he sipped, he thought about his father, who had
taught him everything he knew about business. He really felt
that with the success of The Hollywood Deli he could build the
empire that he had always sought. He envisioned turning it into
a giant entertainment conglomerate. He would roll his own movie
library into the company. Vegas was the next logical step. He
had already spoken to Donny and Dave, and most of the board
members approved whatever they said. Dave suggested that his
daughter Linda be given some responsibilities in day-to-day
activities. Linda had already hired Liz as her part-time
personal assistant. Everyone involved with the company could
sense that this was the next big success to come out of Southern
California.

Sean was finally on his way. It would only take a year
before they could get that new stock issue rolling, and he would
be rich beyond his wildest dreams, at least on paper. The SEC

had rules about when an insider could sell off profits. He had a vision of his father rubbing a lemon around the lip of his beer glass, leaving Sean with an unforgettable taste that he still craved.

Liz had convinced Brian to join the party at Le Dome, if for no other reason than to have a good time. Sean said that he didn't mind. Liz discussed the possibility of getting Brian getting involved in the deli. "He's bright, eager, and he hates working at CAA," she told Sean.

Liz and Brian spoke about it as he drove them to Le Dome. "I'm not interested in business like you are. I mean, I am, but I want to be an agent, not the head of some company that looks like it has nothing to do with show business," said Brian.

Liz replied without hesitation, "Look at Ron Meyer. What about all that money Ovitz got from Disney? Don't you see, it's all part of the same thing? Agenting is no longer just agenting. It's more. The world has changed. We're no longer booking agents. We're…we're evolving. The world of agenting is changing and you can either change with it, or be passed by."

"I guess I'll be passed by," said Brian.

"Come on, Brian. Don't be like that," she said. She moved closer and patted his shoulder.

"Sexual persuasion?" he asked.

"If I thought it would help. Brian...Sean is in the business. You know what he's done. He's talking about making movies here. What about Victor Drai?"

"What about him?"

"He produces movies and owns a restaurant. It's just the way things are going. You know a long time ago Hollywood merged with Washington, D.C., and now food is becoming more entertainment oriented. It was only a matter of time. People need more entertainment. It was inevitable, and The Hollywood

Deli is going to be the first and best to really take advantage of an emerging market," she said, trying not to swallow her own words.

"Liz. You sound like one of those pitch guys on the station where you see a talking head on a telephone and a voiceover giving stock advice, with the lips moving out of sync while the voice says something else."

"That bad, huh?"

"Not your best," said Brian.

"Okay. Forget it," said Liz. "But all bullshit aside, it might be a good investment, and Sean is willing to give us shares for some good P.R., and placements with some of the agency people. What can we lose?" She didn't want to tell Brian that she already owned shares with Brantley and more through her work relationship with Linda.

"Dignity?" he answered.

"Since when is dignity something to look for in business?"

"Good point."

"Yeah. You already knew that," she said. "Will you at least think about it?"

"Okay," he answered unconvincingly.

"Good boy."

"Gosh. I feel like I've just pleased mother."

Liz gave him a playful poke in the arm. "Try to have a good time."

"A good time. Yes, I'll try to remember that, mother."

Liz figured that Brian would soon leave CAA, regardless of whether he got a job with The Hollywood Deli or not. She had seen the scenario before; some people don't have the right DNA to be an agent, or anything else in Hollywood, and yet so many tried, and so many were destroyed by trying.

CHAPTER TWENTY-ONE
Ira, Neil, Mel
Neil, Chris
Brian
Dave, Brantley

Ira forwarded his grandfather a first class airline ticket to visit Los Angeles. He had mailed him several letters telling him of the restaurant's incredible success. Sean had sent Mel an extra fifty-thousand dollars as soon as the first new money had arrived. Mel was promised much more and Sean guaranteed that the additional money would be coming. Certainly when the I.P.O. was engineered, Mel would become a millionaire, several times over.

Neil did his best to persuade Ira to let things alone, and not tell his grandfather about the meat. "What's the difference? You'll only make him unhappy. Why do you want to make him miserable? He's happy now, happy that he's going to leave something when he's gone. Don't you know how important that is to him?"

Under normal circumstances, these would have been reasonable arguments, but Ira could not live with himself if he didn't tell his grandfather what had happened.

The night after Mel had arrived in Los Angeles, Ira sat him down in one of the shiny booths, and told him the macabre tale. Neil sat with his arms folded on his chest, contemplating how

all this should be handled. After hearing the story, Mel stared
into Ira's eyes.

Ira pleaded like a child caught with his hand in the cookie
jar. "It wasn't me, zaideh. Neil did it. Once we got started, it
was too late."

"Ira. Don't be so upset with your friend. He was trying to
help you," said Mel.

"I don't believe this. You think this is okay? My own
grandfather is condoning this?" questioned Ira, his face flushed
with confusion.

"Look. If I tell you something, will you stop nudging him
and let him go about his business?" Mel waited for affirmation.

Ira realized that he was clearly the odd man out. He
nodded, having no idea what to expect. The bad dream was only
getting worse.

Mel continued, almost condescendingly. "Things happen in
business. That's the way things are. I know you want to be a
hero, but there are no heroes, only survivors. Many years ago we
had a problem here on the boardwalk."

Neil listened with his mouth open. He might have been as
astonished as Ira.

"There was a gang of black boys that were terrifying the
stores. One night I got my Louisville slugger baseball bat out
from the cellar. Marty Perfors and I trapped the big leader
named Tiny behind the store, and we let him have it. He went
down like a sack of potatoes. Listen. He got what he deserved.
Marty took care of the rest. We boiled him up, stripped the
flesh off his bones and dumped the remains off a boat about five
miles off shore. Nobody ever bothered our businesses again. Ira.
You do what you have to, to make the business work."

"See? What did I tell you? Come on, have some more French
fries," said Neil. Even he wanted to change the subject.

"You want me to have more French fries. My grandfather just told me he used to be a cannibal," said Ira.

"Cannibal, shmanibal. It was business. Hak mir nit in kop!" yelled Mel. He had heard enough.

Ira jumped up from the table and ran outside toward the sand. The emerging full moon lit the beach with twilight shadows. He stared straight ahead, not knowing how or if he could assimilate what he had just heard.

The business at the beach location continued at a steady clip. Neil had left word for Chris that he would need more meat than usual. One night, Chris picked Neil up right on time. Neil left Ira to close up and hopped inside the van. As they drove along the ocean, Neil brought up the new problem.

"I'm giving you all I can," said Chris.

"But we're opening a third place in two weeks. You said you had a friend at USC," said Neil.

"It's too dangerous. Muy peligrosa. I can't do it."

"I thought he was your cousin," said Neil. Before he could finish the sentence, he realized that Chris and his fellow workers always claimed to be related to whomever they recommended.

"You are asking for almost double what I give you now. It is just not possible," said Chris.

The traffic was dense as they neared the Third Street area where a huge promenade and indoor mall went on for blocks.

Chris turned off to zigzag through the darker side streets.

"Okay. How much more do you want?" asked Neil.

"No. It is not dinero. You pay me good," answered Chris.

Even the side streets were packed with pedestrians. Chris tried one of the alleys. "Oh shit!" said Chris. The alley was filled with about a dozen homeless people. He had to maneuver the van around them.

Neil stared outside the window, hoping that he could come up with a solution. Just about the moment that the thought entered his head again, Chis spoke.

"The city doesn't like these people anyway." He turned to see if Neil understood.

Neil turned to face him, and for a moment when their eyes met Neil was struck with fear from the cold sensation that shot out from Chris' dark little circles. Neil retreated from the nearly hypnotic gaze and returned to his most civilized posture. "That's going too far," he said. "That's murder."

Chris turned back to face the road and maneuver the vehicle around two men going through a big green dumpster. "Do you think there is a difference? The soul is almost gone in these people, just like the medical school ones. Whatever part is left, God will be happy to receive. It is one less lost soul to torment on the streets of Santa Monica. Nobody will know. Nobody will care." His diction was clear. He repeated, "Nobody cares about these people. We will send their souls back to their maker."

"What part of Mexico are you from?" asked Neil. He was shocked by Chris' perfect speech.

"I am not from Mexico. I was born in Brazil," said Chris.

Neil really didn't want to know any more. "You're joking, right?" he said, but knew that Chris wasn't. Besides, he had thought the same thing more than once and had even pretended to joke with Ira about it.

Chris volunteered more than Neil needed to know. "My great-grandfather would tell us stories of the last time his village beat to death a robber from another village. The women prepared the body. They threw away the head. The limbs were cut into sections and boiled in a big pot. The insides weren't eaten,

just the fleshy parts. The rump and the chest, those were the
best parts. Everyone had a little. It was part of the culture.
My grandfather told me all the same stories."

How convenient thought Neil. "When was this?" he asked,
playing the role of an investigative anthropologist.

"In the fifties," said Chris. "Maybe early sixties."

Neil thought, *Instead of watching Howdy Doody on Saturday
mornings and Milton Berle on Tuesday nights, this guy's family
was teaching him how to be a cannibal.*

"What do you want to do?" asked Chris. "Jefe," he sang,
laying on an accent. "It's your call."

"I don't think it's such a good idea." Neil was already
thinking about how to accomplish things so that only Chris could
get caught. *Forget it,* he told himself, but he couldn't. His
mind and body were racing. There was something about the process
that excited him. It was so bizarre, yet so practical, and now
Chris was making it all so easily real. Neil was giving in to
some perverse force of nature that would balance out the system.
He laughed to himself at the thought of getting the City of
Santa Monica to actually pay him for getting rid of some of the
homeless.

Not another word was said during the evening ride.

Soon, Neil found dozens of suggestions for euthanasia
cocktails by talking to the anesthesiology residents at UCLA. He
invited the house staff for a free dinner at the deli. About six
or seven showed up, and were eager to spout the best kind of
cocktail for "doing the Kevorkian". One of the most rapid and
consistently reliable ways was to induce a coma with about a
twenty milligram dose of thiopental sodium, also known as
Nesdonal. By increasing the next drug to about a triple dose,
say twenty milligrams of a muscle relaxant like pancuronium
bromide (Pavulon) or twenty milligrams of vecuronium bromide

(Norcuron), the intended result could be achieved easily. That's if intravenous was the desired way to go. Oral methods could use pentobarbital sodium or secobarbital sodium. Oral was not a rapid way to go and needed to be followed by a muscle relaxant as well. With the oral method, there was always a chance that the recipient would vomit. Last, but not least, there was the suppository approach.

Neil decided on a little oral cocktail that could be followed up with an injection. There were many possibilities, all with the same intended result. He settled on some sort of barbiturate cocktail followed by the muscle relaxant. Finding drug sources in Los Angeles was not terribly difficult. Enough medical students and residents had their own undisclosed sources.

A few nights later, Neil and Chris stopped the van next to a man propped up against the side of a building. He was wearing the hood from his tattered ski parka, and was partially covered in a sheet of bubble wrap. Bandages stuck out from inside the covering.

Neil and Chris approached him. A foul odor filled the air from within the protective plastic around the rest of his body. They offered him some food.

"I don't want to eat. I just want to die. Leave me the fuck alone," said the whiskey baritone voice, his face almost hidden inside the parka.

Neil could see long strands of peroxide blonde hair sticking out from inside the hood. "We want to help you," he said.

The man smiled, and laughed at them. "Fuck off!"

"We want to help," said Chris. "I have something that will make you feel great."

The expression triggered a recorded monologue. The man

spoke in a dispassionate, slow, deliberate speech. "I was an Army brat. My father dragged me all over. I never really knew my mother. He left her when I was a kid. She was drunk every time I ever saw her. The first time my father broke my ribs I was maybe eight." He stopped in order to cough.

Neil could see the pain in his face when he coughed. "Drink this, you'll feel better," said Neil.

"I don't want to drink nothin'," was the answer. Despite his remarks, the man took the little container. His hands were lean, making Neil think that he was an excellent choice. "I used to work as a caddy. I worked Brentwood and Hillcrest. I caddied for some famous people. Harpo Marx, Kirk Douglas, Dinah Shore. I was popular. But I have nothing now. I can't walk. I don't want to go back to the V. A. Hospital. They said I'm not going to live more than a few months."

This was music to Neil's ears. He watched as Chris helped the man take a sip from the potion. By the time the man closed his eyes for the eternal slumber, Neil had disappeared outside the end of the alley. He rationalized that they had done a good deed.

Weeks later, as darkness fell earlier than usual, the boardwalk was almost deserted except for a few brave skateboarders who weren't bothered by the unseasonably low temperatures. It was so cold the last few nights that Chris had left his meat supply on ice outside in protected vats. He was opening the last of them when Neil appeared outside with two large garbage bags.

"Amigo. How's it goin'?" It was Neil's usual insincerity.

Chris continued to work and took one more swipe with a meat cleaver on the nearly frozen carcass. "Señor Neil. Listen. I want to talk with you."

"Just give me a minute." Neil hoisted the two bags into a large trash container. He dusted off his hands by rubbing one against the other, and then wiped them on his already soiled apron. "Shoot."

Chris put the meat cleaver down on the mottled concrete. The cleaver glistened in the setting sun, sending a momentarily blinding reflection onto Neil's face. He shaded his eyes, and moved aside to listen.

"Señor Neil. You and I are amigos, right?"

Neil responded without missing a beat. "Of course." He patted the side of Chris's shoulder to emphasize the point.

"I was talking to my cousin about things, and he said I should get a package," said Chris, deliberately waiting for the term 'package' to sink in.

Neil knew what it was all about. "Chris. This isn't IBM. This is just me." He paused for a second. "And Ira. It's just me and Ira. Your cousin is talking about big business. You know. Companies that can give more benefits. There aren't any kind of packages in a little place like this."

Chris's expression soured. "I'm not stupid." There had been articles in a variety of local newspapers announcing the escapades of Dave Stirling and his boasting about the new deli business.

"Nobody said that you were stupid."

"I don't want to get into anything here," said Chris. He suddenly sounded very Hollywood. "I know where you're coming from, but I don't think you get where I'm coming from. I am doing something very special for you, and I want you to do the same for me."

"Look it, Chris." Neil was getting a little worried. Chris knew what was going on. What if he went to the police? He wouldn't do that. He would lose his job at the medical school

and at the tennis club. These guys knew that by making trouble
they would only create problems for themselves. *I'll throw him a*
bone, Neil thought. "When things get going, maybe we can lease a
new delivery truck for the deli, and you could take it home on
the weekends. How about something like that?"

Chris shook his head. "I know the deal."

"You know what deal?"

"I want shares," said Chris. He was way ahead of Neil.

Neil feigned ignorance. "You want shares?"

"Look. You give me shares. I will take the same gamble as
the others," said Chris. "I'll buy my own truck. Or maybe a
BMW."

At first, Neil was shocked, but quickly realized that it
would have been easy for Chris to eavesdrop on any number of
conversations with Sean, Donny, or Ira. Several members of the
Beverly Hills Tennis Club were involved, and investments were a
source of continual conversational and boasting points. Neil
thought how ridiculous the request was. *Yeah, right. I'll give*
him shares. Then his thinking did a one-eighty. He didn't want
any trouble. He rethought all the parameters. It meant nothing
out of pocket. Why not give Chris shares? Linda Stirling had
arranged for Liz to get extra shares. The shares would have no
real value until the I.P.O. materialized, plus it would buy
Chris' silence forever.

"Okay. I'll check it out."

Chris nodded. "Good."

Neil spelled it out. "It's not the usual way to go, but I
don't see why we couldn't get you some shares. You know they may
never be worth anything, and by taking them you may lose out on
raises and other things down the road."

Chris wasn't finished. "That's not the package I want. You
also get me the usual things like a health plan, and a

retirement account, like a Roth IRA. That's what my cousin got on his job, and we have deal."

Neil felt as if he was talking to someone from the Bloomberg business network. "I'll see what I can do. Amigo?" Neil put out his hand to shake.

Chris smiled and shook his hands and then hugged Neil.

Boy. These guys are too smooth, thought Neil.

Chris returned to cleaving the meat. Once Neil disappeared inside, a wide grin formed on Chris's face.

Liz made a point to speak with Brian as often as possible. The tennis club was walking distance from his apartment building on Palm Drive. She insisted that Brian meet her there for lunch and if she could get away from the office, for a drink in the late afternoon.

"Brian. Why don't you just quit the agency business?" she finally asked one day as they sipped vodka martinis before dusk.

"What will I do?" he asked. His voice trembled with fear.

"Brian. You're bright. You're resourceful. You can do whatever you want. Don't get trapped in the business. Get out now. You know it's not for you."

"Yes. I know that, but I'm not able to quit something. If it isn't working, I blame myself, just like with my teeth."

"Come on. There are a few different things you can do if you come to work for the Stirlings."

The ring of it did have some cachet. "What can I do?" asked Brian.

"How about this? I think you'd make a great manager, for starters. But it's more of a ground floor kind of opportunity. It's worth the gamble."

"You sound very convincing."

"Sean liked you at the Le Dome dinner. I'll set it all up for you."

"Okay-okay. But don't be angry with me if I fuck up."

Within a week, Brian interviewed with Sean at his office. During the interview, Brian asked what seemed to him to be an all-important question. "Do you have dental coverage?"

Sean was slow to answer. "Why? You have bad teeth or something?"

Brian revealed his interest in dental hygiene, and lapsed into his tooth-related disappointments.

Sean had found a comrade. "No problem. Until we have a dental plan, you'll see my guy personally. You know, I have moderate periodontitis." It was a proud confession.

"I'm sorry," said Brian.

"No. I'm fine. It wasn't chronic. Mosher San. He's my guy. I'll line it up. He's the best in town. I know all about this stuff. He'll level with you."

Brian was reluctant, but agreed to go for an initial exam. From the second he entered the office, he felt at ease. Dr. San came in to say hello and then suggested that Brian let the hygienist measure the pocket depths of his gum tissue, probing, and then give him a complete scaling and curettage. Dr. San was a movie-star handsome man with dark skin and a slight accent. The whole time the hygienist worked, she reminded Brian that he had good tissue. "You really must take good care of your mouth," she said. This was a switch from the gloom-and-doom to which he had grown accustomed.

"I do," he said proudly. He knew that he shouldn't become too happy. He knew that she was saving it all for the end.

After polishing his teeth she smiled at him. "Well. I don't think there's much of anything there," she announced, while displaying his chart on an overhead computer monitor.

"You don't?" asked Brian in disbelief.

"You had one 'three' in the back, and one little tissue flap over the back of your last molar, but otherwise okay. There might be a small crack in number thirteen, where you have an old silver filling. That's - "

"The upper left bicuspid," interrupted Brian.

"Hey. How'd you know that?"

"Maybe I'm a little obsessive about these things," he said.

"I think it's cool that you take such an interest. Let me call Dr. San. He has to check you before you go," she said. "You're fine," she added as she gently patted him on the head.

Brian realized that all these years he had been doing a decent job, and that the old office had conspired against him to make him think that he had bad gums and was doing a lousy job.

Dr. San spent another few minutes talking about Brian's treatment plan. "You can have your teeth cleaned here about three times a year. That's plenty for you."

"I was going four times, sometimes five, at the other office," said Brian.

"Too much," said Dr. San. "You can go back to your general dentist to have that cracked tooth taken care of, or I can recommend you to someone else." Despite Dr. San's straightforward manner he was still a businessman and wanted to seize on the opportunity to steer a disgruntled patient to one of his own sources of referral.

"I don't know. I definitely don't want to go there for cleanings anymore," said Brian.

"Why don't you go to Sean's general dentist, Mickey Isles?" asked Dr. San.

"Okay. I guess." At that point, Brian really didn't care. He was happy that someone had finally told him that he was doing a good job on his teeth and gums. It was ironic, that when he finally decided to leave CAA, it would end up helping his oral hygiene.

Shortly after that, Sean suggested that Brian try working nights at the deli beach location. Ira and Neil liked having him on board, and were happy to have another pair of hands filling in wherever he was needed. He showed an immediate affinity for hosting the front door and solving problems for customers. By the next week, Brian was working evenings at the Beverly Hills location.

"I'm a deli man!" he would exclaim as he closed the restaurant after midnight each night. "Son of a bitch. Brian, the deli guy." He really loved it.

Within thirty days, he wrote his official resignation letter to the head of CAA. He didn't have to send it up that high, but he took pleasure in expressing his point of view, even if it never was read by the big boss. Brian knew that it probably wouldn't matter one way or the other, but it was his way of 'having closure', the new catchall phrase for being happy after a questionable period of problems.

After months of duplicitous conversations, Dave finally told me that Walter Mirisch had personally gotten back to him about my screenplay. By this point, I was numb to the whole process. I couldn't believe that Dave was still trying to help with *Small Steaks*. As usual, the phone call came between patients.

Dave read to me from his notes. I was uncomfortable with the fact that Walter went through Dave, without contacting me.

It all seemed so convoluted. I thought I was done with the Mirisch thing.

"He said he didn't like it," began Dave.

I felt a dagger pierce the tissue outside my heart.

Dave continued as if he were Hans Blix describing his assessment of inspections in Iraq. "Doesn't really cover the two guy relationship. Basically just describes characters and nothing else. Doesn't deal with problems or create them. All just character. Need more of a plot and a story. Don't understand why the main character is putting up with the girl. You have to balance plot more with the character. He doesn't want to pass on it, but really can't do anything with it unless you rewrite it."

Dave sent the Mirisch handwritten notes to me. I kept it with my rejection letter collection. The gist of the letters was consistent, while generally less descriptive than the Mirisch one. Mirisch or someone who worked for him had actually read my script.

The regular rejections were piling up.

"I have reviewed the material and determined that it is not something that we would be interested in pursuing."

"Good luck in setting up the project."

"So and so has reviewed your script, and has indicated that he is not interested in the subject matter, therefore I am returning it to you.

"Best of luck with this project."

In hindsight, I would have been better off with this: "Give up. You have no idea what you are doing. Maybe some psychiatric help will cure you of this mad escapade."

I thought more about my book idea, a collection of characters, conversations, and intersecting plots without a major hero. Maybe if I succeeded as a sympathetic character   -

someone trying to survive against insurmountable odds in
Hollywood - that would help. But I knew that there was nothing
terribly appealing about me or my life. I would have to just
report the experiences, and hope that what I witnessed or was
told by others would be interesting enough to please a reader.
Whatever happened to Sean still seemed important, since he was
at the other end of the Hollywood spectrum from someone like me,
and represented the struggle from within the industry. I knew
the book could never fit a conventional format. Ironically,
Mirisch's comments fueled me to work harder on compiling
information for the book.

CHAPTER TWENTY-TWO

Dave

Sean

Frank

Heather

The obituary reported stated coldly that Dave Stirling had
died from some rare virus. Nobody knew for sure, not even the
family. Dr. K. said it was the result of a degenerative
neurological disease, one only recently discovered. It made no
sense to anyone, since Dave was still quite young for sixty-
five, and although he had been complaining about fatigue, nobody
ever thought that he was that sick. Only Linda doubted the great
Dr. K., suggesting that he had flat out missed the diagnosis. By
the time he and his team of consultants got it right, it was too
late. For nearly two years, Dr. K. kept saying something about a
variant of Epstein-Barr virus (EBV).

Within a week after Dave's death, Dr. K. and his wife set
up his memorial. The big event was held inside the new Kodak
Theater, home of the Academy Awards. One speaker after another
took his place at the podium. A former Dean at USC, the head of
Nutrition at Cedars-Sinai Hospital, movie stars, and elder
entertainment moguls who still owned large chunks of the studios
all spoke. One speech after another had the same central theme.
Dave had made money for all of them.

Not one person spoke of love. Maybe for them, love was money. Even Sean spoke about the deals, and hardly mentioned the man. He told how Dave had once stood up at a meeting and challenged people to match his charitable donation, or otherwise he would rescind it. There was a rumor that Dave even gave personal guarantees to several of the deli investors. A lot of men in business did that sort of thing to satisfy their own egos. At face value, a rather generous offer, but if things didn't pan out by a certain date Dave would have to buy back the investment, picking up more stock in the deli. The investor would be out only the missed interest. But, it gave Dave more control. By covering their losses, he in effect controlled more stock than would have otherwise been allowed by the SEC after the company went public. Up until his death, Dave had been running the entire financial show for the delis.

The Stirling family followed the instructions in Dave's will. He left his body to medical science, providing that he would be cremated and the ashes returned to his family for a ceremony at the famous Hillside mortuary, home of Al Jolson and numerous stars and power brokers from Southern California.

At a Friday night Kaddish service with Linda, Sean asked why they weren't going to the cemetery. "The body is over at UCLA," said Linda. "Something about an autopsy. The instructions were in his will."

Sean wanted to tell her, but he couldn't bring himself to warn her. If he did, he would have to expose the meat source for the deli. Most recently, they had started using some conventional sources, but nobody had told Chris to actually curtail his activities.

Later that week, Sean sat quietly in his usual booth by the window at Kate Mantilini, the very popular destination for show biz types, only two blocks from the Motion Picture Academy of Arts and Sciences. His mind was jumbled by his confusion about love and the needs of the new business. He knew where Linda stood. She would back him up, and that's why he loved her. She didn't judge him by what he did, but by who he was, and always saw his real soul buried deep within the tarnished layers.

Sean's daughter Katherine waved as she entered the room after passing through the rather ordinary front door. He rose from his seat and beamed.

Moments after they ordered, Sean got right to the point. "Katherine. I really want your opinion on something."

"Anything, Dad," she answered in all sincerity.

"What would you say if I told you that there was something really terrible about my new business, something horrible, something that is beyond - ?" He stopped himself, because he didn't know how to express it, without actually saying what it was.

"Dad. What's the matter? You look terrible," Katherine said.

"I've been working very hard on this. Between the movies and the restaurant, I just don't have much time to myself." He paused and had a sip of lemon beer. He thought of switching to a Bloody Mary.

"The horrible thing. Can it be corrected?" she asked.

"It can in the long run, but something horrible has already taken place."

"Dad. You always told me that business is business, and that we should never be ashamed for anything we do in order to see a business deal through, so long as we don't break any laws, at least laws where you can get caught."

"Did I say that?" He laughed.

So did Katherine. "Dad. What is it?"

He shook his head. "I can't tell you. You'll think less of me."

"Okay. If you can't tell me, how can I answer?" she asked.

"You already have."

"You always said that all's fair in love and war and making a buck, and you're just making a buck, right?"

Sean realized that his daughter was trying to be supportive of him, of the things he had told her all her life, but he knew that she wasn't being herself, not after all her morality talks.

After meeting with Katherine, Sean realized that Linda would be the right one to tell. One night during dinner at the Beverly Hills Hotel, Sean began to tell Linda, but only alluded to serving unusual meat. "I just had to tell someone. It's been eating at me and eating at me. I had to tell someone."

"I don't want to know any more. So you've been buying lousy meat. It's not the first time I've heard that. My grandfather was practically giving away chicken lunches in his stores. I'm sure it wasn't the best poultry, but nobody ever got sick. Besides, the lunch counters were right next to the pharmacy," said Linda, trying to lighten up Sean's mood.

"That's not it. I wish it were. The meat was a good quality. Well, what I mean is that the meat was fine, it's where it came from," said Sean.

"I don't get what you're saying." Linda tapped her fingers on the table.

"Well. Let me think of how to say this. It was - " He paused. "You're right. It's no big deal."

For a split second Linda entertained the idea that Sean was really too weak to run this type of company. He was acting more nervous and less in control. It worried her on two levels. She was concerned for Sean personally, but also had the new responsibility of protecting her father's estate, which included a lot of stock in the deli.

Frank didn't hear another word said by his money manager over the car speakerphone. He didn't even blink when it was suggested that he sell his black Bentley Turbo and the customized Hummer.

As Frank drove, his anger grew. It was the only emotion he knew when he felt that life had cheated him. His life experiences had left him disillusioned and embittered. Cheated by his father and by his brother. It was their fault that Frank never became as successful as them. They stopped him. They put him down, and he had spent most of his adult life trying to show them that he could

be a player, too. He had lost. It was those damned big birds. They had let him down, after Frank had cared for them so well.

Frank parked his car in front of the main house on the expansive property. He walked over to a corral where a solitary ostrich was grazing, following a day of shots to keep it healthy. Frank stared at the bird for what seemed like a long time. He couldn't believe it was all over. He was broke.

He remembered turning his collar up and trying to close the top button on his shirt. Was it five minutes ago or was he there longer? He glanced at his watch. He had been staring at the ostrich for about fifteen minutes.

He ambled back to the house. Once inside, he checked the food supply. The refrigerator was stocked with prepared foods from Gelson's grocery. An open bottle of California Chardonnay was being cooled in the refrigerator. The red Palmer was also opened and breathing.

Frank took a bottle of pills from his pants pocket. He took one, and washed it down with a glass of Chardonnay. While he

sipped his wine, he dialed a number on the telephone. "Heather.
It's Frank," he announced.

She did her best to sound sincere. "Yes. Frank. Oh, yes.
How are you, darling?"

"Listen. I got the pills. I popped one just before I
called."

"Well. That does sound interesting. Do they work?"

"I don't know, but if they do, maybe you and I will head
over to Viagra Falls."

Heather laughed. "That's funny, Frank."

"I know. I heard a few others that are real winners. Get
your behind over here, and we can have a little show and tell.
Hey. I think it's working already. Is it possible?"

"How should I know? Give me about an hour and a half," she
said.

"An hour and a half?" he moaned.

"Frank. It's got to be at least an hour in the car if I hit
any traffic."

"Get here as soon as you can."

"Okay, darling. See you later."

Frank drank a second glass of wine and decided to take a
second Viagra pill. He never believed in taking the recommended
dose of anything. He marched to the liquor cabinet and removed a
bottle of Jack Daniels. He yanked the cork off of the bottle and
took a swig on his way to the glassware, which was stored in a
floor-to-ceiling mahogany cabinet.

Moments later, he sat inside the living room of the long
ranch home, in front of the burning logs, staring at the moose
head that adorned the wall above the fireplace mantle. He wasn't
much of a drinker, but tonight he sipped from a Waterford shot
glass with only one purpose in mind, to shut down his brain and
get some relief from his agony.

So far, it wasn't working. It was only dredging up horrible memories of his father's voice, a voice that never brought comfort, only fear, criticism, and a continual sense of his overbearing self-importance.

"That Begley kid is smart," was all Frank's father said, years ago when Frank was younger, after attending a birthday party for Milton Berle's adopted son.

A lot of celebrity parents had attended with their sons. The Fords were naturally invited since they were one of the wealthy local families that made up the cornerstone of Beverly Hills.

Frank knew that Ed Begley, Jr. was smarter than he was, but that wasn't the point. All Frank's father could do was carry on about Ed, Jr. To Frank's ears, it meant that he must be stupid or that he had disappointed his father in some unspoken way.

Frank kept his lips to the bourbon, sticking his tongue in the liquid in order to feel a little stinging sensation. He mumbled to himself as his thoughts wandered, layering harsh memories one on top of the other until rage began to bubble up from the dismal emotional cauldron of Frank's life.

Frank rose and walked to the kitchen to locate the paper report that had triggered the earlier phone call to his financial manager. When he had arrived earlier, he had left it on the walnut island counter. He read the last paragraph out loud. "On the basis of the review we made this month, the best course of action would be to sell the farm. At this point, you can cut your losses by breaking even on the real estate, leaving you with an actual loss of five million dollars, based on your initial investment and operating costs. We have two brokers who can market the sale of the equipment, and are presently looking into the sale of the ostriches. There is one firm in Canada that has expressed some interest and we suggest that you accept any firm offer."

Frank was worth a lot less money than anyone could have imagined. He received trust disbursements - enough cash flow to cover his expenses. Frank's father had given full shares of the family company proceeds to his brother and cousins. But, not to Frank.

"Fucking accountants. God-damned fucking accountants!" Frank ran from the kitchen and threw the papers in the fire. There was no way Frank was ready to give up his ostriches.

He lost his footing for a second, falling to one side, but regained his balance by placing one hand on the corner of the thick leather sofa. He clumsily staggered back to his chair, picked up the bottle of Jack, and headed outside.

"Don't do that. Only schmucks do that," he heard his father say.

He remembered the first time that he had heard his father call him a schmuck. Frank had been trying to get a screw into a hole that had been started by his father. He was only eight-years-old, and didn't have the strength to tighten the screw any further. Frank took a hammer and tried to pound the screw into the wood. The system was working until the screw was close to the wood, and then it wouldn't go in any further.

"Hey. Don't do that, you schmuck!" His father laughed as he took the hammer away from Frank.

Frank was still angry at the ostrich. He staggered back to the corral, sipping his bourbon. Once at the corral, he stopped and stared. The moon was bright in the sky, and a few stars twinkled over the perverse western wilderness. A yellow hue from a tall halogen light illuminated the corner of the corral.

His father's voice trailed him. "Frank. You're a dreamer. A dumb dreamer, like your mother. At least your mother knew her

place and did a fine job of bringing up you and your brother.
But Frank, you know you're never going to make a dime on your
own, so you might as well come work for me."

That was Frank's only job offer, which he took and
regretted his decision the rest of his life. He let his father's
words run his life, and make him into a failure on so many
levels.

Frank drank from the bottle as he yelled over to the
ostrich in the corral. "I'll get even with you little bastards,"
he said as he walked toward the enclosure. His mind was a dark
cloud, and his thoughts were twisted. "You disgust me, and I'm
going to get even."

Frank started to sweat and flail his arms about as he
spoke. He felt any rational thought slip away, and he let his
fury take over his inebriated mind. "Don't laugh at me. Don't
you eyeball me. You think you've won. You haven't won anything.
Old Frank is still going strong."

Frank's vision blurred for a second or two and he steadied
himself on one of the corral posts. He opened the gate to the
corral and moved alongside the ostrich.

"Frank always has the last word," he said. He pulled the
leash on the ostrich closer to the stanchion, so that the
ostrich's lateral movements were somewhat inhibited.

"I'll show you. You want to fuck with old Frank. Well, then
let's see how well you can handle this."

Frank opened his belt buckle and slid his pants down around
his calves. He reached inside his shorts and felt his throbbing
penis. "Well now. Old Little Frank is back." He grabbed the
sides of the ostrich and tried to ram himself inside.

"Take it in the ass you reprehensible piece of shit!" he
screamed.

He lost his footing as the ostrich flailed and tried to shift to one side. He felt dizzy. He used his right hand to cushion his fall as he hit the ground. The ostrich's leg moved with blinding speed, and caught Frank hard on the side of his head. He laughed as hard as he could as he rolled away. The next thing he knew, he was flat on his back, dreaming about his childhood girlfriend with a few buttons on her white blouse undone, lying on the back seat of his mother's Chrysler Imperial.

Frank remained on the ground near the ostrich. Blood ran freely from the side of his head. His only pair of Ferragamo loafers were covered with mud, and his gabardine trousers from The Polo Store in Beverly Hills were twisted and locked around his ankles like a pair of leg irons. They were his two most expensive articles of clothing; things that he had purchased to impress Heather. He glanced to his side and could only focus on the ostrich's right eye. It was the last thing he saw before blacking out.

Soon, Heather pulled up to the front of the house. She wore black low-rise jeans with a white blouse tied in a knot a little above her waist. She left the keys in her new yellow Jaguar convertible, leased to Frank through one of his friend's businesses.

"Frank. Frank. I'm here," she shouted as she opened the front door.

Heather skipped around the house, stopping to help herself to a glass of the Chardonnay. She exited the house through the kitchen door, sipping her wine as she strolled. She could see the light on near the corral, but went back inside to take one of the large portable Magna Lights that were used by the staff.

Outside a minute later she yelled, "Frank. Are you out there?" as she walked slowly toward the corral. She could see the ostrich, tied to the post. Frank's body blended in with the corral, just out of reach of the light. It wasn't until she was right on top of the post that she saw Frank.

"Frank. Are you drunk?" she asked.

She put her glass down and entered the corral. She poked Frank in the side with her foot. "Oh, my. Has my little Frankie had a stroke or a heart attack? My, oh, my," she said as she sighed. She picked up her wineglass and rushed back to the house.

Once inside, she dialed 911, and told them that she thought Frank had fallen or something from a heart attack. While she waited for the police and ambulance to arrive she made another call. "Hi. Bob. It's Heather. Fine. Fine...Right...I can make it after all...Right...I'll be done here in about an hour or so...I just have a few things to attend to...No. I don't care where we go...Anyplace...Spago would be better than Mastro's. You can get in, can't you?...Good...I'll just meet you there in a couple of hours or so...Right...Thanks. You're a doll."

After the call, she went into the kitchen. There was a piece of Gelson's poached salmon sitting all by itself on the refrigerator's center shelf. Frank had probably intended to serve it as an appetizer. By the time she heard the ambulance siren, she had devoured the salmon with a second glass of wine.

Heather quickly went into Frank's private office. The papers on his desk were for his investment in the Hollywood Deli. Heather swept the papers off the desk and into a little shopping bag from Gelson's. She folded the bag into small sections, and jammed it inside her black Fendi purse.

The next day, the obituary in the *Los Angeles Times* said that Frank had died from a fall while working at his ranch.

The conversation in the card room at Hillcrest Country Club continued into the next week.

"I spoke to the coroner myself," said Robert.

"He's dead," said Chuck. "Leave it alone."

"You're going to like this one," said Robert.

"He's going to tell us whether we want to hear it or not," said Stanley.

"One of the ostriches kicked him in the head," said Robert, holding back his laughter.

Chuck tried not to smile, but did, ever so slightly, and then pronounced that "that's an awful way to go".

"What about this? His zipper was open and his dick was hanging out," said Robert.

Stanley got up and left the room.

Chuck could no longer control his laughter. Robert laughed, too.

"Go get Stanley. I'll deal the cards," said Robert. "And see if you can get that new guy, the dentist, A.B. whatshisname to sit in. We're going to need another player with Frank gone," said Robert.

"I wonder if we can buy up Frank's shares in that Hollywood Deli deal," said Chuck.

"Why would you want more?" asked Stanley. "Didn't you buy a whole private share initially?"

"I hear from Dave's daughter that this thing is going to be super big," said Chuck. "Super big," he repeated.

For the next few minutes, the card game continued without any discussion. Chuck had dropped a bomb with the key phrase "super big". The 'insider link' line meant that more big money was being lined up to keep the expansion afloat. No more discussion was necessary or appropriate. They had all been part of the drill before. The less said, the better. If either of them were ever interviewed for any improprieties, they would have nothing to tell the SEC.

CHAPTER TWENTY-THREE
Brantley
Sean, Brantley
Sean, Gary, Bob
Ricky, Brantley

For reasons completely unknown to me, I was soon working
hard on *Beverly Hills Cannibals*. I tried to spend as much time
as I could in Beverly Hills, making sure that the screenplay had
an authentic look and feel. I was determined to make the most
out of what seemed like my last opportunity – every opportunity
felt as if it were the last. It was a far cry from what I had
originally envisioned about being a screenwriter, but it was a
start. I labored over the setup before submitting the scenes to
Sean a second time.

INT. SPAGO. NIGHT

The elegant restaurant is filled to capacity. Glamorous
people pace the bar area, waiting to be seated. A MAN in a
business suit argues with the HOSTESS. She is young and
looks like a fashion model, as do half the people at the
bar. They are in the middle of an argument.

                    MAN
I called twice this week. I even had my secretary
call. What are you trying to say, that after all that,
you don't have a table?

                    HOSTESS
                 (annoyed)
Mr. Mosk. I can have a table for you in about two
hours. Do you care to wait or would you like to come
back later?

                    MR. MOSK
I don't understand. We called and accepted an early
reservation for six-thirty and so…and so what, we
arrived at six what, six thirty-one? Come on. This
isn't right.

The Hostess cocks her head to one side in order to clear
the hair that was blocking her view of the room. She
glances across the room, as if she were looking for an
empty table.

                    HOSTESS
As you can see, we are just overbooked.

Mr. Mosk reaches into his pocket and takes out a folded
twenty-dollar bill. He folds it a second time and places it
in the Hostess' hand.

                    MR. MOSK
Please see what you can do.

HOSTESS
I'll do my best.

She stares over his head, a signal for him to go away so
that she could deal with the group waiting behind him.

As Mr. Mosk walks away, he mumbles loud enough for
everyone to hear.

MR. MOSK
I've been eating in this damn restaurant since day
one. You'd think Puck would treat his clientele
better.

I had written several scenes similar to that one, some more
pleasant than Mr. Mosk's experience, but I felt that that one
captured the spirit of the local Beverly Hills dining patrons.
The intent was to set up the evening of the big earthquake, to
show what was going on in town when the big one struck.

After submitting the new pages, I was summoned to meet with
Sean at the Grill. That time I got to eat something - overcooked
pasta and a gristly steak. Some chefs punish anyone who orders
steak medium or medium-well. At this joint, I was chastised
quickly for asking that my steak be "on the well side" of
medium, with the reinforcement coming later from the chef in the
form of the worst cut of meat he could find.

Sean initially sounded professorial. "First of all, it's
too long. Second of all, I told you not to do that kind of
insightful bullshit opening. The tone is thrown off, although

it's a decent start for establishing the theme." Then he became
curt. "Tits and ass. That's the restaurant scene."

"But I put in the model like you suggested," I said.

"It's all too long. The earthquake has to happen around
page twenty-five. Better at page twenty. Even sooner. Maybe even
five minutes into the movie, boom! All hell breaks loose. Lock
it in earlier."

I thought that Sean was clearly wrong. I was sure that the
setup in movies like the *Poseidon Adventure* was much longer, and
contributed to making the world of the story abundantly clear.

"Don't you think we should finish the screenplay first, and
then decide how long to make the setup scenes?" I asked.

Sean stared at me. His face became expressionless. "No, but
I shouldn't have to answer an asshole question like that. Let's
get something straight. This screenplay is going to be no more
than one hundred and ten pages."

"But I thought the rule of thumb is one-twenty."

Sean continued to stare. "No. Now you made me say it
twice." He picked at a chicken Caesar salad. "This has got way
too much cheese. Sort of like your writing."

I hoped that he wasn't going to stop in order to complain
to a waiter. "I read a copy of *Moonstruck*. That was way over
one-fifty." I wanted Sean to know that I had been studying as
much as possible.

"I don't believe that, but what's the difference? Look.
Kid. It's about a minute a page, but we're going to have to show
the earthquake and how it affected each of the setups. We
haven't even decided who the main survival group is going to be.
And the stakes have to be crystal clear."

"You mean it's not the people I've written in for Spago?"

"It could be. I mean we have to pick no more than five people that will be involved in the cannibal act. And I don't think the sous chef from Spago should be part of it."

I remembered that Sean had originally told me that the earthquake would occur when people were stuck in their homes or in restaurants. He wanted nothing to do with schools or hospitals.

"Do you want to show the earthquake at Spago or just after dinner, like in the people's houses?" I asked.

"I think both. Think about it. What's worse? Being trapped in this elegant restaurant, and wondering if the last thing you were ever going to do was watch some movie star get hit over the head by a falling pillar while eating lox on a pizza. But the people at home, that's a little more typical. I want one of the people at home to have an upset stomach. I want him angry. He's just spent over two hundred bucks for dinner and now he's in the can. Sick and angry. and then the earthquake hits."

"This is a character we don't like? Not our protagonist?"

"Sort of. He turns out to be moral in the end. He helps save people or something. But in the beginning, the guy is a bastard in his office. Make him an attorney. No. There are too many bad attorneys in the movies. Why not make him a plastic surgeon? Yes. A prick plastic surgeon, who does boob jobs and Botox and the like all day and eats dinner at Spago. That's the ticket…Dr. Sugar. Call him Dr…" He paused, fishing for the brilliant creation. "Dr. Sugar…Dr. Daniel Sugar."

Sean watched as I made copious notes on a yellow legal pad that was attached to a clipboard.

"So?" asked Sean, drawing out the word.

I looked up. He had a puzzled expression on his face.

"So?" he mimicked himself. "That's a great name, isn't it?"

I responded with little enthusiasm. "I guess so."

"You don't like it. It's perfect. Dr. Daniel Sugar. Can't you hear it on those Dolby speakers in the movie theater, blasting out into the room the first time one of his patients or a nurse better says the name. 'Dr. Daniel Sugar.' It's just got that, I don't know, that right sound to it." He paused. "If you don't like it, call him whatever you want." And with that, Sean returned his focus to his salad.

I knew by then that naming characters wasn't really up to me. I was beginning to feel that little if anything I said mattered. There was only one thing that I knew was for certain. I was writing Sean's screenplay for him, and the experience was making me feel more like a personal secretary than a writer, sometimes worse than dealing with Ricky.

Sean and I spoke for almost an hour. Toward the end of the meeting, Sean finally got back to the scene I had actually written.

"You can't make fun of Spago. That's not what it's all about. Have the character treated royally. This movie isn't about bad service in Spago. It's about something else."

"But I've been there. This is what really happens," I said. I buried my head in my crumbled New York cheesecake. I hadn't been eating it, only twiddling it with my fork. The waiter soon removed the mess I had made out of the dessert.

"Brantley. We're making a movie, not a documentary about Beverly Hills. You have to trust me on this. Nobody wants to see a movie where a guy doesn't get his table for dinner. Look. This is only the setup. We want to show the glamour, the excess, the great life that all these people have before they eat each other. If the guy has trouble getting his table, what the fuck has that got to do with an earthquake and people eating each other in order to survive?"

I was so exhausted by that point, I agreed. And the question did not appear to be unreasonable. "Okay. I'll change the scene again." I felt as if my thinking had become transformed and similar to Data of Star Trek fame.

"Good. Because Wolfie is a friend of mine. He plays tennis at Jerry Weintraub's house. I want to keep on good terms with both of them," added Sean. He sipped a double decaf espresso. "They have great espresso here."

Then I spoke again, not wanting to give in entirely. "What if we don't call it Spago? What if it's just a restaurant? Any restaurant."

"That's a very interesting idea, but I like the idea of shooting it in Spago. I don't know that we'll eventually shoot it there, but let's not waste any more time on this. Agreed?" Sean sounded slightly agitated.

"Fine," I said. I knew I couldn't win, but felt better that I had expressed my opinion, which Sean obviously deemed worthless.

"Do you want some dessert? They have great cheesecake here."

I decided not to remind him that I already had tried one. "No. Thank you. I'd better get going and do the rewrites," I said.

"Okay. You can take off. I've got the check," said Sean. "Here. Take this."

Sean handed me back the pages. While I put the papers in my folder, Sean signaled to a waitress for the check. He said, "Some of the other stuff is okay."

Ever since I invested in The Hollywood Deli, Sean had begun picking up tabs. I would have preferred to think that it had something to do with my writing, but it clearly wasn't. What did

I expect? The deli deal put me in a different perspective, having come up with hard cash, mostly borrowed from Liz.

"This could be a major credit for you," said Sean. "Absolutely fucking major. I was talking to Bob and Gary and it looks like we might go as high as ten million for this one. It's going to look great."

"It's very exciting for me. I just hope it all works out," I said.

"It will, boychick. It will. Go. Bring me back some brilliant writing."

At the next meeting, Sean appeared subdued. He was preoccupied with the newest Hollywood Deli, set to open in West Hollywood on Sunset Boulevard, not far from the original Spago on Horn. I took Sean's sedate behavior as a sign that the screenplay was coming along better.

We sat in the lobby bar of the Four Seasons Hotel on Doheny. I sipped a martini and Sean had his now usual beer. This time he asked for a lemon and a lime on the side.

A group of what I took to be rap musicians sat across from us on sofas surrounding a heavy coffee table. The waitresses were all abuzz, making extra stops around the portly leader. Later, I would see the boys pour their entourage into customized vans, guarded by suspiciously over-dressed members of the Armani army.

Sean showed a deeper, more detailed, legitimate concern. "I want to read that scene again. This is the one where everyone is devastated. The power is out, and the water supply is shut off. Now the announcement comes over public radio that somebody or something has dumped anthrax toxin into the food supply."

I had hit another plot problem. "That's the part I don't understand, either." Sean, like with everything else, didn't recall that he had told me to construct it that way. "It won't get into the whole food supply."

He was finally relinquishing some control. "You figure it out. Make it a toxin that spreads or something. Make it science fiction. I don't care. Just make it so they have no food. I want them to have the proper motivation for eating each other. Make it worse. Make it botulism and anthrax. Then you don't have to go the sci-fi route. It's something that could really happen. Haven't you heard of all the false alarms that have been called in last year with the anthrax thing? It's a real possibility. Do it that way. It will be more believable. We're really on to something here. Don't you feel it?"

"Yes." My response was muted.

Sean went over the story, again. Each time, it was a little different, but there was no doubt that he would eventually end up with something that pleased him, and made him feel like the creator. "Make sure you have the part with the botulism and then the anthrax. I want the first person eaten to be one of the maids. As bodies get scarce, then they start eating the rich people."

I couldn't argue with the logic. I worked out the scenes as discussed with Sean.

EXT. DR. SUGAR MANSION. BEVERLY HILLS. DUSK

DR. SUGAR is standing outside the main house with MR. MOSK. In the BACKGROUND we can see the other organizers doling out a box of scones from Starbucks.

        DR. SUGAR
We eat the help first.

                    MR. MOSK

That's right. Everyone except Claire. She's been with me
for years.

Dr. Sugar winks.

                    DR. SUGAR

I know what you mean.

                    MR. MOSK

Why don't we agree on a process? The ones
with green cards will be eaten first.

                    DR. SUGAR

We'll go door to door. There'll be plenty to go
around. But why start with the green cards? Shouldn't
we do this with some form of democracy?

                    MR. MOSK

That's right. If we survive, we don't want anyone
to hold this against us. Your point is a good one.
Illegal aliens will be consumed first. Then the green
cards, and if we run out of food we will have to eat
U.S. citizens. But only then.

                    DR. SUGAR

Come on. Let's tell the others about our plan.

                                  CUT TO:

EXT. SUGAR BACKYARD

CLAIRE, Mr. Mosk's longtime housekeeper and lover overheard the conversation. She steps out from behind the shrubs. She reaches into a knapsack and takes out a small microcassette recorder. She has the conversation on tape.

For the next meeting, Sean picked the upstairs bar lounge at Mastro's. I was getting taken to all the 'company' hangouts. The experience pushed all the right ego buttons. *Hey. Look at me. I'm talking about my screenplay.*

Sean suggested that we split the Kansas City steak. "It's too early for dinner. I can have them slice it, like an appetizer." He insisted that we also drink single malt Scotch. No arguments from me.

"I think the script is coming along fine," said Sean.

"I'm glad you like it." I didn't know what else to say.

"I'll have Gary read through it one more time, and make some editing notes for you."

I bristled at the idea of having Gary make more changes in the story. We had never done it that way before. "I didn't know that Gary did the final editing work for you."

"Gary's the best. I would never go ahead until he approved the script. What's the problem?"

"No problem." My voice had given me away.

"Brantley. This is how we get a good product. Screenplays are written by committee. You should be glad you're not at one of the big studios. The script would have already been rewritten a dozen times. Who knows? In the end your name might not even be on it."

"It's just that we spent so much time on this already."

"Time? This is nothing. What has it been? A few months. That's all. People spend years writing these things. You've got a crash course here, and for free. I've already got the investors in line for this one. We can probably start shooting it in a few months. And pretty soon after that you'll be at the premiere and see your name on the credits. You've got nothing to worry about."

I listened to Sean's talk about the big money investors and the actors who would appear in the movie. Occasionally, Sean threw in expressions like "overseas distribution" to spice up the dialogue. By that time, I had a sinking feeling in my gut. Sean had nothing in place, and needed the script finished in order to sell the movie to investors. That made more sense. People wanted to see a finished script, not a few scenes. Whatever the realities, I was glad to see that the process was coming to an end. I was also glad that I had the notion early on to put all of what had transpired down in a book. The book was starting to appear more viable, but I had to question who would care about or believe my experiences in Hollywoodland.

After our meeting, Sean drove back to his office. When he arrived, Bob was holding court. He had just returned from the Sundance Film Festival - the big extravaganza held each year in Park City, Utah. Sean handed Bob a copy of *Beverly Hills Cannibals*.

Sean said, "It's ready to fix."

Bob said, "There was this guy who made a slasher movie, *Coven*, Mark Borchardt. But this other guy, Chris Smith, makes a documentary about the other guy making his slasher movie. Hey. It was good P.R."

"Did you see the movies?" asked Gary.

"Yes, dumb nuts. I do go to the movies when I'm there," said Bob. "And don't give me that sarcastic tone shit."

"I thought it was so you could hit on all the chicks," said Sean.

"That too," said Bob. "It shouldn't be a total loss."

"I liked one about this Jewish woman who meets this guy up in the Catskills," said Bob.

"Sure. With all the good stuff you pick the most mainstream," said Gary.

"I guess I've gone mainstream," said Bob.

"Did you see the Tim Roth movie?" asked Sean.

"Yeah. I walked out. I'm not a big fan of graphic incest," said Bob.

"Just a little fan," said Gary.

"Right," said Bob. "Anyone got a cigarette?"

"I put a carton in your desk drawer last Monday," said Sean.

"That was last Monday," said Bob.

"I thought you were cutting down," said Sean.

"I am," said Bob.

"Look in the first aid kit. I hid a few extras there," said Gary.

"My hero." Bob opened the bottom drawer of a file cabinet and took out a small plastic box. He located a pack of cigarettes amongst the band aids. He tore open the top of the pack. He rushed to light cigarette. He was already inhaling his first puff before the flame disappeared on his purple disposable lighter. "Sean. I don't know if you heard about *Ravenous*," he said as he exhaled the smoke into the room.

"Open a window," said Gary. He rose and moved to the other side of the room.

"Just turn up the air conditioning. It's on low. Put the fan on high," said Bob.

"What's the deal with *Ravenous*?" asked Sean.

"Cannibals," said Bob.

"Cannibals?" asked Sean.

"Yeah. Antonia Bird. Cannibals," said Bob.

"So what? My movie won't be ready for a year. It makes no fucking difference to me."

"Minimum," said Gary.

"I thought I'd mention it. Don't shoot the messenger," said Bob.

Sean spoke with finality. "All cannibal movies are derivative. There is no such thing as an original cannibal movie. It won't have any effect on our chances." With that, he left the room, satisfied that his pronouncement was accepted.

"What's he pissed about?" asked Bob.

"He doesn't like you smoking in the office," said Gary.

"Tough petunias." Bob puffed away.

"He owes three months rent," said Gary.

"I know. And there's nothing going on," said Bob.

"Sean offered us some shares in his deli company, in lieu of rent," said Gary.

"Take it. You know Sean. That means he has no intention of paying the rent. So just take the shares. It's better than nothing."

"But you know they're worthless," said Gary. "It's all paper profit."

Bob rolled his eyes up and then moved his head in circles. "Dats right Kingfish. You're not getting me into one of these serious conversations, are you? Let me read through this piece of crap."

"Okay. Is that the cannibal script?'

"Yeah. Why?"

"Sean wants me to read it when you're through," said Gary.

"Sure. Do you want me to make notes on it like I always do for you?" Bob began flipping through the script.

"Please. And highlight those scenes that you think are important, so I can get the general idea," said Gary.

"You got it, boss. And Gary?"

"Yes."

"Don't ever bother me about the rent again. Next time, take whatever it is Sean is proposing. That's what always happens. It will help cut down on my stress level."

"Yes, darling. Is there anything else I can do for you or can I go back to my desk now?"

The telephone rang. "Hello. Production," said Bob. "Gary stepped out for a while. Who should I say is calling? Brantley Benjamin. Brantley, how the hell are you? Great. I'll have Gary call you back when he gets in…sure…right…take care." He hung up.

"Call him back tomorrow and tell him I'm on a location, out of town," said Gary. "Set up some kind of story meeting. You know the drill."

"Check," said Bob. He inhaled deeply and hid his head in his hands.

"What's the matter?"

"I don't know. Last night I was so desperate I watched an infomercial. After five minutes, I realized I had seen it before."

"I actually find them more entertaining than some regular programming. I like to watch George Foreman. To me it's just as entertaining as watching a cooking show like that guy, what's his name?"

"What guy?"

"The guy from New Orleans."

"Emerson?" Bob knew the proper name.

"That's right. Emerald, or something."

"Whatever. I know what you mean."

"And that guy who's been doing it for years. The Pocket Fisherman guy."

"I know him. Ron Popeil. He's a hoot, isn't it?"

"Yeah. I saw this show where he was cooking all this stuff in this little, bitty kind of convection oven or something. He does get into it, doesn't it?"

"Yeah. What are we going to do about this script? It sucks, you know." Bob easily recognized it as Sean's scene structure.

"I know. I guess we'll have to have the story meeting with the Doc, and make some suggestions."

"He's green at this. Do you think he'll go for it?"

"Look. Sean wants to stick with him. The script can be fixed. It's not that bad, right?"

"The guy can write, but these kinds of movies don't need a writer. Look at this section, where someone is talking about an article in *The New York Times*. This is supposed to be a story about cannibals. His characters are too smart to be in this movie. And what about his jokes? He's got some really dark stuff in here. Funny, though."

Gary was hopeful. "I know what you mean." *Not really*, he thought. "But it's funny, right?"

"Gary. That kind of funny won't sell tickets. The script is like Woody Allen meets Les Craven. It's not going to work unless he can take the Woody Allen out of it."

"I know what you mean. Call him and tell him we don't need Woody Allen for a movie about cannibals in Beverly Hills. And tell him to take out things like *The New York Times* and put in *Beverly Hills 213*, you know, that local piece of crap with all the shiny ads."

"I think you should tell him at the story meeting. You're the better one at manipulating and lying to would-be writers." Bob forced a smile.

"Asshole." Gary returned to his usual desk spot.

Ricky called Liz in order to convince her to side with him about altering the Mal screenplay to Ricky's specifications. She set up a lunch meeting with me and Ricky at the Beverly Hills Tennis Club. She insisted that I be present at the meeting. Ricky balked at first, yelling something about switching to "the Morris office." Liz ignored his shtick and told him. "Either show up or I'll drop the project and you can take it to any agency you want."

Well into the meeting, things were still going well. Ricky was paying more attention to his club sandwich, French fries, and chocolate shake than to the substance of the conversation.

"Ricky. Don't you think you want to at least include your mother in the scenes dealing with the casinos?" asked Liz. "Wasn't she there?"

Ricky stopped chewing his food.

"Ricky doesn't want her in the story," I said.

Ricky continued to chew his food.

"I see," said Liz. "Well. It looks like a good story. It needs a little more Mal."

"Oh, I get it," Ricky whined. "It's two against one. I'm not that stupid. You're not going to drag my balls along the patio floor. Not here. I was here before either one of you. You know Mal used to belong here, so cut the crap."

"Ricky. Nobody is ganging up on you," said Liz. "It is going to be tough to sell Mal to a network without a little more about Mal. That's just a fact."

"This is not a story about Mal. It's about my life. Mal is just a part of it. If you don't think you can handle the project…" He paused and stared her down. "There are plenty of agents in this town who will."

"You don't have to talk to Liz like that," I said.

Liz shot me one glance. I could tell that she was through.

Ricky threw his napkin into his food. He pushed himself away from the table, and reached inside the inner breast pocket of his tattered Members Only black windbreaker. A shiny object was whipped into the air. "I warned you not to fuck with me. Nobody fucks with Ricky V. Rose!" he yelled, now brandishing a glimmering chrome gun.

Liz spoke to him as if he were five years old. "Ricky. Will you cut it out? That's a gun, isn't it? You brought a gun to our meeting. Well. Isn't that nice? Sit down before you get us all in trouble."

I didn't know if she was bluffing, but she was doing a hell of a good job.

Godfrey spotted the fracas from inside the glass-enclosed office and dialed '911'. "This is Godfrey at the BHTC. Get here right away. One of the guests is running around with a gun. That's right. 340 North Maple Drive."

Ricky laughed. "I told you not to do this. I could blow your fucking head off, Brantley. But I won't, because I'm fair, and I want to give you a chance to finish this thing."

Sirens could already be heard in the background.

Once Ricky saw the police hustling across the patio, the gun disappeared into his pocket. "No problem, officers," he said in a calm voice.

With her gun initially drawn, a female police officer and another officer behind her calmly escorted Ricky to a deserted area of the patio. It appeared that she knew Ricky. He was all smiles. There, he forked over his weapon. They stood and talked for about a half-hour.

Meanwhile, another officer spoke with us. We refused to file any complaint.

As it turned out, the gun was licensed and belonged to Mal. Ricky was arrested on a brandishing charge and released soon after Kyle Bixler showed up at the police station, glad-handing all the officers. Bail was posted and Ricky would be arraigned a few weeks later.

Ricky made the most out of the publicity. He reenacted the incident for *Access Hollywood*, the tabloid-styled news show on NBC. He took a lot of liberties in the new version of the event.

Kyle asked Liz and me to meet him in his office. We did, and listened to him for almost one-half hour. He wanted to be certain that we would not pursue Ricky legally. It was unclear whether what he had told us was intended to dissuade us by intimidation or he only wanted to point out the pathetic nature of his client. "Everyone always thought that Ricky was just a wiseass kid. Sure. That part was true, but most people have no idea how dangerous Ricky can be. He once pulled a gun out on a 747 bound for Japan. How I got him out of that I'll never know. He once beat up a film school professor who gave Ricky's younger cousin an "F" on a term paper. The class was about basic screenplay technique. Ricky thought that he was a great writer, so he told his cousin that he would help him write something for the class. It was Ricky who actually received the failing grade. Then there was the time he got into a fight with a security guard who had asked him to stop after the metal detector went off as he went through the lobby of a building. The guy was closer to seventy than sixty, and Ricky let him have it in the face. I kept helping him because of Mal. With Mal gone, I have tried to have nothing to do with Ricky, like everyone else in this town, except for you, Brantley. Everyone else told Ricky to get lost, and I mean everybody. I bailed him out this last time because Arnie begged me to do it in memory of Mal."

I didn't know how to feel; I was still working with a pathological product of Hollywood.

Soon, Ricky called and pleaded with Liz. When she got off the phone with him, she called me to tell me to forget him, and give up.

I didn't. Ricky insisted that we meet again at the Loews Hotel on the beach, never telling me that the last time we were there he had stiffed them on the check. The same manager was not on duty when we had arrived for an early dinner. Ricky soon ordered enough food for six people.

Ricky was exuberant, perhaps manic, or maybe only pretending to be. "I'm in a great mood tonight. I feel everything is going to be great after tonight," he said as he dipped a quarter of a bacon, turkey, and avocado club sandwich into a sea of thousand island dressing. He had ordered an extra side of all the ingredients so that he could add to each section of the sandwich as he consumed it. His favorite appeared to be wrapping bacon around the outside of the sandwich like a greasy belt, trapping a piece of avocado as the mushy buckle. He kept a tray of dim sum close by, occasionally popping one in his mouth between bites of the sandwich.

I found it very difficult to get my little speech out, but it was time to put on the brakes. "Ricky…I think you should understand something. I have a finished screenplay and that's what it will remain for time being, finished." I expected Ricky to blow up. "I'm not doing any more work. I've added more about Mal like Liz suggested. If you don't want to take the deal with Sean, we have to wait to see what Liz can get us." I had learn to lie; Liz wanted nothing to do with Ricky.

Ricky's response was unexpected and wonderful. "Hey. You've made my day. That's great." He grabbed two dumplings in his hand and drowned them in a combo of soy sauce, mustard, and duck sauce before swallowing both with little chewing. The darkish sauce dripped in a thin line over his wrist, suggesting blood from ancient sci-fi movies.

By the middle of the meal, Ricky spotted the manager who knew him. He headed toward our table, trailed by a security guard.

"Not this asshole again," said Ricky. "Let me handle it."

"What? What's this about?" I asked.

"I'm sorry. You'll have to leave," said the manager loudly, while he was still a table away.

"What's the matter?" I asked.

"I owe him some money." Ricky took out two one hundred-dollar bills and placed them on the table. He smiled at the manager. "Are we okay?"

"Okay," said the manager. He quickly scooped up the money and disappeared with the guard.

"Mal was right about these little people. He had a nickname for them. Jerrys. He always said to watch out for the Jerrys."

Was this the new Ricky? I had no idea what brought about the sudden change, but I wasn't going to question it. Medication crossed my mind.

After dinner, I walked Ricky to his truck, which was parked on the street in back of the hotel. It was getting dark, and the area was poorly lit. I had used the valet parking, and after goodbyes would need to walk back up the hill and around to the front of the hotel. I was still stunned by the sudden change in Ricky's personality. Maybe he had realized that Liz and I were at the end of our rope or maybe he was on new prescription drugs. Then it all became abundantly clear.

"Brantley. I think we're ready to go ahead and get this thing produced. I think it's time I inserted myself more in the process, and took over."

"What do you mean?" I asked.

"Well, for starters, I'll completely edit the script before we send it anywhere else."

"It's been edited. What are you talking about?"

"You're a lousy speller. I've noticed you can't spell or you don't care, and that's a sign that you don't care about the finished product. You're new at this. I've been in the business my whole life."

"This is crazy." I felt my pulse quicken.

Ricky tried his usual logic. "Isn't it true if we send something out with spelling errors it will lessen our chances of getting it produced?"

"Ricky. Why are we having this conversation about spelling again? The script is great. Let it go out."

"In good time. Look. I have to take over here. You've done a good job, and I'll see to it that you get story credit."

"Story credit!" I screamed.

"It's my life story. Not yours. How can you expect to get a screenplay credit?"

"That's it, Ricky. I can't take this anymore. It's my screenplay as much as it is yours."

"Ha," snorted Ricky. "I knew you were like everyone else, wanting to use me, not caring. Look. I've been through that with Mal, and I don't need another Mal in my life.

"Fuck off. I'm calling an attorney." I began to hustle up the hill. Instinct told me to turn back.

Ricky had another gun. It was larger and he was pointing it at me. "Now you're not even going to get story credit. See how you've ruined everything for yourself." He pursued me with his full waddle.

I ran across the street toward the parked cars. I heard a shot and kept running. My arm was stinging and it grew very warm. My neck throbbed. When I reached the top of the hill next

to the hotel I could see that my arm was drenched in blood.
Ricky had shot me. I felt my legs give out for a moment. I
propped myself up on the outside of the cashier's kiosk in front
of the hotel.

I looked at my bloodied appendage; a dark band had formed
on the outside of my jacket. A voiceover from an old Western
comforted me. "It's only a flesh wound, son." Or was it? What
the hell did the voiceover know?

This was way beyond my root canal training. I felt faint.
The Mexican valets began running around like jumping beans. The
young girl inside the kiosk had the sense to dial 911, so I
excluded her from my justifiable-at-the-moment racist thoughts.

"Get my car!" I shouted. I felt that I could drive. I
wasn't going to rely on the valets for getting me medical care
or an ambulance.

One of the valets ran to get my car, while the others
conspicuously kept their distance. Before the paramedics
arrived, I was on my way to nearby Santa Monica Hospital. I
hoped they had someone on emergency duty with a little
experience with weapons. After all, Santa Monica was not
Compton.

Ricky couldn't start his truck. He got out and walked
around to the other side of the hotel. He planned to call a tow
truck from the hotel.

"Don't move motherfucker!" said a low voice.

Before Ricky could turn around, there were two men at his
sides. A third pressed the barrel of an assault weapon into
Ricky's back. One of the men grabbed Ricky under his arm.

Ricky thought he could handle them. "What do you want? I've
got money!"

"Just give us your money and shut up," said the first man.

Ricky reached in his pocket and pulled out his gun. "You want to fuck with Ricky V. Rose?" he screamed, as he wrestled his arm free. He turned to face his attackers.

Ricky's bloodied body was left in an alley frequented by the homeless. I would much later find out from Chris that he was making deals for bodies with some of the criminals who did business in Santa Monica. He eventually told me about Ricky, as it was told to him.

It turned out that the old western voiceover was right. My wound wasn't so bad, but I don't think that I ever recovered from it. I felt weak for months, and I still envision what happened, both in my cold acute memory and the twisted accounts that show up in nightmares.

Liz and I had initially concluded that Ricky had left the country. The police couldn't locate him, only his jacket and an empty wallet. We initially thought that it was some kind of ploy, a publicity stunt, something typical of Ricky. Nobody wanted to touch the screenplay until Ricky resurfaced. End of that deal. But not the end of me wondering why I had held on to Ricky for so long.

CHAPTER TWENTY-FOUR

Linda

Sean

Ira

Sean regularly confided in Linda about all the continued pressures involved in operating the newly named Hollywood Deli Company. He desperately wanted to start principal shooting on *Beverly Hills Cannibals*. Without telling me, he paid another writer, not quite A-list, to do a rewrite based on Gary's notes. I was out of the loop, but I would not know that for some time.

One night, while Linda and Sean sat on the plush sofa in her apartment, he tried to explain that he didn't think he could handle both running the new company and making movies. "Linda. I was never a businessman like your father. I was just a full steam ahead kind of guy. People were afraid to fuck with me because I was an athlete, well connected, and I had tons of momentum. People were friends as long as the money was there, but lose them a nickel, and they turned on me as if we never met. I don't mean acquaintances, I mean guys from my childhood. People would pretend to be my friend, buy me gifts, take my silly-ass late night calls, schmooze, profess love, send cards, and bring me medicine and chicken soup when I was sick. You name it. It all means nothing. These people are not my friends. They are often seductive, charismatic, charming beyond anything anyone can resist, but they all want something, and if you fail to deliver that something to them, you are no longer their friend."

"I'm sorry that you feel that way." Linda saw it as a clear weakness. She would soon speak to Donny about "a new problem with Sean".

"There's more," said Sean.

"Oh," she said. She didn't want to hear more.

"The meat. Remember when I told you about the meat?"

"Yes."

"It was originally coming from a human source."

"Very funny," said Linda.

"I mean it. It was. I mean we stopped. Well, we've almost stopped."

"Sean. You're delirious. Let me get you another drink." She moved toward the bar and poured heavily from a bottle of Stoli. He was back on a steady diet of Bloody Marys.

Sean leaned back and appeared to sink into the soft sofa. His hands felt moist. He rubbed them on his face, and then on the sides of his hair.

"Here," she said. She handed him the vodka straight.

He took a sip. "Linda. It's cadaver meat. We get it from UCLA Medical School mostly, at least that's where it started, but I don't know anymore. I want to stop the whole thing."

Linda was simultaneously struck by several thoughts. The first was that she may have consumed part of her father at some point, or at least a portion of him was eaten by someone in one of the delis. The other was that Sean was a clear threat to the success of the company if any of this was true or not. Her major concerns were with the latter; Sean was becoming a liability. He was the last one she had thought would ever pose a problem. She heard her father's voice. She knew what she had to do.

Over the next few weeks, Linda had several conversations with board members of the company. She spoke mostly with Donny, who didn't need to be coaxed to give his opinion. "The deli was Sean's brain child. He set it up, and he's getting plenty of stock for it. We have to think about hiring someone who has restaurant experience. Even that won't be enough. With the I.P.O., there will be plenty of cash to perhaps integrate. Who knows? We need someone who knows the ropes. That's all. It happens all the time."

"Do you mean bringing in an outsider?" asked Linda. She said it with the perfect amount of naiveté, just like her father Dave would have. Dave had given her the lecture on more than one occasion. Many companies were set up by people who had little or no practical experience running any kind of a retail establishment. Companies always needed good 'help', someone who didn't have an emotional stake in the company, a hired gun who could come in and make things work. Some of these people enjoyed great reputations for building new companies, while others with nicknames like Chainsaw enjoyed less popularity.

Linda knew what Donny had in mind, but she didn't want to commit one way or the other. "You know me, Donny. I don't know the first thing about this. I'm here to protect my family's investment." It was far from the truth. She knew the ropes, and was privy to every nuance of Dave's deals. That's all he ever spoke about during dinners or weekend brunches.

Donny thought, *I'd better back off*. He said, "Well, I've talked to a lot of the board members. Let's see how it goes. Maybe it can work out with Sean. There was some talk of a co-chairman situation. We'll see." Donny had no intention of keeping Sean. He also was pleased by how coy Linda was playing the whole situation. She had learned well from Dave.

About a week later, Sean stepped out of his car and into
something soft on his driveway. He lifted up one of his legs and
turned his Lucchese boot inward. "Damn plumbers!"

There wasn't any water spurting that time, but there was a
constant flow at ground level, which washed the loose soil
across the driveway toward the house. He opened his front door
to see that the darkened water had leaked inside. With the
interior lights on, he had a clear view of how the water had
seeped in near the base of the walls. His carpets already had
dirty oval stains.

Sean marched back out into the mud. He looked over at the
area where the plumbers had worked. They had left a broken piece
of pipe on the lawn. Sean knew what he had to do. He took the
broken pipe and put it in the front seat of his car.

Almost an hour later, as it was getting dark, he stopped
his car in front of Jack Reilly, Inc. He slowly walked to the
glass front, and when he was as close as he could get he threw
the pipe as hard as possible through the old window. It
shattered nicely, taking all of the business name and logo with
it. He glanced around. Nobody saw him. Even if somebody had,
what Sean did was a common thought amongst locals when it came
to plumbers. Most would say that Sean had let them off easy.

He quickly returned his car, and drove off into the bright
lights of Beverly Hills. He had gotten his revenge, at least
momentarily. He knew that he would have to sue the plumber as
well as his own contractor, which in Hollywoodland was business
as usual.

The next day, Sean called Linda from his car. "Can you meet
me?" he asked.

She could sense the urgency in his voice. "Sure. Where?"

"Beverly Hills Hotel, okay?"

"Sure. I can be there in half an hour," she said, glancing at her Picasso-styled wall clock.

With the hour, Sean and Linda sat alone in a corner booth in the Polo Lounge. It was a little after three-thirty in the afternoon, and there was only one other booth taken and that by big drinkers who had stayed on after lunch.

"Sean. It was wrong. I'm agreeing with you," said Linda.

"I can't quit. There's too much involved."

"Sean. I don't want you doing this."

"It's just business," he said. "I'll adjust. It all got to me."

"I guess that's why I never liked business."

"It was only supposed to be for a little while."

"I've seen it before. My father said he was only going to sell guns in his sporting goods store for only the first year, and then he would tell the other partners that he wanted to stop."

"What happened?"

"They kept expanding until they were the biggest retailer of guns west of the Mississippi," said Linda.

"What should I do?"

"You don't have to do this. Stop fighting yourself, and stop fighting me. If you don't quit this you'll end up like some of those old miserable bastards at country clubs, walking around mumbling about what was, and seeing who they can make miserable along with themselves. Don't end up bitter."

Sean leaned back and looked directly into Linda's eyes.

"That's some speech."

"Sorry. I didn't mean to preach. I'm sorry. It's your business," she said. "I'd better go." She picked up her plain, black leather purse.

"No. Don't go."

Linda turned to face him. "You really mean that, don't you?"

Sean nodded in the affirmative and slumped down on his side of the booth. He covered his face with his hands. Linda sat down next to him.

"It's funny," he said.

"What is?"

"You really love me, don't you? Even with all of the horrible things I've told you about myself. After all the mean things you've heard me say to Bob and Gary, you still love me."

"Sean. It's okay," she said. "I know it's not you. It's an act."

"Okay. I'll tell them that it has got to stop."

"Thanks," said Linda in an almost indiscernible voice. She realized they hadn't been talking about the same thing. Sean was still preoccupied about the meat. Linda was talking about him quitting the business entirely.

They said nothing else about the deli. Each left with a clear agenda, diametrically opposed from the other.

Sean called Donny first. Donny had a plan. "Don't tell anyone else. I'll arrange a meeting of the board, tonight, at my house. I'll get deli food from Nate 'n Al's. Don't tell anyone else what you've told me. Got it?"

Sean agreed.

That night at Donny's house, Sean told the board about the meat problem and offered to resign. After a little murmuring, Dr. K. took over.

"We don't want you to resign," said Dr. K. "This matter can be rectified, and we don't need to make it public."

"I don't think I want to be a part of it anymore," said Sean.

Donny spoke. "Sean. Go home. Think over what you're saying. Get a good night's sleep." He convinced Sean to leave without making any commitments.

When Sean left to go to his car, Donny turned back to the board members. He looked toward the back of the room. "Neil. What do you think about all of this?"

Neil cleared his throat, and stood up from his seat in a shiny leather swivel. He knew that none of this could go any further, and he already had a solution.

Later, Sean drove home along Malibu Highway. He felt free for perhaps the first time in his life. He would try to get a good night's sleep.

The telephone rang early the next morning in Sean's house.

George Roy barked, but Sean didn't pick up the telephone.

The voicemail feature kicked in. "Hi. It's Linda. I thought you were marvelous at the meeting last night. I think everything is going to be okay."

A few hours later, Sean's daughter pulled up and parked next to his car. She rang the doorbell on and off for fifteen minutes. There was no answer. She went back to her car and left a message on the answering machine. "Daddy. I guess you're with Linda. I'll call you later."

Another message came in on Sean's machine. "It's Donny. The board has asked that you assign your shares to other members. We'll buy them at current valuations, that's if you still want out. But I don't think you should do it. The rest of the board members don't care about the past. We want to move ahead."

Soon after that night, Linda called Liz to confirm the next board meeting.

"I remember my father's words," said Linda, "and I want to do this for him."

"I understand," answered Liz. "I emailed you a statement that I intend to read at the meeting."

"It sounded fine. By the way. Did you give them notice at the agency?"

"I'm out of there at the end of the week," said Liz.

"Fine. Then I can let the other board people know that you're coming to work for us fulltime."

"Yes. I'm glad to be going. Ever since Ovitz decided to go back into business, things around here have gotten worse. And now he's done. Everyone is watching his back. Clients are defecting. That Robin Williams thing really blew everyone away. I wouldn't be here if it wasn't for Ovitz, and now he's long gone from the scene."

"All's fair in love and war, and business is war," said Linda.

"Another one of Dave's?"

"Yeah. He was full of them. But I'm beginning to see that he was right about almost everything. I'll see you over at the meeting."

"Right."

Not a word was said about Sean.

At the meeting, Liz read from a prepared statement. "I know all of you have read about the unfortunate disappearance of Sean Daren. In the meantime, Linda Stirling will be taking over his duties in seeing that the I.P.O. is carried out on schedule. I'm certain that no objections will be raised."

Neil and Ira sat quietly in the back of the room.

"Neil. What do you know about this?" Ira asked.

"Ira. Leave it alone. It's done. Just leave it alone."

"Are you saying what I think you're saying?"

"Ira. They did it to him; they can do it to you."

"Who did it? Who are you talking about?"

"Look. I think we should both keep our mouths shut."

Ira made up his mind to go public with what he thought had happened. He suspected that Chris had something to do with Sean's disappearance.

That night, Ira sat alone in front of his computer and anonymously emailed the *National Enquirer*.

"I have a story about The Hollywood Deli," was all he wrote. He stopped himself because he realized that someone would have to call him back. He didn't want anyone to know that he was the source for any article.

Instead, he packed his personal things. He was going to stay with his grandfather in Florida. He had no idea what he would do, and he didn't care. He wanted to leave. Maybe if he gave some of the money to charity, it would somehow make up for how the money was made. Ira wanted the truth to be told.

Ira decided to call the newspaper directly. He dialed from a telephone booth because he was afraid the company's caller I.D. system could identify his number. He was connected to a reporter who spoke with what he thought was an English accent. He told him the whole story.

"Cannibals, you say", the reporter repeated, as if he were saying "vegetarians".

One week later, the story was printed near the center of the tabloid, near an exposé about extraterrestrials. The headline about the deli was so extreme that it was laughable. "Missing Beverly Hills Producer Likely Eaten By Partners."

Other tabloids like the *Star* picked up the story as well. "Hollywood Is Eating More Than Just Raoul". And in the *Examiner*,

"Move Over *Sweeney Todd*. Hollywood Deli Serves Up Dead Human Flesh."

A curious reporter from the *Los Angeles Times* called the offices of The Hollywood Deli for a response.

Linda and Liz decided to use the opportunity to call a press conference in order to capitalize on the growing publicity.

Liz read the official statement. "Our attorneys are looking into the ridiculous matter as we speak. In the meantime, our plans to open another Hollywood Deli at Universal Studios will continue. By the summer, we expect to have six Hollywood Delis in Southern California."

Ira wrote a letter to his stockbroker, Manfred, instructing him to sell his shares in the business as soon as it was legally possible, and mail half of his proceeds to his grandfather's address, and the rest to a P.O. box in Stony Brook, Long Island. He had applied to transfer to the medical school in Stony Brook.

Then he wrote a letter to his grandfather.

Dear Zaideh:

As I told you on the telephone I'm coming out in a few days. I will let you know the exact day and flight. I guess I've just about had it here. I've learned one thing. Anything good gets destroyed in Hollywood. Just like what they do with the movies, they take a good idea and turn it into something twisted and mediocre. That's how a lot of things work out here. Look at what they've done to the movies. Every Christmas it's the same old story. The main character is a sexually active Santa who is friends with a snowman with a multiple personality disorder. Then they throw in some wisecracking children on Ritalin, who live in happy but broken homes. I can't remember the last time that I saw a movie in which the children lived with both of their parents. I hope I'm not rambling on. I'm looking forward to seeing you. I guess I'll stay with you for a few days and then head back to New York. I've arranged to transfer to Stony Brook to finish medical school. I guess I'll make a better doctor than I did a businessman,   although Manfred says the stock should fetch a hefty sum. I'll leave you with this happy thought. A good person hasn't got a chance here, like a good idea. Both get eaten alive or disappear altogether.

Love,
Ira

EPILOGUE

I continued writing my book with a new found passion. By then, I had endless recorded conversations. I wanted to add as much as I could learn about Sean, before and during the aftermath of his disappearance. I felt that his Hollywood story was as emblematic as anything I had personally experienced or heard about.

Bob wasn't so hot on the idea in the beginning, but eventually became more forthcoming, supplying me with endless stories about the office and his own situation. "The police didn't bother me too much about Sean. I went in the hospital for what was supposed to be a routine procedure through the ribs. They always told me I had this prolapsed thing, but since I was working on one lung anyway, and my blood pressure wasn't so good, they talked me into this procedure. It didn't work so good. I had to come back and they put in a pig stent that was supposed to make me perfect. A couple of weeks after that I'm in bed with Heather and I think I'm going to die. Turns out I was. We ended up in the emergency room in Century City. I think I scared the hell out of the young guy who was watching the 'store'. He said that I'd better get over to wherever my surgeon was. That was the last thing I heard. Heather told me the kid hung onto me all the way over to Cedars. I had a heart attack

and two bypasses, and now I've got a back problem from staying
on my ass so long. Sean? I know what you asked. Listen. This is
a tough town. It's not like in the movies, where the good guys
wear white. The black t-shirt is the uniform of everyone around
town. Just because you put on a light suit over it, it doesn't
hide the black undershirt, and most people in this town have no
fear of showing a little black underwear. Think about it. Sean
knew all the bad guys and all the good guys. You figure it out."

Rabbi Ermis was much less candid. "Sure. I knew Sean Daren.
He was a nice guy, but never quite made it to the top. No. I
won't talk about his disappearance. I think he's probably living
somewhere else, under an assumed name. People do that to get
away sometimes, although he was on the verge of a great success
with The Hollywood Deli Company. Did you know they were making
movies now? The last time I saw Sean he was at Norby Walters
house. I would smoke cigars there once in a while with Charles
Bronson, Sean, Milton Berle, Jason Alexander, Richard Dreyfus,
Michael Lerner, and Richard Lewis, you know - the nervous
comedian. I think he's on *Curb Your Enthusiasm* now. It's a funny
show. The guy who created Seinfeld is doing it. Larry
whatshisname? I would sometimes see Richard and Milton at the
Peninsula Hotel in Beverly Hills. Richard would sit with a
script, right in the middle of the bar lounge and study his
lines. Milton was always Milton, doing his old routine, handing
out cigars to everyone. He carried about thirty with him in a
pouch. I heard his son wrote a book about him. I didn't think
his son had any writing talent. I bought the book, and it wasn't
bad, but I know the guy who really wrote it. I heard it wasn't a
walk in the park to deal with Milton's son, either. I think both
of them came off looking bad in the book. It was a sad story.
Oh, yes. Sean. Yes. Sean got along with everyone. He was a nice
guy who just never made it to the top. That happens in this

town. Maybe he wasn't strong enough. I don't know. I don't like to make those kinds of judgments about people…Do I think he was moral? Yes. Yes, of course I do. Sean was a moral man. He was like most Jewish men who work in this town. It is a town of dreamers; everyone here has to be a dreamer. Here, a Jewish man can become as assimilated in the culture as he wants, because it is Hollywood, and along with Washington, that defines our culture to a great extent. Jewish men here are not concerned with whether they are too Jewish. It was always the other extreme. If anything, men like Sean were worried if they were Jewish enough. That's mostly what I would hear. It's a strange situation, and it won't change, not as long as Hollywood survives."

It was easier then to make Sean the central character of my book. He was connected to so many people I had met, and most all of them were willing to spill their guts about his life, including intimate details.

The first official shareholder's meeting of The Hollywood Deli Company was held in the main ballroom of the Regent Beverly Wilshire Hotel. It was quite an affair. Every shareholder received a box of clothing bearing the logo of the new public company. Four little pushcarts wheeled around the room, each serving different foods from the deli. Chris Perez manned one of the carts. Gibby worked another. Chris' special talents were no longer needed, but he made a donation anyway. Chris personally supplied morsels of Ricky V. Rose. Chris had made plans to soon move to South America, where he already had transferred a lot of the money he had saved and placed his stock holdings in an international investment bank. Before he left town, he let me record hours of tape under two conditions. I would never use his real name and he would not have to say anything about Sean. Kyle

Bixler had seen to it that Chris received all of his promised
stock, including a cash 'travel' bonus, although Bixler warned
Chris about using certain South American banks. I also agreed to
give Chris a fixed fee, providing my book was published. My best
guess was that Chris felt if he ever said anything incriminating
regarding Sean's disappearance, I would be forced to go to the
authorities. He sensed there was no love lost regarding Ricky.
Yet, he must have known that once my book was published someone
might begin to take the tabloid stories more seriously.
Certainly, his participation in chopping up an icon like Mal
would raise a few eyebrows. Chris didn't care; he spilled his
guts quicker than a criminal in front of an MSNBC microphone
right after signing a book deal.

The hotel banquet room was filled with movie stars and the
Hollywood elite. Neil made a dazzling presentation about the
company's plan to release at least four movies a year. Sean's
film library assured them of a constant cash flow, particularly
since *Beverly Hills Cannibals*, a movie produced by Neil, Gary,
and Bob under the new company umbrella, had gone to video & DVD
after a decent worldwide distribution, and was beginning to
develop a cult following around the world.

I had filed a grievance with the Writer's Guild before the
film was released. The final version was so different from my
script that I was left out in the cold. Gary had reams of notes
showing that it was all Sean's idea anyway. Sean, Gary, and Bob
also had a company that was not a signatory or member of the
Writer's Guild, designed for situations like mine. So even if I
had proven my case, I was not entitled to any compensation under
the Guild's jurisdiction. I had agreed to do the work for Sean
'on spec'. It happened all the time. So much for regular
channels. Kyle Bixler came to the rescue after I mentioned my
disappointment. He only had to make a few phone calls, the first

one to Neil. I ended up with a 'story by' credit for the movie,
a check for over seventy-five thousand dollars, plus something
for getting screwed around, and some miniscule net percentage
known in the business as 'monkey points'. The new company could
not afford any negative publicity, especially since I was a
shareholder. I had learned how easily 'muscle' worked in the
industry. It was a mixed blessing; for the rest of my life, I
would always be connected to *Beverly Hills Cannibals*.

Bob stood in one corner talking with Linda. He wore jeans,
t-shirt, and a faded blue blazer, his most dressed up apparel.
She had taken to wearing dark Armani suits.

Bob spoke nonchalantly. "They removed most of my palate.
I'm wearing an obturator, but it doesn't bother me. The chemo
has kicked in. They say I can go another five to ten years." He
lit a cigarette. "Hey. In ten years I'll be sixty-eight. That
ain't such a bad run."

"After all you've been through, I'd have to say you're a
real survivor," said Linda.

Bob laughed. "Yeah. They marked me off years ago."

"What are you going to do with your stock money?"

"I don't know, make movies. That's what I've always done."

"Let me know. I'll make sure that Neil takes a good look at
the material."

"You bet."

"You really are a survivor," she repeated.

Bob shuffled away. His gait was uneven. His head bobbed
side to side with an almost imperceptible rhythm that made him
look as if he was about to topple over with his very next step.
He spotted two young men in the corner. He moved closer to hear
their conversation. It seemed that they had just begun speaking.

The first spoke with a cool, knowledgeable air, akin to Lou
Dobbs' financial report on CNN. "*Rodger Dodger* is doing business
in Australia."

"That's a joke, right?"

"I thought it was interesting to know that they like all
kinds of movies."

The second young man discovered what may writers also had
discovered before him. "I don't think any of that matters. We
have to write what we want to write and that's it. We can't
worry about the money when we're writing."

"Look. The top ten of all time should be something we
should look at. *Titanic, Star Wars, E.T., Jurassic Park, The
Lion King, Forrest Gump, Return of the Jedi, Home Alone*. I can't
remember the others, but doesn't that tell you something?"

The second man sounded dejected. "Yes. It tells me that I
can't write for the movies."

Bob moved closer, thinking that perhaps they had a story
for a screenplay. He felt a cigar inside his jacket that he had
been saving to celebrate. Maybe he would invite them outside for
a smoke.

Eventually, I asked Barry about people like Bob. "Maybe one
day they'll find a gene that drives people like Bob. They'll
have to call it the Hollywood gene. What else could they call
it? There is nothing like it anywhere else in the world. Only a
select group of people in the business have it, something that
leaves its own genetic imprint inside every cell of its
existence, and every one of its owner's transactions. It's just
something people have or they don't. It's not something you can
learn or something that people even set out to teach. Bob is one
of those people who had what it took to survive in a town where
people were consumed by the process. So did Linda, by the way."

I suggested to Donny that he write a book. "Me write a book? Are you nuts? Because nobody would believe some of the things I've seen and heard. As much as has been written about the Hollywood scene, it's something that someone has to experience on his own. Wait. That's not really what I mean, what I mean is that it's something people would be better off without experiencing."

Neil was way ahead of me by the time he agreed to a formal interview for my book. "I really cover a lot of what you're asking in my new book, *Chicken Soup Can Be Cash In The Bank*. I tell mostly about how I got started. I never intended to be a CEO of anything. I always thought that I was going to finish medical school, but things change. I have a vision now. I see us in competition with everyone. We are no longer just a food company, but we are an entertainment company, and we have to compete on the Internet, like everyone else. Even Microsoft is someone I see as a competitor. It's a great time for expansion. Have you seen our new corporate logo? It's a corned beef sandwich inside a little satellite."

Soon, a civil action materialized. Dr. K was not afraid to speak about it with me. "Yes. I heard about the lawsuit. I understand the suit is about the disposal of cadaver remains...I doubt if UCLA really improperly disposed of eighteen thousand bodies...Yes. I heard that, too. It goes back to 1993, when some funeral at sea company found that there was medical waste mixed together with human remains. We put a stop to that right away, and the school crematorium was shut down...The whole thing is ridiculous. I know that it was a rumor going around for a few years, but come on now, cannibalism? Here? The school stopped mixing human remains with medical waste, animal remains, scalpels, blood samples, and aborted fetuses. Since then, I have only heard good things about the program at UCLA...No. I don't know the outcome of the legal matters. I assume that everything is in order."

Linda agreed much later to be interviewed, but didn't offer much help. "That's funny. I heard all those rumors too, how we were serving less than high quality meat in the beginning. The Hollywood Deli always served the best quality meat available in Southern California. You know we've sold out our food division to another management group, but we still own it. We're more entertainment now, but the Hollywood Deli is a historic memory that our company will never forget. Have you seen our remakes of some of those old sci-fi movies? You know we have one of the largest film libraries in the world. I think we'll easily do a hundred million on this new one. It's based on a cult movie of a few years ago called *I Spit On Your Pasta*."

One of the funniest encounters with a patient came about when I received a phone call from a referring general practitioner telling me that Henry Mancini, the famous composer, needed a root canal surgery. I had a break before his arrival, so I went down the hall to the bathroom. While I was urinating, a man pulled up in the tall, ancient urinal next to me.

"Hi!" he said.

He was overly friendly, way beyond public bathroom protocol. I guess that he felt comfortable talking to me since I was dressed all in white. I was either a doctor or the long defunct Good Humor man. We were both old enough to remember the ice-cream vendor and his all-white truck and outfit.

After a beat or two I recognized him. "You're Henry Mancini, aren't you? I think you're coming to see me."

"Right you are. Dr. Benjamin, I presume?" He was a charmer, and had a knack to make people laugh.

At his second visit, Mancini proposed a plan. "You know your fee is very high." I knew what was coming, but he developed a unique twist. He continued as if his survival was dependent upon his negotiation skills. "What about a trade? I'm teaching my nephew how to play the piano. Do you want to trade for piano lessons?"

I smiled. "Will I be able to write a million-selling pop tune when we're through?"

Mancini laughed and shook his head. I received his payment promptly by mail.

A great deal of time had passed before I realized that I suffered from some kind of arrested development. It's not a bad attribute for writing; I don't think it's a good fit for much else, perhaps only acting. I had always felt that people from my past thought about me the same way that I did about them, wondering how they were doing, and if they had fond memories of the time we had spent together. I still think of my childhood school chums, high school girlfriends, teachers, bagel bakers, and professional associates as if it were yesterday.

I have finally gotten rid of the notion that people really care that much about their pasts. They prefer to live moment-to-moment, fueled by some bizarre mix of intangibles that feeds a cruel short-term memory. After all, I live in the foothills of the Hollywood sign. At least now I know what to expect.

Katherine Daren summed it up this way: "I've been around people in the business my whole life. I never thought much about it as a child, but now I have doubts about how the whole moral structure works. It's strange that my father was part of that structure. I always thought of him to be a moral man. I guess it has a lot to do with definitions, the way you want to look at it, maybe the way to explain the whole thing. It may be a DNA thing, and that's the end of the story. If you have moral DNA, then, you know…If you don't, you don't. But there is also some kind of behavioral thing. People in the business tend to stay amongst themselves - eat in the same restaurants and travel to the same places. They stick up for each other, at least when a problem is with someone perceived as an outsider. Look at that phony trial for Winona with Peter Guber on the jury. Guber ran Sony when Ryder made three movies for Columbia Pictures. And a programming development executive for an entertainment company and the husband of a Disney big shot. Who are they kidding? The judge even said, "I think we have all the studios represented." They come to each other's rescue, but god help you if you are a stranger. That's probably why it is so hard for outsiders to get into the business. I laugh when I talk about it, but here's the best example of how the business works. Vampire bats don't exactly have the easiest diets to satisfy. They need blood every night just to make it to the next day. But if one of their own doesn't have blood, another bat will share blood. In return, the bat that got some free blood better remember, and the next time around better share. Somehow the bats know who fucks up, and if they don't cooperate, they're out. This kind of communal system assures that only the bats that share the blood will survive. Sound familiar?"

Other than meeting Liz, the completion of my book seemed like the only positive thing that could come out of my overall experience. But there was something more. My stock in the Hollywood Deli nearly tripled. I decided to work fewer hours, eventually selling my practice, and devoted most of my time to writing. I, too, became a Hollywood survivor of sorts, albeit within the limitations imposed on those who stick around. Once I knew that Hollywood ate its own, I was always on guard.